Buddhist Fury

Buddhist Fury

Religion and Violence in Southern Thailand

MICHAEL K. JERRYSON

OXFORD
UNIVERSITY PRESS

OXFORD
UNIVERSITY PRESS

Oxford University Press, Inc., publishes works that further
Oxford University's objective of excellence
in research, scholarship, and education.

Oxford   New York
Auckland   Cape Town   Dar es Salaam   Hong Kong   Karachi
Kuala Lumpur   Madrid   Melbourne   Mexico City   Nairobi
New Delhi   Shanghai   Taipei   Toronto

With offices in
Argentina   Austria   Brazil   Chile   Czech Republic   France   Greece
Guatemala   Hungary   Italy   Japan   Poland   Portugal   Singapore
South Korea   Switzerland   Thailand   Turkey   Ukraine   Vietnam

Published by Oxford University Press, Inc.
198 Madison Avenue, New York, New York 10016

www.oup.com

Library of Congress Cataloging-in-Publication Data
Jerryson, Michael K.
Buddhist fury : religion and violence in southern Thailand / Michael K. Jerryson
p.   cm.
Includes biliographical references.
ISBN 978-0-19-979323-5; 978-0-19-979324-2 (pbk.)
1. Buddhism and politics—Thailand, Southern.   2. Violence—Religious aspects—Buddhism.
3. Thailand, Southern—Politics and government—21st century.   I. Title.
BQ554.J47 2011
294.3'37273—dc22   2010040326

1 3 5 7 9 8 6 4 2

Printed in the United States of America
on acid-free paper

CONTENTS

4. Militarization   114

5. Identity   143

Conclusion   178

FIGURES AND TABLES

Buddhist Fury

Introduction

> It is also an erroneous idea to suppose that the Buddha con-
> demned all wars and people whose business it was to wage war.
> Many instances could be quoted to prove that the Buddha recog-
> nized the necessity of defensive war, and such may also be
> inferred from parts of the following allocution itself. What the
> Buddha did condemn was that spirit miscalled "Militarism," but
> which is really intolerant and unreasoning hatred, vengeance,
> and savagery, which causes men to kill from sheer blood-lust,
> and a religion that tolerates such a brutish spirit is not worthy of
> the name of religion!
>
> —King Vajiravudh, Rama VI *

"We need to find peace," said a seventy-five-year-old southern Thai Buddhist monk I will call Ačhān Pim during an interview at his monastery August 14, 2004.[1] Ačhān Pim was referring to the growing divide between Buddhists and Muslims in the region, which had suffered sporadic unclaimed attacks against monks, armed forces, teachers, workers, and pedestrians. His monastery is located in a region within Thailand's three southernmost provinces that border Malaysia (*sāmčhangwat chāydāenphākhtai*). Eight months before our January 2004 interview, the Thai government declared martial law in the three provinces of Pattani, Yala, and Narathiwat. However, the Thai government's declaration, together with its policies and practices, proved ineffective in quelling the seem-ingly random bombings and murders. If anything, the imposition of martial law intensified the political nature of the conflict.

Among the many victims were Buddhist and Muslim rubber workers. The rubber industry was a major economic commodity for the region. Ačhān Pim explained, "When Muslims threaten Buddhists, sometimes Buddhists need to be violent in return. The people need to rise up and harvest the rubber trees. They need to unite and resist this form of extortion."[2]

Since January 2004, there have been more than 4,100 deaths and 6,509 casu-alties attributed to the violence in the deep south.[3] The conflict has had many det-rimental effects upon local Thais, among them distrust and suspicion between

Muslims and Buddhists.[4] In my interviews with over thirty abbots (*čhao āwat*) living in the war zone, which occurred during visits in 2004, 2006, 2007, and 2008, I came to realize that Ačhān Pim's militaristic view was not unique. Rather, his perspective reflected those of many monks and laity living in a dangerous and frightening climate. Ačhān Pim's call for Buddhists to embrace violence was a recent development in Thailand's southernmost provinces. International and Thai analysts largely overlook the Buddhists' call to arms when they attempt to explain the spikes of violence in the war-torn region. This is a serious oversight. Religion changes the contour of a conflict and infuses it with cosmic relevance.[5] Although they are not the primary agents, *Buddhist monks are armed participants in the southern Thai conflict*. And, if the epigraph for this chapter suggests anything, it is that the Thai Buddhist views on violence are much like those in any other religious tradition. Violence becomes a religiously justifiable action so long as it is defensive. This seemingly sound qualification yields a slippery slope, for who sees themselves as true instigators of a conflict? In many ways, the focus of this book contrasts with the most general assumptions of Buddhist traditions and monasticism.

Buddhist monasticism entails the separation of one's self from life's vulgarities. Theravāda Buddhist traditions like Thai Buddhism involve the practice of young men taking temporary ordination for this very purpose. This is a time for them to separate themselves from the regular affairs of the world and their community and direct their time and attention to Buddhist teachings and monastic practices. In addition to intrapersonal merits, their ordination builds merit for their family and grants them social status in their community. Thais view Buddhist monasticism as a break from the regular habits and vices of life. It is commonly assumed that Buddhist monks live apart from everyday politics, corruption, and economic issues. As the fading lineage of Thai forest monks (*thudong*) reveals, the more a monk appears separate from society, the greater the social veneration. And, why not? A forest monk embodies the commonly held beliefs of what Buddhist monasticism should be.[6]

It is, thus, a great shock for Thais to hear about monks equipping themselves with handguns or affiliating themselves with military activities. Monks are not immune to political tensions. One of the most recent examples of this is the Thai Buddhist monks' divided affiliations during the violence that took place in Bangkok between March and May 2010.[7] The involvement of Buddhist monks as both victims and agents of violence significantly alters the conflict's parameters; in particular, it strengthens a perceived religious dimension to the conflict.

While the conflict is distended with causes, actors, and motivations, there are some threads that stand out among the rest. The first of these is education—or specifically, the public recollection of the region's religious and political heritage. The Thai colonization of the Malay Muslim kingdom of Patani and its manipulation of public memory have resulted in the violent treatment of Malay Muslims, who are a religious and ethnic minority. The second of these threads is the relationship between the Thai State and Thai Buddhism. At the heart of this work is an assessment of the centralized authority—the Thai network-monarchy, bureau-cracy, and subsidiaries, which collectively I refer to as the Thai State—and its close symbolic associations with the Buddhist monks who comprise the Thai *sangha*.[8]

Thai Buddhist studies scholar Suwanna Satha-anand postulates that a Thai Buddhist hegemony allows Thai Buddhists to tolerate different religious groups.[9] Hegemony always creates a comfortable space for the privileged; however, the Thai Buddhist hegemony is contested in the southern context. What I ultimately conclude through fieldwork and archival analysis is that the State-*sangha* con-nection furnishes a hegemonic script that subjugates, silences, and alienates the Malay Muslim minority, their history, and their identity. This hegemony fuels the Malay Muslim insurgency in the southern region. There is a panoply of studies that review the Malay Muslims, just as there are studies on the relation-ship between the Thai State and Thai *sangha*. However, this is the first study to assess the role of Thai Buddhist monks in a religio-political conflict and contrib-utes to the study of Buddhist traditions and their relationship with warfare.

Backgrounds

Southern Thailand is home to a diverse population. Among the more unique characteristics to the conflict are religious demographics. Whereas Buddhists represent a majority in the country overall, they are a minority in the south-ernmost provinces (see figure 0.1), which are predominantly Muslim. This dis-tinction is reflective of the specific history and development of the region, which is rich in religiously pluralistic activity. Southern Thailand is a border region and much of its diversity is due to this. At the same time, border areas are also known for conflicts, but, as Ravina Aggarwal cautions in her examina-tion of the Buddhist/Muslim community of Ladakh, the tendency to map such regions as sites of violence or idyllic utopias is at best problematic.[10] Conflicts arise from specific circumstances and historical contexts. Southern Thailand is no different.

Since the escalation in violence, we find numerous agents involved in the fractious conflict of the deep south; however, the two largest political combat-ants in the violence are the Thai security forces (such as the military, volunteer militia, and police) and the Malay Muslim separatists. Although Buddhists are the minority in southern Thailand, Buddhist principles dominate the political and military stage nationally. This presence is not portrayed in the media, which often references the conflict as an Islamic conflict without the necessary corol-lary—a Buddhist conflict.[11] The inclination to label the conflict as Islamic is due, in part, to global pretensions.

Malay Muslim separatists are fueled by political and religious tensions dating back to the sixteenth century when the three southernmost provinces were an

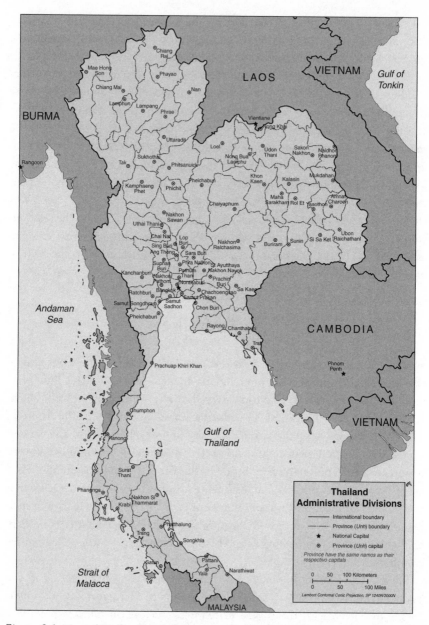

Figure 0.1 Map of Thailand's Administrative Divisions, by U.S. Central Intelligence Agency, 2005.

Islamic kingdom called Patani, which paid tribute to Siam.[12] Southeast Asia's national boundaries are contentious, much like other regions beset by colonial pasts. Nestled amongst Burma, Cambodia, Laos, Malaysia and China, the Siamese State began to fight for an identity and for the preservation of its borders. Although the now nation-state was never colonized formally, Siam's borders were internationally drawn by French and British colonial powers. The southern border of Thailand was a direct byproduct of Siam's struggle with the British, who had colonized what is now Malaysia. Within the boundaries of Siam's struggle with the British lay another internal one, the kingdom of Patani's fight for independence, which persisted from the 1300s to 1800s. In 1817, after Patani made multiple attempts to separate from Siam, the Thai State partitioned the kingdom into the smaller present-day province of Pattani and several other principalities, which are collectively known as the provinces of Yala and Narathiwat.[13] This tactic was effective in diminishing the solidified force of Pattani's resistance, but it did not end the area's strong claim for independence.

Patani's struggle for independence became redefined in relation to modernity and the advent of nation-states. During the early 1900s, Siam was intent on nation-building and congealing the disparate ethno-religious groups together into a national identity. In 1902, the last sultan of Pattani, along with the previously constructed provinces, refused to yield further local control to Siamese authorities. As with past attempts, this effort failed; the ethnically and religiously distinct population of the south became part of the new, centralized Siamese society. Throughout the twentieth century, the southern provinces of Pattani, Yala, and Narathiwat continued to contest State authority and evolved with each new political tension and context. This continual tension led the Thai State to direct troops in southern regions to deal with organized resistance from groups like the PULO (Pattani United Liberation Organization) or the BRN (Barisan Revolusi Nasional). Separatist groups like PULO and the BRN are still active in the three southernmost provinces, but many believe the majority of attacks are led by a new grassroots organization loosely affiliated with the older resistance groups, such as the BRN-C (Barisan Revolusi Nasional-Coordinate).[14] In 2006, Don Pathan, a leading journalist who covers the conflict in the southernmost provinces for the Thai newspaper *The Nation*, and Andrew Marshall from *Time Magazine* reported,

> In an interview with TIME, a high-ranking insurgent leader confirms what the teenager suggests: a new generation of militants is tightening its grip on the south, employing increasingly brutal methods that threaten to wreck an uncommon mood of conciliation in Bangkok. The leader, who calls himself Hassam and commands 250 fighters, claims there is now at least one militant cell in 80% of southern villages. His and Ma-ae's rare testimony help to illuminate a shadowy insurgency remarkable for its secrecy, resilience and bloodiness.[15]

Although the Malay Muslim separatist movements, which were predominantly formed in the 1960s, remain relevant, their silences after large-scale attacks on Thai military and civilian targets suggest the presence of different and more recent local parties. This consideration was echoed more recently by anthropologist Marc Askew, who reveals a system of misclassification in which private and drug-related murders and injuries are reported as insurgency-related due to financial compensation. Only victims of "security-related" violence are eligible for government compensations.[16]

Amid the private and drug-related attacks that also take place in the chaotic region, is an insurgency. From its inception, the separatist movement was distinguished by ethno-religious identifications and calls for autonomy. Surin Pitsuwan places the genesis of the Malay Muslim liberation movements to the final incorporation of the Patani region into the Thai kingdom on December 20, 1902. Since then, "sporadic movements and violent uprisings have been very common."[17] The fuel that sustained the resistance and the later militant developments is primarily found in the Thai State, which has made poor—at times disastrous—political decisions.

In his ground-breaking work on the conflict in southern Thailand, McCargo summarizes some of the more prolific political clashes prior to the 2004 resurgence:

> The region has a long tradition of resistance to the rule of Bangkok, and political violence has emerged at various junctures in modern history. Some of this violence was perpetrated by the Thai state. Landmark events included the 1948 Dusun-nyor incident (in which dozens, perhaps hundreds, of Malay-Muslim villagers were killed in Narathiwat); the 1954 arrest and disappearance of prominent Islamic teacher Haji Sulong, at the hands of the Thai police; and mass demonstrations at the Pattani Central Mosque in late 1975, triggered by the extrajudicial killing of some Malay Muslim youths.[18]

Intermittently, the Thai State has attempted to reconcile itself with the Malay Muslims. After the failure of Thai operations that targeted Muslim "terrorist" activities in the 1970s, Prime Minister Prem Tinsulanonda (1980–1988) devised a temporary solution to the southern violence by establishing the Southern Border Provinces Administrative Centre (SBPA) in 1981.[19] The stated purpose of the SBPA was to address and resolve the issues and dilemmas in the three southernmost provinces. The SBPA was largely successful in redirecting Malay Muslim discontent through political and civilian, rather than military, channels; however, State dishonesty and abuses of power gave rise to a Malay Muslim generation in the 1980s that, unlike groups such as the PULO, opposed negotiating with the Thai State.

This new generation of militants did not surface until twenty years later and, more importantly, not until after Thailand's democratically elected prime minister Thaksin Shinawatra disbanded the SBPA in 2001, thereby eliminating an important socio-political outlet for Malay Muslims. This was followed by a removal of the 41st and 43rd Ranger units, paramilitary groups of hunter-soldiers (*thahān phrān*), to the Malaysian border. The first of these new collective attacks took place on January 4, 2004, with an organized raid on a military base in Narathiwat. Within weeks, southern schools were bombed and Buddhist monks were shot while on their morning alms round. The Thai State responded by imposing martial law over the three border provinces. In response, militant attacks in the border provinces became even more politically relevant throughout the country. The declaration of martial law made the southern issue a matter of national security and raised the State's stakes in the conflict. Since the declaration of martial law, there have been three large conflicts between militants and the Thai State, two of which occurred during 2004. The first was the conflict at the Khru Se Mosque, the second was the Tak Bai massacre, and the third was a series of attacks on the Chinese New Year, 2007.

On April 28, 2004, Malay militants waged a comprehensive attack throughout the southern provinces of Songkhla, Pattani, and Yala. Malay Muslim youths, labeled by the media as "separatist militants," charged seven police outposts before dawn. Some, dressed in fatigues with red cloth strips wrapped around their heads, were said to be as young as fifteen.[20] One of the more critical clashes climaxed at the Khru Se Mosque in Pattani. After exchanging fire for six hours, Thai police and military shot tear gas and rocket-propelled grenades into the mosque, leveling the mosque and killing the thirty-two Malay Muslims inside. The overall body count for the day's attacks exceeded one hundred, nearly all of whom were Malay Muslims.[21] The destruction of the famous mosque and the heavy-handed approach to the militants resulted in increased religious tension between Buddhists and Muslims in Pattani province.

On October 25, 2004—six months after the multiple attacks and the assault on the Khru Se Mosque—the Tak Bai massacre in Narathiwat added to the Malay body count. More than two thousand locals protested outside the Tak Bai police station. Reports vary as to which group instigated the violence. Regardless, the police response was brutal. According to the International Crisis Group, the 45th Ranger Regiment arrested and transported protestors from the Tak Bai police station to the Ingkayut military base in Pattani.[22] Over 1,300 protestors were arrested and more than seventy-eight people died en route to provisional quarters in Pattani Province.[23] In addition, others were shot by police firing into the crowd.[24] Unlike the conflict at the Khru Se Mosque, most of those who died at Tak Bai were Muslim civilians.

Analysts such as Ukrist Pathmanand dubbed these events the "Achilles Heel" of the late Thaksin administration and highlighted the injustices of the Thai State.[25] Violence escalated throughout the southernmost provinces as a result of the controversial and inflammatory manner in which Thaksin handled the conflicts at the Khru Se Mosque and in Tak Bai.

Violence in the south continued to play a key political role on the national stage following a military coup that ousted Thaksin from office in September 2006. On February 18, 2007, anonymous attacks were waged on commercial, residential, and *wat* (Buddhist monastic compound) property throughout the three provinces.

According to the *Bangkok Post*, the attacks represented the "biggest wave of coordinated bombings, terrorism, and murders ever reported across the four southernmost provinces."[26] As the December 23, 2007, democratic elections for a new prime minister drew near, candidates such as Aphisit Wechachiwa and junta commander General Sonthi Buiyaratglin listed the southern violence as their top priority.[27]

Yet, the concerns and inquiries into the more recent spate of violent episodes do not address the murders, bombings, and beheadings of Buddhist villagers that occur on a daily basis in the southernmost provinces. Human Rights Watch's report for August 2007 states:

> Increasingly, and particularly since the beginning of 2007, separatist militants seem to favor a new brutal tactic: victims—all of them Buddhist Thais—have been set on fire after being shot or hacked with machetes, sometimes in front of many eyewitnesses.[28]

Human Rights Watch is incorrect in its claim that Thai Buddhists have only recently become special targets; however, their statement does highlight the recent trend toward more overt and public acts of violence against Thai Buddhists. Militants also target Malay Muslims, some allegedly *munafik* (traitors to religion) because of their work for the Thai State or for their moderate views.[29] The State's inability to address these attacks weighs most heavily on local authorities such as village and district leaders, who are also common targets of violence.[30]

As separatists continue to target the Buddhist minority in these provinces, southern Thai Buddhists express frustration and disappointment over the lack of attention to their plight. As of January 2010, statistics show that over 38% (1,559) of the deceased and nearly 60% (3,894) of the injured were Buddhist.[31] While Muslims represent a higher rate of mortality, they also represent a significant majority of the population. Factors such as these contribute to a level of frustration that is mixed with fear. Unaware of the historical significance of the Malay Muslim's resistance against the Thai State, some southern Buddhists believe that the violence in their villages is a byproduct of the global Islamic resistance to the "West" in the popularly coined "Al Qaeda" network. These Thai Buddhists see themselves as natural targets precisely because they are not Muslims and, therefore, stand in the way of Islamic expansion. This mentality often results in Thai Buddhist animosity toward Malay Muslims. Amporn Mardent, a lecturer from Walailak University of Nakhon Sri Thammarat, argues that the media's depiction of bandits (*čhōn*) in the southernmost provinces often underscores a link between the violence and Islam. To emphasize this point, she retells an episode in the southern province of Trang in which a Buddhist man on a bus yelled at a Muslim female passenger sitting next to him who was wearing a *hijab*. The Buddhist shouted that the Muslim woman was an assassin of peace in Thailand and that she should move to Malaysia.[32]

Assumptions by southern Buddhists about transnational militant activities are relevant, albeit nominally. According to the International Crisis Group,

> The recruitment process follows a pattern similar to jihadi organizations elsewhere in South East Asia, with selection, separation, oath-taking, indoctrination and military training. The difference is that recruiters in this conflict appeal to Malay nationalism and the oppression of Malay Muslims by Buddhist Thai rulers rather than invoking a universal Islamic state or a global war against the "international Zionist-Christian alliance."[33]

Southern Malay Muslim separatists apply similar training and recruitment methods, but they are specifically tailored to the region. Separatists are not without international aid, nor do they shy away from using warlike jihadic rhetoric. In recent years, anonymous leaflets have circulated in the southernmost provinces and abroad, some of which call for a jihad to take back the land from the "infidels."[34] Malay Muslim militants use these leaflets to communicate anonymously with locals. It is difficult to assess this communication because it is unclear if the leaflets are disseminated from one group or from disparate parties. Nonetheless, they clearly reflect the sentiments of the Malay Muslim militants.

Like the training of militants, most of leaflets focus on regional issues, such as the occupation, and call for Buddhists to move out of the three southernmost provinces. One of these leaflets found its way to Wat Chang Hai, in Pattani during the last week of November 2006. Signed as "a group of fighters gathered to restore the independent state of Pattani," (*lao nak rob kŏb kū ekarācharat pattānī*) the leaflet was printed in Thai and advised Thai Buddhists:

(1) Move out or migrate outside of Thailand's three southernmost provinces;
(2) Do not collaborate with any of the police and soldiers;
(3) You are forbidden to get involved with police and soldiers entering the villages because they are our main targets. Where there are police and soldiers, there is a war. Please know that the soldiers and police will not be able to protect you all the time.[35]

The anonymous leaflet indicated that the conflict was primarily between the Thai State and the separatists; however, it also contained important religious undertones, and was sent to a *wat* that served as a Buddhist center. The Thai language and word choices, such *khon thai* (Thai person) used throughout the leaflet, implied a specific ethno-religious identity, Thai Buddhist. This characterization contrasted with the writers and their ethno-religious affiliations, who were Malay Muslim. These identity politics are notable in their first demand that Thai Buddhists move out of the three southernmost provinces.

Islam is not the cause of the violence; rather, reactive social forces against the practice of Islamic traditions have become the locus of contestation in southern Thailand. One example of this is found in the Malay Muslim desires for Islamic education. Malay Muslims are united in their disapproval of the Thai educational system and its centralizing effect on their *pondoks* (schools). As a result, parents began sending more of their children to study in Muslim schools located in other countries, most particularly Malaysia, Pakistan, the Middle East, and Egypt. Egypt's Al-Azhar University, the most respected Islamic university in the world, is known to have produced a number of southern Malay Muslim leaders in the 1960s. Other international links come from Malay Muslim separatist training camps in Libya, Syria, and possibly Saudi Arabia;[36] however, while the notions of violent jihad and transnational Islamic movements have impacted the nature of violence in the three southernmost provinces, they are neither the cause, nor the motivation for this violence.

For centuries, Malays have fought to reclaim their regional autonomy from the Siamese State. Since the sixteenth century, the primary cause of intermittent conflict in the southernmost region has been the issue of nationalism and sovereignty. Yet, the context of the violence has apparently changed in the three southernmost provinces of Pattani, Yala, and Narathiwat. In recent years, the Thai State has framed the conflict as a standoff between independent guerilla actors or seditious regional groups and a secular nation-state.[37] However, locals consider the conflict more complicated with the added components of ethnic and religious divisions.

Some southern Thai Buddhists perceive the violence in their villages as a product of the conflict between radical Islam and Thai Buddhism. Within these perceptions we find a process similar to Tambiah's *nationalization* and *parochialization*:*globalization* and *parochialization*.[38] Whereas for Tambiah, *nationalization* and *parochialization* denote the reproduction of a national issue in diverse local centers, *globalization* and *parochialization* describe the reproduction of a global issue in diverse local centers (in effect, a phenomenon similar to Roland Robertson's *glocalism*). Conversely, many southern Malay Muslims perceive the conflict to be between Malay Islamic separatism and a hegemonic Buddhist State. These visions denote polemical religious identifications present within the conflict. With the presence of religious significance, any steps toward quelling the violence in the southernmost provinces will require more than economic policies; it will require religious reconciliation. And religion, at its core, addresses the issue of identity.

Approaches to Religion and Violence

Religion and violence are two words that remain ambiguous and highly contested, yet continue to collude in contemporary global analyses. I do not think these juxtapositions are by accident, but I will delimit their properties before

I discuss their relationship. In my attempt to isolate my use of these terms, I am aware of different critiques about defining or using "religion," one of the more prominent from anthropologist Talal Asad.[39] However, I feel that deconstructive arguments such as these act as an ideological Tower of Babel.[40] Although "religion" is located in a specific cultural etymology that delimits a particular understanding, I use this term (which is difficult to avoid as a scholar of religious studies). As such, I have a view of what "religion," is, and to avoid a disclosure of this simply masks my perspective.

What I find operable in my examination of Thai religious systems is Clifford Geertz's explanation of religion as a worldview and a code of conduct in that worldview.[41] The historian of religion Charles Long further elucidates Geertz's stance in his definition of religion when Long writes, "For my purposes, religion will mean orientation—orientation in the ultimate sense, that is, how one comes to terms with the ultimate significance of one's place in the world."[42] When this becomes pertinent in the discussion of violence and religion is the individual's orientation, specifically in respects to the world and ethical behavior. This rather loose and fluid definition operates well within the Thai Buddhist term for religion, *sāsanā*.[43] Thai Buddhists understand the world through their *sāsanā* and form a merit-based behavior pattern for it.[44] Among the many different ethical boundaries drawn is one demarcating the nature of violence.

What constitutes a violent act and, more importantly, what forms of violence are acceptable (and perhaps more importantly, when are they acceptable)? These questions have nettled the very best of scholars and have provoked larger treatises on the subject. To draw from its Latin root *violare*, violence is the violation of another, most often for the purpose of domination. Violations are not confined to physical actions; Gayatri Spivak's term "epistemic violence" is a form of structural violence that constitutes the colonial subject as the Other.[45] Walter Benjamin devises the axis of law and justice to explore the parameters of violence, which provides a fertile heuristic to understand State-affiliated violence. Natural law regards violence as a product of nature "as if it were a raw material," whereas positive law sees violence as a product of history.[46] Whether natural or historically produced, physical conflict and warfare represent the more widely identified forms of violence (*khwāmrunrāeng*). Both physical and abstract elements of violence exist in southern Thailand. Religion becomes apparent in the discussion of *acceptable* violence—as condoned violent behavior—a distinction that Benjamin frames between justice (ends) and legality (means).

The amalgam of religion and violence has been a global theme for centuries. Most recently, the phenomenon surfaced in such disparate places as Ireland, Nigeria, Sri Lanka, Bosnia, the Philippines, and Chechnya. Violence in these areas is caused by a plurality of contexts that Mark Juergensmeyer considers "cultures of violence," contexts that include environmental issues, economic grievances, and deep racial divisions.[47] However, in each case religion becomes a perspective in the violence that either condemns or condones the acts. In his comparative study of religiously motivated terrorist acts, Juergensmeyer locates the resurgence in religiously motivated violence within the larger geopolitical theatrical landscape. People define themselves and their cultures against that which they are not—a trend that James Aho has calls the "dialectic of heroism."[48]

The dialectic of heroism is not exempt from Buddhist traditions and often is exerted through the political mechanics of warfare. There are a limited number of books that follow the relationship between violence and a Buddhist tradition. Stanley Tambiah's *Buddhism Betrayed?* (1992) is one of the first to follow the Theravāda Buddhist–inspired acts of violence in Sri Lanka during the 1980s. Tambiah's work was followed by other exemplary studies of the recent Sri Lankan civil war, most notably H. L. Seneviratne's *Work of Kings* (1999). There have been several works on the role of Japanese and Chinese Buddhist traditions and violence. One of the first is Brian Victoria's *Zen at War* (1997), which is a comprehensive account of the Japanese Zen Buddhist monks' roles in twentieth-century warfare and required a new interpretation of one of the United State's earliest progenitors of Buddhist traditions, D. T. Suzuki. The history of Chinese Buddhist traditions and violence is vast, but little has been written on its contemporary relevance. Xue Yu provides a recent account with startling connections between Chinese Buddhist monks and twentieth-century warfare in *Buddhism, War, and Nationalism* (2005), Additionally, in a forthcoming study, Jacob Dalton addresses the violent elements in the Vajrayāna Buddhist–inspired acts of violence in Tibet.[49]

As the various Buddhist traditions spread across Asia, Buddhist principles were incorporated into military activities and warfare. This is found in the contemporary conflict in Sri Lanka, Japanese military activities during the Russo-Japanese War (1904–1905), the Sino-Japanese Wars, World War II, and early sectarian battles in Tibet during the rise of the Gelug-pa (14th–17th centuries). Paul Demiéville's detailed and comparative history of Buddhist militarism in 1957 was significant because of Buddhists' vast and repeated relationship with violence throughout Asia.[50] In each of these occasions, religion was mixed with State interest. This confluence makes for a unique branding of power.

Sociologist Saskia Sassen provides a poignant observation on distinguishing power between religion and State. For Sassen, State power is related to territory or bounded space, whereas religious power is not spatially confined, but instead is located in the rhizomatic appearance of authority.[51] States like the United States and Thailand operate within the parameters of territory—although, with the advent of the Internet, the notion of space or territory is no longer bounded physically. Religious authority from non-State-based religious traditions, such as Malay Islam, is not derived from governance dictated by spatial considerations. A Malay Muslim school teacher returning from a visit to Indonesia could claim authority based upon his religious experience and views. Unlike a governmental bureaucracy, which oversees and legitimates territory, the Malay Muslim school teacher needs no political body that oversees and legitimates his religious status. Rather, his status comes from religious systems of education, becoming a hajji (having performed the Hajj to Mecca), thus being conversant in Islamic beliefs. However, this distinction is lost when a State appropriates religion, as the Thai State does with Thai Buddhism. The confluence of religious desires to extend/preserve authority and State designs to expand/protect territory appears to lend a propensity for violent reactions.

Thailand is the largest Theravāda Buddhist country in the world, with over 61 million adherents. Although Thailand is more than 92% Buddhist, the three southernmost provinces are over 80% Muslim, making southern Thai Buddhists, such as the elderly Ačhān Pim, both a local minority and a national majority.[52] The authority of the Thai *sangha* becomes tenuous in such an environment, which coincides with the Thai State's fragile hold over the region. As noted earlier, southern conflicts historically arose in Thailand during times in which the State was politically and/or economically weak. The most recent resurgence of violence resulted from the Thai State's economic fragility following the global market crash in 1997, the Thaksin administration's support of a contested democratized secularism from 2001 to 2006, and the subsequently embittered administrations.[53]

The Thai State's current struggle for control over the southernmost provinces contains Buddhist dimensions, which are outlined in the subsequent chapters. However, to avoid any ambiguity, let me make clear that I do not claim that religion (or Buddhism for that matter) is violent.[54] People are violent and these people adhere to all sorts of religious beliefs and practices. My attention to Buddhist dimensions is heuristic in order to draw out the agency of Buddhist monks and the Thai State, as well as include Buddhist actors in the discourse on religion and violence.

Negotiating Subjects

There is a significant amount of Buddhist militia, civilians, and military involved in the conflict, but I have chosen to narrow the focus of this study primarily to southern Buddhist monks. One of the reasons for this is the sheer immensity of such a project, for although this scope would allow for a greater degree of gender equality in my subject, it would undoubtedly require a staggering amount of resources. However, another and more important reason calls upon the politics of authenticity. In an attempt to chronicle the relationship between religious persons and violence, there is always the critic who claims that the person who commits religiously inspired violence is not a "true" Buddhist—or Christian, or

Muslim for that matter. However, it is a different matter to disregard the actions of monks, whose religious identity is upheld and legitimized through a religious institution. Thai Buddhist monks are involved in the violence, and to refute their Buddhist personas is the same as to refute the legitimacy of the Thai Buddhist *sangha*.

Yet, before my selection of monks, I already had selected one specific religious group in the conflict. In order to understand the genesis of the violence and issues surrounding separatist movements in southern Thailand, it is imperative that scholars assess Malay Muslim views, values and history.[55] One indicator that is relevant to the contemporary violence is the conception of Malay Muslim identities, which are tied to the earlier local Islamic Malay kingdom that existed prior to Siamese colonialism. Throughout this work, I draw upon Malay Muslim historiographies and perspectives, particularly in chapters 1 and 5, to understand the structural components of violence; however, I do not supplement the historiographies with extensive ethnographic data from Malay Muslims for two reasons. The first is a stronger need to address the Buddhist lacuna in the study of religion, most particularly Buddhist studies. The second is feasibility.

The first reason for the lack of a Malay Muslim voice in this work is the need to address a lacuna in academics—southern Thai Buddhists. One of the greatest voids in the contemporary academic study of Thailand is the southern Thai Buddhist voice. As of 2010, there is very little historical, anthropological, or sociological work focusing on southern Thai Buddhism, or southern Thai Buddhists. The most recent and defining contributions to the area come from a collection of essays under the leadership of Duncan McCargo in the *Journal of Southeast Asian Studies*.[56] The field of Thai studies is replete with work on Thai Buddhism and Thai Buddhists, most of which are located in northern Thailand in places such as Chiang Mai, northeast Thailand (known as Isan) or the greater metropolitan area of Bangkok. Much like northern and northeast Thai Buddhists, southern Thai Buddhists practice variations of rituals, beliefs, and retain local histories, but these are nominally treated and reviewed in Thai studies to date.

In contrast to the dearth of scholarship on southern Thai Buddhists, there is a healthy amount of work that focuses on southern Malay Muslims, such as in the contributions of anthropologist Raymond Scupin, political scientist M. Ladd Thomas, and Islamic scholars Andrew Forbes and Arong Suthasasna. Most of these scholars correctly see southern Malay Muslims as important because of what they represent: marginalized identities within the Thai Buddhist State. Because we study these marginalized groups, we also must study the local marginal southern Buddhists who carry the double identity of being both a local minority and a national majority. Moreover, in any study of conflict it is important to consider multiple perspectives. Until recently very little attention was given to southern Thai Buddhists. Therefore, my intent is to redress this imbalance.

The second reason for omitting Malay Muslim perspectives is feasibility. When I traveled to southern Thailand, I found most people living in villages divided along Buddhist-Muslim identities. While this division does not exist in every village, nor is it recognized by every individual, the practice is widespread, especially in pockets of Pattani and Yala where there are larger concentrations of Buddhists. This contrasts sharply to the southernmost province of Narathiwat.

Ethnographic Disclosures

The southern Thai Buddhist tradition, like any religious tradition, is performative.[57] Buddhists live out their ideals and beliefs through a series of actions, reflecting the fluid and ever-changing aspects of their lives and environment, as opposed to nation-building doctrinal sources written in the early 1900s. In order to examine the role of Buddhist monks and acts of violence, I deliberately avoided adopting the traditional Buddhological approach that relies predominantly on textual sources. I am aware that, like other traditions such as Christian and Islamic, Buddhist traditions have a long and rich history of alternative interpretations and translations of texts that address violence, as well as different views on the *vinaya* (monastic guidelines). These textual sources are important when assessing Buddhist scholastic stances on violence; however, my aim is twofold: to assess the Buddhist monks' impacts on the violence in southern Thailand (more specifically, to what extent do monks increase or decrease hostilities or alter the parameters of the conflict); and to ascertain the violent environment's impacts on the Buddhist monks. As this objective is sociological in nature, it requires a focus on human activity. For that I draw upon ethnographic sources, such as participant observations and personal narratives, to provide contemporary Thai Buddhist monastic views on violence. This approach enables me to view and understand Thai Buddhism as a *lived tradition*, one that is fluid, diverse, and often distinct from the idealized tradition found in narratives.

Throughout my fieldwork in the three southernmost provinces, I primarily acquired testimonials from Buddhist officials, monks, and laity, who were predominantly male. I recorded these initial testimonials in 2004 with the assistance of a local translator. Subsequent interviews were conducted without a translator between August 2006 and October 2008. In my references to these testimonials, I contextualize these conversations in order to locate the statements in a specific time and place. As with many other contemporary ethnographers, I chose to use "I" in order to make myself visible and situated in the fieldwork, rather than mask my involvement in the data collection.

Ethnography involves a series of negotiations between the ethnographer and her/his informants. In studying Buddhist monks and their relationship to violence in southern Thailand, I had to decide between developing ties with Malay

Muslims or Thai Buddhist monks, since prolonged public relations with one of these groups would inevitably result in limited accessibility to and trust from the other. As a result, I largely omitted Malay Muslims from my ethnographic research. The focus on Buddhist monks also enhanced a male-oriented data source, which is unavoidable due to the strong patriarchical monastic system.

One of the first of my fieldwork experiences began in July 2004, when southern abbots permitted me to visit their *wat* and interview them. After visiting more than a dozen *wat*, I considered visiting the mosques and meeting with Malay Muslim leaders, but I ultimately decided against this. Since the rise in violence, Malay Muslims tend to avoid Buddhist monasteries, which represent a separate cultural community in many southern Thai villages, where I conducted the bulk of my research. It would have been incredibly difficult to win the respect and trust of local Malay Muslims, imams, and tok gurus while visiting the *wat*. In addition, it would have been nearly impossible to retain the trust and confidences of the Buddhist monks if they heard that I was visiting Malay Muslim homes.

One of the first and most difficult hurdles I faced was gaining the trust of the Buddhist abbots and monks in the conflict areas. I managed to get access to these initial contacts through my students who, as Buddhist monks, served as intermediaries. In 2003, I worked as a visiting lecturer at the College of Religious Studies at Mahidol University in Nakhon Pathom Province, less than an hour west of Bangkok. At the college I had the unexpected privilege of teaching religious traditions to both laity and Buddhist monks.[58]

When I arrived in August 2003, I planned to research Thai Buddhist activism. I was in the midst of examining Thai Buddhist monastic interactions with environmentalism and gender equality when acts of violence erupted from the southern provinces. The date most often referenced is January 4, 2004, when militants organized a raid on a governmental military base in the southernmost province of Narathiwat, bordering Malaysia. They stole a substantial cache of weapons and soon after, Thai prime minister Thaksin declared martial law over the three southernmost provinces of Pattani, Yala, and Narathiwat, which is still in effect today. I decided that, due to these recent developments, I should observe Buddhist monastic activities in the new militarized zone. I realized that, from a Thai perspective, issues such as environmentalism and gender equality were culturally relative and not necessarily viewed as natural offshoots of activism. In contrast, peace-making was a more culturally congruent form of activism in Thailand. The erupting violence in southern Thailand produced a setting in which I could view the way monks were involved in communal healing, interfaith dialogues, and peace movements. My intention was to observe southern Buddhist monks and note how violence affected their lifestyle and, conversely, how the monks affected the violence.

I was further motivated when I learned that, among the numerous NGOs, state-sponsored programs, and scholars writing about the region, very few were examining southern Thai Buddhism. In April 2004, following the conclusion of Mahidol University's academic year, I traveled to Pattani Province and arranged a series of interviews with abbots there. I decided upon the province of Pattani for three reasons. First, as a region it is a rich historical hub of the Malay Muslim insurgency. Second, the highest number of *wat* are found there; and, third, the most violent and emotional conflict at that time, which was memorialized at the Khru Se Mosque, took place on April 28, 2004, in the capital district of Pattani.

At my request, my Thai Buddhist monk students made phone calls in advance, notifying the abbots about me and my proposed project. This unique networking allowed for some very frank discussions with Buddhist abbots about the violence. Ultimately, I interviewed twenty abbots from eight districts, which accounted for over 22% of the abbots in the province. Interviews occurred in person or over the telephone, and all were conducted with the assistance of a local Buddhist translator.[59] These monks were extremely cautious when talking to strangers, even more so if they did not know whether the strangers were Buddhist. My students informed me that, when they called in advance to arrange my interviews, they had to convince the monks that I was partial to Thai Buddhism rather than Islam. Because of these delicate conditions, I chose a Thai Buddhist graduate student who came from Pattani Province.[60] I asked twenty standard questions that primarily pertained to demographics, which were followed by a question-and-answer session, found in the appendix.

During the rainy season of 2004, there were very few white people in the capital district of Pattani. Although more came later, at that time I came into contact with only two *farang* and had heard about a third. Two of the *farang* were Germans, hired as visiting professors at Prince of Songkhla University. The third was a Canadian who purportedly came down once a month from a neighboring province to teach, but only did so under armed guard. I decided to keep a low profile, but also tried to publicly support Malay Muslim establishments. Due to my dietary restrictions and deep appreciation for beef, I frequented Malay Muslim restaurants. I would often walk to these restaurants in the middle of the day and bring home leftovers for dinner. Very few wold walk after dark at this time, even in the capital district. It was simply too dangerous.

People would stop me during my walks and ask me questions about my identity and my purpose in Pattani. Rumors began to circulate that I was working for the CIA, for why else would a white man visit militarized Buddhist *wat* in this region? These rumors made it difficult to procure help with translation work. Many of the students I met thought I was working for an intelligence organization and did not want to get involved. I made a practice of not wearing jackets or taking bags with me—which could signal that I was armed. I also consistently pointed to my academic affiliation with the University of California, Santa Barbara; however, the existence of the rumors appeared more powerful than my claims. In late July, it became more difficult to find help. Professors called me, requesting that I not ask their students for help. It was too dangerous to journey outside the campus grounds.

On August 7, I had dinner at the C. S. Pattani Hotel, which was adjacent to my apartment. After dinner, I was stopped in the lobby and interrogated by an inebriated Malay Muslim. He was keenly interested in my religious affiliation and wanted to know whether or not I was a U.S. citizen. Although honesty is one of the principle values in ethnography, I answered in my typical fashion. Early on I decided that I would try to distance myself from the Bush administration. In short, I would lie and say I was Canadian. This proved costly, as lies only add to the power of rumors. I was never sure if the man believed me or not, but this encounter became more relevant later.

Three days after this, I received a call from a colleague at Prince of Songkhla University. I learn that a week earlier, one of the German visiting professors heard that a professional hit had been put out on "an American masquerading as a Canadian." He had not bothered to tell me about it until he received further information that credited the source, and recalled that I was the only U.S. citizen he knew in the area. This news coupled with the recent encounter close to my apartment was enough to merit concern. My informants booked a safe ride for me to Hat Yai, the nearest international airport in the adjacent northern province of Songkhla Province. I traveled from Hat Yai to Bangkok, spent less than a week in Bangkok, during which time I concluded some of my interviews over the phone, and then returned to the United States.

I did not return to southern Thailand for two years, during which time I developed a higher proficiency in Thai and evaluated the preliminary data I acquired. The 2004 interviews had collectively shown the need for more research; monks commented on their fears, violent attacks, and cursory proto-Buddhist nationalism. I realized that in order to gain further information and depth to these perspectives I would need to spend more time in conversation with the monks.

Although I visited my earlier contacts, I kept my visits short. I conducted subsequent interviews without a translator during these periodic visits from August 2006 to October 2008. Before each visit, I contacted the abbot of the *wat* by phone and then worked out travel arrangements with a driver I met in 2004. This enabled me to travel in and out of the conflict zone with very little time in-between field sites. Instead of living in an apartment and eating in public restaurants, I spent most of my time living in the *wat* that I visited in 2004. Throughout this time I suffered what I later learned was ASD (Acute Stress Disorder). However, due to my precautions, I did not have encounters with locals like I had back in 2004.

At the *wat*, Buddhist abbots and monks periodically tested my allegiance, sometimes by serving me pork. Thai and Chinese Buddhists eat pork, whereas pork is a forbidden food for Muslims (Arabic: *haram*). The acceptable, or "clean" food (Arabic: *halal*) is similar to the Jewish preparations for kosher food. In this context, one of the first visible signs of a person's conversion from Thai Buddhism to Islam would be their dietary habits, as in, they would stop eating pork.

During interviews, monks explained their views of the violence, and why they felt certain *wat* in Pattani, Yala, and Narathiwat were most affected. I learned that, as in 2004, most of the monks were not engaged in activities that specifically addressed the violence. Their passions and interests were directed toward their chosen livelihood, namely, practicing and disseminating the *dhamma* (Buddhist doctrine). The monks believed this was the best way to deal with the violence, which they perceived as political and, therefore, something to avoid. This point was exemplified when I was with a thirty-three-year-old monk I will call Phra Man. I asked Phra Man if southern monks were actively responding to the violence and he quickly replied, "No. We cannot be active in this [violence] because it is political. Monks should not be involved in political matters and this is political."[61] Phra Man's response was similar to those of most monks I interviewed in 2004. These sentiments signaled an important social disjuncture between the way monks saw themselves and the way their communities saw them. Monks viewed themselves as apolitical actors; however, contrary to these internal reflections, local Malay Muslims and local Thai Buddhists saw monks' identities and actions steeped in political relevance.

Monks also described the varying degrees of the conflict according to the demographics of violence, which was depicted through quick color references. The most dangerous areas with the most murders and attacks were called the red zone, followed by the yellow and green zones. Initially, these were military designations that referred to the number of incidents and casualties in an area. However, as Marc Askew astutely reflects in his study of Songkhla Province, "local people have appropriated this colour 'red' as a metonym to designate their own dangerous places in their local landscape."[62] These color-coordinated designations were reconceived and remapped into subjective spatial categories in the minds of the abbots. A handful of abbots acknowledged that they lived in a red zone, but the vast majority thought they resided in yellow zones. Interestingly, not one monk felt that he lived in a green zone. The green designation was always a signifier used in comparison to other areas (and to some extent, this was the same for red zones). Consequently, the abbot at Wat Suan Dok felt his *wat* was situated in a yellow zone, but that all of the *wat* in the capital district were in a green zone. On the other hand, a few abbots in the capital district felt they were living in a yellow zone, while all the *wat* in Khokpo district were in a green zone.[63]

Throughout these interviews, I discovered that most monks felt isolated and alienated from the rest of the country and the world. They reacted to my presence and questions in different ways. Some were uncomfortable addressing specific and disturbing events in their daily lives, while others displayed an enthusiasm that could be seen as cathartic. With nearly every encounter, the monks reflected how very few people seemed interested in their lives, problems, and thoughts.

An abbot from Yaring District in Pattani Province explained that he remained isolated because of the violence; it was simply too dangerous to visit him. "I have no role because I have no one to talk to. No one comes to the *wat*... . If anyone does come, they stay for only a short time, so I cannot teach."[64] Like many other abbots, his identity was tied to his actions, chief of these being the ability to teach the *dhamma*. These performative duties stopped or were severely diminished after the State declared martial law over the southern provinces. It was not because of martial law that less people came to the *wat*, but rather lay reactions to the climate of fear that preceded the declaration of martial law.

For some monks, this sense of isolation from the community was coupled with a sense of isolation from the world. Before I left Thailand in 2004, I had an extended phone interview with Ačhān Subin, the secretariat to the Pattani Sangha leader. I was in Bangkok, but still wanted to try and contact some of the remaining monks on my list. Ačhān Subin argued,

> Foreign reporters only interview the ones who cause the violence; they
> do not ask the monks. They just ask the ones who instigate the violence,
> not the victims. You should ask the victims, not the ones who are act-
> ing, because those who are causing the violence will give false and dis-
> torted information.[65]

As Juergensmeyer argues, terrorism is a term best defined by the victims, not the perpetrators or outside observers.[66] In the southern Thai conflict, local Malay Muslims and Thai Buddhists were terrified; however, these people were not being heard. And, according to Ačhān Subin, the situation was even more pronounced in the case of Buddhist monks. It was in fact Ačhān Subin's claim that became one of my reasons to return to Thailand in August 2006. If nothing else, I felt obligated to hear the monastic views and perspectives about the violence.

In order to assess varying degrees of stress and violence, I chose to examine three of the *wat* more closely. The overwhelmingly majority of monks indicated that Wat A was in the red zone, Wat B in the yellow zone, and Wat Chang Hai in the green zone.[67] From August 2006 to August 2007, I traveled frequently to Thailand, where I stayed for a few days to a few weeks at a time in each of these locations. As mentioned earlier, throughout these trips I was without a translator. However, I benefited from the previously created social network I made in 2004, which assisted me in establishing local trust. This independence allowed me to enjoy longer and more open discussions with monks, many of whom found release in the ability to discuss the violence with an outsider. From living in these violent areas for brief periods, I witnessed how daily fears greatly affected everyone. From the monks' perspective, it did no good to complain or discuss the fear among themselves; however, I was a newcomer and was eager to hear anything. The monks did not have to worry about disclosing their inner fears as they might were I a Buddhist layperson or a local. Although I never made any declarations of religious affiliation, these monks saw me as a Christian. Here, my positionality as an interviewer and observer was racialized with respect to religion. Most southern Thais assumed that white U.S. citizens practiced some form of Christianity. Often when they asked about people in the United States, they were surprised to hear about religious pluralism. But it was their initial assumptions that I was Christian (and not Muslim) that appeared to encourage the monks to vent their anger and frustrations.

Reaching a field site was one of the biggest challenges I faced during my fieldwork. Typically, I would fly or take a bus into the southern international center, Hat Yai in Songkhla Province. From Hat Yai, I would board a regional minivan that traveled back and forth between the capital districts of Pattani, Yala, and Narathiwat each day. While affordable, this service was slightly dangerous.[68] From there I had to drive a few hours to reach Wat A, Wat B, and Wat Chang Hai. The roads to Wat A and Wat B were considered extremely dangerous and, although the roads to Wat Chang Hai are generally considered safer than most, locals expressed concern about traveling these roads. Due to the risks, I hired a driver who worked for the Prince of Songkhla University and supplied him with hazard pay.[69] I carefully coordinated the times of my pickups and drop-offs. For example, my driver would drop me off at a site and return to his village before sunset because nighttime was an opportune time for militants and bandits to attack vehicles.[70] I developed relationships at each location with the monks, novices, assistants, regular patrons (laity), and the military. Wat A was home to over thirty soldiers, Wat B to forty policemen, and Wat Chang Hai to over thirty soldiers.[71]

While I lived at these *wat*, I traveled with the monks to different locations for rituals and ceremonies, or to investigate outbreaks of violence, thus extending my fieldwork to peripheral examinations of five other *wat* associated with Wat A, Wat B and Wat Chang Hai. As a participant-observer staying at these *wat*, I became acutely aware of the varying degrees of communal value placed on each *wat*. For instance, Wat A was a center of trade, where Malaysians came to sell their goods to locals and soldiers. Wat B hosted sporting events, such as basketball, as well as non-religious education, such as English classes. Wat Chang Hai was an international Buddhist pilgrimage site and a center for monastic learning. All three were favorite spots for locals to gather and socialize.

As multipurpose communal sites, the *wat* also were connected to different villages, districts, and provinces by communal and monastic infrastructure. Wat A provided services to more than two hundred Buddhists from different districts. The abbot there maintained regular contact with different abbots and villagers throughout his province and beyond. *Wat* throughout Thailand performed in similar fashion, but southern *wat* communities in the yellow and red zones became like extended families, supporting each other through difficult times. Buddhist laity and monks worked hard to maintain their relationships through the weeks and months of bloodshed. They readily integrated the soldiers and police into their intimate communal space in order to preserve the familial integrity of the *wat*. By the end of my fieldwork, my study of Buddhist monks and their habits ultimately yielded a snapshot of an internal complex social infrastructure consisting of negotiated identities, economies, and politics within a very violent external environment.

Chapter Overview

This work is divided into five chapters that compose the body, together with an introduction and a conclusion. Each chapter addresses one Buddhist dimension of violence in the three southernmost provinces. Although each dimension is examined separately, they all are interrelated through shared spaces, actors, and causes. What distinguishes these chapters—in addition to their subjects—are the Buddhist elements, which are integral to the justification of, and escalation in, violence throughout the southernmost provinces. Chapters 1 and 5 focus on abstract Buddhist qualities that dramatically alter social views of history and race. Chapters 2, 3, and 4 center on the relevance of Buddhist spaces and Buddhist monks. More specific information about each chapter follows.

Chapter 1: "Histories" describes the impact of historical narratives on the southern conflict. Thai Buddhist authorities, southern teachers, and Malay Muslim separatists adopt different historiographies that are lined with religious connotations. These historiographies become mytho-histories of the region to southern locals and provide them with justifications for the violence.

Chapter 2: "Representation" examines the symbolic power of southern Buddhist monks and its connection to the violence. The Thai State politicizes Buddhist monks through State rhetoric and official programs, thus transforming them into embodiments of Thai nationalism and Thai Buddhism. As political entities, the monk physically becomes a military target in the conflict, thereby escalating religious tensions and violent reactions.

Chapter 3: "Practice" shifts from the analysis of the symbolic role of Buddhist monks to the performative aspects of Buddhist monks. Personal narratives and accounts from the three southernmost provinces display how Buddhist monks reassert their politicized roles and call for a stronger form of Buddhist nationalism.

Chapter 4: "Militarization" focuses on Buddhist soldiers and police in the southernmost provinces and the State's role in militarizing Buddhist identities and areas. In addition to examining militarized Buddhist temples and the advent of the military monk (soldiers who simultaneously work as monks), it compares the military monk phenomenon with other military monk occurrences throughout the history of Asia.

Chapter 5: "Identity" expands the analysis of the conflict to the issues of race and ethnicity. It traces the genesis of racially charged terms from South Asia to Thailand, and looks at how this structural form of violence fuels the problems in the southernmost region.

The conclusion provides an existing model of religious pluralism that mitigates the ethno-religious tensions. While the Thai State's policies and actions politicize the role of Thai Buddhism and exacerbate the violence, a minority of monks work to retain Thai Buddhism's communal and interfaith characteristics in the southern provinces. By reducing their political roles and increasing their community ties, these monks offer hope to the region and, more importantly, a platform of action to develop in the area.

Language Notes

Throughout this work I use the National Library of Congress's style of transliterating Thai words. Following this method, Thai words are separated in the Roman script (as opposed to being read without spaces between words in Thai). There is no plural or singular differentiation in Thai; thus, words such as *wat* (monastery) are written the same regardless of plural or singular connotations. To address this ambiguity I inserted English articles before these words to note the singular form. The omission of an article indicates the plural form (for example, "The *wat* were close to my home," versus "This was a *wat* different from others in the region."). In addition, I follow the Thai custom of using *wat* as the initial marker for a proper noun with respect to monasteries, while not italicizing the name (for example, Wat A, Wat B, Wat Chang Hai). The National Library of Congress style of transliteration requires that I not italicize a Thai word once transliterated into Roman script; however, for the sake of clarity and consistency, I decided to italicize transliterated Thai words. I acknowledge that there is no standard form of Thai transliteration and some scholars choose to improvise with their own styles.

Acknowledgments

I am above all deeply indebted to the Thai monks and the people of southern Thailand for permitting me access to their homes, lives, and memories. Much of my fieldwork would not have been possible without the assistance of Paulpone Petdara, Thanaporn Maliwan, Chanyanunt Siriparnithipakorn, Waranya Pimsri, Jinanggoon Rajanan as well as southern locals and students who wish to remain anonymous. Archival work was done with the assistance of Sophia Hajisamae and her staff at the Institute of Southeast Asian Maritime Studies at Prince of

Songkhla University, as well as help from Don Pathan of the Thai newspaper, *The Nation*. But, in the end, my fieldwork in Thai would never have been possible if not for the dedicated and inspiring work of Ačhān Kannikar Elbow of the University of Wisconsin–Madison, Ačhān Suthiwan Titima of the National University of Singapore, and the Ačhāns of the Advanced Study of Thai program at Chiang Mai University. Though often underappreciated, language *ačhāns* are the gardeners of the academic nursery.

Any project such as this has a chronology of important influences and influencers. The first of these began in my undergraduate studies with Harold Scheub at the University of Wisconsin–Madison, who introduced me to the medium of ethnography, particularly through the use of oral narratives. During a pivotal time in my graduate studies, Charles Hallisey and Thongchai Winichakul modeled memorable levels of critical thinking in the discussions of Theravāda Buddhism and Thailand. Upon arriving at the University of California, Santa Barbara, Mark Juergensmeyer and Stanley Tambiah were principal mentors in the conception of this project and have remained supportive throughout its development. During the off-site research stage in Singapore, Irving Johnson of National University of Singapore posed definitive questions and prompted important reflections and future observations. Michael Montesano of the Institute of Southeast Asian Studies gave more time than I thought possible to help sharpen my knowledge of Thai history. It was also at this time that I had the good fortune of working with Duncan McCargo who guided me through parts of the fieldwork and academic matters.

My dissertation committee outperformed any expectations I could have conceived. During the first incarnation of the project Justin McDaniel of University of Pennsylvania and Vesna Wallace of University of California, Santa Barbara braved countless revisions and offered frank and insightful comments with each version, which resulted in global and specific changes. Mark Juergensmeyer provided invaluable ideas, structural suggestions, encouragement, and moral support. At times, his ability to articulate my interests and arguments surpassed my own.

The dissertation work would not have been completed without colleagues. I discovered the depth of support possible through the periodic sessions with Torsten Sannar, Staci Scheiwiller, and Beth Wynstra, who took Jody Ender's seminar of academic writing to a new level of productivity.

Since the dissertation stage, the work underwent important transformations. Saroja Dorairajoo, Irving Johnson, Michael Montesano, Duncan McCargo, Charles Keyes, Rudy Busto, Johari Jabir, Lawrence Chua, Amy Speier, and Deborah Bensadon generously read chapters and provided the feedback that helped the work transform into what it is. The development of the chapters was also aided by Charles Keyes, Suwanna Satha-anand, Francis Bradley, Alicia Marie Turner, Jovan Maud, and Rohit Singh, who generously shared their related work.

I also am indebted to the feedback in collective settings at the Ninth International Conference of Thai Studies at Northern Illinois University (2005), East-West Washington Center and Institute of Defence and Strategic Studies Singapore Workshop at the C. S. Pattani Hotel, Pattani (2006), the American Academy of Religion in Washington D.C. (2006), Association of Asian Studies in Boston (2007), the International Workshop on Buddhism and the Crisis of Nation-States in Asia at Asian Research Institute of National University of Singapore (2008), and Center for Southeast Asian Studies Friday Form at the University of Wisconsin–Madison (2009).

However, it is not until the classroom that this work gained a new dimension of meaning to me, and this was only possible with the help of U.C. Santa Barbara students in my *Buddhist Warfare* course and Eckerd students in my *Asian Religion and Warfare* course in 2009. These students were living testaments to the value of scholarship and research that occur in the undergraduate classroom.

Eckerd College has provided an amazing environment in which to finish this project. Lloyd Chapin, Dean of Faculty, secured funding for my research and professional development. Julienne Empric, chair of the Letters Collegium, devoted many hours to my pedagogical and professional needs. My Religious Studies colleagues David Bryant and Davina Lopez are a veritable warehouse of energy, guidance, and academic modeling. I am also grateful to my extended academic family that includes Andrew Chittick, Bill Felice, Heather Vincent, Carolyn Johnston, and the "Grits for Thoughts" crew.

I am indebted to the *Associated Press*, *Bangkok Post*, and Muang Boran Publishing House for the use of their photos and to the editors of the *Journal of Southeast Asian Studies* for their permission to reproduce portions of chapter 5. Thank yous are also much deserved to Cynthia Read, the anonymous reviewers, and her editors at Oxford University Press for their support and meticulous guidance in the development of the manuscript.

Special thanks are due to those who sacrificed their time in and out of academia. Aysha Hidayatullah, Chris Joll, David Kessler, Nathan McGovern, Chloe Martinez, and Jamel Velji provided companionship, faith in me and much needed intellectual support. Shirley Ronkowski, Susan Jarrett, Rhella, Kessler and Fawn Jerryson provided ceaseless help in converting my convoluted phrases into coherent sentences.

However, ultimately it was through the gifts of kindness and compassion from Fawn, Sienna, and Parker that I was able to see this work to completion. These gifts are immeasurable and they enrich my life on a daily basis.

While these acknowledgements indicate how much I owe my support networks and informants, I want to make clear that any interpretations or errors are strictly my own.

1

Histories

The teaching of history is an exercise of power, a way of shaping remembrance. It is also a way of shaping identity. With this in mind, we should ask: how do Thai southerners teach their own history? In a private office at the College of Islamic Studies, Prince of Songkhla University (PSU), I spoke with Ačhān Dolmanach Baka, who teaches comparative religions and offers a course on Islam in Thailand. I asked him, "How do Islamic Studies students learn about the history of southern Thailand?" Ačhān Dolmanach Baka's students were mostly Malay Muslims from the three southernmost provinces. Not more than five years ago, students from all over Thailand enrolled at PSU's Pattani campus; however, the enrollment has changed, which is a byproduct of the volatile and dangerous environment. Ačhān Dolmanach Baka appeared taken back by my question and frowned. "I'm not sure. They didn't let us study Pattani history in the past."[1]

Students in the three southernmost provinces receive very little formal education on their region's history.[2] The scarcity of knowledge is partly due to the Bangkok-centered bias prevalent in elementary and secondary curricula (*laksūt prathom mathayom*).[3] Another more specifically regional reason is the danger inherent in teaching the regional history of the south. The general teaching profession is under attack in the three border provinces. Since the Phibun administration (1938–1944, 1948–1957), the Thai State has used education as a means of "making Malay Muslims into *Thai* Malay Muslims."[4] With this State focus on education, it is not surprising to find that militants have directed many of their attacks on public schools and teachers. Since January 2004, over three hundred schools have been destroyed and more than one hundred teachers have been murdered or gone missing—nearly 10% of the total murders in the region.[5] Teachers of the southernmost provinces are in danger, more so if they offer controversial subjects (such as southern history). The danger in teaching southern history lies in the politicized context embedded within the subject matter. The educator either would have to present a history that refutes the Malay Muslim insurgency's claims to the region, or offer a version of history that refutes the Thai State's authority.

A historian's construction of a narrative is a product of knowledge, or as Michel Foucault puts it, an attempt to memorialize the monuments of the past in documents. In this manner, historians galvanize a history behind a conceptual model, calling attention to specific instances, causations, actors, and artifacts. These conceptual models comprise the skeletal structure of a narrative. Thus, historians apply methods of periodization and teleology that affect the way readers interpret history. Perhaps one of the better known examples of this comes from Buddhist recollections of the Buddhist tradition's demise in India. In a popular narrative, causations, actors, and specific periods treat Muslims as the scapegoat. I have heard Mongolian, Thai, Sri Lankan, and Chinese Buddhists recount the pivotal destruction of Nalanda, the world-renowned Buddhist monastery and college of northeast India, by Muslim invaders in 1202 CE.

The story of Nalanda's destruction serves as a historical marker for the decline of Buddhist traditions from the subcontinent and for those responsible. However, this narrative is simply not true. Buddhist traditions persisted in the area of Nalanda well into the thirteenth century and as late as the seventeenth century in the subcontinent. But why does this inaccurate portrayal of history persist? In his critical work on Buddhist-Muslim interactions, Religious Studies scholar John Elverskog writes, "There are numerous possible explanations for this and they range from the Buddhist prophecies of decline to the problems of contemporary scholarship. However, rather than addressing such concerns, one can simply begin with the power of story."[6]

Story is powerful. In the authoritative role as history, it is a subtle, yet powerful dimension to the violence in contemporary southern Thailand. Buddhist and Islamic sentiments are enmeshed in the competing histories of southern Thailand, working to justify either the Thai State's or Malay Muslim's rights to the area. Many histories focus on providing justifications, or as historian Richard Evans argues, an "inspiration for political and social movements in the present."[7] Traditionally, the historical focus on justifying social movements has been prominent during times of war, wherein opposing political factions need to justify and inspire the populace through calls to renewed nationalism. Histories also contradict one another in their embodiment of people's interests present in wars and conflicts. Janet Abu-Lughod draws direct parallels between conquest of a war and conquest over narratives. For her, "If history is written by the victor, then it must, almost by definition, 'deform' the history of the others."[8] In this chapter, we will examine the contradicting narratives of southern Thailand found in Buddhist and Islamic historical narratives and their justifications for violence.

The Didactics of a Master Narrative

In intra- or international wars, each faction retains a version of history that lends an explanation to the conflict. In Thailand's southernmost provinces, there are two prevalent historiographies: the master narrative, in which historical accounts acknowledge the Siamese/Thai State's continuous rule over the three southernmost provinces for centuries, and counter narratives, in which historical accounts depict the provinces as the Islamic kingdom of Patani, colonized in the contemporary era by the Siamese/Thai State.[9]

The master narrative serves as a Foucaultian example of how power produces knowledge. In this situation, the Thai State produces the record of itself. This form of State-sponsored narrative is present throughout the world and is endemic to the region of Southeast Asia. Chris Baker and Sunait Chutintaranond, who challenge master-narrative styles in *Recalling Local Pasts: Autonomous History in Southeast Asia*, begin their volume with a cautionary statement: "The history of Southeast Asia—especially mainland Southeast Asia—has been written as a history of kings and states."[10] In Thailand, this monarchial history is evident in contemporary textbooks, which follow the chronology of central Siamese/Thai rulers and their kingdoms.

Thailand's rulers have been at the helm of its history-making.[11] Thai historian Charnvit Kasetsiri finds that while the cadre of authors remains consistent, the themes fluctuate over the previous centuries.[12] The Thai method of writing history endured several transformations over the last five hundred years, but the principle influencers remained with the royal courts and Thai *sangha*. In the present mold, the master narrative upholds the legacy and integrity of the current Thai State, venerating the current Chakri dynasty and Thai king Bhumibol Adulyadej through a favorable and heroic development of past events leading up to the present. Each successive reign of kings in the Rattanakosin lineage led Thailand to develop and embrace modernity. The Thai State profits from such a narrative inasmuch as the monarchy and State bureaucracy are intimately connected. As a result, it has taken measures to insure and protect the narrative.[13] For instance, any work critical of the monarchy is perceived as a form of *lèse majesté*, and this State position includes the subject of history (and its monarchical focus).

The multiple Thai historiographies denote changes in the social and political milieu. In this fashion, we can use historiography as a window into the State's identity-building exercises. History making is a didactic form of identity-formation or, in this contemporary case, nation-building. Benedict Anderson's comparison of an infant with that of a nation is apropos here. Personhood—or nationhood—is imagined through a recollection of the past, "which, because it can not be 'remembered,' must be narrated."[14] This identity-making is not simply national, but religious in significance. The first administration of the Rattanakosin kings, that of Rama I (1782–1809), provided significant influence over the official Thai historiography, and much of this carried Thai Buddhist sentiments.[15] This religious infusion to the writing of history was due in part to the small cadre of intellectuals centered on the royal court and the Thai *sangha*. The narration of Thailand was, until the early 1900s, entrenched in an educational system that was systemically Buddhist. Buddhist monks had been the traditional facilitators of education in Siam, and their interrelationship with State-sponsored learning extended into the southernmost provinces.

When Siamese Buddhist monks opened educational facilities in the southernmost provinces, Malays immediately rose to protest. They wanted an education that was neither dependent on Buddhism, nor on the Thai language.[16] However, nationalist curriculum was still present in the 1970s, when Chavivun Prachuabmoh found that students "learn about the Thai migration to Southeast Asia, the biographies of national heroes, the institution of kingship and the socio-economic conditions."[17] As historian Francis Bradley succinctly explains,

> Discussion of Pattani's gilded Islamic past has often been muted because it has served as a rallying cry for many of the Patani independence movements since 1367/1948 and is thus seen as threatening to a broader view of the Thai nation.[18]

Historian Thongchai Winichakul considers the monarchical institution and Thai Buddhism the two most important elements of the nation; indeed, they are integral parts of the national-identity marker: Thainess (*khwāmpenthai*).[19] In this manner, the master narrative continues to act as a harbinger of Thainess in Thai history textbooks, academic works, and government archives. Thai primary and secondary school history textbooks adhere to the Ministry of Education's guidelines and utilize sources from the National Library's bibliography. These textbooks also reflect a central-Thailand bias in history-making.

In the 2007–2008 history curricula for the capital district of Pattani, students from Mathayom 1–6 (secondary education, ages 13–18) focus primarily on four eras (*yuk*) constructed around the ruling of Thailand's central dynasties. Sukhothai is the first dynasty, and this chronology imposes significance with a point of inchoation in time, place, and content.[20] Here the focus is on the development of the central region, its dynasties, its peoples and their traditions. Table 1.1 provides the general parameters of the six years of history provided in Thailand's secondary education, whether a student attends school in Chiang Mai Province, the former region of the kingdom of Lanna, or Pattani Province, the former region of the kingdom of Patani.

Mr. Adam is a thirty-two-year-old history teacher at Thamavitya Mulniti School (*rōngrīenthammawithayā mūlnithi*) in the capital district of Yala Province. Thamavitya Mulniti School is the largest Islamic public school in the southernmost provinces, with almost seven thousand students attending for primary and secondary education. Mr. Adam has been teaching Social Studies to secondary-education students at Thamavitya Mulniti School for ten years. Each year Mr. Adam follows the prescribed historiography of the Ministry of Education and spends the majority of his time discussing the Ayutthaya period. The

Table 1.1 **History Table for First Year Secondary Education, 2007–2008**

Name of Era	Capital City	Time Period
Sukhothai	Sukhothai City (*krungsukhothai*)	1249–1463 (B.E. 1792–2006)
Ayutthaya	Srī Ayutthaya City (*krungsrī'yuthayā*)	1350–1767 (B.E. 1893–2310)
Thonburi	Thonburi City (*krungthonburī*)	1767–1782 (B.E. 2310–2325)
Rattanakosin	Bangkok (*krungtēpmahānakhon*)	1782–Present (B.E. 2325–Present)[i]

[i] *Prawatisātm. 1: chan mathayom sūksā pī thī 1* [History, Year 1: First Year Education for Secondary Education] (Bangkok: *aksončharōenthat*, 2007), 11.

Ayutthaya period is an important time for the southern region according to both the master and counter narrative accounts because this is the period in which the Patani kingdom became a vassal of Siam. Nevertheless, the Patani kingdom is not mentioned in the classroom for purposes of this or any other discussion.

The only times Mr. Adam discusses southern history is when he touches upon the early Buddhist kingdoms of Langkasuka or Śrīvijaya that existed prior to the first of the Thai empires, Sukhothai. When discussing the two southern kingdoms, Mr. Adam primarily limits the lessons to aesthetics.

> We don't cover Śrīvijaya, but we discuss the art and ancient places of Śrīvijaya and Langkasuka. For instance, there are many *stūpas*, *chedis*, and other artifacts from the Śrīvijaya period in Jareh and Yarang. We teach about the art of Śrīvijaya and Langkasuka, but we don't teach or talk much about the kingdoms of Śrīvijaya and Langkasuka.[21]

Buddhist references to southern Thailand, albeit nominal, link southern history to the Thai Buddhist dynastic compilation. Mr. Adam is one of the two Social Studies teachers in his department. Both he and his colleague Mr. Azam would like to teach more about the two southern kingdoms but, as Mr. Adam explained, teachers in the three southernmost provinces are not given sufficient information to do so. Mr. Adam's discussion of southern Thai history is not unique to his school. An examination of the six different history books for Thai secondary education in Pattani Province confirms his assertions.

In secondary-education history books, the history of southern Thailand is confined primarily to topographical snippets, with no reference to the region's Islamic heritage. Thai history textbooks do not specifically omit the discussion of Islam. Chavivun Prachuabmoh notes that local criticism over the lack of education on Islam may have prompted the Ministry of Education to alter the curricula in the 1970s. By 1980, any primary school that was more than 50% Muslim included the subject of Islam.[22] However, this change has not altered the manner in which southernmost history is taught. For example, Pattani's fifth-year history textbook contains a short section on the role of Islam during the development and growth of Southeast Asia.

> Southeast Asia contains many models of governance. In the first period, [the models of governance] were influenced by India. All ideas concerning kingship and doctrine came from Buddhism, and this model of governance was used in many kingdoms. For example: Thai, Burmese, Cambodian, Lao, Indonesia and Malaysia. Later, Indonesia and Malaysia turned to Islam. The model of governance changed as well, by having sultans as the head of the country.[23]

The section continues with the development of Vietnam and the Philippines, and then addresses the Eurasian colonization of Indonesia and Malaysia. As evidenced in the excerpt above, the textbook acknowledges the conversion of parts of Southeast Asia from Buddhisms to the Islamic faith; yet, the developmental scheme, the status and identity of the southern region, is missing. The entire existence of the Patani kingdom, which scholars have called "the cradle of Islam in Southeast Asia," and which existed from the period of "Islamification" in Indonesia and Malaysia to the subsequent period of Eurasian colonialism (over four hundred years), has been omitted (and is not present in any of the earlier or subsequent history books for the curricula).[24]

Mr. Ali is a thirty-one-year-old history teacher at a private Islamic school near the Thamavitya Mulniti School. Approximately 1,500 secondary education students, many of whom graduate and attend Prince of Songkhla University's campus in Pattani, go to the school. Mr. Ali, like Mr. Adam, would like to teach about the kingdom of Patani as well as the early southern Buddhist kingdoms, but he explains that the educational system inhibits teaching on the subject. "There is nothing on the subject, because it's not in the Ministry of Education's curriculum."[25] The absence of the Patani kingdom from the history textbooks is significant, and Mr. Ali's students sometimes ask him about the kingdom. Mr. Ali explains,

> That is a problem. Sometimes, I cannot answer the question because it's related to security. If we do answer [those questions], people will think

that we are provoking violence, and so I must answer that [Patani] has been part of the Thai kingdom. Usually, I answer like that.[26]

Mr. Ali's concerns are common among Buddhist and Muslim teachers alike in the three border provinces. The Pattani Educational Administration (*sāmakngnankānsuksā*) in the capital district oversees the public-school curriculum in half the province.[27] None of the Social Studies teachers offer classes on southern history and all cite concerns similar to those of Mr. Ali. Mr. Wila at Bengama School in Pattani Province explains that the teachers are too afraid to discuss the subject.[28] Militant violence and martial law in the three southernmost provinces present a political context in which teachers cannot offer alternatives to the master narrative. This problem extends beyond secondary education; researchers find similar problems in higher education as well. In an attempt to explain the political climate around researching the local history of Pattani, Prof. Dolmanach Baka explained:

> The Council for National Security only gave two or three historians access to conduct research on Pattani's history. They wrote what they wanted based on the questions they received in advance. These historians did not have their doctorates. They didn't write the truth. I don't know how and who will correct this. I have been looking into this.[29]

Through the Council for National Security, the Thai State holds immense power in controlling the content and dissemination of history. Thus, the master narrative operates through both transmission and omission, as the Thai State controls the history of southern Thailand. The Council for National Security is the interim political body that was established following the coup in September 2006. It has the power to adjudicate which researchers have access to archives and, moreover, who can write about southern Thai history. Information concerning this region is scarce and often contradicts academic work conducted outside of Thailand. In Pattani's second-year history book, one of the few references to Pattani depicts the region as a province (*hua mūang*) of the Ayutthaya State, which was associated with and fought against the Siamese State in the 1400s.[30] Here there is no mention of the kingdom of Patani or its Islamic heritage.

The Didactics of Counter Narratives

Just as the master narrative confirms the centrality of power in the State, counter narratives substantiate a form of resistance to the State. However, the method of dissemination is different. Master narratives possess a central

governmental agency that advocates and oversees dissemination. Counter narratives depend on individual and communal actions to survive.

There are a variety of counter narratives on southern Thailand. Some reflect
Thai Buddhist perspectives, while others represent Malay Muslim points of view.
Whereas the master narrative assumes a normative role in Thai society, an examination of counter narratives displays a polemical discourse that is beset by
interpretations. The Buddhist counter narratives assert the presence and importance of Thai Buddhism in the southernmost provinces; authors use historical
references, distinguishing themselves and southern history from that of their
Malay Muslim neighbors. Conversely, Malay counter narratives maintain the
historical legacy and importance of the Malay Muslim kingdom, thereby distancing Malay Muslims from Thai Buddhists. Through this polemical discourse,
each counter narrative advocates a religious-nationalist account of the border
provinces and continues to reinforce the ethno-religious divide, as well as the
sacred duty, vested in the current conflict.

Buddhists in southern Thailand offer a counter narrative that is different
from the master narrative, one that places greater emphasis on the details of the
early southern Buddhist kingdoms of Śrīvijaya and Langkasuka, in addition to
the importance of southern Thai Buddhism.[31] While recalling the two kingdoms
as Buddhist strongholds, Buddhist laity and monks often neglect to mention
that they are also a part of an important part of Malay heritage. Thais living
outside of the southern provinces have limited knowledge, if any, of Langkasuka.
In fact, there have been some recent pop-cultural references that promote the
legendary status of the Langkasuka kingdom.

The most recent reference to this kingdom occurred in 2008, when Thai film
director Nonzee Nimibutr released his movie *Queens of Langkasuka* (*bunyai čhom
sa lad*). It was initially titled *Queens of Pattani*, but due to the violence in the
southernmost provinces, the name was changed to *Queens of Langkasuka*, though
neither title was appropriate to the context of the story. The movie is set in the
seventeenth century, with a fantasy-based script. There are only nominal references to the southernmost region and its culture.[32] As with other pop-cultural
references to Langkasuka, the substance lies predominantly in name. Archaeo-
logical evidence suggests a much richer and more substantive account of the
kingdom. According to historian David Wyatt, the kingdom of Langkasuka
became a Buddhist stronghold in the Gulf of Thailand and managed to preserve
its autonomy until the eighth century when it became a vassal of the Śrīvijaya
thalassocracy.[33] Contrary to the master narrative's centrist perspective, there is
evidence suggesting that Langkasuka's socio-religious properties influenced
what later became the central region of Siam, not the reverse as was previously
thought.[34]

Like Langkasuka, Śrīvijaya's Buddhist activity was quite pronounced. The
beginning of Śrīvijaya occurred in the seventh century and expanded with the help

of a twenty-thousand-strong army.[35] Some of the oldest inscriptions from Java refer to the development of Mahāyāna Buddhism in Śrīvijaya. From these Sanskrit inscriptions we have learned that the sacred center of Śrīvijaya was the Buddhist park of Śrīksetra, which was founded by King Jayanāśa and Bukit Senguntang.[36] According to Buddhist pilgrim Yiqing, the capital of Senguntang was an international centre of Buddhist learning, with over a thousand Buddhist monks.[37]

As a genre, counter narratives are often diverse, in part because they reflect the fragmentation of peripheral power (political and/or economic). Nonetheless, there are common tropes throughout counter narratives, one of which is victimization. Current southern Thai Buddhist counter narratives tell of a golden age that has come and gone. Southern Thai Buddhists may be part of the ethno-religious majority in Thailand, but their regional heritage places them outside normative Thai culture. Southern Thai Buddhist readings of southern history are not found in the official curricula because Langkasuka and Śrīvijaya are only peripherally important to the current central government as the State's legacy in Thai history.[38] Thus, southern Buddhist narratives differ from the master narrative in detail and regional focus, but not in ideology. Both the master narrative and the southern Buddhist narratives provide justifications for Thailand's rights to the southernmost provinces, in addition to the region's great importance to Thai Buddhism.

The dominant Malay Muslim counter narrative frames its discussion of history on the Islamic kingdom of Patani and the subsequent Siamese colonization of the kingdom. Just as the master narrative supports "Thainess" and the Thai normative identity, the Malay Muslim counter narrative supports the Malay Muslim minority identity. Prachuabmoh writes of the Malay Muslims, "the history of Patani makes them conscious of their previous existence as a political entity independent from the Thais."[39] According to this counter narrative, prior to being annexed, the three southernmost provinces were a Malay Muslim kingdom called Patani. Like the southern Buddhists' narrative, most of these narratives are presented in oral form, although the Malay Muslim counter narrative also exists in academic works outside of Thailand. There are local written accounts, but these are extremely difficult to locate.

Outside the John F. Kennedy Library at PSU in Pattani, I met with Ačhān Kaimōk, the only academic at southern Thailand's prestigious university who offers courses on southern Thai history. She is passionate about her work and the numerous challenges surrounding this subject. Ačhān Kaimōk considers the current political climate detrimental to Malay Muslim perceptions of available local historical archives. She notes a stigma associated with the study of history in the three southernmost provinces, one of the many hurdles Ačhān Kaimōk faces as she researches southern history.

One time a teacher named Songchai was writing about the history of Pattani. He went to gather information in the area that he was researching and said he came across a record of southern Thai people on animal skin. This was an ancient method of recording history. After making this discovery he returned to the site to see it again. But, when Songchai asked about it, the villager was afraid. He quickly set fire to the skin and threw the remains into a pond. The villager did this because he was afraid that whoever possesses such historical evidence would be viewed as an insurgent.[40]

Ačhān Kaimōk's story of Songchai illustrates the power of history during wartime. Historical narratives are political stories, and particular political stories become instrumental during times of conflict. In his study of the Patani educational system, Francis Bradley locates the primary indicator language:

> In addition, much of the discourse on the history of Thailand's south has been conducted in Thai, based on Thai-language sources. Malay sources in Jawi script ... aside from the *Hikayat Patani* (Story of Patani), have often been ignored. The numerous stories I encountered in the border region that told of old Jawi manuscripts being burned—either by Thailand's state forces or locals who feared such as possession would lead to undue attention from government officials—further suggest that these writings have been marginalized.[41]

Ačhān Dolmanach Baka also notes that it is far easier to research and study the history of southern Thailand outside of Thailand, such as in Singapore, Malaysia, or the United States. There are individual centers that operate semi-independently and serve to support Islamic counter narratives. In 2007, 136 private Islamic schools and *pondoks* and 249 *pondok* institutes officially operated in the three southernmost provinces.[42] To a large degree, these educational centers supported counter narratives, but lacked the systemic qualities of a State. One of the more prevalent counter narratives is the *Hikayat Patani*, which is available in both English and Malay.

The *Hikayat Patani* is one of the most popular counter narratives of southern Thailand and was written in the late seventeenth century.[43] It posits that the southernmost provinces are part of a region that was the cradle of Islam in Southeast Asia. In opposition to the master narrative, the *Hikayat Patani* places southern Thailand as the focus of its narrative and relegates the Siamese/Thai State to the role of antagonist. Because the *Hikayat Patani* was originally written in Bahasa Melayu (Malay) and promotes Islamic identity, it stands in direct contrast to the "Thainess" found in the master narrative.

The reading of religion reveals a crucial dimension to the history of Patani's resistance. According to the counter narrative, one prominent factor in Patani's distancing itself from Siam was its conversion to Islam in the fifteenth century.

This change in the region's religious identity is of great significance to the contemporary Malay Muslim resistance and extends beyond the resistance to the majority of Malay Muslims who see their identity tied to a nationalism formed by the creation of the city of Patani.[44] Beyond its academic properties, the Malay Muslim counter narrative provides a postcolonial discourse that offers credence to the Malay Muslim insurgency.

Due to the counter narrative's use of Islam as a distinguishing identifier, most accounts of Buddhists in Patani are swept away in an effort to centralize the binary religio-political struggle between an Islamic tributary kingdom and a chief Buddhist kingdom. In this polemical discourse, the origin of Patani's loss of autonomy and subservience to Siam differs with each historian. A few scholars posit that Patani never had complete autonomy. Some cite its tributary status in the sixteenth century as the reason, while others identify the date of its subjugation as being in the eighteenth century.

Counter narratives and master narratives are powerful tools for legitimizing power. The difference between these historical media is that counter narratives lack a uniform account of Patani's autonomy. For example, in the *Hikayat Patani*, there is a clear indication that Patani was a tributary of Siam during the Ayutthaya period. However, this status denoted influence, not ownership. Another popular version comes from pseudonymous Ibrahim Syukri, who published the *History of the Malay Kingdom of Patani* in Malay during the twentieth century.[45] Syukri concedes much less and places Patani's loss of autonomy in the eighteenth century. Like the master narrative, Syukri views control in absolute terms. For him, Siamese influence is "incomplete or non-existent" in the political history of Patani.[46]

The *Hikayat Patani* and Ibrahim Syukri's *History of the Malay Kingdom of Patani* reflect not only the written tradition, but the oral tradition among Malay Muslims. According to the International Crisis Group, it is not uncommon for *ustadz* (Islamic teachers) to discuss the glorious past of Patani prior to its annexation by Siam in 1902 and to frame the period since then as a struggle of the Patani people against the Buddhist kingdom.[47] Ačhān Kaimōk finds that many of her Malay Muslim students come to her classroom with preconceived notions of what southern Thai history is, even though it is not present in the official curriculum. Often their version of history matches that of the written counter narratives:

> Last term, I taught Pattani history. One of my students came from Yala. He studied at a pondok. He had learned history from the [oral] transmission of locals. He told me that his teacher was a Tok Guru who taught and traded. I got the idea that I should have the students who are studying the history learn from the actual area in question. I told my class that whichever student had studied the history of Pattani

probably understood the history better than me and that they could serve as a mode for oral transmission. They had studied in the local area from their ancestors, so I asked who wanted to speak.Then, Adunan raised his hand and said, "I am pleased to talk about this." He [went on to say that he] could tell us about Pattani from the beginning of the ancient kingdom to the present. His version of history is similar to Ibrahim [Syukri's version].[48]

While the master narrative is evidenced in the public classrooms and history textbooks, the counter narratives are very much alive in international publications and oral traditions. Each narrative embodies a religious and regional scope that is intimately connected to forms of identity and nationalism.

Problems of Periodization

One distinctive influence among the counter narratives and the master narrative is the style of periodization. In the official Thai curricula, historians often distinguish periods by noting changes in political/military rule. This is a common means of conceptualizing history, as opposed to other methods like ecological calamities, social movements, ideologues, and so on. The choice of periodization not only influences the way history is read, but reflects the author's worldview.[49] In the case of southern Thailand, particular styles of periodization justify and legitimize one side of the conflict over another.

The master narrative and counter narratives' biases and perspectives have become especially apparent during the last seven years with the Thai media's consistent application of the master narrative's periodization. Due to the use of this style, most Thai journalists frame the conflict as a contemporary event, not a symptom of a long-term struggle against Siamese/Thai colonialism. The accounts depict a homogenous south in which southern Thai Buddhist activities are frequently obscured by the growing violence in the border provinces. Aside from reports of deaths and injuries, southern Buddhists often go unmentioned on the front pages of Thai or international media. Instead, Thai and international scholars chronicle the southern Thai violence around the Malay Muslims and their interactions with the Siamese/Thai government. These chronicles commit a series of mistakes, including the propensity to link southern violence with international Islamic movements such as Al Qaeda, thus relegating it to a strictly modern context and phenomenon.

The country's Thai and English newspapers depict the violence as relatively new. Articles from the *Thai Rath*, *Matichon*, or *Bangkok Post* discuss the violence in short statistical blurbs and sensationalize it for their readers.[50] These short pieces also lead the reader to misinterpret the violence as a recent phenomenon,

using a periodization that begins in January 2004.[51] Thais find the incomplete
historical portrayal of the conflict confusing. An example of the ubiquitous mis-
intrepretations of the southern violence appeared in a *Pǎchǎriasǎn* editor's interview with the NGO worker Nārī Čhěriypholpiriya. The editor complains,

> If we reflect upon the series of events we have heard about [the violence
> in the south] we cannot deny the bad news, which airs on TV every two
> minutes, or the news about daily murders in the newspapers. The media
> present an unexplained phenomenon, thus acknowledging situation,
> but unable to improve our understanding [of the events].[52]

Even top military officers lack the information to explain the southern violence.
In a *Matichon* article, a Thai military general raises two popular questions
concerning southern violence that plague Thais and journalists alike: "But, the
biggest question is who the negotiators are and, moreover, who do they negotiate with?"[53]

The without a historical context, the explosion of violence in 2004 appears seemingly random and chaotic. The resulting chaos has furthered the anonymity of
the militants. Unlike attacks by the LTTE (Liberation Tamil Tigers of Eelam) in
Sri Lanka, the Hamas in Israel, or the Maoists in Nepal, no organized group
claims credit for the attacks that occurred in southern Thailand between 2004
and 2008.[54] Of the different stories and speculations about the southern "militants," two explanations stand out as the most compelling. One theory comes
from journalists Don Pathan and Andrew Marshall, whose articles suggest that
the cause for militant silence is the sheer inexperience of its separatist leaders,
who come from grass-roots organizations.[55]

The second explanation comes from Nidhi Aeusrivongse, considered by international scholars to be one of the most eminent living Thai historians. Akin to a
Gramscian reading of the conflict, Nidhi explains that the absence of southern
militant accountability is a symptom of the State's failure to understand its
"small people" who are currently staging a millenarian revolt.

> An authoritarian state does not often pay much attention to the small
> people who participate in social movements. It never conceives that the
> common people could mobilize a political or social movement by them-
> selves. It always assumes that they must have been incited by someone
> else to take part, or else have been lured into it through bribery or
> deception.[56]

Gramsci's work on subalternity and hegemony carries with it very striking and
applicable parallels to the Thai context. The early twentieth-century neo-Marxist
theories from Antonio Gramsci address the internal colonial efforts on southern

Italy. For Gramsci, it was not just class, but also geographic factors that led to oppression of the southern Italians. Coining terms such as "hegemony" and "subaltern," he explains how a dominant group undermines subordinate ones through a normative network of subjugation. This subjugation eventually leads to disenfranchised individuals who, ironically, the Italian State could not interpret.[57] Both the Southern Malay Muslims' relationship with the Thai State and the State's inability to interpret their actions suggest that Nidhi's allusions to Gramscian theory are applicable. Although Don Pathan's and Nidhi's explanations acknowledge the militants' agency, both explanations minimize that agency by following the master narrative's contemporary periodization.

The Thai master narrative never acknowledges the kingdom of Patani as an independent or autonomous polity. The narrative claims that the Siamese governed the region from the time of Siam's first dynasty—Sukhothai (1238–1376)—until the present. One of the more dramatic examples of this continuous reign over the region comes from Prince Damrong Rajanubhab (1862–1943), who helped found the modern Thai education system. Prince Damrong claimed that "Patani has belonged to the Thai [kingdom] since time immemorial."[58]

This grandiose statement exposes Siam's *need* to govern Patani. Prince Damrong's statement of Siamese ownership over Patani was a political statement employed to ensure the legitimacy of Siam's international borders. Thai historian Thanet Aphornsuvan contends that this nationalist account of the southernmost provinces is tied to the narrative of Thai independence:

> The national history of Thailand, the predominant form of historiography in the country since the emergence of modern historical writing in Siam in the late nineteenth century, maintains that the Thai kingdom possessed the Malay states in the South, including Patani, Kelantan, Trengganu, Kedah and Perlis. The intensification of Western colonialism, however, forced Siam to cede parts of its traditional territory in order to preserve its independence. The discourse on Thai independence was thus structured around the loss and preservation of its territory.[59]

Colonial pressures had an enormous impact on the Siamese royalty during the time of Prince Damrong.[60] This defensive strategy bonded Siamese ownership of the southernmost provinces to twentieth–twenty-first century notions of Thailand and Thainess. In effect, a Siam without the three southernmost provinces was an incomplete Siam.

This is not the first time colonial pressures influenced a nationalist articulation of history. The British East India Company (England) initiated its occupation of the southern Malay Peninsula in the 1800s and manipulated the Siamese into a defensive position. In an effort to halt British advances, King Rama IV,

Mongkut (r. 1851–1868) entered into negotiations with the English over respected national boundaries. Mongkut was already experienced in these matters. When the French claimed rights to the province of Siemreap, Mongkut used "history" as a means to justify his own claims.[61] When he discussed matters with the British, Mongkut used the Buddhist history of Patani to legitimize Siam's ownership over the region.[62] Like the later comments from Prince Damrong, his son, King Mongkut's claims to the current provinces of Patani's seven principalities were bound by a nationalist agenda of preservation.

The Siamese view of nationhood changed dramatically after the "1893 Crisis" in which a French blockade and seizure of the Siamese palace for days "represented a sharp break in geographical concepts and practices and the displacement of the old notion of nationhood."[63] This new type of nationhood was formed with consistent international (and colonial) scrutiny. Less than ten years after the French blockade, Rama V mirrored the act of aggression in Patani. He dispatched navy warships to the Pattani River and imprisoned the last sultan of Patani. According to Tamara Loos, Siam's ability to negotiate modernity and to prove its status among the foreign powers was contingent upon this form of imperialism.[64]

In the colonial world, Thailand's various provinces became viewed as appendages of the nation, but as an exercise of history, appendages such as the deep south *always existed as such*. Therefore, any accounts of Malay Muslim autonomy, or efforts to separate, run counter to the master narrative. The contemporary setting of the conflict—and the absence of an autonomous Patani—depicts the Malay resistance as enigmatic and cancerous.

Thai Malay Muslim counter narratives also create problematic periods of history in order to further support the resistance. At times, oral narratives collapse distinctions between different time periods and their corresponding conflicts and weave together the disparate and intermittent Malay Muslim uprising into a continuous movement. The portrayal of continuity sometimes results in mistaken dates or locations. This creates symbolic similarities to conflicts when, in fact, there are none. One of the more popular misconceptions is the alleged connection between: (1) the Dusun-Ynor revolt on April 26 and 27, 1948; (2) the arrest of Hajji Sulong on January 16, 1948; and (3) the conflict at the Khru Se Mosque on April 28, 2004.[65]

Hajji Sulong was an immensely influential religious leader for Malay Muslims in the southernmost provinces. In addition to reforming Islamic education there, he mobilized over a hundred Muslim leaders to form the Patani People's Movement (PPM).[66] In 1947 the PPM, under his leadership, presented a list of seven demands to the Thai State. The demands outlined the designs for a limited autonomy for three southernmost provinces, in effect making way for Islamic rule.[67] The Thai State, then guided by the liberal-minded Pridi Phanomyong, considered Hajji Sulong's terms. However, in January of 1948, before Pridi could act, he was ousted from power in a coup. The Ministry changed and Field Marshall Plaek Phibunsongkhram became the new Prime Minister. Unlike Pridi, Phibun displayed little patience with requests for limited autonomy and summarily had Hajji Sulong arrested on January 16, 1948.[68]

In the same year that Hajji Sulong was detained, the infamous Dusun-Ynor revolt occurred in Narathiwat. Surin Pitsuwan was the first scholar to write a comprehensive account of southern Malay Muslim nationalism in 1985. Surin considered the violence in the village of Dusun-Ynor to be a landmark event, providing inspiration and justification for Malay Muslim resistance to the Thai State.[69] The State's military response was extremely violent. The massacre of Muslim villagers, who were armed mostly with pitchforks and knives, became emblematic of the oppressive State. Provocations for the violence are unknown; both local Malay and Thai State accounts differ as to the causes of the revolt. However, what is undisputed is that the violence occurred on April 26 and 27, involved one thousand combatants, and resulted in the deaths of four hundred Malay Muslim villagers and thirty Thai police officers.[70]

Malay Muslims were so emotionally charged by the arrest of Hajji Sulong and the massacre at Dusun-Ynor that the two incidents are recollected as one singular event, a reaction that typifies highly volatile and emotional periods in a collective memory. At times, the incidents are referred to as "The Hajji Sulong Revolt," when, in fact, the Dusun-Ynor violence was entirely independent of Hajji Sulong's arrest.[71] To add to the politically disastrous events of the year, the Thai State memorialized the Dusun-Ynor massacre. One year after the event, the provincial police station of Narathiwat was presented with a monument of a bullet.[72] For many Malay Muslims, the events of 1948 helped crystallize a need for a unified front against the Thai State.

The conflict at the Khru Se Mosque occurred on April 28, 2004; the month and day are almost identical to the Dusun-Ynor revolt of April 26 and 27, 1948. Because of the similarity of these dates, many people, including scholars, think of them as interrelated events, as if both had occurred on April 28.[73] Thanet Aphornsuvan argues that, after the conflict at the Khru Se Mosque, the "historical meaning of the 'April 28 Killing' has not been lost to the public."[74]

The Malay Muslims and Thai State's mistaken notion of connections between the Dusun-Ynor revolt, the arrest of Hajji Sulong, and the Khru Se Mosque affair is due to the collapse of horizontal and vertical memory. Oral narratives, through memory, manipulate factual details and chronological sequences in order to secure symbolic, psychological, and formal associations. According to historian Alessandro Portelli,

> The discrepancy between fact and memory ultimately enhances the value of the oral sources as historical documents. It is not caused by faulty recollections . . . but actively and creatively generated by memory

and imagination in an effort to make sense of crucial events and of history in general.[75]

The corollary between the conflict at the Khru Se Mosque and the Dusun-Ynor revolt is realized through the experience of trauma. This constructed parallel and eventual periodization is a means by which scholars and Malay Muslims attach understanding and symbolism to the killings and to the destruction of the Khru Se Mosque. Examples like this illustrate how oral counter narratives also contribute to a more polarizing reflection of the Thai State's relationship with Malay Muslims while sustaining the communal memory of a historically continuous Malay Muslim struggle.

Identities outside Polarities

In public spaces, Buddhist and Muslim identities are distinguished and emphasized through the use of language, performance, and narratives. Thai Buddhists read and write Thai, attend rituals at the *wat*, and subscribe to either the master narrative or the Thai Buddhist counter narrative. Although many Malay Muslims speak Thai, a sizeable number speak Bahasa Melayu and write in the Arabic script, attend mosques and *halal* restaurants, and subscribe to the Malay Muslim counter narrative. After the rise in violence, many Buddhists stopped frequenting *halal* restaurants and most Muslims stopped visiting *wat*.

The separate practices and habits of Buddhists and Muslims in the southernmost provinces allude to a region consisting of homogenous religious groups. However, this is far from the truth. Aside from the mythologizing of monolithic ethno-religious collectivities (there is a very long and healthy legacy of Malay Buddhism in the southern region, some of which still persists in Narathiwat), there is an academic and media tendency to collapse different ethnicities within the separate religious denominations. Whereas there are many Muslim ethnicities such as Pathan and Indian in the border provinces, Malay has become the dominant signifier for Islam. In the same vein, there are many Buddhist ethnicities, but Thai has become the dominant signifier for Buddhism. One of the largest ethnic groups absent in this conflict-spawned polarity is the Chinese.

Although the Chinese have critical roles in the economic, religious, and social development of the southernmost provinces, neither the master narrative, nor the dominant counter narratives afford space for Chinese agency in southern history. As in any polemical discourse, there is the need to present two groups in a war of domination. In the Thai context, the conflict revolves around the Thai Buddhists and the Malay Muslims, precluding the agency of other ethno-religious actors. Indeed, the inclusion of the Chinese in the history of the southernmost provinces would problematize such a polemic discourse.

Chinese immigrants had a profound impact on early southern Thai and Malay communities. From early history until the twentieth century, Chinese immigration to Patani was exclusively male.[76] Chinese immigrants in Patani more often than not led to *lūkčhin* (Chinese offspring) of Chinese fathers and Siamese or Malay mothers.[77] Kenneth Landon argues that the absence of Chinese women prompted Chinese males to marry Siamese women and to adopt Siamese customs. This practice of inter-ethnic marriage has resulted in a saying among local Thai Chinese, often expressed jokingly. In a somewhat proud, yet whimsical manner they explain that they are the ethnic glue that brings southern Thais and Malays together.

Chinese women began to immigrate to Siam in the early twentieth century. As a result, there was a sharp decrease in the number of inter-ethnic marriages and an increase in "close-knit Chinese communities" in the southernmost provinces. It was because of these "close-knit Chinese communities" that the Chinese were able to distinguish themselves as a distinct group, separate from the Malays and Thais. Kenneth Landon explains that Chinese communities in the late twentieth century placed more emphasis on what is deemed Chinese "cultural life" than on acquainting themselves with their Thai communities[78] The "cultural life" Landon mentions includes the Buddhist practices of ancestor veneration, vegetarianism, and other Sino-Mahāyāna Buddhist customs.[79]

While inter-ethnic marriages declined, the Chinese continued to interact with Thais and Malays through trade. Thai Chinese rose in economic status through successive generations in the kingdom of Patani, creating the association of success with Chinese identity. The genesis of Chinese wealth lay in the capitalization of the major labor industries (tin and rubber), which usually employed recent Chinese immigrants. Hence, many Chinese worked in the tin-mining industry, while some opened local businesses and conducted specialized professions such as dentistry.[80]

The influx of Chinese laborers and merchants to the southernmost provinces did not overly trouble the Malays and Thais. Chinese immigrants from Malaya (the former kingdom of Malaysia) began to work in the rubber industry in southern Thailand in the early nineteenth century and, by the mid-twentieth century, they had entered the rice market and were the dominant ethnic group both in tin mining and rubber.[81] In the late 1930s, there were more Chinese living in Thailand than in any other country outside of China—Landon estimates three million.[82] By the 1990s, Thai Chinese worked at local markets and owned the majority of the shops in commercial areas.[83]

There are varying accounts of Chinese and Malay relations in the southernmost provinces, but it is widely thought that, while the Chinese practiced Buddhism, they were more sensitive about Malay Muslim habits and preferences than the Thais, thus supporting the local Thai Chinese self-referential "ethnic glue" claims. Their businesses were predicated on their ability to sell—to Malays or Siamese. Unlike their Thai competitors, Chinese merchants aspired to speak the Malay language in order to improve their trade. As such, Chinese merchants spoke Malay and catered to their Malay customer's religious preferences, respecting *halal* rules as much as possible. Anthropologist Louis Golomb notes that, in the late half of the twentieth century, "Chinese merchants who open shops in Muslim neighborhoods are careful to respect the sensibilities of their neighbors by not openly selling pork or alcoholic beverages."[84] This sensibility is absent from the Thai Buddhist–Malay Muslim polemics.

In the late 1990s, Thai Chinese eventually found themselves caught in the middle of the Thai-Malay conflict. For centuries, the Chinese traded with and immigrated to the Malay Peninsula, enriching Buddhist traditions and ethnic relations in the area. Coinciding with these social processes was a healthy Malay economy, in which the Chinese participated. The historical trend of prosperity and positive relations between Malays and Chinese turned a sharp corner in the 1990s. This economic downturn led to increased tension between Chinese and Malays. Alexander Horstmann believes the crisis revolves around Chinese and Malay entrepreneurs. He notes the Malays see the Chinese as exploiters of the "Malay peasantry without mercy." Chinese, having historically played the middleman in the marketplace, are now being weeded out in order to keep transactions between Malays.[85]

As the southernmost provinces grew steadily poorer, the success of Chinese traders and the rise of Chinese ethnicity in Thai popular culture became something to resent rather than admire. The apparent "assimilation" of the Chinese into Thai society allowed them greater political and economic power, but pulled them further away from their intermediary status among the Thai Buddhists and Malay Muslims. Prior to the imposition of martial law, socio-economic disparities between Thai Chinese Buddhists and Malay Muslims created tensions in southern communities.[86] Some southern locals believed their local strife was the result of an ethno-economic divide between the Thai Chinese and Thai Malays. One space that exemplifies the Chinese-Malay divide is the Khru Se Mosque in the capital district of Pattani, which was rebuilt after it was bombarded during a standoff between insurgents and Thai military in the conflict at the Khru Se Mosque on April 28, 2004.

Legend holds that a Chinese man converted to Islam in order to marry a Muslim princess. He was in the process of building the mosque when his sister visited. His sister demanded that he renounce his faith and return to visit his sick mother. The brother refused, prompting his sister to curse the completion of the mosque just prior to hanging herself from a cashew-nut tree. A local Pattani explained that some time back, Thai Chinese Buddhists tried to pay homage to the tomb in the mosque, but wanted to bring pork for the ritual. Malay Muslims made a human barricade, blocking the Chinese from bringing pork into the mosque. The conflict ended when the Chinese pulled the tomb outside the mosque.[87]

However, whether the Thai Chinese are conciliatory or antagonistic in their communities, attention to their actions or, more importantly, to their identities would complicate a binary narrative. In the narrative of southern Thailand, we find that ethno-religious tensions between Thai Chinese Buddhists and Malay Muslims are subsumed in the larger narrative of the Thai Buddhist State versus a Malay Muslim insurgency.

In the last five years, militant attacks have targeted Malays, Chinese, and Thais alike. However, the Chinese have suffered the greatest financial losses from the bombings, with militants frequently targeting Thai Chinese businesses. This reflects a growing religious perspective concerning the conflict, as well as the lack of power behind the Chinese, who once served as "ethnic glue."

While the State remains hegemonic, the influences are not static. Anthropologist Jovan Maud recounts how as late as 2001, State activities "*under-pinned* hybridity, and even the ability to speak in terms of hybridity."[88] These forms of hybridity continue to exist outside of the militarized region and are finding new and dynamic expressions in and around the urban centers of Bangkok and Chiang Mai. In the south, Chinese Buddhist practices are present in contemporary times with Tang-Ki rituals and vegetarian festivals in the Songkhla city of Hat Yai,[89] and embodied in Guan Yin statues, the Chinese incarnation of the Bodhisattva Avalokiteśvara. However, portrayals of hybridity within the war-torn southernmost provinces are largely absent. One of the symptoms of violence is the polarization of identities, and master and counter narratives reflect this polarization within the deep south.

Conclusion

The transmission of history is a means of retaining and disseminating culture, as well as acculturation. That is why teaching history—or general education for that matter—is a focal point for conflict. One of the most visible threads of conflict and education is in the making of the colonial world. In his excellent work *Imperial Encounters*, Peter van der Veer follows the ways in which education was a primary instrument for the religious conversion and political expansion of colonial interests in India and one of the platforms from which muscular forms of Christianity and Hinduism emerged.[90] Education helped to remake Indian identity both in reflective pasts and in current selves. This is no less a purpose for militants that target schools in the postcolonial terrains such as Afghanistan, Pakistan, and southern Thailand.[91]

The motives for targeting schools in southern Thailand are multifaceted; however, one unmistakable reason is ideology. Social scientist Hans-Dieter

Bechstedt observes that religious instruction is one of the *primary* educational goals of the Thai elementary school system. "At school the child will learn about the life of the Buddha and will be instructed in some of his famous texts about ethics, morality, and proper behavior."[92] In addition to this Buddhist inclination, the Thai State has sought to preserve nationalism through the master narrative, which supports the State and its sovereignty. Throughout the world, States employ master narratives to legitimate their rule, while religious groups use counter narratives to justify a violent return to their traditions. In some instances, the master narrative becomes a discursive protectorate for the imagined community's heritage.

For example, the Iranian State has excluded female agency from its master narrative in order to legitimate its preferential consideration of masculinity.[93] During the Apartheid Era the South African State assumed control of public education under the Bantu Education Act (1953) in order to maintain its racial vision of the nation-state over the populace.

> Their language was unique, and most Afrikaners experienced little but the Nationalist world perspective from cradle to grave: at home, in Afrikaan-language schools and universities, in Dutch Reformed churches, in social groups, on radio and television, and in books and newspapers. In particular, their schools imbued them with a political mythology derived from a historiography that distorted the past for nationalist purposes.[94]

The South African State sought to retain its legitimacy by controlling language—and historiography. The same techniques were employed for darker purposes in places like the socialist government of Mongolia during the mid-twentieth century. The Mongolian People's Republic shut down Buddhist monastic educational centers after centuries of service and authorized revisionist accounts of history that supported the Mongolian State and its subsequent genocide of Buddhist monks.[95]

The history presented in the State's master narrative also serves to polarize and intensify ethno-religious relations. This is evident in the British colonial use of the Hindu-Muslim divide to create its master narrative of India's conflicts. The polarization of Hindus and Muslims helped to increase Hindu-Muslim animosities, but only through the British whitewashing of socio-economically driven caste clashes.[96] Identities and heritages often inconsistent with the State's normative identity are marginalized or left out of textbooks and research projects, as in the case of the Malay Muslims in southern Thailand's history. A case in point is the traditional absence of Palestinian Muslim accomplishments in Israeli history textbooks, which was recently called into question in the Israeli school curriculum; this provoked the defense of the master narrative by conservative Israeli Jews.[97] As a rule, master narratives are carefully constructed, giving air to particular ethno-religious grievances and conflating events in order to create scapegoats. Historian Michael Sells has shown how the master narrative is actively applied through different time periods to distinguish, and then vilify, Bosnian Muslims. This abstract process triggers a very physical and violent result by the normative group, at times even to the extent of condoning ideological genocide.[98]

While the State uses master narratives to retain control, religio-political groups not aligned with the State generate counter narratives as a means of justifying the preservation of their respective traditions. For many Malay Muslims in the three southernmost provinces, the *Hikayat Patani* voices their desire to reclaim their regional autonomy. Similarly, for Thai Buddhists, oral narratives express a desire to return to the Buddhist community's status as it was in the days of Langkasuka and Śrīvijaya. Yet, to borrow a phrase from Bruce Lincoln, each of these narratives entails a level of strategic tinkering with the past.[99]

The use of master and counter narratives to justify violence is a pervasive global phenomenon seen in places such as Bosnia, South Africa and Israel. In the South Asian Theravāda country of Sri Lanka, Sinhalese Buddhist groups ardently opposed to Tamil Hindus sometimes cite a Buddhist counter narrative, the *Mahāvaṃsa*, as proof of Sri Lanka's Buddhist past and the need to preserve its national heritage.[100] The application of history in this particular context is used against the "other," the Tamils, in order to demonize them.

So how does a society begin the journey that ends in such violent treatment of specific religious groups and traditions? One of the first techniques is the alteration of public memory. This is accomplished through the control of public spaces, memorials, and physical signifiers in communities. However, the manipulation of public memory is also achieved through formal education. In the case of the master narrative, history becomes a heuristic of hegemony, and in the case of counter narratives, history becomes a means to further alternative forms of nationalism. The histories of Thailand's southernmost provinces are no different.

2

Representation

Thai Buddhist monks are walking embodiments of Thai nationalism. For centuries, Thai monks symbolized political and religious power.[1] However, in the southern conflict, the State's escalated use of the monks' signification makes them choice targets for militants. Additionally, as an embodied symbol, a militant attack on a Buddhist monk becomes an attack on the body-politic as well as the Buddhist *sangha*. The potential result of such an attack is one of local and national fury. Attacks on monks act as ethno-religious bombs and can ignite passions and acts of retribution from Buddhists in the border provinces. While on the ground many monks seek to distance themselves from the politics and the violence, their religio-political identities ultimately draw them closer to the conflict and raise the relevance of religion in the violence.

This chapter examines the ways in which Buddhist monks, even as passive agents, become catalysts for Buddhist violence in Thailand. Since Buddhist monks are passive agents in this context, it is not their intentions, but rather the way their actions are perceived, their representative power, that becomes significant. Thai Buddhist monks become symbolic of a concept greater than religious authority; they become representations of the imagined solidarity, the nation. In this particular context, Buddhist-inspired violence requires three conditions: a space of conflict, a politicized Buddhist representation, and an assault on that politicized representation.

Buddhists are motivated toward violence by the murder of monks—in effect, the defacement of sacrosanct bodies—within a conflict zone engulfed by ethno-nationalist and religious strife. Much of the powerful significance of the monk's body is due to the Thai State, which appropriates Buddhist monastic roles and actions to the political stage. The infusion of politics into the depiction of religious agents carries inherent dangers. In this instance, the murder of a monk can act as a medium of transformation and change the conflict over economic and national grievances between the Thai State and militant Malay Muslims into a war of religious proportions.

The Monastic Catalyst

It is a typical early Thursday morning in Pattani Province. Monks in their saffron robes from Wat Noppawongsaram slowly walk outside their monastery and down Magrood road. They are performing their morning alms (*binthabat*), an activity through which they gather sustenance and, in turn, offer Buddhists a chance to make merit. In front of them is a young Thai police officer dressed in army fatigues and holding an M-16. He smiles at me as they pass by, and I notice that there is another policeman following them. The scene is quite common throughout regions under martial law in southern Thailand.

The following day two policemen were on break in the lounge of My Garden Hotel, one of the few hotels that cater to international travelers in the capital district of Pattani. The two policemen were stationed at the hotel to protect both visitors and the property. I decided to sit across from them and ask about the police and soldiers guarding monks. Have any monks been killed, I asked?

Saksin, a policeman hailing from Chonburi province whose partner has an M-16 with a sticker reading "I Love You, Thailand" answered. "Yes, monks have been killed, and if we find these murderers, we'll shoot them on sight."[2]

Military assistance is needed in order for monks to continue their morning rituals in some areas. Although locals in the southernmost provinces are now

Figure 2.1 Morning Alms outside Wat Noppawongsaram, by Michael Jerryson, July 29, 2004.

Figure 2.2 Patriotic Arms, by Michael Jerryson, July 30, 2004.

accustomed to this sight, the military escort of Buddhist monks is a new and disturbing sight for Thais living outside the conflict zone. Since January 2004 Malay Muslim militants have killed and injured over 23 southern Buddhist monks and novices. These numbers do not fully reflect the violence on Thai Buddhist monasticism, as it is difficult to acquire accurate statistics and some attacks are not reported. Recorded attacks predominantly occurred when monks were on their daily routine of collecting alms, but the most dramatic and polarized attacks have taken place in their *wat*.

As indicated in table 2.1, militant tactics might have changed in the last several years, as the highest number of attacks on monks and *wat* occurred between 2004 and 2005. However, we must also consider other variables that may explain this change as well. Since 2004, many *wat* in the red zone no longer have monks going on morning alms, making it more difficult for militants to target and attack monks. The task is also made more difficult by the increase in the number of police and military guarding the monks. The changes in monastic routines and military protection suggest another reason for the decline in monastic casualties in the three border provinces. However, while there is a decrease in monastic casualties, the murder of a monk still provokes intense reaction among Thai Buddhists, especially among the military. In 2007, Non-Governmental Organizations (NGOs), such as International Crisis Group and Amnesty International, saw a rise in Thai military brutality against Malay

Table 2.1 **Monastic Casualties in the Southernmost Provinces, 2004–2008**

	Wat Attacked/Burned	Monks Killed	Monks Injured
2004	9	4	2
2005	4	1	6
2006	1	–	6
2007	2*	–	3
TOTAL	16*	5	17[i]

[i] Personal communication through electronic mail with Srisompob Jitpiromsri, Political Science professor at Prince of Songkhla University, Pattani on February 5, 2008. The asterisks indicate changes that I have made to Srisompob's statistics. Srisompob did not have any attacks on *wat* recorded for 2007; however, on one occasion I witnessed an attack on a *wat* in Pattani Province during the Chinese New Year, February 18, 2007. In January 2010, Srisompob released new statistics and disclosed twenty-three monastic casualties. Srisompob Jitpiromsri, "Sixth Year of the Southern Fire: Dynamics of Insurgency and Formation of the New Imagined Violence," *Deep South Watch* (Prince of Songkhla University: Center for Conflict Studies and Cultural Diversity, 2010): 1–24, 15.

Muslims in the southernmost provinces. Their reports and others cite examples of Thai Buddhist soldiers beating Muslim suspects to death and burning down Islamic schools.[3]

Retaliation and revenge are not universal responses to acts of violence, but for Thai Buddhists such as the policeman Saksin at the My Garden Hotel and General Thammarak, the act of murdering a monk is seen as defacing incredibly powerful and personal values. Thus, the significance of a Thai Buddhist monk's identity becomes fused with Thai Buddhism and Thai nationalism. When someone attacks a monk, they are attacking these two principles, and violent reactions are intense when someone attacks such ideals.

It is not just people who react to the attack on monks; the Thai State has reacted as well. State reactions to the murder of monks began on January 28, 2004, when the Thai State considered imposing a curfew in the three southernmost provinces, which already were under martial law. Thai authorities cited the murder of monks as one of their chief reasons:

> Defence Minister Thammarak Isarangkurana Ayudhaya said [curfew] was being considered following a series of machete attacks on Buddhist monks and students. Three monks have died and one was seriously injured. Two students were also wounded. A curfew would facilitate all-out military and police operations against separatist bandits. "Now that the bandits have gone berserk, our men must become crazed too, to fight them," Gen Thammarak said.[4]

While two students were wounded, it is doubtful that General Thammarak's comments about the bandits going "berserk" were in reference to these attacks. He and his men were ready to become "crazed too" over the murder of Buddhist monks. But, how does the representation of a Buddhist monk become such a powerful concept?

The Power of Representation

In his examination of contemporary South Asian ethnic conflicts, Tambiah argues that interpretive frameworks must include questions of how groups acquire, maintain, and protect their symbolic capital.[5] This inquiry is germane to the discussion of religion and violence; representation is part of an inherent social process of constructing symbolic capital.[6] What we do, and more importantly, *what we are perceived as doing*, bestows a measure of prestige upon us. As such, we follow Tambiah's inquiry in our examination of representations.

The importance of monks in Thai society is due, in part, to their continual visual references in movies, television, newspapers, and local flyers. Thai cultural images of monks can highlight two different dimensions of the Buddhist monk: his sacrality and/or his patriotism. Thais observe the status of monkhood in patriotic venues, such as at the beginning of every cinematic event, when an official obligatory cinematic montage of images of the Thai king Bhumibol Aduladej stops briefly with a still of the young king undergoing ordination. There also are frequent picture books, posters, and images of the Buddha's earlier incarnations, such as Mahājanaka, in the Buddha's rebirth stories, known as the Jātakas (*chādok*).[7] These stories reinforce the image of monks, who model the Buddha's life, as holy men who are devoted to a life without attachments, antipathies, and ignorance. The fact that masculinity is imprinted upon the model of monkhood is not lost in the gender dynamics of Thai society and weighs heavily upon the limits of symbolic capital for Thai women.[8]

The commercialization of amulets and subsequent commodification of monks' charisma reifies the sacrality of monastic images.[9] In rituals, monks infuse images with the charisma and *paritta* (protection) of Buddhist saints or the historical Buddha, a process that Donald Swearer calls hypostatizing the Buddha.[10] Thais regularly adorn themselves with these images, which are often of regional monks, believing that such amulets hold powers of protection and fortune. However, visual imagery alone does not explain how Thais view Buddhist monks. The Thai laity live in the same communities as the monks. Therefore, the visual images are weighed against what Thais see, that is, what the Buddhist monks do. A Buddhist's perception of the monk as an abstract quality or representation is the inverted process of sacralizing art (in which the viewer becomes intimately connected to the abstract through the sacred) or, in accordance with

Jean Baudrillard, is the systemic process in which society converts reality into symbols and signs.[11]

A person's significance is often derived from her/his duties and actions. Moreover, we often conflate the office or profession with the person, who simply occupies or performs the duties of the office. In like fashion, anthropologist Thomas Kirsch writes that Thai Buddhist monks are perceived to be the most auspicious and revered figures in Thailand:

> The Sangha stands as the proximate exemplar and symbolic center of Buddhism; the monk stands as the apex of the Thai religious *and* social order. Further, the monk defines the upper limit of the human dimension of the Buddhist moral hierarchy.[12]

This exemplary platform of morality stems from the doctrinal dimension of Buddhisms. The *sangha* and its members are part of the highly venerated Three Jewels (Pāli: *tiratana*), namely, the Buddha, Dhamma, and Sangha. In the Thai Theravāda tradition, the Buddha may no longer be reachable, but his teachings, which quintessentially concern morality, are accessible and they are preserved by the *sangha*.

One very general Thai custom that exemplifies the elevated status of Buddhist monasticism in Thai society is the perfunctory *wai*. This is a form of greeting wherein two hands are pressed together in a form of deference and respect.[13] According to Thai Buddhists, there are three types of people who require such a display of respect: parents, teachers, and monks, each of whom is seen as mentor of sorts. Within this context, each enjoys a superior social status to the one who initiates the *wai*. But, if we compare these types of people, we find an implicit hierarchy of respect. A teacher does not *wai* a parent, unless the context is such that she or he is no longer a teacher but, rather, a sibling, and a monk never initiates a *wai* to teachers and parents. His elevated status is such that the opposite is expected or accepted.

Outside of a local context, which allows for personal interaction and complex associations, there is a societal identification of monks as sacred actors, worthy of veneration.[14] Part of the monk's elevated status is due to his duties and actions, particularly his pursuit to awaken.[15] Craig Reynolds observes that charismatic authority "adheres to the practitioner of these austerities as a consequence of enduring what is beyond the capacity of most men and women."[16] It is the adherence of authority that becomes crucial in our understanding of a monk's representation. This sacralization of the monk's body is also enhanced by his association to Buddhist sacred teachings (Pāli: *dhamma*). The *perceived* austerity and ascetic practices associated with the monk transforms him into a "field-of-merit."[17] When a Buddhist donates to a monk, s/he helps to sustain this deeply sacred vocation and, in turn, earns merit for her/himself.

To elucidate this abstraction a bit more, we should consider the monks' socially and religiously prescribed functions a part of their individual personas, and in turn, that in specific contexts the monks become embodiments of these functions (among others, the Buddhist aspiration for *nibbana*, liberation). An attack on a monk signifies an attack on the locus of the Buddhist sacred—the embodied path to awakening. Viewing the murder of a Buddhist monk against this backdrop, it is easier to understand why General Thammarak called for his men to become "crazed" in response to the machete attacks on monks and students.

The politicization of monks enables them to represent the Thai State. But, just as amulets represent former monks as well as Buddhisms, monks invoke more than a governmental agency; they also represent the corresponding ideology of the State, Thai nationalism. As early as the 1880s, Thai Buddhist monks have proselytized under official State programs, thereby serving two different institutions simultaneously: the Thai State and the Buddhist *sangha*.

In an era of governments that employ the term "nation-state," there is an inherent connection between the State and its prescribed nationalism. What Tambiah deems the "politicization of ethnicity," which he describes as a transnational phenomenon of ethnic and secular forms of nationalism,[18] becomes a matter of politicized religion, a global phenomenon that pertains to secular and religious forms of nationalism. Sociologist José Casanova notes that in recent years we have witnessed an increased and widespread de-privatization and re-politicization of religion throughout the world.[19] But, while Casanova places the start of this increase in the 1980s, the Thai context existed long before. In a Buddhist society like Thailand, a monk working to spread the Buddhist teachings is seen as serving his State *and nation*. Thus, monks who represent both the religious and national domains of society embody a significant amount of power in the aforementioned associations. All it takes for this power to be fully realized is violence.

The Political Origin of Thai Buddhism

In the summer of 2004, I interviewed southern monks about the violence at the Khru Se Mosque and the random local murders and bombings. While many monks felt that the violence disrupted their daily routines, they were resolved to continue their routines. For them, their most pressing need was to teach the *dhamma* (Buddhist doctrine) and to perform different rituals for the Buddhist laity.

Sitting under a tree within a fortified *wat* at about midday in the summer of 2004, I interviewed one of these monks, Phra Kaew. At thirty-three years of age, Phra Kaew was younger than most of the monks I met and was visibly uncomfortable during the interview, glancing every so often at the military walking about his *wat*. When I asked him what he thought monks should do about the rising violence, Phra Kaew was quick to answer: "We cannot be active in addressing this [conflict] because it is political. Monks should not be involved in political affairs, and this [conflict] is political."[20]

Phra Kaew's aversion to politics is well warranted. Buddhist monks devote themselves to an ascetic lifestyle in an attempt to avoid the detrimental influences of the world (Pāli: *lokiya*). Tambiah, looking at Theravādin Buddhist countries in South and Southeast Asia, draws similar conclusions and argues that, when a monk becomes political, he damages the integrity of the *sangha*.[21] To Phra Kaew and those who maintain a contemporary Thai Buddhist perspective, there is a clear and distinct division between Thai Buddhism and politics; however, this distinction is more fanciful than accurate in recent Thai history. Moreover, the division between Buddhisms and politics was not present in early India either.

In what is now the country of Nepal, Siddhattha Gotama, founder of Buddhist traditions, was a political figure. When canvassing different transnational religions, the genesis of Buddhisms follows that of other Indian religions in that its founder came from royal lineage; Siddhattha was a prince.[22] This status contrasts sharply with the social background of other global religious founders such as Jesus, who was a carpenter's son, or Muhammad, who was a merchant.

Historian Uma Chakravarti shows that, in addition to the historical Buddha's socio-political status, the nascent institutional structure of the *sangha* within the Indian subcontinent was drawn from an indigenous political system, the *gana-sangha*, which was a republican-style government.[23] These early associations between Buddhist monks and the State later developed into an ideological affinity between Theravāda Buddhisms and State power. Rulers of South and Southeast Asian kingdoms used Buddhisms to justify their sovereignty. According to historian Balkrishna Gokhale, State applications of Buddhisms were so pervasive in India that they became an assumed practice.

> The reality of the power of the state is always taken for granted by the Early Buddhist thinkers. For them the state is an organization of force or violence the possession of which is largely restricted to the king and his instruments.[24]

One reason so many States implemented and applied Buddhist doctrine in South and Southeast Asia was the political flexibility of Buddhist traditions.

The Pāli Canon, the scriptural tradition of Theravāda Buddhism, does not explicitly outline the parameters of the State's power and authority; instead, it provides occasional ambiguous references. These ambiguous references allow for States to ethically maneuver their policies within Buddhist guidelines. For instance, while Buddhist principles stress the need for kings to uphold the *dhamma*, this adherence did not preclude previous kings from committing acts of violence. The *Vinaya* (Buddhist monastic codes of conduct) prescribed an implied relationship between the State and violence so that "those who administer torture and maiming are called kings."[25]

Uma Chakravarti argues that power is invariably expressed in Buddhisms through the monarchy. Buddhists, she writes, "do not seem to envisage a political and social system without the institution of kingship."[26] These early political elements in Buddhisms led scholars such as Tambiah to argue that Buddhist traditions are not merely centered on issues of awakening, but also on kingship and a principle polity.[27] Due to the early *sangha*'s need for political support from the kingdoms of Kosala and Magadha and the Buddha's political upbringing, it is highly probable that early central Buddhist laws, doctrine, and beliefs were intended to be accessible and amenable to the State.

Taking this hypothesis further, the role of the famous Mauryan emperor Aśoka, who massacred thousands in the infamous battle at Kalinga and then adopted the Buddhist path out of remorse, would be a realization of the religion's political design, not an aberration or evolution of the religion. Aśoka's conversion to Buddhism may have been motivated by the ambiguous ethics of governing and the comfortably familiar structural similarity between the *sangha* and a political institution. This discussion of State Buddhism does not preclude other forms of Buddhisms that exist beyond the political. Early popular expressions existed simultaneously with State Buddhism, and these popular forms did not always correlate with the State version. While Southeast Asian polities appropriated State Buddhism because of the religious tradition's structural solvency, the laity adopted popular forms of Buddhisms because of its relative easy assimilation of local deities. Yet, as this inquiry pertains to Thai Buddhist monks, we will focus on the trajectory of State Buddhism, which extends out from Bangkok.

Nation-State Building and Monastic Representations

As the global structure of polities changed, so did the State application of Buddhisms. This phenomenon has been comprehensively surveyed by Craig Reynolds (1972), Stanley Tambiah (1976), Somboon Suksamran (1977), Yoneo Ishii (1986), Charles Keyes (1987), Peter Jackson (1989), and others; however, in order to build upon the argument, we must first revisit it. One important and significant change in the State application of Thai Buddhism occurred in the early 1900s. While nation-states developed in Western Eurasia and colonial pressures beset States in Southeast Asia, a new form of religio-political Buddhism surfaced in Siam: Siamese State Buddhism.

Justin McDaniel has succinctly demonstrated that, contrary to popular opinion, most Buddhist education in mainland Southeast Asia has not been canonical.[28] Indeed, the political and religious changes throughout Siam's "internal colonialism" in the early 1900s were limited in the local and peripheral regions, especially with respect to the educational content. However, a structural change did occur and this resonated throughout the Siamese government and its subsidiaries. The institutional form of the Thai *sangha* emerged with a prevailing State Buddhism, nurtured by Siamese and Thai State efforts. Religious and Gender Studies scholar Peter Jackson considers the twentieth century a time in which each Siamese and Thai regime relied upon the Buddhist monks for political legitimacy.[29] One could point out that this is not new; Siamese Buddhism always has been involved in Siamese statecraft.

Prior to the 1900s, Buddhism was inextricably linked to Siamese governments and Siamese sovereignty; however, the *nature* of the monastic politicalization had changed. Earlier Siamese governments were kingdoms more concerned with empire-building than nation-building (*sāng chāt*). Historian Kamala Tiyavanich applies the term State Buddhism in reference to Siamese nation-building, which under King Chulalongkorn created and perpetuated a new form of Buddhism in order to centralize and unify the country, as opposed to a country bent on expanding and conquering more territories.[30]

Since the Sukhothai dynasty, Siamese and Thai polities controlled the representation of Buddhism in order to insure their legitimacy.[31] This is by no means unique to Thailand. Craig Reynolds duly notes that Asian monarchs and emperors alike "saw the patronage of monks and monasteries as both moral duty and advantage."[32] The advantage lies in the monk's representation, which is an indispensable and irreplaceable power in Thai society. Religious Studies scholar Christine Gray frames the power of a living monk's representation around the body-example of the *dhamma*:

> Pure monks are believed to exercise a beneficial influence on all segments of society. Specifically, the sight of such monks is believed to "strike" at the senses of the Buddhist laity and generate moral-mental transformations in their "hearts and minds" [*cit lae cai*], the seat of volition [*cetana*]. Thai monks are referred to as models, or literally, "body-examples" [*tua yang*] of propriety [*kwam riap roi*] and of dhamma. "Visual texts" whose mere presence inspires the most uncivilized men towards minimally righteous behavior, their presence enhances the life circumstances of all men who are reborn together in the same "life" or region....[33]

Gray's mention of monks acting as "visual texts" or "models" for the Buddhist laity underscores the power of a Buddhist monk's representation. This representation was tied to the State very early in the twentieth century. Historian Craig

Reynolds examines Prince Wachirayan's description of monastic roles during Chulalongkorn's State and postulates, "It is possible that Wachirayan was saying that monks were in some sense representatives or intermediaries of the government...."[34] By representing the government, monks were viewed as emissaries of both the *sangha* and State.

The restructuring of the monastic institution to represent (and support) the State was particularly evidenced when the bureaucracy went through a metamorphosis, such as the dissolution of the absolute monarchy in 1932 and the reinstitution of Chulalongkorn's reforms in the 1960s. Chulalongkorn's administration (1872–1910) instituted the creation of the Siamese nation-state, a construction predicated on the *social imaginaire*. Nation-state building is an important element when considering the politicization of Thai Buddhism because the construction of a nation-state requires the re-imagining of citizenship that binds people together under a shared sense of nationalism.[35] While Buddhist monks previously were political tools for Siamese governments, the Chulalongkorn administration marked the beginning of appropriating Thai Buddhism for a new national identity.

Royalty were deeply entrenched in the Chulalongkorn administration's appropriation of Buddhist symbolic capital. Two of Chulalongkorn's brothers, Prince Damrong and Prince Wachirayan, were at the vanguard of reorganizing the order and policies regarding Buddhist monks. Prince Wachirayan was the son of King Mongkut, a monarch who created and supported an entirely new sect of Thai Buddhism, the Thammayut, which exists today as a subtle variation of the larger school, the Mahānikai.[36] Mongkut saw a need to rejuvenate the Thai *sangha*, and did this through his political leadership and patronage. Sharing his father's vision, Wachirayan viewed the State as a vessel for supporting and proliferating Buddhism. In his autobiography, he writes:

> To be able to maintain the health of Buddhism, at the least by administering the monastery, is difficult without the strength of the state's (*phaendin*) support. The state is ever patiently vigilant. Wherever a good monk appears who is revered and respected by the people, he will likely be conferred rank to grant him strength to do the work of Buddhism.[37]

For Wachirayan, the State was instrumental in supporting the health of Thai Buddhism, and he was in an excellent position to enforce this. King Chulalongkorn appointed his brother Wachirayan to the office of the supreme patriarchy, possessing full powers over the Thai *sangha*.

Prince Wachirayan's younger half-brother, Prince Damrong, also was instrumental in the reorganization of the *sangha*. Damrong became the first director of the Department of Education in 1880 and used his platform to consolidate educational reforms that encompassed religious teachings and practices.[38] Both

Wachirayan and Damrong applied broader legal measures under the Sangha Act of 1902, and it was through these acts that the Thai *sangha* became nationalized in an effort to bolster the polity.[39] These laws and reforms fused the Thai *sangha*'s symbolic capital to that of the nation-state.[40] With this fusion came politicization of the Buddhist monastic infrastructure, as monks for the first time became emblematic of not just the *sangha*, but the governing bureaucracy as well.

Perhaps the most comprehensive State appropriation and centralization of Thai Buddhism came under the umbrella of "Sangha Acts." In the last century there have been three Sangha Acts—the Sangha Acts of 1902, 1941, and 1962— with amendments to the 1962 version occurring in 1992 and 2004. Each Sangha Act altered the structure of the Thai *sangha* and enabled the current administration to commission Buddhist monks for national programs and policies. Prince Wachirayan's preface to the Sangha Act of 1902 is indicative of these intentions:

> Although monks are already subject to the law contained in the Vinaya, they must also subject themselves to the authority which derives from the specific and general law of the State....In sum, monks must obey three types of law: the law of the land, the Vinaya, and custom. This Act is the law of the land; thus it should be known, understood, and followed correctly.[41]

Wachirayan's vision was partly realized. Monks of any substantial ecclesiastical prestige eventually subjected themselves to the authority of the State, although localized practices continued unabated on the village level. The subjugation of monks to State law became the means by which the State could affect the direction and activities of the *sangha*, enabling their use of monks as political tools.

Prime Minister Sarit Dhanarajata (1957–1963) enacted policies that heavily shaped contemporary representations of Buddhist monks. Sarit augmented the already intimate relationship between the State and the Thai *sangha* with his 1962 Sangha Act. Like Wachirayan, Sarit viewed Thai Buddhism as an important tool for centralizing Thai society, and he viewed Buddhist monks as important cultural ambassadors of the State. Under the Ministry of Education, the Department of Religious Affairs oversaw many of his innovations, such as Buddhist missionary programs. In 1964, a special program was launched under the auspices of the Department of Religious Affairs called the Phra Thammathut (ambassadorship of the *dhamma*). In the State-crafted missionary project, monks met in Bangkok for a few days of debriefing and were sent off to the northeast and southern provinces for two or three months. The monks clearly understood their purpose in these projects, as Stanley Tambiah explains:

> Finally, it is clear that other monks explicitly or implicitly conceive the *thammathud* program as having the objectives of reducing regional

grievances (particularly of the northeast), of stemming communism, and of mobilizing loyalty to the king and the nation and by extension to the government through the agency of religion.[42]

A sister program called the Phra Thammačārik Project was initiated merely a year later in 1965. Focusing primarily on the minority ethnic groups living in northern Thailand, the Phra Thammačārik sent monks to Karen, Hmong, Shan, and other villages in an effort to spread Buddhist teachings, reduce drug trafficking, and garner more local representatives for the State.[43] In a Phra Thammačārik pamphlet from Chiang Mai, Brawit Dandlanugul explains that the "Hill Tribes" (a collective term for minority ethnic groups) had no knowledge of religion and worshiped demonic spirits (*nabthūa phūtiphī*) instead. These initiatives focused primarily on Thailand's peripheral regions and people, including the Malay Muslims in the southernmost provinces. These State programs politicized Buddhist monks through their official proselytizing of the *dhamma*.

While Sarit was at the helm of these politicized religious programs, he was assisted by another important and later extremely influential partner, the Thai monarchy. Journalist Paul Handley gives detailed accounts of King Bhumibol and Queen Sirikit's interactions and involvement in the orchestration of these Buddhist initiatives, some of which occurred during their development.[44] The monarchy's involvement was strategic. Power over the representation of Buddhist monks was power over their symbolic capital.

The monarchy and State commissioned monks to both expand and protect the integrity of Thai Buddhism, which was particularly ideological in nature. From the 1950s until the 1970s, the Thai State used Buddhist monks as ideological foils against the encroaching communist fighters in the southern and northeastern provinces.

At the behest of Thai authorities, monks argued that Buddhist principles stood in opposition to socialist and communist ideas.[45] Political scientist Somboon Suksamran considers the Thai *sangha*, for the most part, acquiescent in the State appropriation of Buddhist monks:

> Very recently, Buddhism and the Sangha have been used as a government agency for the carrying out of particular policies and also, to some extent, as a force to counteract communism and to unify all classes within society. The Sangha for its part has appeared to co-operate readily with the government not only to set the moral tone of the nation but also as an effective communication channel between the highest national level and the vast majority of the population living in the villages.[46]

Buddhist monks, becoming living "channels" between the national government and the villages, served as ambassadors of the State. Their involvement in State programs, such as those addressing the communist threat, politicized their duties and, thus, their representations.

Prior to the student-led coup in 1973, Buddhist monks were supportive of the Thai State and its initiatives. Public dissent for national directives was nominal, if not altogether absent. However, the Thai *sangha* became divided following this political upheaval and the later junta's bloody re-emergence in 1976. State Buddhism demonstrated concerted opposition to the Thai government for the first time due to military violence and student cries for democratic reform.

Part of the *sangha*'s division was fueled by political events outside of Thailand. Cambodia's genocide of Buddhists under Pol Pot, Ho Chi Minh's victory in Vietnam, and China's backing of communist groups in and around Thailand alarmed many Buddhist monks. Monks also felt pressure from the Thai monarchy. Queen Sirikit voiced her criticism of activists on the left and expressed support of the military throughout the political turbulence in the 1970s.[47] King Bhumibol and Queen Sirikit participated in numerous exercises and activities, such as the inauguration of Čhittiphawan College in Chonburi, to demonstrate support for conservative Buddhist monks. Handley writes that Čhittiphawan was designed to train young monks in a form of activism that defended the State as a bastion of pure *dhamma* practice. As such, any social attempt to change the political structure was "an act of destroying the state."[48]

Publicly divided, Bangkok monks either supported the students and their calls for democracy or denounced them as communists for opposing the junta's power and control. According to Somboon Suksamran, this division resulted in the emergence of a new kind of a Buddhist monk, the political monk. Somboon categorizes political monks from this period into two groups:

> First, those that espouse a cause that demands political action, such as campaigning for the underprivileged, Buddhism, or nationalism and second, those that undertake political action in response to what they conceive of as threats to their personal status, privilege, and position.[49]

These political monks were able to reclaim their symbolic capital for their own initiatives, albeit briefly.[50] This emergence of political monks was a phenomenon for a specific politicized and violent period in Bangkok and receded almost as quickly as it began. The Thai monarchy, government, and media either slandered monks for their political opposition to the State or heralded monks for their condemnation of those opposed to the State. However, while these monks were politicized in violent times, they did not become victims of the violence. The latent power of their representation remained dormant.

The Buddhist monks of the 1980s and 1990s lacked the political solidarity of the 1970s. Monks involved in sex and drug scandals occasionly appeared in the daily newspapers. This period also witnessed the rise of splinter Buddhist sects such as the vegetarian followers of Santi Asoke or the globally business-minded Thammakāy. It is also during this period that Suwanna Satha-anand finds an emergence of a new wave of Buddhist intolerance against other religious traditions in Thailand.[51] These public images of a fractious and unruly group of Buddhist monks prompted the Thai State to restructure its bureaucracy in order to protect the integrity of its Buddhist representations.

In 1992, a new division within the Ministry of Education was formed: the Office of National Buddhism (ONB). This office replaced the Department of Religious Affairs in overseeing the professional conduct of Buddhist monks. The regulation of Buddhist monks was an attempt to protect their public image, that is, their representations. According to ONB Director Dr. Amnat, the duties of the ONB reflect the Buddhist principles implicit in the State. According to Dr. Amnat, the Thai notion of justice (yutithām) shows how the State is built on the "Lord Buddha's teachings."[52] Emblematic of their need to protect the representation of Buddhist monks, the ONB worked with the Thai sangha to orchestrate a special unit of police monks (tamrūat phra), who would monitor monks and report on any irregularities.[53]

The ONB also became responsible for dispersing monetary perks to monks who passed the final level of their State Pāli language exams (parian), one of the educational reforms instituted under Prince Wachirayan and Prince Damrong.[54] Since the time of Chulalongkorn, monks would receive a stipend from the government in accordance with their official titles, and many received significant incomes from the rituals they offered. These monetary practices were characterized as "modest" and not overly publicized. Thus, the monks' connections to money did not adversely impact the public view of Buddhist monks as pure.

However, during the 1980s and 1990s, monks publicly were seen indulging in materialism. Duncan McCargo considers the Thai sangha's power for social change marginalized by these public scandals. Sex scandals impugned the public's association of Buddhist monks with asceticism, such as the case of the "superstar" monk Phra Yantra, who eventually fled to the United States. Thais also became increasingly aware of monks addicted to drugs—a stark display of worldly attachment that conflicted with their supposed otherworldly intentions. By 2001, Manop Polparin, of the Department of Religious Affairs, declared that 10% of monks and novices were drug addicts.[55]

In all likelihood, this "rise" in monastic problems was more an advent of increased media access and mobility than drastic changes in monastic behavior. With a Machiavellian twist, the integrity of monastic representations was not contingent upon monks' actions, but rather the visibility of their actions.[56] Regardless of its authenticity, the media's portrayal of monks had a strong impact on their representations, breaking down previously delimited fields of moral labor and making publicly visible acts that would otherwise have remained hidden. Ultimately, sex scandals and drug incidences temporarily ruptured the symbolic value of Buddhist monks, leading scholars and social critics to demand structural reforms for the *sangha.*[57]

The rise in technology and media and its correlates led to a savvier "*Sangha* and State" with advents such as police monks who oversaw public monastic practices. In this manner, Thai monks and their representations weathered occasional storms of social criticism such as these scandals and continued to stand as beacons of moral authority. While the Thai State remained reliant upon Buddhist monks, we find new expressions of this phenomenon emerging in southern Thailand.

Politicizing Monks in Violence: Volunteer Monks

The Thai State's appropriation of Buddhist monastic duties and roles does not elicit intense, violent Buddhist reactions in three southernmost provinces. Rather, to return to the broader argument, there are three conditions that evoke violence: a space of conflict, a politicized Buddhist representation, and the defacement of the representation.

As we have seen, State use of Buddhist monks for national projects is not uncommon, whether in Thailand or in other Buddhist countries such as Cambodia, Burma, or Japan. However, the Thai State's use of Buddhist monks in times of violence is unusual. Apart from the campaign against communism in the 1970s, the only other time the Thai State used monks during violence has been during the current conflict in the southernmost provinces. This instance is particularly sensitive due to the ethno-religious divisions between the Malay Muslims and the Thai and Thai Chinese Buddhists and, thus, deserves special attention. Due to the already present religious identities and divisions, the impact of politicizing the representation of Buddhist monks has been enhanced.

One recent development emerging in this violence is the targeting of Buddhist monks. In the *Bangkok Post* editorial of January 28, 2004, a reporter noted the following:

> In 30 years of troubles in the South, this is the first such assault on rep-
> resentatives of this most venerated institution. The attacks took place
> on Jan 22 and 24, leaving two monks and a novice dead and a third
> monk with serious injuries.[58]

The editorial failed to establish the proper historical context, ignoring the fact that violence in the southernmost provinces existed for centuries, and it neglected to note previous threats to the *sangha* in the southernmost provinces, such as the 2002 bomb threat at Wat Chang Hai. Nevertheless, the significance of the statement remains. Monks as "representatives" of the most venerated institution were attacked.

The continual attacks on monks prompted Queen Sirikit to marshal a media fanfare to the southernmost provinces. On her birthday, she expressed the need for the nation to unite over the issue of southern violence: "Even Buddhist monks have been killed. I don't want people to sit still. Even I myself have to come out to speak."[59] Her speech included a full disclosure of the power of monks' representation. Now an attack on Buddhist monks became a reason to act.

Queen Sirikit did more than voice her opinions about the dangers to Buddhist monks in the southernmost provinces. In 2004, with the help of the ONB, the Queen formed the Volunteer Monk Program (*phra āsāsamak*) in order to address particular problems in the borderland provinces. The program, popularly referred to as the "Queen's Project," followed the model of missionary programs similar to that initiated by the Phra Thammathut in the 1960s. Its goals were simple—to support the Buddhist laity, increase the number of Buddhist monks, and protect the integrity of Buddhism in Pattani, Yala, and Narathiwat. Monks from around the country were asked to spend at least three months in one of the southern *wat*, many of them in the red zone. Although the Queen's Project was designed to affect only the Buddhist population in the three southernmost provinces, it also became a powerful example of politicizing monks. In addition, as the violence persisted, the need for volunteer monks increased. A senior royal aide explained,

> If the situation persists the country's image will deteriorate. [General Naphon] appealed to everyone to help restore peace in the region. Even monks are afraid to stay in the region. For monks who remain, people have been asked to feed them at the temple so that monks do not have to leave the temples by themselves. Gen. Naphon said he would per-suade monks from elsewhere...to come to the region to give spiritual uplift to local Thai Buddhists.[60]

The Queen's project is not the first time we see the Thai State employing monks to embolden nationalistic sentiments in the southernmost provinces. The Thai government also implemented policies to redress the Thai Buddhist–Malay Muslim imbalance in one of Sarit's programs called the Self-Help Colony (*nikhom sangton-ēng*).[61] One criticism of these projects has been their lack of sensitivity training required for Buddhist monks unfamiliar with Malay and Islamic prac-tices, which is due, in part to the lack of time in the scheduled training program.

Volunteer monk training for the Queen's Project takes place in several loca-tions, the most popular place being at Wat Don Mūang in Bangkok and at Wat Chang Hai in Pattani. In Bangkok, the training occurs two days prior to a monk's relocation. Nearly every volunteer monk attends the training session, which lasts from 9 A.M. to 3 P.M. The morning is reserved for merit-making rituals.

Buddhist laity in Bangkok donate items for the volunteer monks to use during their stay in the southernmost provinces. The merit making is followed by a break for lunch. The afternoon training is led by soldiers, monks, and laity and consists of a seminar on the objectives of the Volunteer Monk program. Throughout the seminar, monks are told about the growing threat to Buddhism and how their presence could help preserve religious order in the southernmost provinces. Only one month after their deployment in 2007, one volunteer monk called Phra Laek from Wat A recounted how they were informed of the physical dangers as well as the symbolic importance of their mission:

> We were told to be careful because there were people who wanted to do away with monks in this area. When there are no monks left, Buddhists will move out, too. They showed us how to live here safely and they showed many pictures of monks here who had been attacked.[62]

The Volunteer Monk training emphasized the national importance of the monks' mission and underscored a Muslim threat.

The volunteer monks' lack of training adversely affected the southern populace, materializing most visibly in the candor and demeanor of the people employed. In conjunction with Somboon's earlier division of political monks, two types of monks generally are attracted to volunteer service in southern Thailand. The first group is resolutely patriotic. They maintain that their jobs are deeply rooted in *kammic* obligations to the king and country and that their stay in these temples is a testament to their desire to help the country and Thai Buddhism. The second type of volunteer monks is more interested in personal gain. They view their work as an opportunity to achieve fame and financial success. Neither group felt they profited from the training exercises. Yet, regardless of their training or intents, missionary projects like the Queen's Project comprise a visible reminder of the disenfranchisement of Malay Muslims from national government. There are no government-sponsored Islamic projects working to spread the teachings of Muhammad and preserve nationalist endeavors.

The Thai State continues to encourage volunteer monks to relocate to southern Thailand. During the beginning of the Buddhist Lent (*khaopansā*) in 2007, 346 monks departed from Bangkok for the "deep south" in order to "instill a sense of confidence in the region."[63] Wat A retained the services of three volunteer monks a year. Most volunteer monks do not stay longer than their minimum term. As a result, the project needed to send fresh recruits in 2006 and 2007. Wat B received one volunteer monk in 2007 who did not stay very long, and none were requested for Wat Chang Hai. These cultural ambassadors are more than links between the State and the localities; they also act as embodied representations of the State and Thai Buddhism. The absence of such a representation would be an absence of State-religious vitality. As the current director of the ONB puts it,

Nowadays, there are a small number of people who want to ordain because of economic and family responsibilities. So, there are not enough monks in the *wat*. Hence, we look for volunteers to ordain. The main reason is to have enough monks in each *wat*. It is important because we don't want people to think that monks are extinct.[64]

The director of the governmental Office of National Buddhism considers it dangerous for people to *think* that Buddhist monks are extinct in the southern provinces; the image of a strong and healthy Buddhist monasticism must be maintained. The Phra Thammačārik Project, the Phra Thammathut Program, and the recent Queen's Project politically and financially support monks to mobilize and strengthen the presence of the State in regions that were deemed "culturally" unstable or deficiently loyal.

Through the exercise of programs like the Queen's Project, we find that the State enhances the political dimensions of Buddhist monks. This politicization has not gone unnoticed by militants. One vivid example occurred when Prime Minister Thaksin traveled to Pattani Province during the Muslim celebrations of Hari Raya in 2005, a few months after the government dispatched new volunteer monks to the southernmost provinces. Awaiting Thaksin in over thirty paddy fields were political scarecrows, warning him of violent reprisals (figure 2.3).

Figure 2.3 Scarecrows, *Bangkok Post* photo/Jetjaras na Ranong. November 4, 2006.

The scarecrows were draped in the national flag and had a picture of Thaksin for a head. They also contained written warnings. One message read: "As you bombed Muslim mosques, Buddhist temples were set on fire. As you shot dead ustazes [Islamic teachers], Buddhist monks were killed. As you arrested Malayu people, we will kill your people."[65]

If we carefully examine the properties used in these political effigies, it becomes evident that the scarecrows symbolized the State, particularly the head of State, then–prime minister Thaksin Shinawatra. But, the effigies also emphasized a particular religious dimension to the State. The national flag wrapped around the scarecrow has been a symbol of Thai nationality since 1917. Its three stripes stand for the nation (*chāt*), religion (*sāsanā*), and monarchy (*phra mahākaset*). While *sāsanā* could stand for all religious traditions, its normative meaning is one—Thai Buddhism. The State's politicizing of Buddhist monks serves to promote this normativity of *sāsanā*. The warning attached to the political effigy of Thaksin illustrated the Islamic militant perspective of the Thai State: the Thai State was Buddhist. Because of this, any State conflict with the militants put the State's "people" (Buddhists), monks, and *wat* at risk. If Buddhists, monks, and *wat* represented the State, militant attacks on them could be equated to attacking the State.

While the State is not currently building *wat* in the deep south or requesting Buddhists to relocate there, they are dispatching volunteer monks to the southernmost provinces, where they serve as living emblems of their nationalism. A volunteer monk from Wat A, Phra Anek, explained his predicament, reflecting the polarizing experience he is undergoing:

> I didn't expect to stay here for Buddhist Lent. I visited the abbot here. But, the abbot asked me to stay here because there are not enough monks. Actually, I wanted to continue my studies for my Bachelor's degree, but he asked me so I decide to stay here for an extra three months. The situation for Thai Buddhists here is so pitiful. They want to make merit, but it is hard for them because there are not enough monks. We are monks and people can make merit because of us, and so this is what I am pleased to do for the people here. This life is worthwhile for me so long as I can do something for my nation. This is why I wanted to come here.... We just can't go out of the *wat* because there are many Muslims outside. They think that we are from a different religion. We have no problems with them. But they see us as the enemy [*satrū*].[66]

Phra Anek experiences two simultaneous effects from his politicization. He senses a patriotic obligation to stay at and serve at Wat A, but also senses that Muslims see him as an enemy. Phra Anek has not done anything personally to the Muslims to feel this way; rather, he is responding to his representation that creates this polarization. He and other volunteer monks continue to be deployed to the border provinces. On July 3, 2009, the Thai State flew 148 Buddhist monks to Pattani Province in order for them to arrive at their posts before the start of Buddhist Lent (July 7, 2009). As in the past, Buddhist monks were brought from the North and Northeast provinces and given minimal training before reaching their assignments among the hundred different *wat* in Pattani, Yala, and Narathiwat.[67]

One byproduct of a politicized representation is the absence of any individualistic and personal associations. Like soldiers and police, monks become extensions of the State. A Buddhist monk who might recently have been ordained in the central province of Chonburi would lose his local identity during his volunteer service in the south. He would become a defender of Buddhism and another target for militants. This consolidation of national and religious identifications in the monk can yield intense and powerful reactions.

Defacing a Representation

As politicized agents, monks represent both the State and the Thai *sangha*. Because of the monk's dual representation, a southern monk's murder defaces a political and religious symbol. If we take into consideration Bruce Lincoln's argument that society is constructed and continually reconstructed through the exercise of symbolic discourse, then an attack on such symbols has potential for greater and more emotionally intense consequences.[68]

An example of such an event occurred on October 16, 2005, when Wat Phromprasit in Pattani Province was raided. Two Buddhist statues were beheaded, two temple boys (*dekwat*) were killed, a seventy-eight-year-old abbot was hacked to death, and the *wat* was set on fire. When Thai newspapers reported on the destruction of the *wat*, they speculated that it was a result of an ongoing Muslim insurgency.

The media placed the attack on Wat Phromprasit in a nationalistic context. Pattani, the *wat's* province, already was under martial law and Malay Muslim militants periodically killed Thai police and soldiers. In cases like this, a journalist may assume local acts of violence under the larger umbrella of insurgency, since this is the most recognizable and largest frame of reference. However, people living outside of the three southernmost provinces were divorced from the violence at Wat Phromprasit, most particularly, from its local context.

For the national newspapers, the murder of the abbot and his temple boys fit neatly into the binary narrative of Muslim insurgents against the Thai nation-state. The *Bangkok Post* reported that the Thai News Agency "said the 15-minute attack on Phromprasit temple in Panare district came after the insurgents touched off fireworks to distract nearby people and security forces."[69] *The Nation* theorized that twenty Muslim insurgents were behind the events.[70]

The violence at Wat Phromprasit was much more than an insurgent attack on State Buddhism. People were murdered in this scenario for specific reasons. In this context, it is important to remember that a Buddhist monk is more than a representation of the nation; he also is a person living in a local community. The power of representation removes this localized element, but this element is necessary to accurately assess an act of violence. To review the attack once more, fireworks were set off before the attack on the *wat*, presumably to distract the community from the attackers' intended victims. There were at least ten attackers (some newspaper theorized twenty) and their onslaught lasted only fifteen minutes. The large number of attackers and the short amount of time suggest a well-organized attack by separatists.

Pattani Thai Chinese and Thai Buddhist residents offer different and localized accounts of the murders. Some frame the conflict in a very personal and localized context. One account reported that the violence began with a feud between one of the *dekwats* and a young Malay Muslim.[71] For many of the locals living near the *wat*, the attack upon Wat Phromprasit was an escalation of a feud between two locals, not a national conflict between Malay Muslim separatists and the Thai Buddhist State.

Reactions to the violence at Wat Phromprasit reflect the latent power of a monk's politicized representation. Michael Taussig, writing on the power of the negative, notes that the act of defacement releases an unprecedented level of sacrality from an object. He explains,

> When the human body, a nation's flag, money, or a public statue is *defaced*, a strange surplus of negative energy is likely to be aroused from within the defaced thing itself. It is now in a state of *desecration*, the closest many of us are going to get to the sacred in this modern world.[72]

In the devastation of Wat Phromprasit on October 16, 2005, a national emblem, public statue, and, to use Taussig's language, "human bodies" were defaced. The motives for this attack remain unclear, but the emotionally charged repercussions rose to a national level. The National Reconciliation Commission (NRC) saw this attack as emblematic of the shift in the local mentalities for violence and deduced the following: "A murderous attack on Buddhist monks inside temple walls thus eroded the cultural boundaries that traditionally served to limit political violence in Thai society since days of old."[73] For the NRC, the act of defacement indicated an escalation in violence. McCargo makes a similar assessment, locating the attack on Wat Phromprasit as a "psychological turning point," after which there became,

Figure 2.4 Renovated Wat Phromprasit, by Michael Jerryson, December 26, 2006.

...a systematic militant policy of targeting Buddhist religious institutions, and triggered a wave of reactions on the part of the Buddhist
community in the southern provinces. These reactions ranged from the
creation of armed militias, to protests against the policies of the Thaksin
government.[74]

Effects of the violence are still visible at Wat Phromprasit. Its location at the end
of a very long and narrow road off the highway makes it susceptible to attack.
When I visited the *wat* on December 26, 2006, those present were off-duty police
officers and the new abbot. Many of the buildings were rebuilt (figure 2.4). The
ONB later explained that it was crucial to fund Wat Phromprasit's restoration
because it was now an "important symbol." The importance came through the
violence, which transformed the *wat* from a local to a national talking-point. The
main pavilion (*sālā*) was behind one of the buildings, and it was there that I
found the abbot and some of the off-duty police officers.

On the floor of the *sālā* was an M-16 and attached to the ceiling were two television monitors. Only one monitor was on, and it was for surveillance. The
screen was divided into four sections, all of which were live camera feeds of the
wat's perimeter. The new abbot was sitting in the middle of the floor and was
reserved, but open to sharing some of his thoughts.

He was originally from Panāre, the district of Wat Phromprasit. Only thirty
years old, the abbot had been ordained merely nine years prior to receiving this
new position in his home district (*ampē*). His age and experience are not considered unique, but they do suggest the lack of more experienced monks to fill the
role. In our brief conversation, I asked the abbot about the conflict. What was the
cause? Who were involved in the violence? The abbot replied that the southern
violence is strictly religious. Attributing the violence to Muslim teenagers influenced by new Middle Eastern Islamic teachings, his perspective is more aligned

with that of the national narrative than of the local laity. When I asked him why his predecessor was killed and the *wat* attacked, he replied that six or seven Muslim teenagers had performed these deeds based on the *wat*'s location:

> This *wat* is in the field and is quite remote. Furthermore, we had no pro-
> tection. It was safe for them. Actually, they said they would set fire to a
> different *wat*. The police went to protect that *wat*. So they changed
> [locations] and set fire to this *wat*.[75]

The abbot thought the *wat* might be attacked again. He requested that I not take photographs of the *wat*'s military equipment because it might compromise its safety. The abbot attributed the current violence to Islamic extremism and excluded the influence of drugs, poverty, and other causes. This mono-causal analysis of the violence is an effect of living within a conflict zone. People lose sight of multiple identities and multiple causes and revert to dualistic perspec-tives.[76] The State's renovation of and enhanced military presence in the *wat* is one more example of how Thai Buddhism and its main actors have become political entities and targets.

Unlike the past, today's media and its globalized effects play an integral role in the interpretation of violence against monks. When a monk becomes a victim of continual political violence, the media often ignores the local context of the conflict and represents it as one of nationalistic concern. This process operates inversely to *globalization* and *parochialization*, as described in chapter 1. Here, this re-appropriation of an incident into a religiously and nationally charged narrative would follow with Tambiah's process of *focalization* and *transvaluation*, which he uses in his analysis of ethnically charged rhetoric:

> This progressive involvement of the ethnic public coincides with their
> coming under the sway of the rhetoric of propagandists and the horror
> tales of rumormongers who appeal to larger, deeper, certainly more
> emotive and enduring—and therefore less local-context bound—loyal-
> ties and cleavages, such as race, religion, language, nation, or place of
> origin. To sum up: focalization progressively denudes local incidents
> and disputes of their contextual particulars, and transvaluation dis-
> torts, abstracts, and aggregates those incidents into larger collective
> issues of national or ethnic interest.[77]

A drug deal gone wrong becomes an organized attack of the Malay-Muslim insurgency. A murder founded in personal revenge becomes the Muslim assassination of a monk. These narratives are accepted not only by international and national audiences, but also by locals such as the abbot at Wat Phromprasit. Not all southern monks accept this type of narrative, however.

At Wat A, one of the monks who served under the Queen's Project from Ang Thong Province in central Thailand was extremely disturbed by the way in which the Thai media depicted the violence. Phra Kwāmsūk arrived at Wat A in 2004 and maintained a light-hearted disposition throughout his time there. He was known for his dry humor and warm smile. Unlike the other volunteer monks who came and left, Phra Kwāmsūk stayed after his first post ended and participated in daily chores such as sweeping the *wat* grounds every morning. He was sixty-six years old, and affiliated himself with the Thammakāy, the commercially powerful transnational Buddhist organization with sixty centers in over twenty-nine countries. The Thammakāy also had a center in Pattani Province. Phra Kwāmsūk was especially upset about the coverage of the recent murder of monks in the nearby district of Maikæn. Generally a very genial and light-hearted man, his eyes narrowed and his voice dropped as he explained how he saw the problem:

> They said that Muslims killed the monks [at a *wat*]. But no. The people who [killed the monks] were people who sold drugs. The monks couldn't pay and delayed payment many times. This was why the monks were killed when they went out to collect alms. That was the original background for when they talked about how people cut monks' heads off and all. But, then people say the Muslims killed the monks and so on. Then the story explodes into a bigger deal. We only blame them [the Muslims]; we don't blame ourselves.[78]

According to this Phra Kwāmsūk, the murder of monks in the district of Maikæn was not politically motivated, but was prompted by a local drug conflict instead.[79] The monks were unable to pay for the drugs they were buying from local drug dealers, but because they are politicized Buddhist representations in a conflict zone, their deaths became much greater than a local drug dispute. Their *transvaluation* and *focalization* led to a much larger narrative about separatism and the nation-state and, consequently, about the vitality of Thai Buddhism.

The implicit danger in attributing religious significance to violence is that it creates a new and uncompromising motive. Mark Juergensmeyer argues that religious violence alters one's view of conflict, raising it from a mundane issue of money or power to one of cosmic relevance. By transposing the conflict onto a divine stage, people become actors in a cause far greater than themselves.[80] Killing a monk who represents the Thai nation and Buddhism itself catalyzes such a cosmic perspective. The conflict in southern Thailand is no longer about ending the separatist movement or quelling the violence, but about preserving Buddhism, a far greater motive than any monetary reason. It also is a much stronger motive.

The militant targeting of Buddhist monks is a recent phenomenon in the southernmost provinces. In an interview with Human Rights Watch, the abbot of a *wat* in the capital district of Yala reflected on the recent change:

> These militants are clearly different from their predecessors. Three decades ago, there were many separatist militants active in Yala's mountainous areas. But, they never hurt Buddhist monks or innocent people. The new generation of militants is more ruthless.... Muslim youths around this temple show no respect to me and other monks. They spit at us, or point their feet at us [a sign of disrespect]. They say Buddhists are oppressors.... It is very much different from before when Buddhists and Muslims lived side by side.[81]

The recent aim to target monks provokes intense reactions among Thai Buddhists.

Buddhist monks living in Wat Phromprasit's district of Panāre remain emotionally charged and feel that the police and soldiers are too soft on the militants.[82] At the same time, State officials carry out acts of religious vengeance, and there have been reports of Thai Buddhist vigilante squads.[83] The International Crisis Group notes groups of Buddhist militias throughout the southernmost provinces training and arming for anticipated communal conflicts. To cast an even wider net, there are Buddhist organizations that seize upon the significance of a defaced Buddhist monk as a means to rally support for Buddhist nationalism. Video CDs with gruesome attacks on Buddhist civilians and monks circulate among the militia and are "often overlaid with fiery rhetoric about the need to protect Buddhist communities."[84] The *United Front of Buddhist Organizations* disseminates booklets and "broadsheets featuring grisly coloured pictures of beheaded Thais and murdered monks," to different *wat* and border provinces to convince people that the insurgents aim to eliminate Buddhism and take over the country.[85] Rumors, as Tambiah so accurately describes, attribute evil intentions and diabolical acts of outrage to the enemy and "have the dubious honor of inflaming the aggressor to orgasms of destructive violence."[86]

Among the groups to display fervent reaction is the national police, composed largely of Buddhists from central and northern Thai provinces, such as Saksin and his partner at the My Garden Hotel. Police and soldiers in the southernmost provinces find that they do not merely uphold order. They also protect the sacred and avenge the nation. Police officers and soldiers do not merely serve the State; they also protect the integrity of Thai Buddhism.

To revisit one of Christine Gray's observations, Thais often perceive monks as living examples (*tūa yāng*) of the *dhamma*. This observation does not display any aberration; rather, this perception is in accordance with the monk's role in the Three Jewels of Buddhism. Yet, as living examples the monks may retain a

political dimension and, within a conflict zones, this has dangerous consequences. Both militants and Buddhist organizations recognize the power of the
monk's representation. The murder of monks may be personally or politically
motivated, but if the murder is located within a larger narrative, it results in
local and national rage. It is through the defacement of these sacred representations that a conflict transcends from mundane matters to divine wars of unholy
acts and exalted retributions.

An Equation for Buddhist Violence

People commit violence for a variety of reasons. In an effort to understand the
conditions in which Thai Buddhists commit religious violence, I isolated three
elements that, when brought together, produce religious motivations for violence: a politicized religious representation, a space of conflict, and the defacement of that representation. Once a Buddhist adopts a religious perspective
on violence, the motivations and passions for the violence drastically change
(as it would for a person from any other religious tradition). Fighting a war or
physically enforcing the law in villages becomes a matter of preserving the
integrity of Buddhism. A look at a massacre of Thai Buddhist monks in the
United States and the murder of environmental Buddhist monks in northern
Thailand illustrate the differential when the context does not contain one of
these elements.

One of Arizona's worst mass murders occurred just outside of Phoenix at
around midnight on August 9, 1991. Two teenagers armed with a 20-gauge
pump shotgun and a 0.22-caliber rifle entered Wat Promkunaram and killed six
Buddhist monks, an unordained nun (mǽchī), and two novices.[87] The bodies
were found "methodically" face down in the living quarters, the telephone cords
ripped out of the walls, but the donations—mostly $20 bills in the form of a
money tree, the Thai Buddhist tradition of offering money—were untouched.[88]
In this scenario, Thai monks were murdered, but were these monks seen as
political figures?

As Thai nationals living abroad, these monks and nuns represented the Thai
State and sangha. The Nation interviewed Somdej Phra Bhuddacharn, abbot of
Wat Saket and a ranking member of the sangha, about the role of Thai Buddhist
monks who went to the United States:

> He said all monks who have to go to foreign countries as Buddhist mis-
> sionaries have to undergo strict screening from the ecclesiastical
> committee at Wat Saket first and then from the Sangha Supreme
> Council before being approved to teach Buddhism overseas. In the US
> in particular, Somdej Phra Bhuddhacharn said, Thai monks have played

an important role by helping propagate not only Buddhism but also teaching the Thai language as well as Thai tradition and culture to the offspring of the Thai communities there.[89]

Charles Keyes notes that, in this particular context, the Thai monks were missionaries not only of Thai Buddhism, but also of Thai culture.[90] But, what underscored the political dimension of the monks' deaths was the initial speculative motive for the murders, which were attributed to the rising anti-Asian racism throughout the Phoenix metropolitan area. Once again, we find a local incident elevated to a national narrative. Racism would account for the defacement of Buddhist bodies and imply an enhanced political dimension to the monks' deaths. The attacks and speculated motive outraged Thais in the United States and abroad. Wat Promkunaram's deaths became an international concern. The Thai Foreign Ministry paid to have the monks' bodies shipped back for a royal funeral at Wat Saket with the special honor of the Thai *sangha*'s Supreme Patriarch presiding.[91]

However, the speculated motive of racism was eventually ruled out. What was initially thought of as a gang-related racial attack turned out to be a violent robbery committed by a Jonathan Doody, a half-Thai teenager, and his Latino friend, Alessandro Garcia. The change in motives for murder directly impacted the way Thais viewed the incident. Charles Keyes notes that once racism was ruled out, Thais expressed less interest in the event:

> When the case of the Arizona *wat* murders went to trial in late 1991, concluding in mid-1993, the story generated only mild interest in Thailand. It was now not a story about a vicious racially-motivated attack on monks who embodied Thai national culture; rather, it was a story about an American teenager gone bad.[92]

The depoliticized—or rather de-nationalized—motives for murder uncoupled the murdered monks' direct association with the Thai nation. While Thais living in Thailand gradually lost interest in the story, it was still intimately a part of the Thai diaspora in Arizona.

The Thai diaspora was sparse in Waddell, an unincorporated town in metropolitan Phoenix. Most Thais from the area were military wives, who reacted with shock and sadness after hearing the news. They commented on their inability to attend Buddhist rituals and the brutal irony of having no monks available to coach them through this difficult time period. Years later, the massacre is still remembered annually by the local community, which works toward healing and forgiving the two teenagers who orchestrated the violence.[93]

The Arizona massacre of Thai Buddhist monks, a nun, and novices involved the defacement of ordained Buddhists who were, for a time, politicized; however, the attacks did not take place within a conflict zone. Because of the absence of this last condition, we find international (and local) outrage absent of violent reactions.[94]

There have been attacks on monks in Thailand that also allow for a politicized context, but as these attacks are removed from an area of conflict as well they do not evoke violent reactions. For example, environmental monks (*phra nak anuraksa thammachat*) have sought to impede the deforestation and pollution of natural resources in north and northeast Thailand and have been murdered for their political efforts.[95] One of the more recent and public murders occurred in Chiang Mai Province on June 17, 2005.

Phra Supoj Suvacano, a twenty-seven-year-old environmental monk, was found dead from multiple stab wounds. The murder of Phra Supoj shocked a network of environmentalists, social workers, and Buddhist activists, but it did not evoke a violent reaction. An informal organization of monks called the Northern Development Monks' Organization demanded a full investigation into Phra Supoj's death with little result. Ong-ard Decha of the Thai online newspaper *Prachatai* writes that, although the murder of Phra Supoj repre-sented a conflict over access to natural resources, "government agencies responsible came out badly from the case with no progress in the investigation after two years."[96]

Phra Supoj's murder contains two of the three elements needed for Buddhist violence (and a violent reprisal). Phra Supoj was a politicized Buddhist monk who was defaced through a violent assault. However, the area in which the vio-lence took place was not part of a nationalistic conflict zone. Deforestation and corporate greed could become a national narrative, but this would require a national conflict. The absence of a conflict zone suppresses the latent power of the monk's representation. As in the deaths of the Arizona Thai monks, nun, and novices, the death of the environmental monk did not provoke violence or reli-gious justification for violence. However, the murders of the monks at Wat Phromprasit in the southernmost provinces did.[97]

Conclusion

There is a rich discourse elucidating the ways in which contemporary religion has become re-infused into politics, or the religionization of politics. In the case of southern Thailand, *we find the opposite*—the State's politicization of monks, which alters the tone of religious activism in southern Thailand.

The theoretical relevance of politicizing religion has vast implications that stretch beyond the scope of Buddhisms or Southeast Asia. It is a global motif in varied contemporary conflicts around the world. The fall of the Soviet Union and the end of the Cold War made way for a new global conflict—contrasting types of nationalisms.[98] In the 1990s, a bevy of self-declared secular governments were under siege, whether it was by the Bharatiya Janata Party (BJP) contesting the Nehruvianism of India, ultraconservative Muslims overtaking Soeharto's government in Indonesia, or the growing evangelical Christian lobby in the United States. While there are scholars, such as political scientist James Fearon, who argue that the contemporary global trends in violence are predicated upon systems of government and economic conditions, they are unable to account for how and why religion becomes involved in conflicts.[99]

In southern Thailand, one social byproduct of the religiously tinged violence is the dualistic or Manichean mentality that eliminates secular associations. Buddhist Pattani locals no longer recognize an unfamiliar woman wearing a *tudung* riding public transportation as a local, female, or Thai.[100] Instead, she is simply a Muslim—and further, a potential threat. This is an unfortunate result of living in an environment saturated with fear. Living in a violent climate robs people of their subjectival fluidity, or, as Amartya Sen explains in *Identity and Violence*, their plural identities.[101] Pervasive and mounting fear leads people to view those around them as being on one side of a set of growing and fractious binary oppositions; in a global context, people are either capitalist or communist, colonizer or colonized, Buddhist or Muslim. In the case of southern Thailand, ethnic distinctions such as Thai Chinese or Thai are often reduced to one appellation: Thai Buddhists (*thai phut*) or Thai (*khon thai*).[102] In a similar fashion, the myriad of Muslim ethnicities as well as civilian/militant distinctions in the deep south are often reduced to one identification: Muslim.

The monk has the potential to make his greatest social impact by being murdered in spaces of conflict. When a monk is murdered, Thai Buddhism and Thai nationalism are defaced. In his work on the destruction of symbols and iconoclasm, Lincoln introduces the term *profanophany* (a revelation of profanity) and posits that revolutionary movements often "make use of iconoclasm as a weapon against the regimes they seek to overthrow."[103] This context certainly applies to the militant attacks on Buddhist monks in southern Thailand. However, Lincoln also argues that iconoclasts act "with the assurance either that the specific image under attack has no such power or the more radical conviction that there is no such thing as sacred power."[104] What is suggestive in this context is quite the opposite. Militant attacks on Buddhist monks are predicated on the assumption that they possess power, a sacred power connected to the nation. Instead, we find that Taussig's metaphor of "atom splicing" the sacred becomes apropos here. By killing a Buddhist monk, his attackers expose the full force of what he represents and, in so doing, propel the conflict onto a cosmic stage. The genesis for this dangerous mentality is attainable through the three previously discussed elements: the defacement of the politicized sacred in a conflict zone, or in this particular case, the murdering of a Buddhist monk in southern Thailand.

A very recent illustration of this fact is the international attention to Myanmar. After more than forty-five years of a dictatorship and consistent violations of human rights, the world became briefly attentive to the atrocities during a public uprising against the Burmese junta in September 2007. As monks took to the streets protesting junta rule and rallying tens of thousands of civilians to their cause, they created a site of conflict in and around Rangoon. But, it was not the hundred thousand protesters that made the junta's army commanders abandon their posts, nor the Burmese students that caught the international media's eye. Rather, it was the Burmese Buddhist monks and what they symbolized—pious men of peace—and the State violence visited upon them (figure 2.5).[105]

This international attention is not unique. Another memorialized event came from the self-immolation of Vietnamese Buddhist monks during the U.S. war in Vietnam. Thich Quang Duc's self-immolation in a busy intersection of Saigon became a lasting symbol of resistance to the U.S.-backed South Vietnamese regime. Thich Quang Duc's death, as well as other public violent deaths of Buddhist monks, unleashed the full power of their symbolism.[106]

Whereas Burmese monks used their symbolic capital to refute the legitimacy of the junta, such as the refusal of Burmese military donations, the Thai monks'

Figure 2.5 Burmese Indian
Protesting Violence, *Associated Press*,
September 29, 2007.

symbolic capital is invested in the legitimacy of the Thai State. This convergence of Thai sacrality and governance is part of an ideological legacy from Indian Buddhism that stretches beyond the borders of Thailand to the nascent beginnings of Buddhism in South Asia.

There are varying circumstances and situations in which the power of a Buddhist monk's representation is unleashed. For each scenario described above, the murder of Buddhist monks occurred in a conflict area. Vietnamese monks opposed to the State and colonial rule invoked the power themselves through self-immolation. During the political protests in Myanmar, the junta's attack on the monks triggered the monk's symbolic power, and in the southernmost provinces of Thailand, monks are killed by militants.

The Thai context is different from the Burmese and Vietnamese in that the southern Thai monks do not react against the State, but rather act in concordance with it. Monks in the southernmost provinces might wish to remain apolitical throughout the conflict, but they are inevitably drawn into the political dimension through State actions. It is through their politicized roles and defacement that they ultimately increase violence in the southernmost provinces.

3

Practice

When I first met Ačhān Nok at Wat A, I asked him, "What are the monks' duties during the violence in the southern border provinces?" He replied simply, "Monks should have guns to protect themselves."[1] Prolonged exposure to a violent environment had changed Ačhān Nok, a forty-two-year-old Buddhist abbot of the small *wat* in a red zone. During the several years I lived and worked with different Buddhist abbots in Thailand's southernmost provinces of Pattani, Yala, and Narathiwat, I discovered that Ačhān Nok's opinions mirrored that of many other abbots in the region. Most abbots in the red zones wanted or owned handguns. While his fears and desires are understandable, Ačhān Nok's request to arm monks clashes with the most general notions about Theravāda Buddhism. Thai Buddhists consider monks above the worldly matters of warfare and violence. Thais might view monks and war as antithetical entities; however, this reflection ignores a legacy of Thai monks who have fought in wars.[2]

Southern monks engage in practices that adversely affect the violence, such as conducting sermons that openly encouraged Buddhists to distrust their Muslim neighbors. Their fears influence their sermons and rituals, and in turn these performances intensify religious animosities and distrust between Buddhists and Muslims.[3] On these occasions it is not simply what monks do, but *how* they do it.[4] The purpose of such an examination is to widen our typical definitions of political power and identity to expose the applications of symbolic power present within society. As such, in this chapter we will examine the impact fear has on southern monastic practices. Due to persistent levels of trauma, monastic practices change and lead to monks exacerbating the violence in the southernmost provinces, specifically through their views, speeches, and actions.

Practice and Performativity

Performance is not located solely on a theater stage; it occurs all around us. People perform their identities through their dress, speech, and gestures. Just as scholars like Judith Butler demonstrate that race and gender are performative exercises, the same is evident for religion. In the southernmost provinces, Malay Muslims perform their identities by wearing headscarves (Arabic: *hijab*) for women and long flowing robes for men. Religious leaders engage in performances that legitimatize their identities, which become self-reflective modes of *habitus*. Tambiah considers performance an indexical value, existentially transferred to and inferred by actors during a performance and conferring on them symbolic capital.[5] Monks perform rituals and in turn accrue authority, power, and other entitlements. However, when a Buddhist monk alters the way he conducts a ritual, or when he allows more participants into a ritual, the ritual changes while the signification remains. In this act of transference, the monk's agency is illuminated.

In this context, the primary means of legitimating religious leadership falls within the dimension of performance. Buddhist monks influence the laity throughout the day with religious performances, whether the medium is a casual conversation of morality under a pavilion while chewing on betel nut, or a sermon on proper behavior during a communal gathering. Performance, as Erving Goffman has shown, is contingent upon influence.[6] But, performance infers a dialectic in which monks become influential due to the participation of the laity.

Southern Buddhist monks believe their primary duty is to instruct the Buddhist laity about the *dhamma*. Unlike evangelical religious traditions, which include the habits of Buddhist schools such as the Thai Thammakāy or the Japanese Sokka Gakkai, southern Thai Buddhist monastic practices are not focused or directed toward gaining new converts to Buddhism. In the southernmost provinces, their audiences are overwhelmingly Buddhist—civilian and military.[7]

Many soldiers and police live within *wat* in an effort to protect the monks from random militant attacks. Sharing living spaces and providing constant protection to monks, especially during monks' stay outside their *wat*, creates a daily venue for the military to participate in monastic practices. This military and monastic interaction blurs the lines of politics and religion and results in a politicization of southern monks' roles. Southern monks often reinforce their own political importance through their practices as seen in their morning duty of collecting alms.

Every morning, Buddhist monks make their way outside the *wat* and into local villages. Dating back to the fifth century B.C.E., Siddhattha Gotama, the founder of Buddhism, and his monks would make rounds with their bowls in the morning to receive the laity's donations of food. This early institutionalized practice of collecting alms became a structural system of giving and receiving merit between monks and the laity. When Buddhists give a monk food, they receive the merit of enabling the monk to continue his ascetic lifestyle. The more ascetic and removed a monk becomes from the worldly affairs, the more he is viewed by laity as worthy of their generosity, and as an auspicious and powerful factor in the donation of sustenance and gifts. Looking at the social implications of making merit, Thomas Kirsch rightly states:

> [T]he main focus of merit-making activities is the monk, or more gen-
> erally, the Sangha, which is ubiquitous throughout Thailand…Monks
> are worthy objects of merit-making activities by others because,
> through their ordination, they have voluntarily given up their attach-
> ments to kinsmen, neighbors, and friends, and the attractions of ordi-
> nary society, to assume the rigorous discipline of the religious life.[8]

The lay practice of donating food was a standard way of making merit in the southernmost provinces until 2004. The southern monks who were allowed to leave their *wat* strolled through predominantly Muslim neighborhoods between 5:00 and 7:00 in the morning while followed by military escorts equipped with M-16s. Buddhists came out of their homes and made offerings of food, providing more than enough for their *wat*. After martial law was declared in the three southernmost provinces by the State of Thailand, the traditional Thai Buddhist practice of making merit changed.

The military began playing an active role in protecting the monks during their daily alms. The importance of protecting the monastic way of life became apparent eight months after martial law was imposed on October 25, 2004, when the *Bangkok Post* reported that, due to intensifying danger, the Fourth Army asked Buddhist monks in the three southernmost provinces to refrain from their morning alms for two weeks.[9] The next day Wassana Nanuan of the *Bangkok Post* made a correction, issuing Lieutenant Colonel Arkhom's statement, which asserts that monks should continue collecting alms as usual, with soldiers providing protection each morning.[10] The media's attention to the halt of alms and Lieutenant Colonel Arkhom's statement underscore the social importance of this monastic-led practice.

The military exerted great effort to enable monks to continue collecting alms and, in the process, lent a national importance to the issue of southern morning alms. It is at this point that the practice of morning alms changed both politically and religiously. The monastic practice had become nationalized and politicized, but the *Bangkok Post* coverage suggests that this change came from the State, which omits an important element—the monks' agency.

Anthropologist Edmund Leach argues that structural systems in which social actions are institutionalized leave an element of agency: "In all viable systems, there must be an area where the individual is free to make choices so as to manip-ulate the system to his advantage."[11] For Leach, the institutionalized practice of morning alms could change through the agents involved in the practice. If we view Leach's comments in the context of southern monastic alms, the monk's agency becomes more readily visible. Monks changed their practice by adding military escorts to their performance, thereby reshaping the scope and the impact of morning alms. By continuing the practice of morning alms, a Buddhist presence in the southernmost provinces was reaffirmed.

In addition to military escorts, some monks in Narathiwat wore bulletproof vests, while volunteers drove others around in bulletproof *tuk-tuks*.[12] This atypical performance of alms enlarged the scope of people who could accrue merit. In this new militarized performance, not only the Buddhist laity made merit by donating food, but also the police and soldiers who guarded the monks. The domain of merit-making activity even extended to those who were making saffron bulletproof vests for the monks. The traditional means of making merit also expanded to include providing physical protection to the monks. This shift in participants of a ritual supports Catherine Bell's view that ritual "as a performative medium for social change emphasizes human creativity and physicality;" it does not mold people, but rather people fashion rituals that shape their world.[13] Society refashioned monks' daily performance of alms in such a way that the merit-exchange through alms remained the same, while the form of the merit making (such as attire, or even mode of transportation) and the number of participants changed. Morning alms also acquired national and political dimensions.

The Thai State's motivation for including military participants in Buddhist performances comes from a widespread fear among locals, monks, and the national media of violent attacks on monks. Through their practices of collecting morning alms, monks indirectly confirm the local Malay Muslim and Thai Buddhist perceptions of them as political agents of the State. This has been a gradual process that became more public and vocal as the fear and violence persisted. The monks' publicly expressed views began to show the toll that violence had on them. This is evident in statements of abbots like Ačhān Nok who, in 2004, advocated that monks should own handguns. His view on this was synonymous with the views of southern monks living in red zones, the most dangerous areas, and undergoing the most traumatic effects of violence, mostly catalyzed by a continual and pervasive fear.

The southern Thai Buddhist monks' daily practices are an extension of their religious identity. This interpretation is not unique in Buddhist Studies, like in the case of young Buddhist monks in Sri Lanka, who learn their new identities through formal and everyday performative measures, which Jeffrey Samuels calls an action-based pedagogy.[14] In the case of southern Thai Buddhist monks, it is their everyday practice and rituals, and not the doctrine, which imbue monks with social significance. The analysis of practice and performance is not new to the study of violence either. Mark Juergensmeyer devotes attention to *performance violence* and looks at religious terrorism as theater. In this manner, terrorism is a public performance of violence with real and symbolic aspects.[15] Juergensmeyer's use of performance elucidates the techniques and motivations of violent actors, but does not directly pertain to our examination of Buddhist monks. Southern monks are not eager to gain international attention and, for the most part, are not directly engaged in violent actions.

The southern Thai Buddhist monks most clearly articulated their identity through their political views, speeches, and actions between 2004 and 2008. In 2005, after a year of continual violence, southern monks began to vocalize their frustrations. As a result, their thoughts and words coalesced into a collective effort of instilling Buddhist nationalism in their localities. In this respect, Clifford Geertz's sketch of the theater-state, the *negara* in nineteenth-century Bali, and Stanley Tambiah's performative lens in South Asian riots are notable antecedents.[16] Along with monks advocating for a Buddhist state, a move to protect Thai Buddhism on the national level worked to equate the integrity of Buddhism with the integrity of the nation. This advocacy only exacerbated Buddhist-Muslim relations in the conflict zone, as it strengthened Muslims' feelings of alienation from the State.

The Routinization of Terror

The context in which monks enacted their new roles is largely defined by a pervasive and unrelenting level of fear. Fear has a strong influence on monks' daily activities and was an inseparable element of southern Buddhist life during the incessant murders and bombings that occurred day after day. This fear does not infect only Buddhists, but all locals of the three southernmost provinces. A local official for two hundred Muslim families living in Tapong District, a red zone near the capital district of Pattani, explained to an *International Herald Tribune* journalist: "Muslims feel fear, Buddhists feel fear. But we don't know who we are afraid of."[17] Part of this fear stems from the sheer randomness of the attacks and the utter brutality in which many of the attacks occur. To illustrate the context of this fear, we will begin by looking at circumstances surrounding the annual Kathin ceremony at Wat A and then proceed to specific cases in which fear has affected monks' political and religious views.

According to local and military sources, Wat A's village, with a population of more than 4,000 Muslims and 100 Buddhists, was one of the 257 villages in a red zone.[18] The actions and events at Wat A reflected that of any *wat* in the red zone throughout the three southernmost provinces. On October 14, 2006 Ačhān Nok, held his annual Kathin ceremony at Wat A. As early as 4:30 A.M., volunteers, monks, and the two dozen soldiers living at Wat A began preparing the area for the traditional surge of Buddhist laity. Soldiers were sweeping and mopping the grounds, and a few regular female patrons were busy preparing the kitchen for several hundred people who were expected to arrive at 11:00. As I watched everyone work, Islamic prayers emanated from a nearby loudspeaker across the street. It was Ramadan, the venerated Islamic month of fasting. These two observances are religiously distinct, but the Kathin ceremony and Ramadan coincided on the same day and on the same block. It was also a reminder of the different lifestyles and performances occurring on this day.

Malay Muslims were practicing their observances away from the Buddhist festival grounds and would break their fast after sunset. The local Buddhists were celebrating and feasting in their religious space, the *wat*. Although these two observances were taking place in separate quarters, the two religious events did not need to be mutually exclusive. In the past, Malay Muslims had attended the Kathin celebrations; yet in 2006 this was no longer practiced, nor was it expected. Wat A's Kathin celebration involving monks, lay performers, and an exclusively Buddhist audience reinforced religious divisions in the village and perpetuated distrust and alienation between Buddhist and Muslim villagers.

The Buddhist Kathin ceremony marks the end of Buddhist Lent (and the rainy season) and is a time when Buddhists offer gifts and new robes to monks. The Kathin ceremony is a great source of revenue for *wat*; it typically provides the largest number of donations each year. Like other Thai Buddhist rituals, its monetary draw relates directly to its merit-making potential. Stanley Tambiah notes that the donation of Kathin gifts is the third most meritorious act for Thai Buddhists. The first is financing the building of a *wat*, and the second is taking the ordination of a monk or having a son ordain.[19] The Kathin ceremony ordinarily draws Buddhists from their local *wat* to neighboring *wat*, uniting them "with a larger Buddhist world."[20] The Kathin ceremony's pan-Buddhist phenomenon did not manifest at Wat A. Many locals I interviewed at that time recalled a time before the violence, when they were able to travel and attend many different Kathin ceremonies on the same day. It was a day of merriment and celebration, when both Buddhists and Muslims from all over the neighborhood attended the festivities.

However, on October 14, 2006, the Kathin ceremony was different. There was merriment, but there also were armed soldiers—embodiments of violence—and a clear lack of Muslim participants at the *wat*. Before the 2004 escalation of violence, local Muslims celebrated with Buddhists at Wat A; now, the Buddhist celebration, underscored by military participation, transitioned into an activity that divided the community. The morning of the Kathin ceremony, some time before the laity arrived, soldiers stationed themselves outside the *wat* along the street. As Malay Muslims walked down the street, the soldiers watched them carefully. The day before the event the Thai State warned of the possibility of Malay Muslim militant attacks on the Buddhist Kathin ceremonies in the south. Dressed in fatigues and armed with their M-16s, soldiers were a sharp contrast in attire and behavior to festival participants (figure 3.1).

Figure 3.1 Boy and Soldier, by Michael Jerryson, October 14, 2006.

By 2006, the sight of armed military personnel did not alarm any of the Kathin attendants, who felt protected from Muslim neighbors. The awareness of continual murders, bombings, and arson attacks became the acceptable norm for the locals so long as the violence did not occur in their immediate (geographic or emotional) vicinity. This was their coping mechanism for dealing with their fears. Anthropologist Linda Green, working with Mayan widows in Guatemala, came to the following conclusion: "Routinization of terror is what fuels its power. Routinization allows people to live in a chronic state of fear with a facade of normalcy at the same time that terror permeates and shreds the social fabric."[21] It is through this routinization of terror that the victims sustain levels of extreme trauma. Many southern Thai monks and lay people tried to live their lives as if nothing out of the ordinary were taking place. This conflicted attitude was exemplified by many monks who were my hosts. In what became a typical conversation, the abbot or senior monk would encourage me to bring my wife and child to the *wat*. On one occasion, Ačhān Nok remarked, "Why don't you bring them here? It is beautiful here. You should bring them." Moments later we watched soldiers rushing out of Wat A to investigate a bombing that had just occurred a few miles away. He shook his head, and as if forgetting what he had said a few minutes ago, added in anger: "This is crazy. No one should live like this."

The Kathin ceremony was an enactment of this duality of normalcy and fear. As Buddhists danced and sang, I watched a boy casually mimic a soldier who was armed with his M-16. The boy exemplified global and local influences simultaneously in a chilling way. He was dressed in a Spider-Man T-shirt, a piece of residual merchandise that came after the release of the global blockbuster movie *Spider-Man 2* in 2004. He also had been playing with a toy gun. Both the T-shirt and toy gun would not seem out of the ordinary for a boy his age. Boys throughout the world own and play with toy guns; however, the context required further scrutiny. Mirroring the soldier's handling of the M-16 with his own toy gun, the boy was reifying the social influences around him. Ačhān Nok would be the first to say that it was not always like this.

Soldiers and police relocated their operations to southern *wat* in 2004. Many villagers were shocked when the military moved into Pattani, Yala, and Narathiwat *wat*. Military activities, weapons, and the reason for their presence were new to many of the locals in the early months of 2004. But, the military were not the only new occupants at Wat A. A few years earlier, Wat A was without an abbot as well. In 2000, no one wanted the position. The *wat*'s finances were depleted and there was a very small Buddhist population to support it. To make matters worse, monks from neighboring *wat* gossiped about the quarrels of the villagers at Wat A. The district's senior monks held a meeting about the situation. According to Ačhān Nok, after a few minutes of debate, his preceptor proposed the following: "Ačhān Nok should be the abbot of Wat A. If he doesn't accept this, I will not accept him as my disciple anymore and, if I die, he cannot come to my funeral."

"He is like my father in the Buddhist religion," Ačhān Nok explained, "so I couldn't refuse him." Ačhān Nok's passion had been living in nature and meditating in burial grounds. After spending a few years traveling around the northern and northeastern provinces of Thailand as a forest monk, Ačhān Nok returned to the southernmost provinces as the abbot of Wat A. Transforming his solitary life of a forest monk (*thudong*) into farming and counseling, Ačhān Nok began to mediate religious disputes among villagers and to cultivate a garden in his *wat*. Although there were problems in Wat A's community between Buddhists and Muslims at the time, Ačhān Nok felt he could address them. Relations between the Buddhist minority and the Muslim majority improved and Ačhān Nok purchased roughly 1.2 acres (3 *rai*) in order to enlarge his garden. The financial status of the *wat* was improving and religious disputes between Buddhists and Muslims had decreased. Then, on January 4, 2004, an army base was raided, four soldiers were killed, three hundred military weapons stolen, and twenty public schools were torched in Narathiwat.

Unlike previous Malay Muslim attacks in the 1970s and 1980s, no separatist organization claimed responsibility for these attacks, although they clearly were organized. The assaults led to immediate changes in Ačhān Nok's district and throughout the three southernmost provinces. Three weeks after the raid, on January 27, 2004, the Thai State responded by temporarily shutting down 1,029 schools, evacuating monks from their *wat*, and setting curfews.[22] Distrust spread among Ačhān Nok's community and soldiers moved into Wat A. A few months later, Ačhān Nok would go on morning alms and local Muslims would threaten him with hand gestures, moving their fingers across their throats.

When Ačhān Nok recounted these events, he raised his voice, scowling. In Thailand, monks generally are highly venerated. When locals make threatening gestures, they not only violate Thai custom, but perpetuate a state of fear. It was no longer safe for Ačhān Nok to leave his *wat* on morning alms. Although he refrained from going on morning alms, Ačhān Nok would leave Wat A sporadically to perform funerary rites for villagers. In the past, the villagers used to come to the *wat* for these services, but it had become too dangerous.

Buddhist monks and laity throughout the southern provinces commented to me on the shift in communal relations since January 2004. Similarly, in a *Human Rights Watch* interview, a Buddhist laywoman recounted the vicious murder of her father and noted "that the killing has terrified her village, where Buddhists and Muslims once lived peacefully together. 'Now most Buddhist villagers think it is no longer safe to stay here,' she said...."[23] These sentiments are most widely expressed by villagers in red zones.

Due to the level of danger and the highly uneven ratio of Buddhists to Muslims, it became difficult for Ačhān Nok to retain monks at his *wat*. After the 2004 escalation in violence, Ačhān Nok became the only permanent monk his *wat*. In 2005, he gained four monks during the Rain Retreat, but lost three of them after the Kathin ceremony.[24] Monks came and left after the Rain Retreat in 2006 as well. In April 2007, there were only two monks at Wat A. The scarcity of monks is symptomatic of conditions for any *wat* in red zones. Another reason is the small population of Buddhists living in the surrounding area. The southernmost provinces have large percentages of Muslims in each village, resulting in a small number of laity who donate to a *wat* and an insufficient number of monks to perform certain Buddhist ceremonies. Nonetheless, areas like that around Wat A retain a very loyal lay following. Throughout the violence Wat A served over two hundred Buddhists living in and around the district.

The first time I spoke with Ačhān Nok was in 2004 during the hot season, a few months after the conflict at the Khru Se Mosque. Tensions between Buddhists and Muslims were high, and he expressed anger and frustration regarding the violence. Moreover, his inability to go on alms, the reduction in visitors, and increased tensions made him feel isolated. In a strong voice he described the environment in which he lived:

> Five people just died in one day here in Pattani. We have no food to eat in the morning nowadays because Thais are going elsewhere. No one gives food or money to the monks. There is no money for repairs and our daily traditions have changed a lot. Some monks have had to go borrow money from the laity to pay for things. No one comes to the

wat, and there are no more ceremonies here (such as the *nansok* or *suk-mon*), so we cannot get any income from them.[25]

Ačhān Nok continued to perform funeral rites and organized the previously described annual Kathin ceremony; nevertheless, there was a significant decrease in ritual activity and, therefore, in income for his *wat*.

Many *wat* suffered from a lack of funds in 2004. The depletion in donations prompted the ONB to provide money and supplies to *wat* in the southernmost provinces. One ONB officer, who requested anonymity, stated that his particular branch was instrumental in dispersing 40–100 million baht (1–2.5 million USD) a year to *wat* in the southernmost provinces. He explained that the funds were dispersed in cash directly to abbots who passed them to others. The ONB intended the money be spent on securing the walls of the *wat* and in assisting abbots to stockpile supplies.[26]

Financial assistance did not eliminate the monks' other problems and their fears. Ačhān Luk, who lives in a southern capital district, recognized the dangers right after martial law was declared in January 2004, when Pattani Malay Muslims requested the Thai State convert a *wat* in Mayaw District into a mosque. Yet, it was not until the conflict at the Khru Se Mosque, on April 28, 2004, that he realized the depths of the ethno-religious conflict.[27]

Fear is not sustained simply through actions, but also through words. During his fieldwork in the deep south, Duncan McCargo collected leaflets pertaining to the conflict. Leaflets are one of the common methods of militant communication with locals because they allow for anonymity, intimacy, and a sense of immanence. Some of the most common leaflets are warnings, many of which urge Buddhists to leave. A leaflet found in Kha Pho, Pattani, on October 29, 2004, read: "Hey! All you Thai Buddhists. If you still stay on our land, we will hunt you down and kill you all. Get out from my territory, or you will have to eat bullets again."[28] Other leaflets that generate fear come from Buddhists, who see this as a means of "waking up" fellow Thais. The *United Front for Thais Who Love the Nation* saw the violence as a justification for "Thailand's Buddhists to take a stand and affirm Buddhism as the core of the nation's identity." Marc Askew considers a five-page photocopied document, which purports an Islamic plot with twenty-nine measures to take over Thailand, one of their disseminations. The document was "headed with the message, 'Urgent from the South', [and] the document bore the title of 'The Policy to Seize Power over Thailand in Ten Years.'"[29]

During my stay at Wat B, I attended the funeral of an old man who was murdered right outside the *wat*. He was a regular patron of the *wat* until the morning when he was bicycling there and got shot in the middle of the street. Militants chopped off his head and set his body on fire. This very public and provocative attack reflects the brazen attitude of the militants and the lack of State power in the area. It also calls to mind Juergensmeyer's theater of terror and the possible global influences exerted as militant attacks in other parts of the world such as Aceh and Iraq may have an influence on the style of attack in Thailand's southernmost provinces.

As of September 10, 2008, there were forty-one beheadings according to the *Bangkok Post*.[30] Terrorism experts argue that the style of many of these southern Thai beheadings is influenced by Muslim militant actions in the Middle East.[31] However, there is more evidence to suggest that Thais are being trained in Indonesia or that the expertise comes from Indonesian-trained Thais who have stronger regional and local connections than countries in the Middle East. According to the southern Thai newspaper *Isrā*, in one instance a Thai *ustaz* (Islamic teacher) who teaches Islam in Yala Province had trained as a commando and studied Islam in Aceh, Indonesia. Among the Thai *ustaz*'s commando training were techniques for beheading people.[32] The globalizing effect of the media has unquestionably had a hand in spreading the style and tactics of terror; however, the transnational effects of the media should not lead to the abandonment of a locality's ability for macabre and creative endeavors.[33]

The police never caught the people who beheaded the old man in front of Wat B, and they never ascertained a motive for targeting the elderly Thai-Chinese man. The police and military's failure to maintain accountability is a reoccurring phenomenon in southern Thailand and is another element that fuels societal fears. At Wat B, the nearness and ferocity of the attack unnerved and angered many of the monks. Several monks outside of the capital districts of Pattani, Yala, and Narathiwat have expressed their feelings of isolation from the government, largely on account of the unresolved attacks.

When faced with attacks on their *wat* or on those living nearby, monks occasionally exhibit a moderate level of suspicion about local Muslims and their activities. The monks' suspicions are understandable and not completely unjustified. Chaotic environments breed paranoia, and southern Thailand is an example of this.[34] For many southern Buddhists, it was the militant violence, compounded by the Thai State's inability to locate or combat the militants, which demonstrated the State's impotence. The destabilization of State power triggers psychological repercussions in citizens, a Freudian phenomenon ubiquitous in every society.[35]

Before martial law, southern monks viewed Islam and local Malay Muslims as part of the community, whereas after martial law many monks began to view Muslim neighbors with a high level of suspicion. This suspicion manifested itself in a variety of ways, one of them being through the everyday practice of eating meals, a practice that extends Appadurai's notion of gastro-politics into a comparative venue.[36] As Theravāda Buddhism and Malay Islam are both orthopraxic, in which importance is placed more on your behavior and actions than your belief (orthodoxy), Buddhist laity and monks use the Islamic rule of *halal* as a litmus test for strangers' religious identities. If a stranger eats pork, s/he is not Muslim and is considered safe. If s/he responds in an awkward manner or simply refuses to eat, s/he is Muslim and possibly a threat. In other Buddhist-Muslim regions, the issue of *halal* is a common source of contradistinction between Muslims and Buddhists.[37] According to Saroja Dorairajoo, an anthropologist who conducted her fieldwork in Pattani Province out of a southern Muslim household, every time she returned from her fieldwork to a nearby urban center, her Buddhist friends would serve her pork, testing to see if she had converted to Islam.[38] I encountered a similar treatment when I stayed at Wat A, Wat B, and other *wat* of the southernmost provinces. For example, at Wat B, following the typical Thai custom, the monks tried to play host and asked me what I wanted to have for dinner. At times, when I asked for chicken-fried rice, *wat* volunteers would bring me pork-fried rice. "It's all right," a monk would explain, watching me carefully, "You can eat pork, right?"[39]

The pork test is a subtle manifestation of Buddhists' growing distrust and fear of Muslims. It is also an example of how Buddhist communities begin to orchestrate rituals in order to establish safety. Buddhist monks and laity practice these rituals due to the violent climate in which they live. The rituals become surrogate safeguards to cope with the lack of security from the State. However, the closer or more frequent the attacks and bombings, the more suspicious a monk may become. This is indicative of Ačhān Pim, whose words began the Introduction. Ačhān Pim felt constantly spied on. In April of 2004, militants attempted to kill a forty-year-old abbot living in the same district.[40] During a phone interview with Ačhān Pim, he relayed that there were no military personnel living at his *wat*, and his emotions were charged as he was expressing these thoughts:

> Muslims have come around and spied on us, but when they see the local volunteers guarding the *wat*, they go away. They have come a few times and want the Buddhists to leave this area. Islam wants to take over the world and make the world one religion. Everyone knows it. It doesn't matter where you are. Islam discriminates against other religions.[41]

Ačhān Pim was convinced that he had to "watch his back" when soldiers were not present because Muslims had the backing of the Thai State. This was a popular rumor among monks in the southernmost provinces. Many suspected that Muslims had some influence over the Thai State because Muslim families received financial assistance while Buddhist families were ignored.[42] Out of fear, Ačhān Pim no longer conducted funerals or other ceremonies after dusk and warned his laity to be on guard. Ačhān Pim's decision to change the time of rituals is a common trait among the abbots of the southern *wat*. The times for the funerals and other ceremonies are due to fear of attacks.[43]

Aside from personifying Islam and accusing it of being bent on world domination, Buddhist monks have come up with other explanations for the reasons
why the militants target monks. One explanation is that the Muslim neighbors
lack knowledge of Buddhist culture. Thai Muslim youths, raised with Islamic
religious training, are ignorant of local Buddhist customs and the role monks
serve in the Buddhist community. To these Malay Muslim youths, the monks are
social parasites who beg for food and fail to contribute to the community.
Although this explanation may seem simplistic, these sentiments are neither
new, nor unique to Buddhism. In many ways, this situation harkens back to the
day of the Buddha's lifetime in India when Brahmanas accused the Buddha and
his followers of acting like beggars.[44]

The issue of collecting alms is now moot for Wat A, along with nearly 30% of
the *wat* in the province. The monks from these *wat* no longer go outside to meet
the laity in the morning; instead, the villagers come to the *wat* to offer food.[45]
Some of the abbots put a stop to morning alms because they felt they were
endangering the soldiers who escorted them. They thought that leaving the *wat*
along the same paths every morning provided militants with an opportunity of
planting bombs on these paths. One of the first monks targeted by militants was
Juladet Jalarakpawin, a twenty-five-year-old Buddhist monk from the capital
district of Yala. He was hacked with a machete and seriously injured on January
24, 2004. Juladet's abbot believes the attack happened because he, like other
monks, was an easy target:

> Pra Juladet took that route every day to take morning alms. He always
> walked slowly with other monks from this temple to collect food from
> the Buddhist villagers. I think the attackers must have followed his rou-
> tine for some time. And also back then, the government did not send
> soldiers to guard monks and temples. We were easy targets.[46]

Even after the Thai State dispatched soldiers and police, there were still some
monks who were prohibited from leaving the *wat* due to the military's inability
to protect them. Ačhān Nok traveled to visit the laity more often than soldiers
recommended. To be as safe as possible, he went by car whenever he left the *wat*.
Every time I watched him leave, he was escorted by two or three armed
soldiers.

Well into 2008, Ačhān Nok experienced local Muslim youths throwing
rocks at his *wat* or spitting in his direction. Nearby, Buddhists continued to
be assaulted and killed. One monk at Wat A lamented about his predicament,
but felt that staying in the *wat* was a necessity. He, too, thought that going
out for alms provided Muslim militants with the opportunity to plan and
target monks and the military alike. For him, it was a monk's duty to stay *in*
the *wat*:

I have not left the *wat* for three years. There is a minority of monks who do go out. It usually happens like this. The first day, second day, nothing... then the third day, something happens. The terrorists know the monks will come again and they can predict which building they would go to, so they bomb the place. So, you see, these are heretical monks. They want to get money and things. Do you understand? For monks, everything we have was given by the people. Why would we be so greedy? Just stay in the *wat*.[47]

Monks in the red zones became more economically dependent upon lay Buddhists than ever before. They waited each day for Buddhists to bring food to the *wat*, an extraordinarily unique occurrence in Theravāda Buddhist traditions, and also received additional funding from the ONB[48] The scenario became bleak for many monks. Another abbot, whom I shall call Ačhān Tam, lived in a red zone and openly admitted this:

I fear for the monks. The daily chanting every dawn and dusk has changed. Now some monks have to stay at the *wat* and keep watch while the others chant, and then we take turns. Some days we don't even have morning services because before chanting we have to ring a bell and the soldiers have just returned from patrol and gone to bed, so we don't want to disturb them. [There aren't any morning services] during these times because the soldiers cannot protect us.[49]

The constant feeling of vigilance caused by fear had an impact on these monks. Their religious activities decreased in frequency, sustenance was irregular, and there was the continual performance of funerary rituals. The deceased often were victims of the continual violence.

During my stay at Wat A, I would sleep in the abbot's quarters (*kuti*). Sometimes, late at night, Ačhān Nok could not sleep. It was in the quiet recesses of the night that the fear became all the more real to him. He would stay up until one or two in the morning thinking about the violence that surrounds him. For him, violence was more than just a personal issue. Violence against monks equaled violence against the nation and the *dhamma*.

One dark September night in 2006 inside the monk's quarters, we discussed the various violent episodes that involved monks. Ačhān Nok became increasingly upset and expressed a desire to do more about the situation. He walked over and picked up a hand axe that was resting on a table next to the backdoor and waved it in the air, swiping at invisible Muslim attackers. A minute or so later his mood passed. He returned the hand axe to the table, sighed, and laughed it off with a grin. This private performance reflected his mounting angst. While displaying a calm and jovial demeanor to the lay Buddhists by day, by night

Ačhān Nok shouldered growing fear and resentment toward the current violence. It was at night, in the absence of an audience, that Ačhān Nok confessed
feeling the most stressed and concerned.

The Power of Words

When southern monks deliver sermons, they engage in an old and traditional
monastic practice; however, just as in the case of morning alms, their performances alter the relevance of the institutionalized practice. After changes of the
traditional sermons and speeches in the early twentieth century in an effort to
standardize topics and dialects, monks often continued to instructing their
audience on the *dhamma* and its social implications. Yet, as the violence
continued, monks' fears and frustrations were manifested in their speeches.
Monks began articulating their concerns and their frustrations became increasingly manifested in their sermons. Their audiences varied from local volunteers
and large lay congregations to battalions of soldiers.

Monks' public utterances can be seen as powerful socio-religious indicators
that affect the laity. Since their social and religious duty is to teach the *dhamma*
and to embody Buddhist ideals (much less follow their role in the Three Jewels),
their words and judgments are seen as expressions of the *dhamma*.[50] For these
reasons, monks remain powerful social figures at the local level, even in the
political arena. Looking at Thai election processes at the sub-district and village
level, anthropologist Daniel Arghiros notes the important and influential role
of monks in local elections. Many monks dedicate their time to canvassing at
their *wat* and use the elections for promoting their community issues and
developing the *wat*.[51] Acting as community leaders, monks affect the attitudes
of their lay brothers and sisters on various issues, including politics. In the
southernmost provinces, they influence their laity's views of Malay Muslims
and violence.

During my survey of Buddhist monks in Pattani Province at the time of the
first year of violence against them, nearly every monk stated that the violence
would not deter him from his ordinary routines. They further explained that
they would not get involved in any conflict-resolution activities, primarily
because this was not culturally seen as appropriate.[52]

Although monks are regarded by the laity as community leaders, very few
southern monks spoke out and used their social capital to mitigate the growing
religious friction in their villages. In the 2004 survey, which included over thirty
wat with abbots and monks, only two interviewees expressed a desire to get
involved in conflict resolution. One came from an abbot who worked with the
local Imam and Muslim leaders in his village, but only surreptitiously. He felt
that if the locals saw him interacting with Muslim leaders, this would endanger

the leaders and hurt their social standings. Another monk who expressed the
same desire was already involved in interfaith dialogue with Buddhists and
Muslims in the capital district.[53] While these two were actively working with
Muslims to ameliorate conditions, they were an exception to the rule. After two
years, only one of the two monks continued his mediating efforts in working
with the Muslim community and its leaders (and this was done covertly).[54] A
large part of the southern monks' initial resistance to interfaith and mediation
work came from its association with politics and violence. One of the few to
openly endorse interfaith work was a local Buddhist monk who became a member
of the National Reconciliation Commission in 2005 and who worked openly on
interfaith work throughout the period. By 2008, monks began to participate
more openly in interfaith activities, largely due to the fact that these activities
were no longer directly sponsored by the State.[55]

The Thai State and society have flexible, but fairly consistent, views on
what constitutes an appropriate context in which Buddhist monks may engage
in politics. For instance, the Thai media generally condones Buddhist monks
who engage in environmentalism. In the north and northeast parts of
Thailand, environmental monks ordain trees and rally people together in an
effort to prevent ecological devastation.[56] The performance of ecological
activism has led the Thai media and academics to use terms such as
"development monk" and "political monk" in reference to socially engaged
monks.[57] However, for Thais the subject of physical violence is antithetical to
Buddhist monks' involvement on the grounds that violence is entrenched in
the profane arc of *lokiya* (worldly matters). Consequently, although fear and
murder are common maladies in southern Thailand where poverty is widespread, Buddhist monks find themselves outside the socially prescribed
parameters of engagement.

Yet, there are monks who disregard the socially prescribed parameters.
Photirak, leader of a splinter Thai Buddhist movement called Santi Asoke, publicly condemned both the previous Thaksin administration and the violence in
southern Thailand.[58] Another Buddhist monk, Kittisak Kittisophano, a disciple
of the recent Thai Buddhist reformer Buddhadasa, condemned government policies as part of a "Thaksinocracy" that needed to stop.[59] However, neither of
these monks belong to southern Thailand, and for many Thais their actions are
subversive. Unlike the environmental monks in northern Thailand, Photirak
and Kittisak's words exceed the boundaries of the imagined world of Buddhist
performances.

One might suggest that initiating practices outside the imagined socio-
political parameters limits the value of the performance. Although Photirak
and the members of Santi Asoke are considered part of the Buddhist world,
they are not recognized as ordained Buddhist monks. Santi Asoke and its
Dhamma Army practice a form of Buddhism; however, according to the Thai

State and official Thai *sangha* their practices are not under the canopy of Thai Buddhism.[60] While Kittisak officially remains part of the Thai *sangha*, perhaps partly under the good graces of Buddhadasa's legacy, Thais are ambivalent toward his views.

In reaction to Kittsak's condemnations concerning Thaksin's administration, Prime Minister Thaksin called Kittisak an "NGO monk," for his "unorthodox form of social activism."[61] Although Thaksin was speaking in self-defense, many Thais shared his view.[62] Thus, monk's performance in Thai society can be limited by the parameters of the agent's *socially* imagined representation. Therefore, monks' compliance to socio-religious interdiction was sufficient reason to initially prevent them from publicly addressing the violence.

For two years, southern monks avoided commenting on the violence and kept to their routines as much as possible, preaching to their patrons and conducting customary rituals. They would explain the dangers in the area to the laity and advise them on how to protect themselves; however, following the guidelines sent forth by the Bangkok-based *sangha*, southern monks' sermons addressed only day-to-day local concerns and left out overarching religio-political factors related to the local violence. Their vocal neutrality did not win them any respite from the militants. Militants continued to bomb monks on their morning alms round and in their *wat*. As Buddhist casualties rose, monks' concerns became a motivating factor in breaking their silence.

The day-to-day murders and attacks made southern monks feel isolated and alone. Many monks felt that the government, media, and NGOs were not aware of the dangers to which they were exposed, or to the dangers to the survival of Thai Buddhism. For the most part, their accusations were correct. But, the focus of the media was on the Malay Muslims.[63] While watching the late-night news with Ačhān Nok in his office, I heard him express his frustration over the lack of attention to the violence around him:

> I was watching TV and there was news that a group of terrorists set
> fire to a *wat*. When I got there I found that one monk was killed along
> with two servant boys who were shot and then burnt and the *wat* was
> ruined, but the reporters said it was just a little damage! Little
> damage! I was furious. These reporters have no ethics. I used to like
> reading the newspaper, but now I don't read it. It's full of nonsense
> and lies.... If you are a Thai, if you are a Buddhist, you would do
> something. You wouldn't let them cut you to pieces. Each time a Thai
> or a Buddhist is killed it's like someone cutting you with a knife. It
> hurts, right? Then, why are you still doing nothing! Police and mili-
> tary, too! They swore before the king to protect the nation, religion,
> and the monarchy, but when they are in the three southern provinces
> they do nothing![64]

Monks like Ačhān Nok found an outlet for their frustrations in their sermons.[65]

Sermons of southern monks have changed substantially over the last century in Thailand in terms of their form and style. The change was due primarily to the Thai State.[66] At the close of the nineteenth century, colonial pressures mounted on Siam's borders. With the English on the western and southern borders and the French on the eastern border, King Chulalongkorn was faced with the task of nation-building and securing his kingdom. Under the leadership of his brothers, Prince Damrong and Prince Wachirayan, his administration viewed monks as integral to nation-building and thus enacted policies and rules that influenced the dissemination of Buddhism.[67]

In her study of wandering monks (1997), Kamala Tiyavanich notes a shift in Buddhist monks' sermons from local- to State-directed content. Monks traditionally used stories of the Buddha's previous rebirths (Pāli: Jātaka) in their sermons. These stories worked as parables. Each story had components that instructed the laity about Buddhist morality (Pāli: *sīla*), but the story changed with each locality. Not only did monks deliver stories tailored to the local context; they also used local languages. Rather than Bangkok-Thai, official Thai educational administrators report that monks along the border provinces often employed a rhythmic oratory style in order to capture the villagers' attention. The abbot of Teung Forest Monastery in San Kamphaeng District, Chiang Mai Province, recounted the sermons of Lūang Po La, who was gifted in storytelling:

> His detailed and descriptive sermons about nature and wildlife drew a large crowd of adults as well as children. When he preached, the whole hall vibrated with his dramatic voice and the audience's laughter and cheers.[68]

The use of local stories, languages, and dramatic styles of delivery contrasted with the principles of Chulalongkorn's State Buddhism. State Buddhism emphasized rationalism, which "insisted that sermons be sober and didactic."[69] Thus, Thai educational administrators instructed monks to focus on the Buddha's last life, not on his previous rebirths, to moderate their speech, and to speak in Bangkok-Thai.[70] The State Buddhist preference of performance became routinized in some areas, but as Justin McDaniel has shown in his examination of local Thai monastic educational systems, the longevity and reach of State Buddhist content was limited.

For the most part, southern monks adhere to State Buddhism's principles of performance, keeping their sermons monotonous and didactic; however, this style of preaching did not preclude them from commenting on the violence. Ačhān Tam explained to nearly a dozen Buddhist laity:

If the people, no matter their religions, are not selfish, we can all survive. But, some people are selfish, people like soldiers, officers, politicians, and ministers. There is the saying, "Love the Nation, the Religion, and the King." How? By leaving our nation like this, in conflict? Subordinates cannot do anything about it unless those in control give a command. They are united and ready, but almost all the Thai Buddhists are dead. That is what the government meant by harmony. Now the government says they love all religions, but they let people burn down *wat* and kill monks. Muslims also brings in false teachings, so then where's the love? They are all selfish and do not really love each other.[71]

As Ačhān Tam conveyed these words, many of the laity nodded in agreement, but a few monks appeared unsettled with their heads and eyes cast downward. These monks were volunteer monks who had come to the *wat* a few months ago. Later, after the abbot's speech, I met with them at the opposite end of the *wat* under a pavilion. A few were apologetic and explained that the abbot had some rather strong feelings about the Muslims in the area. "He does not like Muslims," one volunteer monk said. "He's a southern monk, not like us," another volunteer monk added. Although the monks had differing opinions, they did not publicly advocate them. Besides, it was Ačhān Tam that the Buddhist laity came to hear. He was the one they visited regarding their problems and financial concerns, and he was the one who stayed when the transplanted monks left the *wat* after spending their year as volunteers.

Some abbots and monks began escalating their expressions of caution into speeches about the need for vigilance and fear. Ačhān Nok repeatedly preached to the laity about the need to be vigilant, warning them against Muslims, who are the untrustworthy enemy. Under his pavilion, he told me:

I have warned people many times. Sometimes they do not listen. There was this one Buddhist named Tapian who was shot dead around a year ago. I warned him beforehand that he should be careful when he went out. He didn't believe me. He said Muslim people wouldn't harm him because he had lived there for a long time and they knew him well. He went shopping at a local market and was shot in the back on the way home. He never committed any sin, never stole or had any problems with the government or friends. He only produced good karma, but was shot dead at a three-way intersection. I warned him, but he said every-thing was all right because he knew a lot of Muslims.[72]

Wat A is in a village with a population that is more than 90% Muslim. Following this incident, Buddhist laity took his warnings seriously.

Words are a powerful asset to southern monks as they can provoke people to action or to lull them to inaction. Ačhān Nok has cautioned lay people to act more carefully as well as relax. Early one morning while we were sitting underneath his pavilion, Ačhān Nok recounted how he talked a Buddhist out of moving away:

> A Buddhist villager wanted to sell his house and evacuate so I went and talked to him. I said "Are you sure if you move to Bangkok you won't die? If you won't die, well I'll go with you! You will die if you stay here and Muslim terrorists shoot you—you will die. If you go to Bangkok and get run over by heavy traffic you'll die, too! You can die anywhere, so you don't have to run away." And so he stayed.[73]

Considering the influence Ačhān Nok exerted on the layman's decision, the question arises as to how much power he or other monks would wield with interfaith activities in their communities.[74]

Different monks preached different views to their laity. Some monks were subtler than others, but most made an effort to influence the laity with their views on the violence. This tendency was a clear break from their uniform decision in 2004 to abstain from discussing the theme of the current violence. Not all monks referred to Muslims as the enemy during this time. A few regarded the Thai State and its failed diplomacy as the most dangerous. One particular sermon indicative of this view came from Ačhān Tuk.

Ačhān Tuk is a sixty-four-year-old abbot who resides in Wat B, a *wat* in a yellow zone. Wat B is located in an urban setting surrounded by a strong Buddhist population, roughly 50% according to the abbots' estimates. Even so, violence took its toll on Wat B. Since martial law was passed in 2004, the *wat*'s revenue diminished with each passing year and its monks were leaving. In 2004, there were fourteen monks and two novices living at Wat B (along with fifty-three soldiers). In 2006, there were seven monks, seven novices and forty police officers.

In 2006, there were no volunteer monks at Wat B; every monk and novice had come from one of the three southernmost provinces.[75] Monks there were going out on morning alms until 2007. Wat B was one of the more fortunate *wat* in the three southernmost provinces. It had a strong financial basis, a sizable Buddhist community living nearby, and a steady flow of novices and monks. But, even in this environment, the monks were fearful. One novice confided to me that he was afraid each time he went out for morning alms, but he went out nevertheless. Ačhān Tuk noted the financial impact of the violence on his *wat* as early as 2004. Revenue was diminishing partly due to decreasing attendance at ceremonies, like the Vientien ceremony, a candle-making ritual that occurs three times a year. He explained:

The Vientien ceremony, which is usually on Sundays at 8:00 P.M., has been changed to 4:00 P.M. because it would be too dangerous later in the evening. We would usually receive 6–7,000 baht for these events, but right now we only receive 2,000.[76]

By 2006, there were even fewer ceremonies at Wat B, yet there were still plenty of funerals to host, some of which were unrelated to the violence. One of the most important ceremonies at Wat B occurred on December 28, 2006.

I had been earning my keep at Wat B by teaching English to novices and monks and had grown accustomed to last-minute scheduling. Perhaps because of my personal association with many of the monks, one of the senior monks asked me to accompany them to a special ceremony the following day, on December 28, 2006. I was unable to learn where we were going or what made this ceremony so special. That morning at 6:05 A.M. a van carrying three armed soldiers came to Wat B and picked up Ačhān Tuk, three monks, five novices, and me. Once we were all in the van, a monk from Wat B informed me that we were going to Ingkayut Camp.

Ingkayut is one of the only two military camps in Pattani province and the only one designed for combat missions. Its commanding officer was Lieutenant Colonel Surathep Nukagow, who was second-in-command of all military units in Pattani Province. Surathep was a forty-one-year-old Special Forces soldier and a member of an elite group called the King's Guard.[77] He commanded over 260 sergeants, 15 officers and 441 privates at Ingkayut Camp, a military compound for the 5th Infantry Regiment, 2nd Battalion.[78]

The van stopped at the perimeter and was checked by armed guards with metal detectors. It then carried us into the hall where the monks would chant. Buddhist soldiers were congregating just outside the hall under a tent, and six seats were placed in front of the monks' raised dais for the high-ranking officers and their wives. Roughly 100 feet away from the tent were two dozen soldiers standing together and smoking. These were Muslim soldiers who displayed no interest in making merit. I realized that the entire affair was secretive because various officers interrogated me as to how I had known about this event. I had nothing to offer them; I was just as baffled by my presence as they were.

I learned later from Lieutenant Colonel Surathep that this was an annual event orchestrated in order to give his soldiers a chance to make merit before the New Year. He had never met the Wat B's monks before, but a few of his officers knew Ačhān Tuk and had recommended him. They needed nine monks, an auspicious number according to many Thais, so Ačhān Tuk had invited the monks and novices to come along.[79] I had spoken with Ačhān Tuk before and knew him for his strong feelings against the violence. The senior abbot considered the violence multifaceted and fueled both by the Malay Muslim militants and the Thai State. From his point of view, people from outside the southern provinces were perpetuating the violence. Muslims were coming into Thailand from other countries and stirring up problems while at the same time Thai military officials abused local Malay Muslims. Now Ačhān Tuk had an audience of Buddhist combat soldiers and his views surfaced as he delivered the soldiers' New Year's sermon.

Ačhān Tuk discussed the importance of new beginnings, of a new year, and the meaning of democracy. His tone was somber and methodic and he never raised his voice; he addressed issues pertaining to the military, specifically soldiers' duties and behavior:

> Merit or goodness is applicable to being a soldier. A soldier has to be tolerant. What does it mean to be tolerant? I used to live in the suburbs. I have to be patient with the cold and hot weather, even with the mosquitoes. But, soldiers have to be tolerant with the security of the population. Nowadays, people have no one to take care of them. There are soldiers that can help them. The second meaning of tolerance is to be patient coupled with distress.[80]

After Ačhān Tuk stated this, six Buddhist soldiers at a distance of only fifteen feet began talking among themselves, indicating the lack of their respect for and rejection of Ačhān Tuk's words. Ačhān Tuk was lecturing the soldiers on their conduct (Pāli: *sīla*), and proceeded to briefly discuss astrology and its implications for 2006 (2549 B.E.), the Year of the Dog. He continued:

> There are many kinds of dogs. Some are cruel. So, we should pray for this coming New Year, and hope this Year of the Pig will not be cruel like the Year of the Dog. If this New Year is not cruel, we can have peace. Peace will happen in a society that stays unified. We live in the same land, called Thailand. Thailand has never been under the control of any country. We fight for democracy, but we don't know what democracy is.[81]

It was Ačhān Tuk's last point that had the greatest significance. He was in a military zone surrounded by a combat unit, declaring their country's government undemocratic. Ačhān Tuk was bold, far bolder than he had been prior to this occasion. He was subtly critiquing the soldiers' previous conduct and then criticizing the government and its idea of democracy. Although earlier he confided in me his views about the violence, about the Thai military's heavy-handedness, and the failure of Thai democracies, Ačhān Tuk had not publicly spoken about them.[82] Yet, here at a combat camp in Pattani Province, Ačhān Tuk was sharing his views on military conduct and the Thai system of government. Fear and anger had worn away at Ačhān Tuk's resolve to remain silent, and now his views were emerging in front of more than one hundred Thai Buddhist soldiers.

Aćhān Tuk may serve as an example of how frustration, fear, and violence motivate southern monks to vocalize their views. However, he is of a minority who blame the State for its contribution to the problems. The vast majority of abbots and monks direct their attention and anger toward the militants and express gratitude toward the militias, soldiers, and police. There also are monks who go beyond verbal gratitude and work with soldiers on a regular basis. Performing rituals and ceremonies for soldiers in a time of war raises ideological questions. Lieutenant Colonel Surathep informed me that, since 2004, special monks have been working for the military. A monk called Aćhān Wirapan lived in Narathiwat and worked with Surathep periodically; together, they offered workshops to youths on understanding security. Interactions like these provoke questions. For example, when a monk blesses a soldier or hands him an amulet for protection, is the monk endorsing violence? If this is the case, does action violate the monk's pledge to abstain from acts of physical violence (or the encouragement of them)?

Daniel Kent examines the moral grounds on which Buddhist monks give sermons to Sri Lankan soldiers. He argues that when monks deliver their sermons to soldiers before battle, it does not directly connect themselves to the soldiers' future acts of violence. Rather, the monks walk a fine line between calming soldiers' hearts and detaching themselves from suffering. By calming the soldiers' hearts, monks seek to reduce the solders' collateral damage as well as from its spiritual repercussions:

> As the Buddha points out in the *Yodhājīvasutta*, if a soldier dies in the midst of battle seized by anger, he will be reborn in a hell realm. While it is impossible to control completely the contents of a soldier's heart, many preachers stressed that they do their best to shape them in other directions.[83]

Sinhalese monks who work with the army consider it their duty to increase the soldiers' morale and help them calm their temper and thoughts. In so doing, monks support the nation—and reduce the likelihood of unnecessary violence from soldiers who are ill-tempered or unfocused.[84] While the Sri Lankan monks might compare themselves to nurses who aid soldiers in a time of war, I would argue there is another more subtle process in place that involves actions, not identities.

When a Buddhist monk's audience is an active military unit and the content of his sermon is aimed to prepare soldiers for a conflict, *his performance becomes militarized*. This is not to be confused with the monk's identity. A monk is not necessarily part of the military by virtue of a deliverance of sermons to armies; rather, his actions become part of the military. Regardless of the monk's intention (Pāli: *cetanā*), be it out of compassion or malice, the sermon and its karmic benefits are linked to the soldiers' expeditions.

The military's need for monastic sermons was not lost to Prince Wachirayan, who as Supreme Patriarch of the Thai *sangha* in 1916, explained to King Vajiravudh that a victorious war depends upon a soldier's presence of mind (Pāli: *sati*), knowledge (Pāli: *paññā*), bravery, experience, readiness in commands, and good fighting positions.[85] In such a militarized Buddhist performance we find the sacred and violence intermingled. Ačhān Tuk's deliverance of a sermon and subsequent acceptance of alms enabled combat soldiers to make merit. His duty was to bless their lives and livelihood for the new year. Perhaps it was this very charge that motivated him to critique the soldiers' conduct and the institution they served. But, Ačhān Tuk's sermon at Ingkayut Camp is not an anomaly. Thai soldiers have sought the blessings of Buddhist monks throughout their conflicts in the southernmost provinces. We can draw one prominent example from the conflict at the Khru Se Mosque. On April 28, 2004, soldiers massacred more than thirty Malay Muslim militants who had hidden in the mosque. In the days that followed, forty of the Buddhist soldiers went to a *wat* to make merit.[86] Implicit in the sequence of events was the soldiers' desire to counterbalance the bad merit they had just earned through their acts of violence with their participation in Buddhist rituals.

Scholars like Patrick Jory, Donald Swearer, and Stanley Tambiah have addressed the commodification of charisma and how the Thai Buddhist laity will exchange money for amulets (and merit). It is not a shock to find that soldiers sought to make merit after dealing with violence, but it did underscore how the soldiers felt about their participation. When a soldier killed a person or was involved in violence of any kind in the south, he felt he incurred negative *kamma* (Pāli: action). Monks became a field of merit from which soldiers sought to balance their negative *kamma*.

A Platform for Action: Buddhist Nationalism

In mid-2005, southern Buddhist monks became more engaged with the military than before. They hosted soldiers and police at their *wat* and assisted them in acquiring intelligence on local Muslims in the surrounding region. In addition, they began to distance themselves from the national *sangha*, creating a southern monastic group designed to raise awareness of their situation and work for Buddhist nationalism. These distinctly different practices altered the monks' role in the violence. Monks' active participation with State officials further politicized their roles and confirmed the representations cast upon them. This, in conjunction with calls for Buddhist nationalism, intensified religious frictions between Buddhists and Muslims in the southernmost provinces.

After the September 19, 2006, coup, the newly appointed prime minister, General Surayud Chulanont, took a more conciliatory role in the southernmost provinces than did Thaksin Shinawatra. Thai officials believed diplomacy was the best course of action in addressing the problems in these provinces. However, in many ways the southern monks' actions worked against the State's public efforts, reinforcing Buddhist militarism to the Malay Muslims in the borderland provinces.

Since Chulalongkorn's administration and its nation-building in the early 1900s, Thai Buddhist monks have engaged in State initiatives to promote Thai nationalism. After reforms under Chulalongkorn and the dissolution of the absolute monarchy following the 1932 coup, the political dimension of Buddhist performance changed drastically. Monks not in line with the State agenda were seen as part of the "economic malaise," and were expected to assent through silence.[87]

These initiatives were particularly prevalent under the helm of Prime Minister Sarit. During Field Marshall Sarit Dhanarajata's term (1957–63), national initiatives such as the Thammačārik, Thammathut, and Village Scouts employed Buddhist agents for the benefit of State policies and agendas, although the initiatives were not implemented until after Sarit passed away. These worked to strengthen religious nationalism through the very values woven in the national mantra: Nation, Religion, and King. In these instances, the publicly touted secularism of religion (sāsanā) and king (mahākasat) has very strong Buddhist implications. Under the various Thai constitutions, while a defender of all religions, the king must be a Buddhist in order to fulfill his role as the defender (as he traditionally ordains as a monk for a brief period). Additionally, while religion remained an ambiguous term in Thai society, political programs advocating Buddhism belied a more exclusive reference of religion.

One such program is the Village Scouts, which was formed by Major General Somkhuan Harikul in the 1970s in order to ward off communist ideologies and movements. As government volunteers, the Village Scouts applied Buddhist rituals to "sway a citizenry whose loyalties were in doubt."[88] They were also an integral force in providing support to the State during volatile times, such as the student revolt (and massacre) at Thammasat University in 1973. Other programs, like the Thammačārik, exploited the expertise and cultural capital of Buddhist monks who were sent to populations considered by the Thai State to be unassimilated with Thai society. Jointly sponsored by the Thai sangha and the Ministry of Interior, many newly ordained Buddhist monks went to border provinces and taught the dhamma, "educating" groups such as the Karen, Hmong, and Kachin about Thai customs and religion. Anthropologist Stanley Tambiah writes that the Thammačārik's objective was to convert these peripheral ethnic and religious groups in an "Aśokan assurance."[89] The monks' application of Buddhism to assimilate groups was articulated best by Phradit Disawat, who helped found the Thammačārik in 1964 and was head of the Tribal Welfare Division of the Department of Public Welfare:

[T]he propagation of Buddhism among the different tribal groups would be likely to advance administrative and development goals among the tribal people because the integration of our people into a large community depends upon the ties of custom and religion.[90]

These State-sponsored monastic programs exposed the illusory status of Thai secularism with the strong underpinnings of Buddhist nationalism in State politics. This Buddhist nationalism collapsed State and Buddhist ideologies, creating a national solidarity around an official Thai Buddhism. Thus, to support one, the other had to be supported as well.[91]

The collapsing distinctions between political and religious identifications pose a serious problem for the southernmost violence. When southern locals perceived a State allegiance to Thai Buddhism, it worked against local and national efforts to redress Malay Muslim complaints with the State. Since the official assimilation of the three southernmost provinces into Siam in 1909, Malay Muslims have cited religious intolerance and persecution under the Siamese/Thai State. They were forced to prostrate before Buddhist idols, adopt Thai surnames, and speak Thai. In its exploration to discover ways to mitigate the violence in the southernmost provinces, the Thai State found that many grievances were a result of the alienation Malay Muslims felt from the State. Thai Buddhist actions that are part of the State only intensified these feelings of alienation.

In chapter 2, we learned that monks from provinces north of the conflict zone serve as ambassadors to the State by volunteering to work in the southernmost provinces. These and other actions led the locals to perceive a juxtaposition of Thai Buddhism and the State, which severely hindered State attempts to ameliorate relations with the Malay Muslim majority in the southern provinces. Southern Buddhist monks were instrumental in enabling the collaboration between the State and Thai Buddhists and were the most transparent in their collective demands for Buddhist nationalism. Until the middle of 2005, southern monks kept relatively quiet and abstained from giving inflammatory sermons or making public statements. However, their behavior changed, largely as a reaction to State measures to placate and redress Malay Muslim concerns.

Pressured to change its heavy-handed approach to the southern conflict, the Thaksin administration launched the National Reconciliation Commission (NRC) on March 28, 2005. The NRC was responsible for investigating the conflict and suggesting policies and measures necessary in order to achieve peace in the southernmost provinces of Thailand. Much of the NRC's fieldwork in the southernmost provinces included numerous interviews with southern Buddhists and Muslims. Although the fifty-member commission was composed of many well-respected Thai Chinese, Thai Buddhist and Malay Muslims, many locals felt that there was no power behind their recommendations. In addition, some southern Buddhists complained that the NRC focused too much on Muslim concerns.

In late October of 2005, after the murders and devastation at Wat Phromprasit, southern monks broke their silence and recast their roles. Similar to previous attacks on Buddhist monks, this attack elicited strident reactions from Buddhists living the region. The Pattani Sangha Council's official response was a call to release a twenty-point declaration. Among the points, number 18:

> The fact that Buddhism is the national religion of Thailand should be accepted and declared, for the sake of the security of the nation, religion and monarchy, which would make it possible for Thailand to have enduring peace and security.[92]

Monks interpreted Wat Phromprasit as an example of how violence could freely enter into their *wat*. Violence had metastasized into their homes. The closer the proximity of the violence, the more intense was the fear. This escalation of fear, coupled with misgivings over the direction of the NRC report, drove monks out into the public arena. While the NRC compiled its report for conciliation, senior monks from the southern Thai *sangha* became national political figures by denouncing the NRC's efforts.

Phra Udom Thammakani, head of the Pattani *sangha*, called for the NRC's dissolution. In a conversation with the NRC's head Anand Panyarachun, he and other senior monks from Pattani complained about the NRC's ignorance regarding the Buddhist plights:

> They don't know how local monks suffer from the violence. Many of us are killed, even in the temples. Of course *ustads* [Islamic religious teachers] are killed, but have you ever seen them killed in their mosques?[93]

Phra Udom was reacting to what he and many other southern monks felt was an overarching lack of attention and awareness. Militants were murdering Buddhist monks in their *wat* and during their morning alms round. His condemnation of the NRC was a reaction to their report and to feelings of neglect. Many monks reported that the constant fear and frustration intensified when they felt isolated and ignored. Phra Udom's public statement, which was cited in newspapers across the country, addressed the NRC, a political branch of the government, and the violence. Other monks and a group of *Mahānikai* echoed Phra Udom's sentiments.[94] This was a clear distinction from the previous behavior of southern monks who had publicly avoided discussing these topics. This was only the beginning.

Feeling unheard and isolated from the rest of the country, southern Thai Buddhist monks from the three border provinces met and formed a foundation called "The Center of Buddhist Affairs in Support of the Southern Three Border Provinces" ("CBA").[95] The purpose of this foundation was to elicit assistance and suggestions for protecting Buddhists and Buddhism from threats in southern Thailand. In many ways, the rhetoric used in these proceedings had undertones of Buddhist nationalism. One principle drafted by the CBA correlated the health of the land and the health of Thai Buddhism. It read:

> Buddhism was very prosperous in the border provinces during the period of Śrīvijaya and Langkasuka, which lasted more than 1,000 years. There are many ancient places, art, objects and evidences that relate to the prosperity Buddhism brings. However, as Buddhism has been neglected, new generations cannot succeed in these productive and prosperous ways.[96]

The CBA envisioned a golden age of Buddhism in southern Thailand. Reflecting on early Buddhist kingdoms of Langkasuka and Śrīvijaya, southern monks equated the prosperity of these kingdoms with their devotion to Buddhism. Religious nationalism often harkens to a golden past in order to justify actions in the present. As mentioned in chapter 1, this form of recollection involves a distortion or an omission of key events in order to fit a narrative into a working vision for religious nationalists.

Southern monks from the CBA and from *wat* across the southernmost provinces recalled the Buddhist kingdoms of Langkasuka and Śrīvijaya with pride. Like the CBA, they associated the Thai State's current failure to protect the southern Thai Buddhists (and in association, the southern Thai Buddhist legacy) with the failure to protect the prosperity and integrity of the region.[97] The fabled kingdom of Langkasuka is remembered by southern Thais, Buddhists, and Muslims alike. Cultural memory on this subject has not changed much over the last one hundred years.[98] And like Langkasuka's, Śrīvijaya's Buddhist activity was quite pronounced.

The modern form of Buddhist nationalism in Thailand can be traced back to a speech delivered by King Vajiravudh (King Rama VI) to his Wild Tiger Corps in 1911. Vajiravudh's rhetoric finds a new context with Kittiwuttho and the Buddhist organization Nawaphon during the 1970s to galvanize Thai nationalism against the "encroaching Communist resistance."[99] Devastated after witnessing the atrocities against Buddhists and Buddhism under Pol Pot in Cambodia, Kittiwuttho returned to Thailand fervently embracing a Thai nationalism that did not allow for dissent. Anthropologist Charles Keyes notes the following:

> For Kittivuddho, Nawaphon is the only ideology which a true Thai nationalist (who must also be a Buddhist) can take. Anyone who opposes

Nawaphon must, therefore, be an enemy of the nation, and the monarchy. And, those enemies are to be destroyed.[100]

Kittiwuttho was one of the most vocal and ardent monastic supporters of the
State in the 1970s. An extremely outspoken, right-wing, high-ranking monk,
Kittiwuttho is well known for his condemnation of communism and other
political resistances to the State. His leadership became more pronounced after
1975, when he took control of the Nawaphon (Ninth Force, alluding to King
Bhumibol, the ninth Chakkri monarch), a Buddhist organization formed in
1974 and commonly depicted as ultra-nationalistic. At times, he embodied the
Buddhist nationalism of King Vajiravudh. Although Kittiwuttho gave public
sermons that were deeply political, he did not suffer the backlash that most
monks like Photirak or Kittisak received when preaching on the southern
violence.[101]

In his dissertation on Sri Lankan Buddhist literature, Charles Hallisey, following in the seminal work of J. L. Austin and performative utterances, notes
that the Buddhist language has a performative dimension.[102] This dimension
encompasses the CBA's political and highly emotional postulations. The patriotic rhetoric chosen by Kittiwuttho in the 1970s and the southern monks in
2006 reflects ideals and a worldview born from fear and frustration. For these
monks, the welfare of Thai Buddhism is inextricably tied to the welfare of the
nation. The push for Buddhist nationalism is not a new development, nor is it
isolated in the three southernmost provinces. Historically, monks from various
regions have argued for Buddhist nationalism, most recently occurring during
the rewriting of the Thai constitution in 2007.[103] Sripariyattimoli, a Thai Buddhist
monk and professor at Mahachulalongkorn University, offers his rationale for
Buddhist nationalism:

[To propose] Buddhism as the national religion is not something new,
in fact it exists already as such; [however], due to the ignorance and
cowardice of previous Buddhist politicians, [it is not], even though
other faiths do not object. This proves that Thai politicians are not
faithful enough to the principles and moral codes of their own
religion.[104]

For Sripariyattimoli, the problems occurring in the south are a result of the State
failing to fully implement Buddhist principles, whereas Islamic teachers and
local Malay Muslims complain that it is this very Buddhist nationalism that
ostracizes them from their Thai neighbors.[105]

In addition to the collective effort to galvanize support for the region and for
Buddhist nationalism, southern Thai monks individually engaged in the violence through various practices. Monks like Ačhān Nok built sleeping quarters

for the soldiers living at his *wat*, offered reassurances to the laity in their areas, provided a space for Buddhist community meetings, and made amulets that purportedly nullified bombs. (Ačhān Nok complained that his amulets were so popular that it was hard to keep enough in stock.) They also adopted militaristic behaviors, such as owning and using guns. In 2006, when I was with him in his quarters and the topic of monks and guns came up again, what followed was a startling disclosure of monastic habits in the southernmost provinces. Although appearing radical, his sentiments and actions reflect the majority of monks' views and practices in the red zones:

Q: Monks cannot touch a gun, or involve themselves in politics, right? I read this in the *Vinaya*.

Ačhān Nok: In the three southernmost provinces, the abbot has a gun. If he does not have a gun, a layman or the local sheriff will give him a gun.

Q: Is this in conflict with the *Vinaya*, that a monk has a gun?

Ačhān Nok: According to the *Vinaya*, this is a misdemeanor [Thai: *pāčhittī*, Pāli: *pacittiya*]. A monk who carries a soldier's weapon commits a misdemeanor. To purify oneself and act in accordance with the *Vinaya* one must confess their misdemeanors. This is a small offense [*ābat noi*]. We commit this offense in order to protect *wat*, but we don't use it to kill anyone. We only use guns in order to protect monks. All *wat* in these three provinces have guns.

Q: All *wat*?

Ačhān Nok: Yes. High ranking monks also have guns. It started with the situation at Wat Phromprasit [in Panāre District, Pattani Province] when a monk was killed. Then, monks started to keep hand guns or rifles with them. Some monks buy guns to keep in the *wat*.

Q: But the *sangha's* Council of Elders does not know about this.

Ačhān Nok: They knew.

Q: They knew?

Ačhān Nok: They knew, but they don't talk about this. However, they have agreed to this by saying that we should have some guns. If we have a license, it is all right to keep them.

Q: Do the monks in the south shoot people?

Ačhān Nok: No.

Q: So, they have a gun, but they don't shoot anyone.

Ačhān Nok: One day, criminals [*čhon*] tried to attack a *wat*. The abbot shot into the air and the criminals ran away. Four of the criminals were arrested and two of them were found with guns. If the abbot had no gun that night, he would have surely died. The criminals had big guns. They shot and fired at *wat* and cars. There is another *wat* in Pattani in which the abbot is very old. He cannot go out, so he stays at the *wat* during the time that other monks go out on morning alms. Criminals came to the *wat* and began hacking away at the *wat*'s walls. They found the abbot asleep in the room. Fortunately a high-ranking monk came to visit at this time, and he shot his gun into the air. The criminals ran away. The villagers recognized two of the criminals and from that time on, the criminals were too afraid to come to hurt the monks at the *wat*. And, during the last fifteen days, there was another case. The abbot at one *wat* was shot in the belly.

Q: Really?

Ačhān Nok: Yes!

Q: Where?

Ačhān Nok: In Narathiwat! This was on the T.V. This monk was tossing some food to dogs out back behind his *wat*. The criminal hiding in the forest shot him in the belly. At that time there were many police and soldiers staying at the *wat*. He was sent to the hospital and had to have surgery. He survived. This shows that, if we have guns, the criminals will be afraid to harm us because they think that we might fight back.[106]

Ačhān Nok's comments invite an array of doctrinal questions and disputes, but these are not germane to the current inquiry. Regardless of doctrinal support for his (and other southern monks' actions), Ačhān Nok's account reveals the effects of living with fear on the monastic practices.[107] The southern Thai *sangha* privately condones the purchase and possession of firearms by monks, justifying it with the level of danger and violence to which they are exposed. By 2006, the monks' practice of owning and using a firearm socially altered their status in the conflict, from civilian to combatant. Although monks did not attempt to injure or kill militants, they openly used a firearm to defend themselves, which according to contacts like Ačhān Nok are only for scaring away would-be assailants.

The call to arms is pervasive and stretches beyond the borders of monasteries and the southern provinces to the doorsteps of the Thai monarchy. After the March 2007 attack on a minibus to Yala, which resulted in the killing of eight Buddhist passengers, Queen Sirikit's response was blunt and to the point: "We have to help people there to survive. If they need to be trained, train them. If they need to be armed, arm them."[108] Queen Sirikit's statement, while directed at the Buddhist laity, may well have applied to the monks. Southern monks now openly acknowledge their involvement in the violence, thereby reconstructing their identities. They see themselves as community leaders, supporting the emotional and physical well-being of the Buddhist laity through their words and actions. One day under his pavilion, Ačhān Tam explained, "We [monks] have to preserve Buddhism in this district. For example, we have to buy the land for the *wat* and pay to expand it. [Muslims] invade Buddhist property, so we indirectly invade theirs."[109]

Southern monks from the CBA have distinguished themselves from the rest of the Thai *sangha* by promoting the belief that not only their lives, but also the very integrity of Thai Buddhism, is at stake. For these monks, an attack on monks and *wat* is seen as an attack on the development and progress of Thai Buddhism and socio-economic conditions in the region. By observing the impact fear has on Buddhist monks' practices, we find that the southern monks have re-imagined their roles, which are analogous with those of the State, within a Buddhist worldview. In this way, violence against monks is indistinguishable from violence against Thai Buddhism and the Thai nation. This mentality continues to promote Buddhist nationalism and further divides the community along the line of Buddhist-Muslim identities.

Conclusion

For nearly fifty years, the Thai public has not witnessed monks engaged in warfare. Instead, they observed monks involved in ceremonial politics, practicing asceticism and disseminating the *dhamma* (Buddhist doctrine). Accordingly, monks' daily meditations, studies, and work have been directed toward freeing themselves from worldly pleasures and suffering (and, thus, not involved in waging attacks or insurrections). Buddhists within and outside Thailand largely view monks as people above the vulgarities of war. Akira Hirakawa writes that, as early as the historical Buddha Siddhattha Gotama, monks were seen as noble persons (Sanskrit: *āryapudgala*).[110] However, monks are people and, as such, are subject to social conditions. When monks live in an oppressive, stressful, and traumatic environment, they may exhibit combative and violent tendencies.[111]

In this chapter, we find that Buddhist monks exacerbate the violence in the three southernmost provinces through their everyday performances. Practices such collecting morning alms with a military escort and politically charged sermons accentuate the divide between Muslims and Buddhists and fuel a primary cause for the violence—Otherness. The intensity of participation and reaction to the violence increased steadily between the initial rise in violence of 2004 and the following years of 2005–2007. What began as differing views and opinions escalated into political discourse and, eventually, into militant action.

4

Militarization

In a school at Wat B, a monk in saffron robes sat beside me in a corner of the room where, twenty feet away from us, another monk gave a Pāli lesson to seven novices. We spoke in hushed voices and our conversation was different from most conversations between a person and a monk. I was there to learn more about the issue of military monks. "Why did you decide to be a soldier?"

He explained that this decision was quite typical for a twenty-one-year-old Thai man. We talked about training exercises he went through, the places he stayed, and then paused. In that moment of silence I turned to him and asked: "When you became a military monk (*thahān phra*), did you have to train more?"

"No," he replied. "I finished training when I was twenty-two. Then I ordained as a monk. For this position we start as a non-commissioned corporal and work our way up from there."[1] Our conversation continued, but I could not stop thinking about how publicly, yet at the same time covertly, we were discussing the militarization of monks adjacent to an active Pāli classroom. Later, I would consider this perceived ambiguity between secrecy and openness endemic to the discussion of military monks. But, because of this conversation, I realized that a new space for violence had emerged in the Thai *sangha*.

In chapter 3, Ačhān Nok mentioned that abbots in the red zones owned and sometimes used firearms. These monks used firearms primarily to scare off potential attackers, and they claimed they never planned on using them to harm others. Ačhān Nok explained that the use of firearms by an ordained monk is a misdemeanor under the monastic guidelines, the *Vinaya*. In this context, the monk who handled the weapon would have engaged in a military action. The same argument applies to the context of Ačhān Wirapan, the monk who advises and blesses the soldiers in Narathiwat and Pattani's Ingkayut Camp. While Ačhān Wirapan's practices condone military actions and, hence, can be perceived as militaristic, his social role is still within the domain of a monk. A military monk, however, is quite different from gun-wielding abbots. Military monks retain both monastic and State responsibilities in their everyday performances, constructing for themselves a political identity, which is forbidden according to monastic guidelines. This chapter focuses on the State's militarization of

Buddhist roles as well as the militarization of Buddhist spaces, drawing primarily on fieldwork from trips to southern Thailand between July 2004 and November 2008.

Contextualizing Militarization

The dimension of militarization is absence from most introductory books on Buddhisms in the United States. The perception, by inference, is that militarization is in direct contrast to Buddhist principles.[2] This perception is well-merited, since militarization is grounded in violence and suffering (Pāli: *dukkha*) and reflects a seemingly counter-intuitive approach to one of the core tenets of Buddhisms, namely to overcome suffering. The root word "military" can refer to positions of uniformed personnel in the armed forces, or to the Weberian category of State, wherein organized violence is accepted as a legitimate means of realizing social objectives. Although limited in its scope, the Weberian category locates power (in this case, a monopoly of legitimate acts of violence) in the State. Organizations, such as the Army, act as appendages of the State and coordinate activities meant to ensure "victory in the battlefield."[3]

In his analysis of social power, sociologist Michael Mann distinguishes military and political power similarly and notes that military power pertains to the "social organization of physical force," whereas political power is about "territorial and centralized regulation."[4] Mann's distinction is important and alludes to the overly wide linguistic umbrella if we use military in reference to the State. Therefore, for the purposes of this chapter, "militarization" will refer to the process that invests social, economic, and political responsibilities in armed forces.[5] As such, the Thai State's militarization of Thai Buddhism refers to the process by which the armed forces invest responsibilities in the Thai *sangha*.

Contrary to the attention paid between Buddhisms and governance, Buddhist Studies has paid little attention to the relationship between Buddhisms and militarization; however, the military has been involved with Buddhist affairs throughout the history of Buddhisms. Written over fifty years ago, Demiéville's seminal work *"Le Bouddhisme et la guerre"* provided a comprehensive overview of militant Buddhist activities throughout East Asia. This was the first comparative and detailed account of Buddhist military activity, but the work was not incorporated into U.S. Buddhist Studies.[6] Even more surprising, Demiéville's article did not spark broader discussions about the nature of Buddhist Studies in relation to militarization. The one exception to this trend is the isolated, albeit voluminous, discussion of Buddhist militarism in Sri Lanka.[7]

Thai Buddhist militarism is most particularly visible in the three southernmost provinces, where the State has situated its forces *within* local *wat*. The joint presence of armed forces and monks within the *wat* symbolizes the collapse of any distinction between Thai Buddhism and the State. This intimate relationship is in stark contrast to the distinctive Malay Muslim's culture and religion in the area, which is relatively dislocated from national government and politics. It has also contributed to violence in the area and the targeting of Buddhist monks. Simultaneously with the collapse of any visible distinction between Thai Buddhism and the Thai State comes the State's advent of the military monk.

Military Monks

Military monks are fully ordained monks who simultaneously serve as armed soldiers, marines, navy, or air force personnel.[8] This amalgam—military monks, who embody the militarization of Thai Buddhism and the military—reflects the inherent violence in their identity. For many, the idea of a militarized monk conflicts sharply with a monk's most fundamental duties. While Ačhān Nok's actions might seem inappropriate and unethical, the concept of a military monk's status may appear paradoxical and contradictory, especially to those versed in Buddhist principles of non-violence. A monk's purpose is to avoid life's vulgarities, to aspire toward awakening. A soldier's life is virtually the opposite—one committed to a job that requires confrontation with life's vulgarities.

In addition to these ideological complications, there also is an ecclesiastical interdiction that prohibits soldiers from becoming monks. However, as anthropologist Hayashi Yukio explains in his study of the Thai-Lao of northeast Thailand, a people's religious practice is rooted in experience. For Yukio, Buddhism "does not consist merely of cultivated knowledge sealed in texts, or of its interpretation. Rather it consists of practices that live in the 'here and now'...."[9] While the Buddhist textual tradition clearly disallows the existence of a military monk, lived Buddhist traditions demonstrate a different attitude. Throughout the development of Buddhisms in such countries as China, Korea, and Japan, we find traditions that do not follow the idealized notions of Buddhisms. Similar to Thai Buddhist monasticism, Chinese, Korean, and Japanese Buddhist monasticisms also have had warrior monks.[10]

The Thai Theravāda Buddhist tradition is unique to the previously mentioned monasticisms by allowing men to temporarily become inducted into the *sangha*. Similar to Burmese, Lao, and other Theravādin traditions, it is common for Thai Buddhist men to ordain as monks for a short time at least once in their lives. Anthropologist Charles Keyes notes that Thai men gain considerable esteem by their temporary ordinations, which generally occur during Buddhist Lent (*khaophansā*). By entering the Thai *sangha*, all men, regardless of class, have access to education and a means of increasing their social status.[11] Moreover, in addition to these social benefits, it is popularly believed that, by becoming a monk, a son grants his mother merit to enter heaven.

According to the *Vinaya*, certain interdictions surround ordainment. Many such rules revolve around physical or social characteristics that would preclude their ordination, such as if a person is diseased, a criminal or handicapped. Most of these guidelines resulted from the historical Buddha trying to cope with specific socio-political and economic dilemmas. For example, a prohibition evolved that specifically relates to the ordaining of soldiers:

> During the time of the Buddha there was a war on the border of the
> northern Indian kingdom of Magadha, one of the primary supporters
> of Buddhist monasticism. Several generals who did not want to join the
> battle entered the Buddhist *Sangha*. At the request of the king, the
> Buddha declared that henceforth soldiers were not allowed into the
> *Sangha* (Vin. I, 73–74).[12]

Since this historic incident, the official doctrinal stance for Buddhist *sanghas* has been to prohibit active soldiers from entering a *sangha*, though we have already noted that this interdiction is subject to regional and historical exceptions.[13] Richard Gombrich, a respected scholar of Theravāda Buddhism, has offered a slightly different context for this doctrinal prohibition:

> A minister advised the king that anyone who thus deprived him of his
> soldiers deserved to be executed. As the king was on good terms with
> the Buddha, he advised him that other kings might not take such as
> thing lying down. Reading between the lines, we can deduce that he
> warned the Buddha that for their own good the *Sangha* had better not
> ordain soldiers.[14]

In Gombrich's explanation, the problems of identity become clearer. If a person takes an oath to serve the State and then the *sangha*, at least one of these oaths would have to be compromised.

The Thai State has formally acknowledged and supported the ecclesiastical interdiction toward ordaining soldiers. In 1905, to avoid the overlapping of duties to the State and *sangha*, the Chulalongkorn administration created a legal provision called the Thai Military Service Act exempting monks from military service. The Act also eliminated the tensions concerning the possibility of monks enlisting in the army. Thus, in accordance with ecclesiastical restrictions, the Thai Military Service Act was designed to prevent the monk-to-soldier process. However, in later contemporary Thai society we learn that tension is not the result of the monk-to-soldier process, but the reverse, that is, the soldier-to-monk process.

Through temporary ordinations, Buddhist traditions such as the Thai one allow for maneuverability around these obstacles to the existence of Buddhist soldiers.[15] According to stipulations articulated by the ONB (Office of National Buddhism), soldiers are allotted one four-month paid leave of absence during their service in order to ordain at a local *wat*. Soldiers normally take this leave during the annual Rain Retreat (*khaophansā*), which generally lasts from June until October. They return to duty after the Rain Retreat has ended. This leniency surrounding ordination is extended even further by another and more covert exercise regarding the new status of military monks.

As early as 2002, a covert military unit authorized by a confidential department began directing Buddhist soldiers to ordain while remaining on active duty. Every year since, military monks have been assigned to specific posts. According to two military monks I interviewed, this secret military unit operates semi-independently. Its operations are unknown to most of the military in Bangkok, although there have been numerous reports that implicate the Thai monarchy, especially Queen Sirikit. For example, there have been reports of military monks becoming ordained in honor of the Queen's birthday.

It is difficult to determine how many Thais in the military truly do not know about military monks as opposed to those who know, but who refuse to disclose what they do know. Military monks work in isolation from one another and are sworn to secrecy; thus, it is difficult to locate and speak with them. Furthermore, due to their secrecy, the documentation is security-sensitive and is unavailable to corroborate their reports.

I conducted over a dozen interviews with one military monk at Wat B and met briefly with another in the capital district of Pattani Province. I first learned of military monks when I interviewed a few high-ranking monks in Pattani Province in July 2004. Two years later, when I returned to do fieldwork at Wat A, Wat B, and Wat Chang Hai, I made it a point not to inquire about military monks. My encounters with both military monks came about through my discreet, yet persistent participant observations at the three main *wat* and neighboring *wat*. Following the discovery of military monks, I asked locals, monks, and abbots about this phenomenon; however, the two military monks are my only primary sources. As military monks, they had to protect their anonymity when providing information. This predicament occluded me from acquiring any physical documentation about them aside from their military equipment, the monthly salaries deposited into their bank account, and detailed reports of their training.

In addition to these primary sources, high-ranking monks from the three southernmost provinces, such as Ačhān Mahāwichī and other abbots, independently confirmed military monk activities. Other scholars, such as Duncan McCargo, also received reports of military monk ordinations. In an interview, an abbot disclosed that a batch of seventy-five military monks were ordained at one Pattani *wat* in 2005 and then assigned to various *wat* around the province in a project supported by the Queen.[16] These disparate, yet corresponding sources of information suggest that Thai military monks are a very real and active presence in southern Thailand. However, due to the scarcity of primary sources and lack of documentation, the military monks' reports as detailed accounts should be regarded with a level of speculation.

As the State-appointed guardians of Thai monastic lifestyles and activities, the ONB does not acknowledge the presence of military monks. When asked about their presence, the director of the Office of National Buddhism dismissed the issue, stating:

> Why would soldiers have to dress like a monk? In dangerous *wat*, we have soldiers there to take care of them. And, this point is a really serious point in Thai Buddhism. We can't let something like this exist. The monk can't fight and can't have weapons. People may think this is possible, but it's not.[17]

The official stance of the ONB mirrors that of the Thai Buddhist *Vinaya*. As historian Craig Reynolds notes, the distinction between militarism and monasticism goes so far as to forbid monks from even observing an army in battle dress.[18] Although the director of the ONB argues emphatically that military monks do not exist, they are a very real and active part of many *wat* in southern Thailand.[19]

Accounts of military monks in southern Thailand are cloaked in rumor and secrecy.[20] In numerous interviews with abbots, Thai journalists, and local Buddhists, there are allusions to military monks, albeit short references, but direct confirmations nonetheless. Such brief references to military monks were always followed by bouts of hesitation and reluctance. If not for the fact that I personally and directly interviewed military monks, I might have dismissed the previous depictions as communal fabrication (or collective memory gone astray).

To dismiss this atmosphere of secrecy would be to dismiss the very ideological efficacy of the military monk. Thai Buddhism is viewed as a peaceful, meditative, and socially supportive tradition that is absent of violence. Monks, as embodied agents of this tradition, are considered diametrically opposed to agents of war, that is, the military. Hence, there is a reluctance to talk about military monks. Michael Taussig postulates that truth comes in the form of a public secret. The importance of this public secret is *knowing what not to know*.[21] One clear indication of this tacit social understanding is the result of many interviews with abbots in the southernmost provinces who claim to know nothing about military monks. Contrary to these abbots' assertions, a high-ranking monk in the southernmost provinces whom I shall call Ačhān Hom confided to me that abbots throughout the region met in 2004 and discussed the issue of military monks receiving military stipends.[22] Living in an environment that normalizes bombings and armed attacks, southern monks and some privileged

Buddhist laity are aware of military monks, but they also know that they should not openly talk about them.[23] Such a discussion would combine elements that socially and religiously are considered opposites—Buddhism and violence.

The very concept of military monks represents a powerful clash between Thai Buddhist doctrine and the lived Thai Buddhist tradition. This conflict between praxis and doctrine, when made public, creates discomfort in most Thai Buddhists. One example of this occurred during an afternoon interview with Ačhān Nirut at Wat Chang Hai, a high-ranking monk in southern Thailand, when I asked him about military monks.

He reluctantly nodded, confirming that he knew a little about military monks. Pressing the issue a bit more, I asked his opinion of military monks—was the existence of gun-wielding monks legitimate? After the question was posed, Ačhān Nirut squirmed a bit in his chair, smiled faintly, and let out a series of filler words. Finally, he replied, "I cannot say. It depends on many things." He paused again and I decided to let the silence linger. Frowning slightly, Ačhān Nirut spoke again, this time in a soft voice, "For me, it is not ok. For me, it is not ok."[24]

Ačhān Nirut's struggle to articulate his stance on military monks could very well be a reaction to their changing roles in southern *wat*. Beginning in 2002, and with limited guidance by the Thai *sangha*, military monks went to areas that lacked monks. Their presence at assigned posts was indefinite and depended upon the longevity of the circumstances surrounding their assignment. If a military monk decided to quit his post, another would replace him.

Thai *wat* need a minimum of five monks in order to perform crucial ceremonies, such as the annual Kathin ceremony in which Buddhist laity bestow new robes and gifts upon the monks at the end of *khaophansā*. Populating these understaffed *wat* with military monks enabled *wat* to perform important rituals and grant local Buddhists a chance to make merit. McCargo offers a choice example of this protection, citing a portion of a conversation with an abbot. According to the abbot, military monks carry guns in their shoulder bags when they go on morning alms.[25] However, beyond the defensive posturing lies a deeper and more symbolic element to the presence of military monks—their identity augments the State's presence in the *wat*.[26]

The situation changed in 2004, however, when Prime Minister Thaksin Shinawatra declared martial law. The Thai State found a new use for military monks. Instead of assigning them to specific *wat* to fill voids in the monastic infrastructure, under martial law the stationing of military monks was to bolster their defenses of particular *wat*. Between 2006 and 2008 there were not many military monks in the southernmost provinces, and the ones I conferred with stated there was no networking among them.

Late one evening in 2007, Ačhān Tim, who taught Pāli to monks at Wat Chang Hai, sat with me at a table outside his quarters relaying what he had heard about military monks:

A *wat* in Narathiwat had a few monks. When insurgents attacked the monks moved to stay in the city. The *wat* became abandoned. Muslims went to the *wat* to destroy the Buddha images, buildings, pavilions, and the monk's quarters. The Queen ordered soldiers to become monks and to stay in the abandoned *wat* to guard the *wat* and its religious objects. In this respect, I agree that there has to be military monks.[27]

One clear indication of this strategy is the commissioning of military monks throughout the three southernmost provinces. The majority of military monks are sent to Narathiwat, the second largest group is assigned to Yala, and the fewest to Pattani. These proportions correspond to the level of violence and instability in the three provinces since 2004.[28] Typically, a soldier training in southern Thailand would learn before his graduation that he had been selected to become a military monk. To proceed through full ordination, he would attend a local *wat* as a military monk, one in his home neighborhood, or at more clandestine locations in southern Thailand. From that point in time, the military monk serves as an active and vigilant protector of the *wat* and its monks.

Early one evening, while smoking his hand-rolled cigarette within Wat B, one military monk, whom I refer to as Phra Eks, proudly opened up his saffron robes to reveal a Smith & Wesson tucked beneath the folds around his waist. Although he keeps his M-16 hidden in his sleeping quarters, at night he generally carries the handgun in case of trouble. For Phra Eks, a military monk's primary duty is to protect monks from terrorists (*phūkokānrai*):

> We need to disguise ourselves as monks to protect [the monks]. If we don't do this, in the future there will be no monks in the three provinces. We need to give them moral support, to serve our nation, religion, and army, to foster harmony, to prevent social disruptions (discord), and to prevent people from abusing others.[29]

Phra Eks is thirty years old and comes from a poor Thai Chinese family of nine in one of the border provinces. His father, who died when Phra Eks was very young, served as a soldier in southern Thailand. Being one of seven children, Phra Eks helps his mother take care of his siblings by contributing part of his military salary each month to the family.[30] In this way, he was able to provide his mother with both merit and money.

Phra Eks's disguise is more than a superficial undercover persona or a means of preserving a public secret. Seemingly contradicting himself, he also asserts that he is not pretending to be a monk; he *is* a real monk (*phra čhing*). Because he considers himself to be both a soldier and a monk, I pressed him as to his ultimate allegiance. He replied that his job as a soldier simultaneously fulfill the duties as a monk. For Phra Eks, his duties do not conflict with one another. In the event that the *wat* was attacked and he killed an attacker, he is confident he would remain a monk, although killing a human being would transgress the most important of the *pārājikas* (severe offense that requires an immediate expulsion from the *sangha*),[31] Phra Eks explained the apparent contradiction. He stated that there are certain people who would "clean up" the situation in order to allow him to remain at his post.[32]

Although Phra Eks recognizes the gravity of murdering a terrorist, the defense of the *wat* and its occupants overshadows it. I asked Phra Eks on several occasions why the existence of military monks was necessary. He explained:

> If the nation does not have Buddhism, it is a country of thievery (*mūang čhon*). Buddhism as a religion helps to clean the heart and shape the mind. Buddhism teaches people to abandon their greed, anger, and obsessions, to live moderately. Without Buddhism to teach and guide people, it would be a nation of chaos filled with selfish people....I will use a gun whenever I see someone who tries to attack monks at the *wat*, such as setting fire [to the *wat*], or coming to hurt or shoot the monks, I will shoot.[33]

To Phra Eks, a Muslim terrorist attack on Buddhist monks symbolically is an attack on the moral integrity of the nation. Phra Eks sees the deterioration of Buddhism connected to the deterioration of social order. Without military monks, Thailand would convert to chaos; its people would become selfish. His rationalization is one of prima facie; the ideological threat of moral turpitude overturns the interdictions against violence. Phra Ek's stance on attackers is reminiscent of the rhetoric that ultra-conservative monks used to describe communists in the 1970s. At that time, for the staunch Thai nationalist supporter Phra Kittiwuttho, communism was ideologically anti-nation and anti-religion; a communist was the living embodiment of Māra, the manifestation of desire. In a controversial interview published in the popular magazine *Caturat*, Phra Kittiwuttho explained that the use of violence against communists was justified:

> ...because whoever destroys the nation, the religion, or the monarchy, such bestial types (*man*) are not complete persons. Thus we must intend not to kill people but to kill the Devi (Māra); this is the duty of all Thai.[34]

Kittiwuttho's justification in the 1970s against the communists rests on two concepts: (1) the antagonist to the State is a manifestation of Māra, an embodiment of moral depravity, and (2) killing such a manifestation is not the same as killing a human being—a "complete person."[35] While Phra Eks does not go so far as to dehumanize Malay Muslim terrorists, his justification for violence is eerily reminiscent of Phra Kittiwuttho's reasoning. For each group of antagonists—communists and Muslim militants—the subtext for murder was the group's inability to coexist in civil society, or their inability to be "tamed" (to use the terms in the *Kesi Sutta*, the doctrinal source from which Kittiwuttho derives his justification).[36] Phra Eks is prepared to attack those who seek to bring about a chaotic and selfish nation, a nation which Kittiwuttho would consider dominated by Māra. It is this ideological threat to nation and Buddhist principles that provoked both monks—Phra Eks and Phra Kittiwuttho—to condone the use of violence. Unlike Phra Kittiwuttho's rationale, however, Phra Eks's rationalization enables him to *directly enact violence*. Kittiwuttho became the moral voice of the State during the violent crackdowns in 1973 and 1976.

Military Monks in Buddhist Traditions

This rationale of justifying violence due to an endangered tradition may be endemic throughout different Theravādin traditions. In Sri Lanka, the Janatha Vimukthi Peramuna (JVP) Buddhists have blurred the lines between sacred duty and murder. Sri Lankan JVP monks rationalize the violence they commit through Buddhist justifications and a legacy of Buddhist precedence. They trace precedence back to the Sinhalese mytho-historical chronicle called the *Mahāvaṃsa*. In this second-century work, the Buddhist King Dutthagāmani wages a sacred war against foreign invaders who were led by Tamil King EÂara. The killing of heathens did not constitute murder, since the Tamil warriors were neither meritorious nor, more importantly, Buddhist.[37]

Centuries later, during the 1980s, the JVP monks reconceptualized Dutthagāmani's cause within the ethno-religious war between the secular separatist movement LTTE (Liberation Tigers of Tamil Eelam) and the Sinhalese Buddhist State.[38] As they demanded President Jayewardene's resignation in 1988, JVP monks launched a rash of violent attacks on police, teachers, and politicians. Their threats, brutal physical assaults, and an attempted assassination all became the means toward a more important and justifiable cause—the preservation of the nation and Sri Lankan Buddhism.[39] Interestingly, the justification seen by JVP monks is similar to Kittiwuttho's, and not too different from the mentality of the Thai military monk, Phra Eks. When there arises a need to protect and preserve a Buddhist nation, monks view violence as a necessarily action. This commonality suggests a uniform latent tendency in Theravādin Buddhist traditions for justifying violence.[40]

Yet, this need to defend a Buddhist nation—and the advent of military monks—can be traced beyond the borders of Southeast Asia and beyond the borders of Theravādin Buddhism to Mahāyāna Buddhism. Under the canopy of

Mahāyāna Buddhism, there historically were situations in East Asia in which both *wat* and monks were militarized.[41] In China, there are numerous instances of Buddhist-related conflicts, such as the Maitreya Messianic rebellions during the Sui and Tang Dynasties (613–26), when soldier-monks led revolts and rebellions, in part due to the Buddhist longevity in the region. In 1891, after examining the militant aspect Chinese Buddhism, J. M. M. de Groot, offered the following ideological rationale for the militarism:

> A last reason for the warlike behavior of Buddhist monks we see in an imperative order of the *Fan-mang-king* to all the devotees of the Church, to afford protection to the *Sam-Pao*, or the triad embracing the Buddha, the Law and the Clergy. No one, says the book, can ever hope for the bodhisattva-dignity, unless he conforms in every respect to this most holy duty of all the children of Buddha. Now, defending the *Sam-Pao* is identical with protecting *wat* and sanctuaries against hordes of invaders and rebels, who as is fully proved by China's history of all periods, have never manifested one whit more clemency for religious than for secular buildings.[42]

Throughout the Chinese Buddhist monks' scriptures, we find Buddhist militarism repeatedly justified in order to protect sacred spaces. This phenomenon is not limited solely to China. During the course of defending its borders between the thirteenth and seventeenth centuries, Korean armies enlisted monks as soldiers to fight its successive invaders: Jurchen, Mongol, Japanese, and Manchu.[43] In Tibet, as late as the mid-twentieth century, 10 to 15% of the monks at Sera, Gandan, and Lhasa monasteries were fighting monks (Tibetan: *dobdo*). To stress their militant characteristics, Melvyn Goldstein states that a fighting monk, who often carried long knives and wore different attire, were fighting monks in dress only unless they fought and could win fights.[44] Unlike the military monks in China, Korea, and Japan, the Tibetan fighting monks were largely confined to bouts of monastic muscularity, brawls, and feats of athleticism. However, Goldstein cites different episodes of violence and rebellion by the fighting monks, which suggest that their aggressive tendencies extend into warfare as well.[45]

Perhaps one of the richest histories of militarized monks is found in Japan. Historian Mikael Adolphson cites more than four hundred conflicts involving Buddhist soldier-monks in Japan's premodern era.[46] During this period and beyond, Japanese Buddhist monks saw their roles in relation to the deteriorating health of the world, *mappō*. According to Buddhist cosmology, we are in *mappō*, the last stage of the fourth and final *mahākalpa*. During this time period it is more difficult to cultivate wisdom, compassion, and awaken. The rationale for many of these monks was that their conduct, while unethical, was necessary in this deteriorated state of the world. To put it quite simply, an armed monk was better than no monks at all.

As early as the tenth century under the abbotship of Ryogen, Tendai armies marched into battle. These soldier-monks were well aware of their transgressive behavior and, because of their actions, were dubbed "evil monks." Regardless of this sanction of immorality against them, the monks perceived their tasks as absolutely necessary. Christoph Kleine explains that the monks saw their *bodhisattva* precepts (Sankskrit: *śīla*) as more important than the monastic rules of conduct, even *pārājika* offenses that entail taking of human life. For these monks, once the purpose became cosmic in importance: "[A]rmed monks had an important task to fulfill, for the sake of Buddhism and thus the sake of all sentient beings."[47] Centuries later, during the Warring States Period of the 1500s, Japanese warrior monks (Japanese: *sohei*) became prevalent, and as late as the Russo-Japanese War (1904–5),[48] Japanese Zen monks could be seen marching in the front lines of the military to preserve the nation.

Another reason for monks' willingness to engage in violence may be a latent tendency for aggression, which is not awakened until the *Buddhadhamma* appears in the need of defense. The need to defend the *Buddhadhamma* became evident in southern Thailand for some Buddhist monks, much like it did for Sri Lankan Buddhists, during the ethnic fratricide in the 1980s. In fact, Kittiwuttho's radical demonization of communists was sparked by the Khmer Rouge's violence and the fear of another systematic slaughter of Buddhist monks in Thailand. The fear of such violence might relate to issues of self-defense or defense of the sacred (in this case, the *sangha*, one of the Three Jewels), or it may derive from eschatological fears found within Theravādin doctrine.[49] Eschatological movements periodically arise in Buddhist traditions, such as the Holy Men revolts of northeastern Thailand, but eschatological movements do not always equate to violence.[50] Religious Studies scholar Alicia Marie Turner argues in her study of Burmese Buddhism and colonialism that the welfare of the *sāsana* (Buddhism) became a focal point for Burmese reform organizations. In the decline of the monastic tradition, Burmese Buddhists saw a signal of a cosmological decline that was connected to colonial occupation.[51] The Buddhist community's angst was somewhat tempered by the British reinstatement of the Pāli Patamabyan examinations, an honor's examination in Buddhist literature; still, each Buddhist "organization arose from a concern that colonialism had brought a drastic decline in pariyatti [religious texts] and that the teachings were in danger of being lost."[52] Eschatological fears motivated collectivity and solidarity, but not necessarily violence.[53] In the Thai circumstance, Kittiwuttho did not indicate the symbolism of the act, but simply said it was the Khmer Rouge's violence against monks that awoke in him the need to defend Thai Buddhism. As in the case of the epigraph in which Vajiravudh finds justice in defensive wars, we find the perceived attack upon the *sangha* or a Buddhist nation justifies a militant Buddhist response in Thailand.

Ordinations in the southernmost provinces, which were already uncommon due to the low population of Buddhists, have further decreased in numbers. One of the districts I visited had only one ordination in over a year, and even that was of a young teacher who decided to ordain for only a few weeks. Those who remained saw the existence of Thai Buddhism in the region was endangered. For them, the violence is not merely about worldly existence and mundane matters, but also about the survival of the *dhamma*. Ačhān Tim at Wat Chang Hai explained that his militancy is a necessity:

> It is beneficial to have military monks in order to protect *the* religion. I mean to protect religious rituals, the *dhamma*, artifacts and people.... Buddhist artifacts have been destroyed. It is good to have a guard to keep an eye on these things. The Buddha's teachings, such as the books, are still here. The religious people are still here. If you are asking about the military monk's importance, I would like to ask you back— what if this there were no military monks? What would happen? The *wat* might be attacked and destroyed. When the *wat* are destroyed, what would happen then?[54]

It is in this respect that military monks and some other monks regard Malay Muslims as their enemies. I asked Phra Eks to define Thainess (*khwāmpenthai*):

> Thainess means good human relationships [that are] gentle, [in which each] helps the other. But, now it's not like that here. Thai Buddhists are still the same; they are gentle like [Thainess prescribes], but Thai Muslims have only violence.[55]

Violence against monks and *wat* has activated the latent tendency in Thai Buddhism to demonize the Other and justify violence. It is this mentality that has spurred such atypical, irregular behavior in Thai monks, behavior such as abbots who go to sleep at night with guns next to their beds.

Caught between the conflicting tides of doctrine and practice, a few high-ranking southern monks offer doctrinal justification for the military monks. According to them, although the *Vinaya* (Buddhist monastic code) strictly prohibits monks from any aggressive force, it does allow them to defend themselves. For these southern monks, the advent of the military monk is a manifestation of this allowance.[56] In his analysis of Theravāda Buddhist monasticism, Richard Jones argues a slightly different rationale. Jones considers the monk's most central social obligation is to teach the *dhamma*. Thus, he concludes that *any action* taken to preserve this primary social responsibility is secondary in importance to the repercussions of not teaching the *dhamma*.[57]

If we employ Jones's interpretation, the monks' obligation to teach *dhamma* in southern Thailand would overrule their other obligations. It might require them to volunteer to move down to the dangerous areas and teach the *dhamma*, accept the presence of military monks, or in even more drastic circumstances, to arm themselves. Military monks feel that they are instrumental in ensuring the existence of monks in this region. If there were no military monks, there would be no monks present at all.

Military monks may accept the doctrine and patriotic justification of their actions; nonetheless, they still must conceal their purpose. I once asked Phra Eks if I could take his picture. He quickly refused, explaining "It would be too dangerous." Indeed, Phra Eks does need to be concerned about exposure. A photograph of him brandishing a gun would expose the secret of military monks and subsequently result in his alienation and possible death.[58]

Stanley Tambiah argues that militancy separates a monk from his sacred identity. In a Durkheimian fashion, we can view the identity of the military monk as a collusion of sacred and profane principles. The inclusion of violence—a profane act—into a sacred persona removes the quintessential attribute of the sacred, distancing it from the profane. Referring to the militant activities of the JVP monks in Sri Lanka, Tambiah explains, "The monk who has finally taken to the gun can no longer be considered a vehicle of the Buddha's religion...."[59] In this vein, a picture of Phra Eks could lead to a series of disastrous effects: the portrayal of Phra Eks with a gun could expunge him of sacrality; the one picture could provoke a suspicion of widespread use and could destroy the pacifist view of southern monks; and lastly and perhaps most concretely, the picture would undermine the clandestine nature of the military monk program. The nebulous nature of military monks makes for intractable documentation, but nonetheless displays the embodied militarization of Buddhist roles.[60]

Monastic to Military Compound

In addition to the militarization of Buddhist roles, Thai Buddhist spaces are also militarized. On November 9, 2006, the *Bangkok Post* published a brief article about one hundred Thai Buddhist villagers who fled their homes in Yala, one of the southernmost provinces in Thailand. Women, men, and children abandoned their homes and livelihood and traveled to their capital district to find refuge in Wat Nirotsangkatham.[61] By the beginning of December, their numbers had grown to over 228 people.[62] None of the Buddhist refugees felt they would be safe returning to their villages; instead, they made a temporary home at the *wat*. The villagers were not the only laity then residing at Wat Nirotsangkatham. Thai soldiers were already living at the *wat*, guarding the entrance and fortifying its perimeters.

The military encampment at Wat Nirotsangkatham is one of many instances in which the State has militarized Thai Buddhism. Although soldiers protect the monks and refugees at Wat Nirotsangkatham, they also use the Buddhist space to strategize and execute military commands, effectively converting the monastic compound into a military headquarters.

The most common place signified in Thai Buddhism is and has always been the *wat*, which often has been identified by locals as a communal investment.[63] The significance of the *wat* has changed, however, due to the practices that now take place in them. From the time when martial law was declared in southern Thailand in 2004, through 2007, Buddhist monks reported that Malay Muslims no longer frequented *wat*. Instead of serving communal gatherings, *wat* became spaces of contestation. Military units and covert operatives situated there guarded *wat* against such dangers as power outages and armed assaults. A consequence of this State vigilance and its militarization of Buddhist spaces is that Thai Buddhist identity has also been militarized.

The local investment in a *wat* can be measured from different vantage points. Although there are more, for the purposes of this chapter I will outline only two levels of analysis: the religious and the secular.[64] In religious terms, having a *wat* allows the surrounding community easy access to annual ceremonies and rit-uals, such as funerals, ordinations, and holidays. Buddhist monks who live in the *wat* go out daily for morning alms. This routine provides the local laity affordable and continual opportunities to make merit. But, from a secular perspective, hav-ing a *wat* allows the community access to such common facilities as basketball and volleyball courts, schools, meeting areas, medicinal and therapeutic counseling for people of all faiths.[65] These two different communal functions lead scholars such as Donald Swearer to consider a *wat* the "religious, cultural and social center of the community."[66]

In the southernmost provinces, the *wat*'s religious function becomes domi-nant when it is used to demarcate Buddhist space within every district of southern Thailand. According to the ONB's records in 2006, Pattani Province has eighty-eight *wat*, Narathiwat has seventy-five, with the smallest number found in Yala, which has only forty-five *wat*.[67] Interestingly, Buddhist space is not reflective of the Buddhist populations or percentages in the three provinces. According to the National Statistical Office in Thailand, Yala, with the fewest number of *wat*, has the greatest number of Buddhist at 127,442.[68]

Prior to the State's declaration of martial law in January 2004, a southern *wat* signified a place for communal gatherings and Buddhist veneration. These shared spaces attracted Thai Buddhists, Thai Chinese Buddhists and Malay Muslims. From 2004 to the present, the communal status of *wat* has changed. Southern Thai monks consider the *wat*'s space altered by the contemporary violent context. Emblematic of this difference are statements made by the abbot of Wat Kūaanai in Pattani Province. In a phone interview he explained that, before the increase in violence "Islam was just Islam and Buddhism was just Buddhism. They did not intermingle. But, whenever we had Thai cultural events like Mother's Day or Father's Day, Muslims would come to our *wat*."[69] Locals, whether they were Malay Muslim or Thai Buddhist, gathered together at *wat* for Thai national celebrations such as the Thai New Year (*songkran*) and the Thai king's birthday.

In the past fifty years, Malay Muslim attitudes toward entering a *wat* have fluctuated.[70] Chavivun Prachuabmoh notes that in the 1970s, the majority of Pattani Malay Muslims felt that "if they just watch or study [at a *wat*], it is all right because they do not participate in the religious ceremony."[71] These Malay Muslims also saw the *wat* as a communal resource, a place to sit and chat with other locals about everyday events, a space for celebrations or to work at them (such as *ngaan wat, nora wayang kulit* and *silat* performances). Though engaging in Buddhist ceremonies at a *wat* was shunned, local Malay Muslims would come to borrow supplies or seek medicinal and charm-related help from the monks who resided at the *wat*, such as in the case of de-hexing.[72]

The southernmost provinces have a long tradition of Malay Muslim and Thai Buddhist interaction and coexistence. Kenneth Landon writes that in the early half of the twentieth century "older Malay communities have members who speak both Malay and Siamese and who follow their religion only to the point of refraining from pork eating and wearing the tarboosh."[73] A clear indicator of this surviving tradition is the record of Malay Buddhist monks in the southernmost province of Narathiwat who are venerated for their spiritual achievements.[74] Further north, in the southern province of Satun, familial ties to Thai Buddhism are remembered in practice. Malay Muslims ordain as Buddhist monks in response to boons granted by their Buddhist ancestors. Anthropologist Ryoko Nishii found that in most cases ordinations resulted from Malay Muslim children who had fallen ill. Their parents, believing that the illness was caused by their ancestors, "prayed to the 'Buddhist' ancestors to cure their child. In return for the cure, the child was promised to become a Buddhist monk, novice or nun."[75] These Malay Muslims, who participated in Buddhist activities at *wat* prior to 2004, embody the past unification of Malayness and Thai Buddhism.

The State's implementation of martial law and insurgent violence within Buddhist villages in southern Thailand has resulted in a different function for *wat* in the area. Wat Nirotsangkatham serves as a striking example of this new appropriation. In an early December afternoon of 2006 I talked to the abbot from Wat Nirotsangkatham, who explained that some of the current refugees living at his *wat* had donated money years ago in order to erect the buildings in which they were now living. He added, "Now, the villagers want the *wat* to help them. It's like what they did in the past comes to help them now.... This building where villagers stay now was built by them."[76]

Thai and Thai Chinese Buddhist refugees from Yala's Bannang Sata and Than
To districts viewed the *wat* as more than a religious and communal space; they
made the *wat* their home. Although many Thai Buddhists believe a *wat* is a sacred
space and endowed with protective powers, many of the Yala refugees chose the
location for a more mundane reason: it contains facilities and shelter large
enough to accommodate them. In the middle of the day in December, 2006,
under one of Wat Nirotsangkatham's pavilions, a community leader for the refugees relayed some of their initial considerations for sanctuary, "Other places
were not big enough to fit all of us," and then added, "and it is safer here because
of the soldiers."[77] The community leader's comment about greater safety at the
wat addresses an important social association existing in southern *wat* located
within its violent environment. In addition to their aforementioned functions,
wat were now recognized as some of the most militarily fortified areas in the
three southernmost provinces.

One of the more recent and devastating militant attacks occurred immediately after the Chinese New Year, on February 18, 2007. A number of bombings
targeted restaurants, karaoke bars, shops, and Buddhist homes in Pattani and
Yala provinces. The *Bangkok Post*, Thailand's most widely read English newspaper, described this attack as the "biggest wave of coordinated bombings, terrorism and murders" that has occurred in the southern border provinces.[78] At
the time of these attacks, I was living in Pattani Province in a monk's quarters at
Wat Chang Hai. The *wat*, as well as other buildings in Pattani and Yala provinces,
lost electricity when the centralized power stations were bombed.

Wat Chang Hai, known for its connection to Lūang Phō Tuat, one of Thailand's
most venerated monks of the late sixteenth century, is an internationally
renowned Buddhist pilgrimage site. The facilities at Wat Chang Hai sprawl over
5.2 acres (13 *rai*) of land, which include a school system and supporting amulet
shops. Because of this and restaurants located in its vicinity, Wat Chang Hai represents a local investment. The legacy of Wat Chang Hai is owed largely to the
Hokkien Khananurak family, who financed the renovation of the *wat* in 1936.
Historian Patrick Jory writes that the Khananurak family supported numerous
other Thai *wat* and they exemplify Chinese families in the southern provinces
that enjoyed good relations with the local Chinese, Thai, and Malay
communities.[79]

By 2007, many of these shops had been vacated. They are visible reminders of
the economic impact that violence has had in the southernmost provinces. A few
restaurants remain open, but all close their doors at 5:00, coinciding with the
time that the *wat*'s front gates are locked. Monks and locals explained that, prior
to 2004, stores and restaurants stayed open late into the evening. One restaurant that receives enough business to stay open is a small family-owned establishment with a dozen wooden tables and chairs and a small T.V. mounted on the
ceiling in the back. I stopped at this restaurant the day after the organized

attacks and noted the difference between these customers and their conversations and those from previous days.

That day there was very few customers and all spoke in hushed tones about the recent bombings. The old man who owned the restaurant appeared to be more concerned about the lack of customers than about a potential attack on his restaurant. Wat Chang Hai is surrounded by the heavily Buddhist district of Khokpo. That was only one of his reasons for feeling secure. "There are quite a lot of [Buddhist] people in this area," he explained. "I always leave the lights on at night. Many people walk past [my restaurant] at night. And, the police and soldiers are also around. Terrorists would not dare to come here."[80]

At Wat Nirotsangkatham and Wat Chang Hai and throughout the southernmost provinces, soldiers and national police use *wat* as their primary bases of operations as well as their homes. Thai *wat* have excellent strategic positions. They are near the highest population of Buddhists in a given area, have access to an ample supply of food and water, and contain facilities large enough to accommodate the police and soldiers.[81] Abbots generally feel receptive to the needs of soldiers and police and make efforts to accommodate them. Residing in the capital district of Pattani, Ačhān Tuk explained that the soldiers at his *wat* had no daily stipends: "The soldiers need food and need to use the bathroom, so this is why they stay at my *wat*. The soldiers depend on lay donations to my *wat* for food."[82] A policeman stationed at Wat B also noted:

> There are many reasons [to be stationed at a *wat*]. One is to protect the monks. Another is to help in the development of the *wat*. And, the *wat* is a convenient place for us as well. Because of the *wat*, we do not have to find somewhere else to stay.[83]

However, the occupation of a *wat* is more than a pragmatic act of protection and sustenance. As Pierre Bourdieu states, "Space can have no meaning apart from practice; the systems of generative and structuring dispositions, or *habitus*, constitute and are constituted by actors' movement through space."[84] It is *what people practice in a wat* that *shapes the significance of the wat*. As mentioned in chapter 3, practices within southern *wat* have changed dramatically, primarily due to their new military occupants. Southern *wat* are now militarized spaces.

While the militarization of Buddhist *wat* is not unique within Buddhist traditions, it is still important to assess the social implications in light of the current context. It had been nearly thirty years since southern Thai *wat* were occupied by the Thai military. Thai soldiers have a history of living in *wat* during times of crisis and conflict. During World War II, soldiers occupied *wat* in the northeast and southern provinces.[85] Later, in the 1970s, *wat* were simultaneously used to house soldiers in areas considered hotbeds for communist forces in the southernmost provinces. They also were used as training grounds for the Border Patrol

Police's Rangers and Village Scouts.[86] The current military occupation of *wat* is in the three southernmost provinces.

Since 2002, the *wat* has become militarized by the very existence of military personnel working and living in them. To protect a southern *wat's* occupants from being observed and attacked, the military residing at it usually raises the outer walls and stretches barbed wire around the entrance and the perimeter. They also convert Buddhist pavilions into barracks, transform sleeping quarters into bunkers, and create lookout posts near the entrances (see figures 4.1–4.6).

Some *wat* have over forty police officers or soldiers living in them. Military personnel are armed with handguns and M-16s and wear camouflage uniforms. I was told that both Muslim and Buddhist police and soldiers live in *wat*, but every *wat* I visited was manned solely by Buddhist personnel.[87] This distinction of strictly Buddhist military personnel encourages locals to merge religious and political identifications and to view the Thai State as a Buddhist State, although its constitution (and its many redactions) does not proclaim a religious allegiance.

State police, soldiers, and government officials (*khārāchakān*) maintain that there is no religious preference or requirement for the police and soldiers working at a *wat*.[88] This is an important position for the State to take. Both Thai Buddhist and Muslim residents in the south feel alienated from the State because of reoccurring acts of corruption and illicit activity by local and State government officials. The notorious disappearance of Somchai Neelaphaijit, a popular Muslim

Figure 4.1 Buddhist pavilion before militarization, by Michael Jerryson, December 4, 2006.

Figure 4.2 Buddhist pavilion after militarization, by Michael Jerryson, February 16, 2007.

Figure 4.3 Buddhist quarters before militarization, by Michael Jerryson, December 3, 2006.

Figure 4.4 Buddhist quarters after militarization, by Michael Jerryson, February 16, 2007.

Figure 4.5 Buddhist quarters before militarization 2, by Michael Jerryson, December 3, 2006.

Figure 4.6 Buddhist quarters after militarization 2, by Michael Jerryson, February 16, 2007.

human rights attorney, symbolizes the State's failure to honor and protect the rights of southern Thai Muslims.[89] Due to these and other examples, there is increasing pressure for the State to appear impartial. Having both Muslim and Buddhist soldiers and police working at *wat* might lessen the symbolic impact of having State officials residing at a Buddhist *wat*. However, the absence of any Muslim soldiers or national police in southern *wat* underscores the perception of a State Buddhism in a region ravaged by ethno-religious tensions.

Only a handful of large military camps exist in the southernmost provinces. For instance, in Pattani Province there are only two soldier units, one for combat and the other for community-support activities. Soldiers from these camps and from other bases outside the southernmost provinces are sent to live in *wat* for as long as two years before their next relocation. Once they are ready for relocation, their new site is generally chosen in southern Thailand.[90] The advantage of stationing soldiers in the south is that the extended duration allows soldiers to become familiar with locals and to build up trust and contacts in the surrounding communities. When asked, monks often say they prefer soldiers instead of police as inhabitants of their *wat*, although the decision-making ultimately is not theirs. They characterize soldiers as hard working and more respectful of Buddhist precepts than police during their stay inside the *wat*. Decisions on deployment come from the military, which assesses each location's needs and importance in accordance with governmental funds.[91]

Many abbots in safer areas stress that they did not ask the State for protection. They say that the military is at *wat* due to State concerns. Early one evening, just before the Chinese New Year, I was sitting with Ačhān Dī in front of his *kuti* at Wat Chang Hai. It had just finished raining and he was smoking his cigarette while relaxing on his front step. Ačhān Dī explained to me:

> This *wat* is not in danger; it is not in any dangerous scenario. The *wat* didn't ask for soldiers, but the government sent them. The *wat* has never called for soldiers to be here. But, the government felt worried, afraid that the *wat* will be destroyed. I'm afraid if I go outside the *wat*, but I think in the *wat* there is nothing [to be afraid of].[92]

Wat Chang Hai has over twenty soldiers patrolling its perimeters with entrenched stations at every entrance. Ačhān Dī's position on the violence changed considerably after the Chinese New Year, when Wat Chang Hai lost power for an hour and there was an arson attempt just a few kilometers away. Yet, even during this period of heightened fear and tension, Ačhān Dī's lack of appreciation for soldiers differs greatly from that of abbots who lived in more isolated areas, with higher populations of Muslims and higher rates of murders and bombings.

Some of the soldiers I spoke with at Wat A, Wat B, and Wat Chang Hai have worked outside of Thailand with soldiers from other countries. This experience provided them with a seasoned view of the violence in the southernmost provinces. Many of the soldiers I interviewed in the *wat* have international experience in areas such as Aceh during the recent conflict, which ended in 2005. A few had fought in Vietnam during the U.S. war. They typically assist with the general upkeep of the *wat*, sweeping the grounds and cleaning the latrines. Although they make their homes in the *wat*, they keep their personal habits private within their quarters. Because of their respectful and helpful actions within the *wat* as well as the long-term protection they bring, some abbots and monks have built bunkers and living quarters in their *wat*. While monks generally prefer soldiers to police, they are less enthusiastic about the military commanders who dispatch the soldiers into the area and yet situate themselves outside the sphere of violence. As I sat at Wat A underneath the pavilion, accompanied with four laity and Ačhān Nok, Ačhān Nok bitterly relayed the following:

> The military sent the soldiers here, but didn't provide them with a place to stay, so they have to sleep under the pavilions with the dogs and ants. Because of this, I built a shelter for them. The military officers are really bad. They call themselves men of honor, but they sit in air-conditioned rooms while their privates, who have to follow orders, are sent to sleep with mosquitoes and ants. Military officers sent soldiers down here, so these officers should care for their welfare. An officer came to

check on the situation once, but he left even before his driver came back from toilet! Didn't even walk around to see where the soldiers slept, how they were living, or what they eat. He just came and left.[93]

As the violence increases, there is more interaction between soldiers and monks within *wat*. This is especially true at *wat* in more remote locations that have a higher percentage of Muslims living in the village. The shared isolation of monks and soldiers sometimes encourages a collusion of resources, the two groups exchanging information about locals in the area.

Police come from different provinces throughout Thailand and live at a *wat* in southern Thailand from six months to a year. A majority of the national police who are stationed in the southernmost provinces are originally from central and northeastern Thailand; consequently, they have little experience with or knowledge of the cultures of southern Thailand. Unlike the soldiers, very few possess any international experience. The police rotate on and off duty within the *wat*, which allows them days or nights to relax and drink. At Wat A, Wat B, and Wat Chang Hai, the conduct of police contrasts sharply with that of the soldiers. Soldiers generally keep to themselves and maintain strict vigilance while living in a *wat*. An incident at *Wat* B illustrates one reason for the monks' preferences for soldiers. Policemen had created an outdoor kitchen in which to prepare and eat their food and consume alcohol. This was just meters behind the novices' quarters. After dinner they concluded the evening with a few hours of drinking whiskey and soda beneath the abbot's pavilion. This behavior resulted in empty whiskey bottles overflowing trashcans within the monk's quarters.[94]

The transgressive act of drinking intoxicants within a *wat* is not the only action worth noting. In December of 2006, I asked five policemen on duty at Wat B if the police who reside at *wat* make merit (*tham bun*) through fulfilling their daily duties. The policeman in his mid thirties gestured around at the barracks and his fellow policemen, all armed with M-16s, and responded: "Yes, we do. Actually, our work assists the monks and is merit as well."[95] Just as in the case of morning alms, when those military escorts and those making bulletproof vests make merit, the very act of protecting monks and the *wat* also becomes a means of making merit, a duty inherent to national police and soldiers commissioned in the South. This encapsulation of merit-making in military duties is another consequence of the effects of colluding State and Thai Buddhist elements.

The State's appropriation of Buddhist space has altered the southern Thai *wat*'s significance. Under the banner of a strident nationalism, *wat* serve as home bases for the military; in exchange for this form of nationalism, the *wat* have lost some of their sacrality. Today, if one were to visit multiple *wat* in an area, a common act for Thai Buddhists on pilgrimage, locals might consider their visits indicative of military communication rather than religious devotion. This change in the spatial significance of *wat* has had an impact on its patronage. Buddhist monks report that local Muslim officials in the three southernmost provinces try to avoid contact with the *wat* as much as possible. Ačhān Mahāwichī, a former Secretariat to the Pattani Sangha Leader who has been a monk for over twenty years explains that currently a trip to a *wat* is viewed by many Muslims as a sin:

> Muslims have said many times it is a sin to come to the *wat*....An Islamic village leader who has to sign a paper when someone dies, complains that when someone dies he has to come to the *wat* and get the thing signed, because it is a sin to come to the *wat*.[96]

Ačhān Mahāwichī is the second highest monk at Wat Chang Hai. According to Ačhān Mahāwichī, the *wat* has become a profane space for many Malay Muslims in the southernmost provinces. For an Islamic village leader, entering a *wat* means entering a space of impurity due to its religious designation. The association of coming to a *wat* with the commission of a sin, although not universally recognized, demonstrates a growing public consideration of what coming to a southern *wat* signifies, and what such an action signifies for group identifications.

Local Malays' recent negative attitudes toward *wat* heighten the significance of visiting a *wat*. Entering a *wat* may imply more than simply a visit; it could indicate one's adherence to Thai Buddhism. As there is no specific ritual or official declaration for conversion to Thai Buddhism, it falls upon a person's praxis. Their behavior and actions signify their religious identity. The very public and regular act of visiting *wat* becomes an act of identity-making or identity-reaffirmation.[97] This emerging perception contrasts with local views prior to the declaration of martial law. Before 2004, visiting a *wat* held fewer implications and Buddhist identity was largely denoted in two ways: by participating in specific merit-making exercises and, one could argue, eating pork, (which is still a very powerful religious signifier).

The new significance of visiting a *wat* arises out of a violently charged environment and the Thai State's militarization of its perimeters. For safety precautions, religious practices and ceremonies at southern *wat* either declined or ceased since martial law was imposed. In areas outside of capital districts, funeral rites, which usually occur in the afternoon or night, are now held during the day. In addition, the regular practice of morning alms has ceased throughout the most dangerous areas. At these *wat*, monks rarely go outside their compounds.

One sixty-six year old monk at Wat A, seated on a bench outside his quarters explained: "I want to go out and meet people, give them blessings, all that and more. However, they forbid it because it is dangerous....I listen and obey my abbot and the government, so I don't go out."[98]

The old monk is not alone. For a large part, there is an of absence monks going in and out of *wat*, which is inversely proportioned to the constant flow of military entering and leaving the *wat*. If public perception held sway, southern *wat* would be as much military compounds as they would be monastic compounds.

Militant Practices at the Wat

Appearances are one element to the militarization of Buddhist spaces. There are also militant activities that proceed within the *wat*. Soldiers and police use the *wat* as military headquarters and implement and develop military intelligence while sequestered in *wat* buildings. At Wat A, Wat B, and a few *wat* in their neighboring areas, abbots showed me detailed reports of villagers in their community. The reports describe the areas that should be heavily watched and pages of reports on local suspects. The pictures and information (like those shown in figure 4.7),[99] are a compilation of shared information between monks and the military, and specify which of the local people are (1) arrested (*thūk čhap lǽo*), (2) on the run (*lop nī*) and (3) those whose identities are still undetermined (*yang mai sāmāt phisūt sāp tūa bukhkhon dai*).

Military intelligence does not necessarily impact public perception of a *wat*. Most locals do not know that Ačhān Nok has this information; regardless, it does illustrate the level in which monks and military collaborate and how the *wat* functions as a military headquarter in southern villages.

While these documents are private, military practices in a monastery are not. If a local walks past the entrance of a *wat*, instead of seeing monks performing daily chores, s/he sees fully armed uniformed soldiers standing guard day and night. These habits and practices, according to Pierre Bourdieu, shape the significance of space and have an important effect on the surrounding community. Monks become less visible as the military becomes more visible. The stationing of soldiers and police, together with their military habits, transforms the *wat* into a military space. In doing so, it exacerbates the relations between Buddhists and Muslims in the southernmost provinces.

One acute example of militant activities at *wat* is the armed forces use of torture in places such as at Wat Suan Tham in Narathiwat, or Wat Lak Muang and

Figure 4.7 Military postings of suspects, either arrested or at large, in the *wat*'s community, Wat A, 2007.

Wat Chang Hai in Pattani. Wat Chang Hai's Batallion 24 Army has received the most complaints for detaining and torturing suspected militants. Amnesty International cites complaints dating as early as December 2007 in which soldiers physically assaulted Malay Muslim detainees, gave them meals with pork, and restricted them to praying over the toilet.[100] In these instances, the military activities transform the significance of the *wat* as well as intensify its relationship with the State.[101] This and other forms of militarizing *wat* raise the *wat*'s political value and give rise to further Muslim resentment of Buddhism in the Thai south.

Militarization of Buddhist places and people has extended to the laity themselves. The International Crisis Group (ICG) has documented the most extensive report of Buddhist militia in the deep south. In their report, "Southern Thailand: The Problem with Paramilitaries" the ICG notes that, with the help of the Interior Ministry, Buddhist laity have formed militias designed to protect *wat* and their monks from harm. A clandestine civilian militia based in Yala Province, The *Ruam Thai* (Thais United), provide their own weapons and only receive minimal training (a two-day course on self-defense and security risk analysis). They have purportedly trained six thousand people, of whom only two hundred were Muslim, and have received allegations of carrying out "vigilante-style attacks against Muslims."[102] For some of these militia groups, like Queen Sirikit's Village Protection Volunteer Project (*Or Ror Bor*), which stations Buddhist militia in *wat* in order to protect the monks and the larger Buddhist community, the State helps to train, arm, and pay them. The Village Protection Volunteer Project was initiated in September of 2004 as a response to southern Buddhist demands for extra security. Volunteers, who are almost exclusively Buddhist, spend two months at the Taksin Ratchanives Palace in Narathiwat and undergo a two-week training course, receive rifles and shotguns, and often take location assignments in *wat* or are "explicitly mandated to protect Buddhist minorities."[103]

Contrary to the opinion of local Malay Muslims, 228 Buddhist refugees who stayed at Wat Nirotsangkatham in December 2006 saw the *wat* as a safer space than their villages. According to the refugees, their villages are over 95% Muslim. They say that murders occur almost daily in their villages. While visiting them at the *wat*, there was a funeral for a man from a neighboring village. The sister of the deceased told me that in her village everyone is a target, from the elderly to two-year-old children. She is a farmer and, just like the refugees, considers her village no longer safe to live in. Part of the refugees' decision to come to Wat Nirotsangkatham is the recent conversion of southern monastic compounds into military compounds. Buddhist villagers stay inside the protective perimeters of the *wat* and leave as seldom as possible, only to purchase food. Unfortunately, perceiving a *wat* as a sanctuary from violence does not distinguish it from the violence; rather, it highlights the *wat*'s role and preferential treatment by the State within a violent climate.

Since 2005, there have been more Muslims murdered than Buddhists in the three southernmost provinces.[104] Yet, despite all the fortifications at *wat*, not one Muslim uses a *wat* as a place of refuge (nor does s/he use a mosque, especially after the Khru Se Mosque Affair).[105] Living under martial law in southern Thailand, *wat* have clearly become an exclusive military space for Thai Buddhist and Thai Chinese Buddhists.

Conclusion

As stated at the onset of this chapter, this section was meant to examine the militarization of Thai Buddhist roles and spaces in southern Thailand. Buddhist monks and *wat* have been and continue to be targets for violence in the southernmost provinces. This trend started in 2002, with a bomb threat at Wat Chang Hai in Khokpo, Pattani. In many ways, the attack represented the nascent policy of targeting monks and *wat*. Even in 2004, monks had attributed this act as a strike against Thai Buddhism. Phra Arhom of Pattani Province offered his interpretation of the motive behind this attack:

> People attacked Wat Chang Hai in order to destroy the morale of the Buddhist people. Because people believe that Wat Chang Hai is sacred and since [it is] sacred, bombing it might decrease the degree of sacredness; people might lose their belief in the *wat*.[106]

With sentiments like these in 2004, it is understandable how some abbots felt comforted by the protection offered by soldiers and national police. The militarization of *wat* clearly enhances the protection for some *wat*. According to statistics provided by Srisompob, the protection has moderately worked.[107] However, the State's militarization of *wat* also heightens the association of Thai Buddhism with the State in an ethno-religiously tense region and raises the *wat*'s political value.

State action has also led to the militarization of Thai Buddhism in the form of the military monk. Whereas the militarization of the *wat* resulted in increasing the political value of *wat*, it simultaneously led some Muslims to identify *wat* as taboo space. Unlike the very visible militarization of *wat*, however, the militarization of monks is a covert exercise. Fortunately, it has yet to produce a similar result in how Muslims view monks.[108] Nevertheless, military monks embody the nexus that links the militant State to Thai Buddhist principles. This has the dangerous potential of further politicizing the situation while incurring Muslim derision of southern monks.

While working undercover at *wat* as ordinary monks, military monks fulfill obligations to both the Thai *Sangha* and the State. Their roles are not publicized;

in fact, at times their roles are not even disclosed to the very monks who ordain them. Violence in southern Thailand is saturated in secrecy: anonymous militant actors, disparate grievances, and victims from both sides that often go unnamed. From this blend of secrecy and violence rises another form of secrecy, a communal secret. Some Buddhists living and working alongside military monks are aware of military monks' identities, but choose not to publicize it. Their decision to protect the secrecy of the military monk may be an indirect result of the religious angst they feel concerning the presence of military monks within the *wat*.

In the current Thai milieu and in Buddhist scriptures there is a dearth of support that advocates military monks. This lack of material derives from Buddhist interdictions, which date back to the time of the Buddha. One of the earliest canonical sources prohibits military ordination and derives from a period when soldiers deliberately avoided their military duties by entering the *sangha*. Ironically, the circumstances have inverted, providing the near-opposite reaction. Hand-picked Buddhist soldiers of the army, who wish to perform monastic duties, can now receive a salary, a gun, an M-16, and admittance into the Thai *sangha*. The contradictions embodied in the military monk engender a secret that, if publicly disclosed, would most likely yield intense reactions from Thai Buddhists as well as from the local Malay Muslims.

During the past five years, an attack on a southern monk represented an attack on a victim—a pacifist operating outside of the violence. Unfortunately, this representation is in flux within southern Thailand. One clear example of this is Wat A, which is now a fortified and heavily guarded military base. Police living inside Wat A collaborate with Ačhān Nok and his monks. Another example is Phra Eks, a soldier doubling as an ordinary monk. These components are powerful influences on the local community. As Buddhist spaces and monks become closely associated with the military and its functions, they increase the religious divide between Buddhists and Muslims.

Militarization of *wat* undoubtedly affects the way Buddhists and Muslims feel about each other and themselves. Surin Pitsuwan argues that, due to the socio-religious parallelism between the *wat* and the *pondoks*, *pondoks* articulate ethno-religious differences. We can see this phenomenon even more clearly established in the militarized *wat*.[109]

Now, some southern monks see their *wat* as a fortress of moral integrity. As if embodying the growing socio-religious divide, Ačhān Nok stood on a hill overlooking his *wat* and pointed to the wire fence surrounding his territory. To him this space was divided into religious lines—and it was his *wat*'s perimeter that demarcated the religious space in the community—where Thai Buddhism ended and "Islam" (*tī islam*) began.

5

Identity

"These Muslims in the South," reported Mongkon to his fellow ninth-grade Social Studies students in Central Bangkok, "I don't think they are one hundred percent Thai." He continued in his presentation and described the characteristics that make Thais "Thai" and the Malay Muslims "*not* Thai." Mongkon covered topics such as language (Yawi, a dialect of Bahasa Melayu), clothing (such as the *tudung*, a Muslim woman's veil), and lifestyle (prescribed by the teachings of Muhammad). After Mongkon concluded his report and returned to his seat, his teacher looked at him approvingly, and said, "Very good."[1]

Like others, Mongkon distinguishes southern Thai Muslims from the rest of Thai society through what they are not: Thai Buddhists.[2] This unspoken comparison with normativity is a transnational phenomenon and takes in the components of ethnicity and religion to distinguish the in-group from an out-group. This method of thin-slicing occurs on a daily basis without conscious awareness of the process. Mongkon is not alone in his application of social differentiation; this is a cognitive process endemic to human relations. If we draw back from this process, we find even greater implications of religious iden-tification—most particularly its relevance to national identity.

Contemporary national identities are, as in the past, fluid in nature and rep-resent transformations of the *social imaginaire*, most recently due to colonial influences. One of the transformations is the role of religion in national identity. If a national identity requires a specific religious marker, this dismantles the most rudimentary notions of civic nationalism. Political scientist Liah Greenfeld defines civic nationalism as an *inclusive* category, one that allows people from different ethnicities, religions, and those that practice different customs to share the same citizenship. According to Greenfeld, people acquire a nationality through their own volition.[3] However, religious identity is a means of *excluding* a group from Thai nationalism. Though Mongkon did not label them as Malay, he did not need to do so. The details of his report refer to the Malay Muslims, the largest Islamic group living in southern Thailand.[4]

Michel Gilquin points out that the tendency of Malay Muslims to live within the three southernmost provinces is a geographical reflection of their social status:

"It has its roots in a tacit acceptance of the equation that Thai equals Buddhist, a notion which sidelines Muslims and is reinforced by [their] geography."[5] Malay Muslims are associated with the southernmost provinces and, correspondingly, the southernmost provinces are associated with Malay Muslims.

In contrast to other speculations over the cause of violence in the southernmost provinces, I will argue in this chapter that racial inequality is the primary cause for conflict there. Poverty alone has not fueled the conflict; rather, it has been State-led exclusionary policies, together with impoverished conditions, that provide fertile ground for separatist militancy to grow. Throughout this process, Thai Buddhism acts as a hegemonic force in this inequality; its identity reinforces the continued marginalized identity of Malay Muslims in the deep south. Malay Muslims are displaced from the normative identity twice-fold, since they are neither ethnically Tai, nor religiously Buddhist. In order to examine this hegemonic role of Thai Buddhist identity, I will approach the subject through three contexts that build upon each other: (1) the relationship between Thai race and religion, (2) Thai concepts of race as evidenced in historical sources and, (3) contemporary Thai race relations in the three southernmost provinces through ethnographic accounts.

Race/Ethnicity in Thai Studies

An examination of race and ethnicity illuminates systemic and hegemonic processes that cut deep into the economic, political, and social domains of the country. Race and ethnicity also refer to interrelated, but distinctive and commonly used identity markers of peoples in the three border provinces. This, above all else, necessitates time spent on the subject, but the topic also has a secondary and equally important purpose. The focus on race and ethnicity reveals the biases implicit in academic investigations into Thai economic, political, and social processes. For these reasons, we will first define race and ethnicity and then look at how significant cultural factors influenced the way that scholars studied peoples in Thailand.

Race is a complex and commonly misused term. To avoid many of its pitfalls, I will employ the terms "racial project," and "racial formation" in my discussion of race in accordance with the categories established by sociologists Michael Omi and Howard Winant. Omi and Winant argue that race is "... an unstable and 'decentered' complex of social meanings constantly being transformed by political struggle."[6] Though unstable, the race identification is continually affirmed through a public sphere saturated with racial projects—physical and oral references that essentialize peoples, such as significations found in Mongkon's report. In a likewise fashion, racial formation is a process "by which *social, economic, and political forces determine the content and importance of racial categories*, and by which they are in turn shaped by racial meanings [emphasis added]."[7] While Omi and Winant's work is specific to identity formation in the United States, as a theoretical rubric their work offers an analytic to assess the process of grouping and discriminating peoples in societies such as Thailand, which share common trends of applying skin color, class, and immigration politics toward national selfhood.

In contrast to race, I use ethnicity as an endonymic nomenclature, which derives from the reflection of self-ascribed groups of people, rather than a name given to peoples. Tambiah expresses the collective, yet internally derived identification quite clearly in his orientation of ethno-nationalist violence in *Leveling Crowds*: "Ethnic identity is above all a collective identity: we are self-proclaimed Sinhalese, Malays, Ibos, Thais, and so on."[8] In this regard, ethnicity is an internally derived social marker, which falls prey to just as many primordialist claims as those that are externally derived. The difference between race and ethnicity lies in who does the naming.

Both ethnicity and race have been used in academic analyses of Thailand. Thomas Hylland Eriksen reviews the connections between ethnicity and Thai nationalism and draws upon the seminal work of Michael Moerman.[9] For Eriksen, cultural difference between two groups "is not the decisive feature of ethnicity." Instead,

> the groups must have a minimum of contact with each other, and they must entertain ideas of each other as being culturally different from themselves. If these conditions are not fulfilled, there is no ethnicity, for *ethnicity is essentially an aspect of a relationship*, not a property of a group [emphasis added].[10]

Thus, "Tai" and "Malay" refer to shared relationships that come from *emic* references and relations, whereas racial labels such as *khaek* are imposed terms used to aggregate peoples from different groups into one category (South Asians, Malays, etc.).[11] The importance of assessing ethnicity together with race not only applies to the data, but extends to the way in which that data is collected by the scholar.

In Thailand, people with dark skin pigmentation suffer from a racial bias that is endemic to the region. Jan Weisman found through her dissertation research that *khaek* had particular physical connotations that included a dark complexion, an aquiline nose, and, in men, facial and/or body hair.[12] Racial inequality is not a cause of the bias, but rather an outcome of closely associated socio-economic and political processes with people having darker skin colors. However, social scientists studying Thai society often place racial inequalities under a larger umbrella of ethnicity and apply the inequalities to an assimilation model, (e.g., minority ethnicities retain inequalities because they have not assimilated into society yet). Although the focus of their studies is Thailand, we find a problematic classification of ethnicity under an assimilation model, which derives from the legacy of an "ethnicity paradigm" prevalent in the studying of racial inequalities within the United States.

Distinctions between ethnicity and race reflect the perception of the scholar as much as the peoples perceived. Whereas my distinction between ethnicity and race is ultimately one of power relations and issues of signification, some scholars distinguish these terms on biological and static suppositions. One applicable lesson drawn from Edward Said's seminal work *Orientalism* is that scholars are part of the knowledge-making exercises of identity. Through the social scientific work of scholars, the rhetoric of a modernity transforms the ways in which alterity is perceived, understood, and acted upon.[13] One acute manner of this is through the sociology of the United States. Sociologists in the United States produced social schemes and models from the greater context of their particular modernity to understand the role of immigrants in U.S. society.

During the 1920s, U.S. social scientists used ethnicity as the initial taxonomy of peoples in an effort to oppose biological frames of categorization. It was through theories of ethnicity that race became a *social* category. Yet, what was consistent among scholars such as Nathan Glazer and Daniel P. Moynihan, working within what Omi and Winant consider the ethnicity paradigm, was their focus on immigration patterns and the application of assimilation models (or as Omi and Winant express it, the dynamics of incorporating minority groups into the dominant society), which ultimately played into a *bootstrap* rhetoric. Scholars explained that the inequalities between ethnic groups were due to internal problems; the fault was a deficiency in Mexican culture or Korean traditional values, not the result of external variables or systemic racial projects and policies, which erected and/or sustained levels of inequality.

Bootstrap rhetoric aside, the fallacy with the assimilation model was the very idea of assimilation, a veiled process of recasting people along a sliding scale of normative identity. People were compared against an unspoken category of quintessential U.S. culture, namely, Whiteness. In this case, Israel Zangwill's 1908 vision of a melting pot melted in one direction: toward a whiter United States. However, this lens was not merely applied inward on U.S. society, but outward as well. The ethnicity paradigm was reflected in the work of U.S. scholars specializing in regions outside of the Americas who used the assimilation model in different social contexts.[14] In Thailand, one of the earliest assimilation models constructed by U.S. scholars was for Chinese immigrants.

Serving initially as a missionary in Thailand, Kenneth Landon is one of the earliest U.S. scholars to write about the Chinese living in Thailand. At the same time Robert E. Park's ethnicity theory was becoming popular in the United States, Kenneth Landon published his accounts of Thai society. According to Landon, during the 1930s the Siamese State determined that "turning Chinese into Thai, requiring generations, needed to be speeded up," which Landon found achievable by means of the economic arena.[15] Landon's assessment of Chinese assimilation was continued in future scholarship, which also pointed to the social discrimination against the Thai Chinese and Chinese peoples.[16] G. William Skinner provides one of the most comprehensive assessments of the Chinese in Thai Society. However, despite Skinner's claim that Chinese immigrants were encumbered by racist policies, he adopts an assimilation model to assess Chinese status in Thai society.

> This survey indicates that local political factors have considerable influence on the course of assimilation of an immigrant minority such as the Chinese in Siam. The very nature of the political elite has been of great importance in Thailand. That it has always been Thai has stimulated Chinese assimilation to Thai society throughout the country's history. That it acquired a *racist bias* early in the twentieth century retarded assimilation. And that the new power elite of the second Phibun administration lacked a stable economic base encouraged a pro-assimilationist rapprochement with the Chinese merchant class [emphasis added].[17]

Despite the fact that his social analysis uses an assimilation model, Skinner's contribution to the study of the Chinese of Thailand is invaluable. However, what we find in Landon's and Skinner's accounts is a theoretical lens of racial relations endemic to the United States.

Another eminent scholar of Thailand, Charles Keyes, considers ethnicity to be rooted in culture and shared descent, a perception that corresponds with scholars who work within the ethnicity paradigm and see ethnicity as the dominant lens.[18] In 1976, Keyes writes,

> Thus far, I have attempted to establish that ethnic groups must be conceived of as a type of descent group whose members validate their claim to shared descent by pointing to cultural attributes which they believe they hold in common. Ethnic groups, unlike races, are not mutually exclusive, but are structured in segmentary hierarchies with each more inclusive segment subsuming ethnic groups which were contrastive at another level.[19]

Keyes's important study critiques the early sociological use of race, in which race served as a biological marker, and argues in favor of a fluid marker of personhood that accounts for intersecting identities and commonalities. Nonetheless, Keyes adopts an assimilation model in assessing the different Thai ethnicities, as seen in table 5.1.

Since the 1920s, U.S. scholars have used assimilation models to explain Thai demographics. In these accounts, Chinese, Malay, and different nations such as

Table 5.1 **Keyes's National Ethnoregional and Ethnic Composition of the Population of Thailand**

Category	% of Total pop.
"Thai"	
"TRUE THAI" (*Thai Thae*)	
Domestic speakers of Standard Thai (not including Sino-Thai)	9.0
Central Thai	27.0
"REGIONAL THAI" (*Thai Phak Tangtang*)	
Isan (Northeastern Thai)	27.0
Khon Muang (Northern Thai)	10.0
Khon Pak Tai (Southern Thai)	8.0
Other Tai Speakers	1.0
"ASSIMILATED THAI"	
Sino-Thai (*Luk Chin*); domestic speakers of Standard Thai	6.5
Domestic speakers of Mon-Khmer languages; bilingual Standard Thai	2.5
Total	91.0
"Ethnic" ("Problematic Thai")	
Chinese (*Chin*)	2.0
Thai-Malay	6.0
Hill Tribes (*chao khao*)	1.0
Total	9.0
"Not Thai"	
Refugees (mainly Burmese)	na
Expatriate Workers (mainly Burmese)	na
Illegal Migrants (mainly from Burma)	na[i]

[i] Charles Keyes "Ethnicity and the Nation-States of Thailand and Vietnam," in *Challenging the Limits: Indigenous Peoples of the Mekong Region*, ed. Prasit Leepreecha, Don McCaskill, and Kwanchewan Buadaeng, 13–53 (Chiang Mai: Mekong Press, 2008), 25.

the Karen or Shan (which together are enveloped under the racial project "hill tribes" [*chao khao*]) are placed within an assimilation model, a method of analysis that is unable to account for racial inequalities. Scholars such as Chan Kwok Bun and Tong Chee Kiong alter the traditional parameters of assimilation and de-centralize normative identity. They argue that assimilation is a two-way process, by which Chinese become Thai and Thai become Chinese. The discussion of fluid identities for both Thai and Chinese corrects one of the problems with the assimilation model. However, the continued absence of race from their discussion prevents a full account of identity formations and relations in contexts like Thailand.[20]

Scholars are just as affected by racial projects as the peoples they study. One of the repercussions of this is an academic tendency to avoid or misrepresent the subject of race. This tendency must be shelved in the examination of the conflict within the southernmost provinces. Thai society contains racial projects and racial formations, and these processes are at the heart of identity politics that drive the conflict.

Thai Identity and Religion

Political scientist Surin Pitsuwan writes extensively on the importance of Islam in the Malay Muslim resistance to the Thai State. The greatest frame of his argument is a religious one; Malay Muslims suffer under a State yoked to Buddhist cosmogony. Surin asserts that Islam is the "strongest element of the Malay Muslims' identity. It is also the element that most decisively isolates them from the mainstream of the nation's population."[21] In the three southernmost provinces, the fusion of Malay identity with Islam happened through centuries of Malay Islamic governance and the government's contestation with a Siamese Buddhist kingdom.[22] Surin also places strong emphasis on the role of race. He writes, "The racial tension grows in such an atmosphere and religious differences become the dividing line between the two conflicting groups."[23] While Surin considers race and religion as being separate, he views both elements as being at the root of the Malay Muslims' resistance in southern Thailand.

I seek to advance Surin's premise with the argument that the identifications of Islam and Malay ethnicity displace Malay Muslims from Thai society on two levels because they are neither ethnically Tai, nor religiously Buddhist. Historically, Malay identity does not necessarily denote Islam, although this may be a popular assumption in contemporary Thai and Malay societies (some of the earliest inhabitants of the area that now constitute three border provinces were Malay Buddhists). Instead, Malay is an ambiguous term that at best is difficult to locate. At the onset of their edited collection of Malay-identity essays, Timothy P. Barnard and Hendrik M. J. Maier confront this with their initial question,

> What is the meaning of "Malay"? The question seems strange and unnecessary. "Malays" live in Malaysia, where they are the major population group. "Malays" are found in Indonesia, in Sumatra and

along the coast of Indonesian Borneo. At first glance, it all seems very straightforward, but for centuries definitions, boundaries, and origins of this word in the world of Southeast Asia have proved elusive, and it seems unlikely that the word will acquire any greater precision in the future.[24]

Malay is an ambiguous and fluid term, which may explain the power context has over it. Within Thailand, the identification of Malay becomes one of two means of differentiating and isolating Malay Muslims from the dominant society. The other means is the Islamic affiliation connected to Malay. This double-bonded alienation is similar to postcolonial feminist Trinh Minh-ha's notion of the "triple-bind," in which women of the Third World are oppressed under the colonial structure and then further marginalized through their race and gender.[25] It is through the intersecting marginal identities of class, race, and gender that Vietnamese women are obscured and isolated. Likewise, the intersecting marginal identities of ethnicity and religion place Malay Muslims on the fringe of their society.

Franz Fanon and other postcolonial scholars argue that racialization is the handmaiden of colonial rhetoric, and this would coincide with the thoughts of Malay Muslim intellectuals such as Surin, who critique the Thai State for the imposition of colonial policies.[26] However, the internal-colonial structure is not what prevents Malay Muslims from gaining acceptance in Thai society.[27] It is the legacy that comes from their previous colonial status. Malay Muslims suffer alienation principally through their racial formation, which encompasses ethnicity and religion. This process began over a century ago, but is sustained through racial projects. It is also further complicated due to the self-ascribed nature of Malay Muslim identification.

Malay Muslims view their ethnicity and religion as one and the same, a trait also found in some Buddhist traditions, such as Tibetan Buddhism. To ask a Tibetan if s/he is Buddhist often elicits a response that, at best, patronizes the questioner. For most Tibetans, their identity inherently implies a Buddhist identity, especially those living in diaspora. This association of Tibetan identity with Buddhism conflicts with other Tibetan identities, such as the Khache (Tibetan: *kha che*), who are Tibetan Muslims.[28] We find this collusion of ethnicity and religion within Burmese Buddhism as well. The Young Men's Buddhist Association's slogan in 1906, "To be Burmese is to be Buddhist," reflects a coterminous boundary of religious and national identity in Myanmar.[29] In a similar fashion the three border provinces of southern Thailand are predominantly Muslim, but the region also contains Malay Buddhists and Christians. In reviewing the issues surrounding the conflict in the three border provinces, the National Reconciliation Report detailed the local distinctions between Malays and Thais.

When villagers in the area are asked who they are, the answer they give is "Muslim Malay," which means ethnic Malay of Islamic faith. Some identify themselves as "Islamic person," in a tone of voice that shows pride and indicates a high degree of religious devoutness. Some reply that they are *"aukhae nayu"* (a Malay), not *"aukhae siyae"* or *"aukhae siyam"* (a Siamese). It is possible that they are afraid of saying "a Thai" because in the understanding of some people, "Thais or Siamese are Buddhists." Answering *"aukhae siyae"* might make that person guilty of *"murtad,"* or apostasy. In this sense, language and religion have long and intensively shaped the identity of Malay Muslims in the area.[30]

How a Malay Muslim sees him/herself is indicative of his/her place in Thai society. In the three southern provinces, Malay Muslims view their religion and language as critical components of their identity, a collective identification that is simultaneously separate and distinct from the national identity. Forms of alterity operate within the national consciousness and manifest as racial projects. One such racial project is the pejorative identification of Malay Muslims: *khaek.*

Different societies exhibit varying means of constructing and classifying race. In the United States, politicized discourse on biology continues to determine racial classifications. One prominent example of this is the infamous law of hypo-descent, or the "one-drop rule" that posits one drop of non-White blood occludes that person from the category of Whiteness.[31] In Latin American countries such as Brazil, racial classification is more ternary than biological; racial formation is contingent upon appearance and economic status.[32]

In Thailand, however, both biological and physical elements determine a person's race and whether that person is more or less than "a hundred percent Thai." The offspring of a non-Thai and a Thai is identified as *khon khrung* (half person) due to inheriting only half of his/her genes from a Thai. There are also categories that are contingent upon skin pigmentation: *khon khaek* (brown people), *khon kham nigon* (black people).[33] These terms are fluid and their application is not uniform throughout Thailand; they are not based on shared heritage or culture, but are, rather, identity markers that aggregate groups of people together.

Although Buddhist identity is not the defining characteristic in these appellations, it is an important identity marker that allows different ethnicities to qualify in one of the varying degrees of acceptance in Thai society. Thai Chinese Buddhists are the largest non-Thai Buddhist group and retain a distinct racial identity (*lūk čhin*). Although they suffered from prejudice and discrimination throughout the early and mid-twentieth century, in the 1990s Thai Chinese Buddhists gained status owing to their economic success and the corresponding changes within the popular culture.[34] A large part of this increased status was due to a shift in class relations. Chinese businessmen played an integral role in

the creation of a new middle class that emerged in Thailand during the 1980s
and 1990s. This period is sometimes referred to as the "Age of the Thai
Godfathers" (*čhao phō*).[35] In addition, much of the Thai pride and public display
of Thai Chinese identity in the twenty-first century parallels China's global rise
in power and its increased prestige.[36] However, economics was only part of the
Thai Chinese Buddhist success. In this reworking of Thai popular culture, the
shared spiritual rituals and beliefs of Buddhism also provided an important
bridge for the Chinese Buddhists that will never be a part of dialogue between
the Malay Muslims and Thai popular culture.[37]

In Thailand, the religious identity of Malay Muslims becomes an identifier
that excludes them from Thai society. This division is predicated on the normative socio-religious identity: Thai Buddhist. In this, both the Malay Muslim and
the Thai Buddhist identity work in tandem, a hierarchy of one (the former)
behind the other (the latter). This is comparable to other hierarchical social dia-
lectics that include such distinctions as Orient and Occident, Black and White,
and primitive and civilized. The main impetus for the invention of "Orient" was
so that Eurasians could construct their own identity, the "Occident."

Examining either side of the social dialectic furthers our understanding of how
such identification leads to the process of alienation and subsequent marginalized
identity. As in any hierarchy of difference, the unspoken normative used is the
dominant identity. In the United States, for example, Whiteness is the normative
identity from which other identities are measured. Identity is always constructed
through opposition to another or, as the eminent Thai historian Thongchai explains,
in the process of creating Thainess, one also creates "negative identification."[38] In
order for a Thai to designate Malay Muslims as lacking in "Thainess" s/he must con-
ceive a model for comparison. In this case, the comparison is to Thai Buddhists.
Thais place great importance upon their ethnic and religious identities, which often
blur into one identity through racial designation.[39]

The racial designation *khaek* encompasses not simply physical attributes, but
religious markers as well. Historian Patrick Jory finds that, near the close of the
nineteenth century, Bangkok elites employed such terms as "*Melayu*" (Malay) and
the derogatory classifier *khaek* when referring to Malay Muslims. The latter term
is a word that "signified people of a different religion."[40] The religious implications
of *khaek* can go much further than a negation of a dominant identity. With his
more recent work in southern Thailand, Charles Keyes locates the association
between *khaek* and the legions of Māra, who in Buddhist traditions is typified as
the Buddha's antagonist. In figure 5.1, the scene of the Buddha's trials before
enlightenment comes to life on the ordination wall of Wat Watchimawat in
Songkhla Province, a southern province adjacent to Pattani. Keyes observes,

> My attention was drawn to the 'Destruction of Māra' (in Thai *Māra*
> *phacôn*) because the cohort of Māra includes not only beings that are

Figure 5.1 "The Defeat of Māra," from nineteenth-century temple painting at Wat Matchimawat, Songkhla, Southern Thailand. Photo courtesy of Charles Keyes.

clearly demons, but also humans. Among these are dark figures of several bearded figures who clearly represent Malays or South Asians whom Thai call *khāēk*.[41]

The color-coded images reflect not only a Thai, but also a South Asian bias toward light skin pigmentation.[42] Initially, the term *khaek* implied a guest or a stranger; however, in contemporary times it denotes peoples who are not part of the Thai dominant society.[43] While the art history of the mural deserves further study, the religious symbolism is pronounced enough to recognize its social implications. Here, the dialectic in play is the Buddha and his nemesis, Māra, who stand as visual reference points to the lighter skinned Buddhists and the *khaeks* of southern Thailand.

Racial formations are sustained through racial projects, some of which are overseen by the Thai State. For the Thai State, the national promotion of Thainess is simultaneously a promotion of Thai Buddhist identity. One example comes from the Office of National Buddhism, which, among other activities, publishes and distributes Buddhist doctrine handbooks to international hotels in southern, northern, and central Thailand. International guests often find the renowned Buddhist monk Phra Payutto's Buddhist doctrine handbook in their top dresser drawer as the intended replacement for the Christian Gideon's Bible.[44] The ONB furnishes this handbook as a national promotion of Thai values. This presents more than an association between Buddhism and Thainess; it creates an implied connection. This implicit connection between Buddhism and Thainess is also found in Thai literature. Chart Korbjitti's novel *The Judgment*, one of the more popular Thai novels of the late twentieth century, is a biting social critique of popular assumptions and beliefs about village life and Thai Buddhism. The protagonist is socially transformed from the village's prodigal monk to the village pariah, based on false assumptions about his behavior. However, Chart's portrayal of a Thai village lacks religious diversity, as his version of the typical village life is Buddhist. This is exemplified in Chart's use of an old Thai proverb to contextualize his main character's (Fak's) need to disrobe: "Rain will come, shit will out [*sic*], children will be born and monks will disrobe: these four events no man can prevent."[45] This association between Thainess and Buddhism may change with the development of alternative ethnoscapes and mediascapes. Thai Internet chat rooms and forums debate the connection between Thainess and Buddhism and reflect a growing consciousness of the ethnic/religious collapse of distinctions in Thainess. One such example is the thread entitled *"khon thai tang pēn khon phut?"* (Do Thais Have To Be Buddhist?). However, the presence of such e-communities and their queries may simply offer a better reflection of what has always existed—alternative voices to normativity.[46]

The subject of Thainess is evoked often in my conversations with Buddhist monks in the three southernmost provinces. In one instance, I asked Ačhān Subin, the secretariat to the Pattani *sangha* at Wat Mutjalin in Nongčhik District, why there were more *wat* in Khokpo District, Pattani than in any other district in Pattani. He replied, "There are more Thai people and the area is bigger. And, there are more villages there, more Thai people."

In an effort to clarify his answer, I asked, "Thai people, as in Thai Buddhists? Or, do you just mean Thai people?" Ačhān Subin answered,

> Thai Buddhists. When I refer to Thai people, I do not mean Thai Muslims. They are referred to as Thais by the government, but they are not real Thai people, because they are forced to be Thai citizens. Real Thai people should be Thai Buddhists, and they [Thai Muslims] are not Buddhist.[47]

Although the context of the conversation clearly denotes Malay Muslims, Ačhān Subin did not specify which Thai Muslims are not "real Thai," and, thus, leaves unanswered his view of Thai Muslims like General Sonthi, who have a Persian background, and are not Malay.[48] However, his view of Malay Muslims exemplifies the power of religious identifications in the Thai normative identity. The Thai State's push to assimilate marginalized identities is more than simply a push for minorities to make a secular decision concerning citizenship; the decision to assimilate also confirms one's citizenship, which inherently carries Buddhist implications.

Race is embedded within the Thai social structure. It serves to justify the inequalities between Thai Buddhists and marginal groups such as *khon farang* (white people), *khon khaek* (brown people), *khon kham nigon* (black people) and others. The umbrella of peoples under the term *khaek* reveal a much broader spectrum than simply religion and point to a socio-political grouping of people into a minority category. Tourists and frequent travelers to Thailand may notice that service industries, such as Thai Airways and others, prefer to employ lighter skin Thais instead of darker skin Thais, who are generally Malay, Lao, or Cambodian and may or may not be Muslim. In Thailand, white skin is considered beautiful. This bias is not an adoption of Eurasian prejudices, but a result of a continuous interplay between global and indigenous prejudices. Thais who work outside and toil under the sun have darker skin and traditionally represented a lower socio-economic class compared with the lighter skin upper-class Thais who did not have to partake in manual labor. The global media has only reinforced this perspective.

Economics is a factor that contributes to violence; it also becomes an identification that benefits or hinders a group's social mobility.[49] Thai racial categories include an economic hierarchy in which Malay Muslims are perceived as poor people.[50] During the 1990s, nearly 70% of Malay Muslim youth were unemployed, and 40% of Malay Muslims had to work outside of their villages.[51] According to the National Statistical Office, the average monthly income levels in Pattani and Yala provinces were moderate compared to the seventy-four other provinces; Narathiwat was statistically much lower, as seen in table 5.2.

What the statistics in table 5.2 do not reveal is the vast disparity between the wealthy and poor living within these provinces. Malay Muslims are most commonly the poorest social group in the three provinces. To overcome such oversights or misleading statistics, the Office of the National Economic and Social Development Board provides more detail. It was determined that nearly 45% of the population in Narathiwat lived below the poverty line (earning less than $20 USD a month) in 2005.[52]

Southern Thais living outside martial law often associate darker skin tones, Islamic customs, and poverty with Malay Muslim identity. Skin color, religion,

Table 5.2 **Ranking of Average Income for Southernmost Provinces in Relation to 77 Provinces**

Province	2000 (2543)	2002 (2545)	2004 (2547)
Pattani	26th	33rd	32nd
Yala	33rd	32nd	45th
Narathiwat	64th	61st	66th[ii]

[ii] Information derived from National Statistical Office, "Rāydai-rāyčhāy čhangwat" [Provincial Income and Expenditures], (Bangkok: Prime Minister Office, 2003).

and low financial status have become an amalgam of intersecting social characteristics, an amalgam that also perpetually reinforces the Malay Muslims' sense of inferiority. Both Thai Buddhists and Malay Muslims associate the Malay Muslim identity as being outside civic nationalism. Malay Muslims' feelings of marginality in the civil sector are due largely to historical factors.

Historical Influences

When anthropologist Walter Mignolo scrutinized Immanuel Kant's categorization of Eurasians into discrete groups of "pagans" and "foreigners," he concluded: "Thus, God was and still is an empty signifier you can appropriate and fill to your taste in private life or in the public sphere."[53] Reviewing the historical application of the divine in the Eurasian context, we find the appropriations are limitless in terms of legitimating the dehumanization of peoples and practices. If we place Mignolo's point within a wider context, we find that all religious traditions, not merely monotheistic ones, serve as active fulcrums for racializing peoples, habits, and dispositions. The formation of citizenship with religion was most prominent in Thailand during the Eurasian colonization of Southeast Asia. Eurasian colonialists dominated Southeast Asia during the mid- and late 1800s, and it was through their colonial exertions that the Siamese reconstituted their borders and their conceptions of nation.[54] The ultimate development of the Thai normative identity (and the exclusion of Malay Muslims) became cosmopolitan in scope, pulling from early South Asian notions of ideology and integrating colonial influences within the local framework of Siamese society. It was also a process that formed the basis of the current conflict in the southernmost provinces.

Siamese society had contained racial formations prior to the influences of the British and French colonialists; however, the impetus behind much of the *contemporary* Thai racial formations originated during the Eurasian colonial era. Near the end of the nineteenth century, British and French colonial forces pressured the Siamese government to rethink its geographic boundaries, international image, and social values, all of which were interconnected under global politics. During this period, Eurasian powers exerted an incredible influence over the cultural (as in meaning-making) fabric of Southeast Asian societies. Among these influences were new forms of alterity, which was a necessary condition of empire-building as Ann Laura Stoler and Frederick Cooper explain,

> The most basic tension of empire lies in what has become a central, if now obvious, point of recent colonial scholarship: namely, that the *otherness* of colonized persons was neither inherent nor stable; his or her difference had to be defined and maintained [emphasis added].[55]

To define and maintain colonial differences, French and British strategies focused on concepts of race. According to Paul Gilroy, race lacked clarity in relation to nationality; this ambiguity became an asset in the colonial nation-building process.[56] In one of many tense diplomatic exchanges with foreigners, the Siamese State received French claims of sovereignty over Siamese regions based upon the race of the Siamese territories' occupants. The French rationalized that the non-Siamese population fell under the jurisdiction of France. The rhetoric of race, which included religion, became a common means of justifying colonial jurisdiction. The Siamese State was acutely aware of colonial identity politics and their need to assert sovereignty over their territories. The State issued a barrage of educational and bureaucratic reforms that re-conceptualized what it meant to be "Siamese" (*kwāmpensiyam*). The peoples who fell under the umbrella of "Siamese," and the land they occupied, would legally become part of Siam. Siamese nation-building, which inherently sought to legitimatize territory, became an exercise of defending and incorporating marginal groups into citizenship. Under Siamese rule, people became Siamese/Thai solely for the sake of retaining sovereignty.

Looking at the historical nuances of this conversion, David Streckfuss notes, "At its most basic level, this creative adaptation of race categories was achieved by merging the concepts of Thai nationality, as in a Thai national (*chon chaat thai*), the Thai race (*chaat, chu'a chaat*), and Thai citizenship (*sanchaat thai*), within the single, malleable, term *chaat*."[57] This merging of nationality and citizenship with race highlights the mutability of race as a category. However, what Streckfuss fails to note is that, within this new concept of *chāt* (race), there was a crucial religious dimension: Thai Buddhism.

Exploring the etymology of *chāt* is necessary in order to understand the identity politics of Siam's nation-building. As Streckfuss already points out, the word *chāt* is used to indicate race, ethnicity, and Thai nationalism, all three fused together to create one identification. Thai Buddhism, as it is practiced, derives much from early South Asian Brahmanical and Buddhist principles. One illustration of this is the word *chāt*. Like many Thai contemporary words, the term *chāt* derives from the Sanskrit—*jāti*—a word used to indicate a person's birth, rank, caste, family, race, and lineage.[58]

In South Asia, the Brahmanical *varṇa* system or caste system (to borrow the Portuguese term, *casta*), was developed around concepts of purity and pollution, sacred and mundane. One's *jāti* reflected not merely a social or economic status, but also a religious one. Religious status originated from a cosmogonic hymn, the "Puruṣasukta" of the Ṛg Veda. In a later reworking found in the *Śatapatha Brāhmaṇa*, a text scholars date between 900–600 B.C.E., four separate groups of people were given symbolic reference to the anthropomorphic deity, Prajāpati.[59] The *brāhmaṇa* (priests) came from the head, the *kṣatriya* (warriors) from the chest, the *vaiśya* (merchants) from his arms, and the *śudra* (servants) from his legs. In addition to linking function with status, this hierarchy was based on a racial formation. Siddhartha Gautama was not immune to socio-religious hierarchy. Donald Lopez notes that

> In describing the buddhas of the past, he [Siddhartha Gautama] said a buddha is never born into a vaiśya or śūdra family, but only as the son of brahmans or kṣatriyas, depending on which of the two is more highly honored by society at the time of his birth—the implication being, of course, that he himself chose to be born as a kṣatriya because it was the superior caste of his day.[60]

From the Brahmans to the buddhas, those who claimed Aryan ancestry have been associated with the lighter skin color and, correspondingly, with a higher social status, a social distinction still evident in contemporary times. It is implicit that the *jāti* system, which merged social, economic, and spiritual status, and exerted a very tenacious and hegemonic hold on South Asian marital customs and commercial relationships.[61] As colonialism took hold of the subcontinent in the nineteenth century, *jāti* was used to refer to "nations."[62]

This Sanskrit term *jāti*, together with its religio-political context, became the means by which King Vajiravudh (r. 1910–25) promoted Thai notions of citizenry and the subtext of race. Owing partly to his education at the Royal Military Academy Sandhurt and in Christ Church at Oxford, King Vajiravudh conceptualized the three ideological canons (*lak thai*) of Siam as "Nation (*chāt*), Religion (*sāsanā*), and Monarchy (*phramahākasat*)," a striking similarity to England's "God, King, and Country."[63] He presented the three ideological canons in a speech to his nationalist party, the Wild Tigers Corps, on May 26, 1911, fusing together the principles of religion and nationalism under citizenship.[64] In his famous speech to the Wild Tiger Corps, Vajiravudh used religion as a synonym for Thai Buddhism.[65]

> The second element fundamental to the survival of the nation in Vajiravudh's discourse was the Buddhist religion.... Vajiravudh described religion as an essential and necessary form of discipline and went so far as to suggest that those members of Thai society who abandoned the Buddhist faith were not really Thai.[66]

Vajiravudh made the national identity contingent upon religion, a derivation from biological suppositions, but nonetheless exclusive in the peoples it would permit into the nation-building *imaginaire*. It is in King Vajiravudh's introduction of the three canons, which later serve as the Thai national flag, that religion serves as a synonym for the Buddhist tradition.

Eurasian colonial powers took pride in their own legal systems and viewed the legislative branch as evidence of a country's departure from savagery, a category reserved for particular races. Conversely, because legality became the means of demonstrating civilization, it also became a justification for labeling other countries as primitive. Matters of oppression and race manifest in jurisprudence in which racial categories create legal vulnerabilities for groups of people. In her examination of Thai family law, historian Tamara Loos argues that a conflation of Siamese Buddhism and State power was codified under Siamese law. This was the pivotal means by which Siam proved its "civilized" status to foreign powers.[67] During the late nineteenth and early twentieth centuries, the Siamese State became acutely aware of the international relevance of its legal system. At the same time, it was deeply invested in the performance of civilized discourse.

One example of this derives from *siwilai*, the Thai cognate of the English word "civilized." Thongchai Winichakul persuasively argues that the racial discourse of civilized people (*siwilai*), in contrast to the jungle people (*chaopā*), evolved partly out of colonial anthropology in the nineteenth century.[68] The civilized always needs its antithesis, and as James C. Scott poignantly explains, this dialectic is invested in the State *imaginaire*. "Barbarians are, then, a state effect; they are inconceivable except as a 'position' vis-à-vis the state."[69] But, it was the manner of what was to be the civilized that took on a *farang* allure in nineteenth-century Siam. In addition to appropriating the language and rhetoric of the Eurasian colonizers, the Siamese intelligentsia asserted their superiority over marginal identities by other means. They sought to appear civilized, or rather, more similar to the appearance of Eurasians.[70] Hence, the Siamese constructed categories using differences in education, attire, and habits in order to inscribe superiority. It was during this period that the Siamese adopted the Eurasian method of eating with a fork and spoon.

The Siamese monastic system was easily subsumed into this hierarchical distinction between civilized and primitive. King Mongkut (r. 1851–68) and his son and successor, King Chulalongkorn (r. 1868–1910) oversaw measures that favored the logic and philosophical aspects of Siamese Buddhism. They did all they could to suppress what was deemed popular and superstitious forms revolving around Buddhist cosmology, ancestor worship, and localized tales and beliefs.[71] Siamese Buddhism became "part and parcel" of Siamese racial identity; as such, it was protected by the State. Modeling the Eurasian Enlightenment pursuits that heralded reason above faith, Siamese kings envisioned a Buddhism that was based on logic and devoid of superstition.[72] This demonstrated one of the means by which the *sangha* was an "active shaper" of Thai society and falls within the classical-turned-modern narrative of development and nation-building throughout Asia.[73]

One corollary to the Siamese State actions is found in its neighbors to the west. King Thibaw Min (r. 1859–1916) used the civilized/barbarian discourse in his attempts to rally the Burmese to protect the nation, such as his "Declaration

of War against Burma" and "Royal War Order," which combined the integrity of
Buddhism with that of economic and political stability. However, unlike the
Siamese, the Burmese nation was under attack by the British. The barbarians
became the English, and the desire became the preservation of Buddhism.[74] The
Burmese and Siamese circumstances were quite different, especially with the
formal British colonization of Burma, but both States saw Buddhist identity as a
viable means of acquiring civility and recognition. Thai Buddhism became a
social mechanism that denoted the dispositions of the popular classes, a means
of accumulating cultural capital, whereas other religious traditions became the
dispositions of the disenfranchised classes. In this light, monastic education
became a means of grooming Siamese to enter civilized society. Peleggi notes
that young males who matured from novice to monkhood went from being called
khon dip (raw person) to *khon suk* (ripe person).[75]

Under the newly formed religious and colonial framework of Chulalongkorn's
(Rama V's) State, a normative Siamese identity was constructed, leaving out
the Malay Muslim identity. During this process of identity-building, the
Siamese State assessed the racial demographics of the three southernmost
provinces. In 1906, these were collectively referred to as Monthon Patani. The
Siamese State separated the southern people into three categories: Malay,
Siamese, and Chinese. While the Chinese designation was tied to language and
immigration, Siamese and Malay designations were predicated on language and
religion (table 5.3).

Even though Chulalongkorn made efforts to include Malay Muslims in
his new nation-state, he could not change the present structural biases.[76]
Malay Muslim identity was especially marginalized due to its ethnic and
religious differences from Siamese Buddhism. In addition, it occupied a
spatial and linguistic identity distinct from the Lao, Cambodian, Vietnamese,
and even Chinese immigrants, the majority of whom adhered to Buddhist
principles.[77] One of Chulalongkorn's most trusted Buddhist servants, the
Minister of the Interior Chao Phraya Yomarat, in his initial reports, revealed
the following:

Table 5.3 **Official Race Statistics for Southernmost Provinces in 1906**

Race	Raw Population	% of Population
Malay	208,076	85.96%
Siamese	30,597	12.64%
Chinese	3,332	1.38%[iii]

[iii] Information cited from Chavivun Prachuabmoh, "The Role of Women in Maintaining Ethnic
Identity and Boundaries: A Case of Thai-Muslims (The Malay Speaking Group) in Southern Thailand,"
(PhD diss., Department of Anthropology, University of Hawaii, 1980), 32.

... Siam's leaders *did* think of the Malay Muslim population as foreign and backward compared to Bangkok, which are key characteristics of a colonial state's rationale for rule. Siam's view of Malay Muslims as uncivilized and foreign may have had its origins in native elitism, but the attitude toward these differences was newly deployed to Siam's advantage.[78]

While we can find evidence of racist tendencies against Siamese Lao or Chinese immigrants in King Vajiravudh's *The Jews of the Orient* (1914),[79] it is Chao Phraya Yomarat's sentiments regarding the Malay Muslim provinces ("semi-barbaric states") that reflect a particularly distinctive conception of Malay Muslims and relegated them outside "Thainess."[80]

Twentieth-Century Developments

Following the advent of modern racial formations, the Thai State applied different measures to assimilate marginal groups within the state borders into the normative structure.[81] As the Thai State developed, so did the intensity of the efforts to homogenize its populace. The twentieth century brought with it a new-found sense of nationhood and a desire to protect and nurture it. This sense of fragility was followed by escalated efforts to assimilate the Malay Muslims within a Buddhist system. The policies led to even greater ethno-religious tensions in the southernmost provinces.

During the twentieth century, language was one of the key instruments for the Thai reconstitution of identity. This reconstitution is framed either as a bootstrap rhetoric of assimilation (through the State), or neo-imperialism (through those speaking against the reconstitution).[82] Different Sino-ethnic groups in the north and central regions (such as the Hokkien, Teochew, or Hainanese) suffered political attacks due to their private language schools and non-Thai surnames.[83] Likewise, Lao and Khmer Siamese in the northeast were told they could no longer converse or conduct business in their local languages. These were all public forms of identifying the normative Thai identity on the basis of linguistic distinctions.[84] The same was true for Malay Muslims, who were forced to learn Thai and to attend non-Islamic schools. This method of assimilation proved to be largely unproductive in the three southernmost provinces. In Pattani Province during the 1970s, Chavivun Prachuabmoh noted the anchor religiosity had on Malay Muslim identity,

> The Muslims themselves in theory distinguish *ada'* (or *adat* in standard Malay)—the Malay tradition or custom—from *ugamo*—the Islamic religion. In their belief, any behavior or institution connected with reli-

gion cannot be changed since it is considered to be *doso*—wrongdoing; against God's will.[85]

Although custom was fluid, religion was not and, according to Prachuabmoh, most Thai Malay customs were already linked with Islam. Thai minority groups such as the Chinese, Lao, and Khmer suffered alienation from normative Thais primarily due to ethnic differences, which encompassed distinct histories, traditions, languages, and habits. Despite their different languages and (retained) different customs, these minority groups largely consisted of Buddhist adherents, which enabled them to achieve a measurable acceptance in Thai society. Perhaps one of the most prominent measuring sticks for the acceptance of marginal identities by a State and society at large was its reaction to interracial marriages.

Anthropologist and historian Ann Laura Stoler found that, in the Dutch-colonized East Indies of the nineteenth century, the most contentious debates about identity revolved around the institution of marriage. While legal disputes over marriage were ostensibly about gender relations and State recognition of a marriage, the legal context and background for discussion was founded in religion. One example comes from the Dutch decree of 1617, which forbade marriages between Christians and non-Christians. Later, this formed the basis for the Dutch Civil Code of 1848, in which ethnic criteria replaced religious criteria.[86] In Thailand, marriages between Thai Buddhists and other Buddhist ethnicities such as Chinese, Vietnamese, the Lao, or Burmese generally did not evoke social unrest or disputes over rites and rituals. However, in the case of interracial marriages between Thai Buddhist and Malay Muslims in the southernmost provinces, social unrest or disputes did occur. In the event of a Muslim-Buddhist marriage, the Chinese or Thai Buddhist spouse would often convert to Islam due to socio-religious pressures.[87] Chavivun Prachuabmoh writes that marriages requiring Islamic conversions do not,

> tie the families into a kinship system since the married persons are likely to be cut off from the original families; either their parents are angry with them or they themselves, because of their conversion to Islam, are no longer permitted to participate in their original family's activities, which may be related to religious rites.[88]

In the event of a Muslim spouse embracing the Buddhist faith, the couple would usually be pressured into moving outside their community of origin to avoid criticism. The anthropologist Louis Golomb notes in the 1970s that central Thais behaved in similar fashion:

> Muslim-Buddhist marriages are quite common in central Thailand. A majority of such alliances are between Muslim men and Buddhist

women, with the wife converting to Islam. Buddhists are far less hesi-
tant about conversion than are Muslims and have no fears of suffering
in hell as a consequence. Where one spouse converts to Islam, the
couple is normally expected to settle in a Muslim community. Should
the Muslim partner of a mixed marriage renounce his or her religion,
the couple will move well outside that partner's community of origin to
avoid criticism.[89]

Abbots from the districts where I conducted my fieldwork could not recall the
last time they witnessed a Muslim converting to Buddhism in their village.
Though all of them concede that this has happened, they claim it has not happened in the last several years (since the beginning of martial law over the southernmost provinces). Buddhist monks explain that this phenomenon is due, in
part, to the taboo in Islam for apostasy. There is no such interdiction in Thai
Buddhism (in fact, there is no specific ceremony or ritual to convert to Thai
Buddhism as opposed to a tradition such as the Korean Chogye Buddhism). In
this sense, an act of apostasy from Islam could signify one's affiliation with Thai
Buddhism. In the deep south, a linguistic way of demonstrating a shift in identity would be to call oneself Siamese (Bahasa Yawi: *aukhae siyae*). However, perhaps the most blatant form of conversion to Thai Buddhism has to do with
relocating the habits of space; frequenting a *wat* and making donations there
relegate the actor to a Buddhist identity among his/her peers.

Pressure to conform to Islamic rules and taboos was much greater in the
southernmost provinces, where Malay Muslims are the majority. Because an
interreligious marriage creates a liminal identity fraught with social pressures
and conflicting obligations, a Thai Buddhist or a Malay Muslim spouse would
convert to achieve marital homogeneity and social acceptance.[90]

Unlike Lao, Vietnamese, and Chinese, the Malay Muslims collectively and
actively resisted State measures to assimilate their identity and lifestyles into
the twentieth-century nation-building. During a fresh wave of proto-nationalism under Field Marshall Phibun Songkhram (Phibun), Malay Muslims were
stripped of their citizenry through educational, legal, and social reforms. Surin
attributed a part of Phibun's ethno-nationalist policies and ideas to his admira-
tion for the Japanese, who at the time were asserting their imperialistic force
throughout Asia. According to Surin, Phibun "created a disturbing concept of
the racist state: the state for the Thai race (*Thai Rathaniyon*). Only cultural fea-
tures of the Thai people of the central region would be tolerated and, indeed,
promoted."

Surin's translation of *thai rathaniyon* as the "Thai race" would better translate
as "cultural mandates," but serves as an example of how the use of culture, an
ambiguous and fluid entity in itself, becomes a means of racializing people.
Under the new mandates, Malay Muslims were no longer allowed to wear their

traditional dress, retain their own Malay-Arabic names, or use their own language.[91] The Thai State's colonial attitude became the catalyst that triggered
Malay Muslims to rebel and commit violence.[92] Phibun became the Prime
Minister in 1938 and began implementing his aggressive policies toward Malay
Muslims shortly after taking office. His policies toward Malay Muslims were a
stark contrast to the position of the Thai Department of Defense which, in 1940,
asserted that "these Vietnamese, Laotians, and Khmers were of the 'same
nationality' as the Thai, 'as if they were of the same blood.'"[93]

The Thai State's relations with Malay Muslims did not dramatically improve
over the course of the following five decades. However, anthropologist Raymond
Scupin notes a shift in governmental policy beginning in the 1960s. At that
time, the Thai State implemented an assimilation policy, which included some
recognition of ethnic diversity. Nonetheless, despite this slight recognition of
diversity, the Thai State discreetly continued to support the dominance of Thai
Buddhist identity.[94]

Since the alienation of Malay Muslims was twofold, Malay Muslims underwent a marginalization unlike most groups in Thailand. One meter for this marginalization is their racial designation, *khaek*. As mentioned earlier, *khaek* is a
racial term that distinguishes people from the dominant majority, that is,, Thai
Buddhists. Anthropologist Chavivun Prachuabmoh notes the Malay Muslim
sensitivity to the term in the 1970s:

> The Thai-educated Muslims are sensitive if they are identified as *khaek*
> by the Thais who are likely to refer to the Muslims by this term. Many
> male Muslim informants told me that at school, they fought with Thai
> students because of this. They felt they were not strangers to Pattani
> and should not be identified as *khaek*. Some also point out that the
> Thais use this term to refer to them with contempt. There is a growing
> feeling among the Thai that they should not use this term to refer to the
> Muslims, at least not to their face. Many lecturers at the local univer-
> sity train their students to refer to Muslims as Thai Muslims and not as
> *khaek*.[95]

Racial signifiers such as *khaek* encompass an alienation conceptualized through
religious and ethnic distinctions.

Such distinctions are apparent within the Malay Muslim educational system.
The Malay Muslim *pondoks* (Malay Islamic education centers) focus on Islamic
education taught in Bahasa Melayu with Arabic script. Because they are important traditional institutions for Malay Muslims, the *pondoks* are a focus of con-
troversy. Public education was a key ingredient to nation-building; Thai Buddhism
was intimately involved in its conception and dissemination. In 1898,
Chulalongkorn's school system was initiated in *wat* throughout Thailand.

According to Prachuabmoh, the extensive education (patterned on the standard Thai curriculum) tends to separate and minimize exposure to the study of Malay, Yawi, and the Koran. Perhaps this is why Malay Muslims view the Thai/Siamese language (Bahasa Melayu: *baso siye*) as a separate and distinct cultural entity.[96]

From the 1960s onward, the Thai State attempted to secularize the *pondok* educational system. It required instructors to teach the national (and Buddhist) rhetoric in the Thai language. These requests are in direct contrast to the functional goals and religious identity of the *pondoks*. Raymond Scupin argues,

> The *pondok* tended to reinforce ethnic and religious differences through symbols and rituals which affected individuals throughout their entire lives. In the process these enculturation rituals created problems for Thai Buddhist legitimacy in the south.[97]

The characteristics of the Thai educational system are symptomatic of a larger and more systemic influence: Thainess.

As the Thai State developed, so did its tactics for using Thai Buddhism to chart levels of assimilation (i.e., delimit the distance minorities stood from the dominant society). We can pull one example from the Wat Srisoda's Dhamma Jarika Project in Chiang Mai. High-ranking Buddhist ecclesiastical officers and the State's Social Welfare Department sent Buddhist monks to teach minority groups and "remote people" (*chon thin*) in northern Thailand. The goal was to "make them realize [that they belong to] the same nation, religion and king, pledging loyalty to the king and the nation as their refuge and worship Buddhism."[98] This was a contemporary extension of the Thammačārik program, which targeted the Meo, Yao, Lisu, Lahu, Akha, Karen, and other nations that could impact the State's security.[99] Vajiravudh's three pillars of Thai nationalism—nation, religion, and monarchy—became the rationale to convert "remote people" into "regular people," through the service of Buddhist monks. (Keyes notes early attempts to convert the different nations proved largely unsuccessful.)[100]

The Thai State's efforts to assimilate the Malay Muslims in the twentieth century only furthered a sense of alienation that has continued until the present day. Conducting fieldwork in the late 1950s, Thomas Fraser notes:

> Because they were, in a sense, a conquered people and because a system of government suitable for Thai villages was imposed upon their culturally different society, the Malays tended to dislike and fear the power of the men who were sent to administer them. Although at present the villager has almost no contact with any part of the administrative hierarchy above his local district and relatively little at the district level, he resents what he feels to be a superior and discriminatory attitude on the part of the officials.[101]

Duncan McCargo's recent work in the three southern provinces reveals that the Thai Malay Muslim sentiments in the 1950s did not improve. Thai Malay Muslims at best tolerate, rather than accept, Thai rule.[102] According to Fanon, groups like the Malay Muslims must decode the systemic inequalities present in their society. Once they recognize this form of racism, they need to alter their inequalities. Fanon's answer was not simply violence, but rather a systemic reworking of the *signification* of people within a society to change the social fabric of classification and to redress the biases of colonialism. This rationale may explain part of the legacy of violence that persists in the southernmost provinces. If we infuse the psychological component of race into the southern conflict, the Malay Muslim violence is a move to refute the assimilatory aura of the Thai State.

Race, Religion, and Violence

The recent surge in violence along the Thai/Malaysian border stems from racial inequalities there that are predicated on religious and ethnic identifications. Both national and international media stress the lack of a unified voice for the current insurrection; however, the militants' voices and motivations are clearly presented in their choice of targets and victims.[103]

On February 18, 2007, soldiers stationed at Wat Chang Hai were following the prescribed guidelines established by the abbot, Ačhān Tūat, after martial law was declared in 2004. At 5:00 P.M. the soldiers shut and locked the front doors to the wat. Shortly thereafter, at 5:30, the bell rang, signaling the monks and novices to gather at the temple (*bōt*) to chant. At 6:00 P.M. the monks and novices retreated to their quarters. If not for the dramatic increase of daytime visitors for the Chinese New Year, one would have considered this an ordinary day at Wat Chang Hai. Just after 6:00 P.M. that evening, I encountered Ačhān Tūat sitting on one of the steps outside his quarters, smoking a cigarette. His shoulders were relaxed and his face calm, unlike his stern countenance earlier in the day when addressing laypersons' requests. After exchanging pleasantries, Ačhān Tūat asked me why the Malay Muslims considered speaking Thai as a sin. "They learn Chinese, Malay, and English. They can speak quite well," he explained, "but they say that speaking Thai is a sin."[104] Although neither of us knew it at the time, the abbot's question would hold larger relevance before the night was over.

At around 8:00 P.M. that evening, lights in my room flickered and were then extinguished. Cell phones rang throughout the monks' quarters, which were adjacent to each other in the two-storey apartment structure. I received a text message from a student at Prince of Songkhla University (PSU), stating that the capital district of Pattani, as well as most of Yala Province, had lost power. After this event, the police reported that earlier in the day they had received messages from militants who threatened to bomb the generators. The PSU student informed me that she received a message saying, "Buddhists are banished from the South." For her and many other Thai Buddhist laity, the bombing of the generators incited panic.

Some monks and novices gathered in the courtyard below the monks' quarters. Within moments a monk came to tell us that a nearby *wat* had been set on fire, but no monks had been injured. After ten minutes, the monks and novices returned to their rooms for the night. The following day many of the monks, including the abbot, expressed shock and frustration over the militant attacks. This incident occurred five months after the bloodless coup of September 2006 that toppled the Thaksin administration, yet the shifts in political power had not deterred the militants from waging continued attacks, this one scheduled during the Chinese New Year.

According to government and media sources, on February 18, 2007, the night of the Chinese New Year, at approximately 7:30 P.M., power generators for Pattani and Yala provinces were bombed. This militant action was followed by attacks on civilian commercial areas such as karaoke bars, malls, hotels, car dealerships, and theaters. These attacks constituted the largest financial damage in southern Thailand since the declaration of martial law in 2004. The militants also claimed responsibility for the numerous attacks on religious spaces, such as the arson attempt at a *wat* close to Wat Chang Hai, and for a small number of coordinated attacks on Buddhist homes.[105] At Wat B, one monk recounted hearing three bombs explode outside the wat. The police there were unable to act because the road leading out from the *wat* was covered in nails.[106] Nails also covered the road leading out of Wat Chang Hai the same night.

Attacks in the southernmost provinces that have taken place in recent years reflect the growing racial tensions between Malay Muslims and the Thai Buddhist State. Scholars like Ukrist Pathmanand speculate that part of the escalated violence in the areas populated by over 80% Malay Muslims can be attributed to the heavy-handed policies of the late prime minister Thaksin Shinawatra.[107] Although this may have been a factor in intensifying the violence, occurrences such as the Chinese New Year attacks of February 2007 demonstrate that there are other elements in play.[108]

After the Thaksin administration was ousted on September 19, 2006, the new administration, led by Prime Minister Surayud, made active conciliatory efforts in the three border provinces. On November 2, 2006, Surayud traveled to Pattani Province and publicly apologized for the deaths during the 2004 Tak Bai Affair. In the same speech, he told the audience that he was against the hard-line policies of the Thaksin government.[109] A few days later, on November 8, Surayud was in Yala promising to end the blacklisting of Islamic teachers and the end to the military's hostile searches.[110] This new direction headed by Surayud paved the way for new relations with Malaysia and tentative agreements to work together. However, the subsequent escalation in violence that culminated in the events of February 2007 signaled that the militants had other grievances aside from the policies of the heavy-handed Thaksin administration.

When Ačhān Tūat mentioned the Malay Muslims' dislike of the Thai language, he was referring to the Malay Muslims' tendency to view the Thai language as a cultural entity that includes both Thai Chinese and Thai Buddhists. The targeting of predominantly Chinese commercial areas in addition to Buddhist sites suggests that militant grievances center on racial disparities that, according to Omi and Winant, inherently include issues of class. If the normative identity is religiously and ethnically positioned, it is no surprise that the violent actions on the Chinese New Year were directed at Thai Chinese Buddhists and Thai Buddhist secular and religious places.[111]

Buddhist monks and soldiers in southern Thailand exacerbate the racial distinction and Otherness of Malay Muslims. Often, this accentuation of differences is marked by the color-coded *khaek* reference. While staying at Wat Chang Hai in Pattani Province, I once had the opportunity to speak with Ačhān Nirut, the second highest ranking monk in the southernmost provinces. Ačhān Nirut was forty-three years old and had come to Wat Chang Hai in 1986, two years after his ordination. He was from the southernmost region and had been ordained at a *wat* in Yala Province. Like other aspiring Thai monks, he originally pursued his Buddhist education in India, earning his bachelor's degree at Nalanda University and his master's degree at Mahākasat University in Bihar.

In the following conversation held in his office at Wat Chang Hai, Ačhān Nirut explained that the *wat* was safe because soldiers were present to protect the monks and their visitors.

Q: How do the soldiers protect the wat?
A: They are on patrol all day and all night.
Q: All day and all night?
A: Yes, all day and all night.
Q: What do they do? Do they stand and protect?
A: Oh, no, no, no. Sometimes they walk around and look for some certain people who come.
Q: Oh, so they come and check the people when they come in sometimes.
A: No. Not like that.
Q: They don't check people?
A: No, no. How can I say this—they check only some people who look—how can I say—black skin.
Q: You mean those who look like khaek?
A: Yes. If you look like a Muslim or, how can I say, not like a person in Thai Buddhism.[112]

Ačhān Nirut's aforementioned description of the security measures at Wat Chang Hai reveals the Thai military and monastic racial profiling of visitors and further underscores the physicality of Muslim identity in the southernmost region. Ačhān Nirut's way of differentiating Thai Buddhists from other people was their black skin, which he quickly corresponded with Islam. Buddhist monks like Ačhān Nirut presume one's religious identity by one's skin pigmentation, a product of racialization and the corresponding term *khaek*.

In the three southern provinces, *khaek*, which would include Arabs, Malays, and South Asian ethnicities, becomes more than a religious signifier. As a racial modifier that is inherently fluid, *khaek* becomes a color-coded reference that, as we will see later, provides complications in distinguishing "Thai Buddhist" from "Malay Muslim." The derogatory connotations for *khaek* are present even though Wat Chang Hai is an international tourist site for both Buddhist and Muslim travelers. Traditionally, visitors would come from Malaysia, Singapore, and Indonesia to Wat Chang Hai to buy amulets of Lūang Phǒ Tuat, a venerated Buddhist monk. After the surge in violence, however, in accordance with Ačhān Nirut's view, soldiers who lived and worked at Wat Chang Hai checked the identification of visitors with dark skin. The presumption was that darker skinned people were possibly Muslims and, hence, potential terrorists.

Aside from racial profiling in and around the southern *wat*, the structural violence of such racialization becomes most pronounced when applied to Malay Muslim women. Frantz Fanon was the first to note that the colonial racial gaze eroticizes the Black body, whether male or female. When a group is racialized to a subordinate or inhumane level, their bodies, particularly female bodies, become fetishized. One can see this clearly in the U.S. depiction of African, Asian, and Latin Americans who only maintain a presence in the media as caricatures of specific stereotypes, or as eroticized bodies. Scholars such as Cornel West argue that racial rhetoric focuses on and degrades the bodies of the oppressed. The primitive, uncivilized body is one that must be tamed or conquered.

Cornel West argues the rhetoric of blackness in the United States often employs the identification of blackness as a "political and ethical construct" used against African Americans. This racial reasoning focuses primarily on the degradation of the African American body: "White supremacist ideology is based first and foremost on the degradation of black bodies in order to control them."[113] This mentality, whether homoerotic or hetero-erotic, complements the patriarchic attitude that dominates colonial and racial discourses.[114] Although there is not enough evidence to point to a clear parallel in the southern provinces, there is enough information to suggest the need for further inquiry.

Rapes are seldom reported, even less so in the three border provinces under martial law where there is very little trust of the State. While working in the area, anthropologist Amporn Mardent identified discrimination against Malay Muslims in the southern provinces. Among her examples she discloses a painful account of Yoh, a young Muslim woman raped by a soldier as an example of the ways in which a woman, through her identity, becomes targeted and sexually assaulted by a military officer. Amporn Mardent writes,

> Rape and sexual abuse of women are often used to terrify people and make one's opponents oppressed and embarrassed. Such a tactic satisfies the soldier's sexual desire and shows men's power during unpeaceful times.... Yoh explained, "And [that man] said further, 'Go back and tell your bandit leader that if you shoot us, we will come back.'"[115]

Prototypical patriarchical responses to rape consist of remarks such as "the woman 'asked for it'" based on her actions or on what she was wearing. However, even these sexist claims are inapplicable to this scenario.

Geography and Racial Metastasis

Geography determines the fluidity in which Buddhists and Muslims interact in southern Thailand. The behavior of Buddhists and Muslims living in regions outside the areas of violence, which is demarcated politically through martial law, reflect greater degrees of tolerance for each other despite the strong distinctions between their identities. One instance of this is exemplified by the family tree of a monk from Wat Chang Hai. Ačhān Tuk's family reflects the fluid interactions between ethno-religious identities in the southernmost provinces.

Ačhān Tuk is a thirty-five-year-old monk who teaches Pāli at Wat Chang Hai. He was born and raised in Phatthalung, a southern province that is north of Pattani and Songkhla. He earned his master's degree at the Buddhist college of Mahāchulalongkorn University in Bangkok. Every year his extended family (khrabkhrūa khayāi) meets for a reunion in Songkhla. Ačhān Tuk's father is Malay and his mother is Chinese, perhaps Hokkien, although he does not know for certain. Ačhān Tuk explained with pride that his father's earliest Buddhist ancestor immigrated to Thailand from Java during the reign of King Rama I (1782–1809). This ancestor was born Muslim, but ruled (čhaomuang) over an area that was overwhelmingly Buddhist. In order to develop a strong rapport with his subjects, Ačhān Tuk's ancestor and his immediate family converted to the local Buddhism. The rest of Ačhān Tuk's ancestors from his father's side are Malay Muslims who immigrated to the southern region in 1605 during the Ayutthaya period (1350–1767). Even during the years of civil war in the southernmost provinces, one could attend Ačhān Tuk's annual family reunions and witness everyone eating and celebrating together: Chinese Buddhists, Thai Buddhists, and Malay Buddhists and Muslims.[116]

There are two important distinctions present in Ačhān Tuk's situation: his family's history and geography. Much of his family's diversity occurred over a hundred years ago when relations between Malays and Thais were less tense. In addition, his family does not live in the three Malay Muslim–dominated southernmost provinces or under martial law. Both of these factors contribute to different and less fractious relationship between Malay Muslims and their Buddhist neighbors.

The effect of geography and racial formation becomes more pronounced within regions sustained by conflict. Thais who experience trauma in the southernmost provinces blur identifications and individual nuances with systemic stereotypes. Askew observes that southern Thai Buddhists see the violence as unnatural, since "Thais love peace/tranquility."

> In using this stock phrase (a prominent phrase in Thailand's national anthem), speakers did not necessarily use the term 'Thai' here as an ethnic label, but as a normative statement of national values affirming coexistence and tolerance among all people in the country. Yet 'Thai' constantly slipped into use to refer to 'Thai Phut' (Thai Buddhist) when responses to violence were mentioned.[117]

This collapse of identifications is endemic to trauma-related victims, and more specifically, to people living in areas of conflict. However, larger ramifications lie in the common misconception that trauma-related phenomena are restricted to an individual's imaginary. Contrary to this, bleeds into larger social connections or into what Charles Taylor and others call the *social imaginaire*.

Thais' fears and anger over the violence in the southernmost provinces become a mechanism for racist rhetoric and views to metastasize from Malay Muslims to all subjects living in close proximity to them. Michel Gilquin notes that Thais also apply the term *khaek* to non-Muslims living in Muslim-populated regions.[118] Ačhān Nirut's measure for identifying Muslims becomes part of a larger problem because some southern Thai Buddhists, like Malay Muslims, have darker skin tones. *Khaek* becomes so affixed to Muslim identity and their spaces that Thais use the term *khaek* for any dark-skinned person—regardless of religious identity—living in the southernmost provinces. As a result, because of their shared geographic and physical similarities, southern Thai Buddhists living in the regions under martial law suffer alienation and persecution similar to that directed at Malay Muslims.

This form of racial metastasis is typified in the case of a Thai Buddhist woman I will call Wān. In 2007, Wān was a twenty-seven-year-old graduate student at Prince of Songkhla University (PSU) in Pattani Province. Like most students at PSU in recent years, she is a native of the southernmost provinces and has spent her entire life in the region. Even when the violence erupted in 2004, Wān decided to stay in Pattani and continue to study, primarily for two reasons. The first was based on her family ties. Her father was a governmental officer in the province, supporting the family of four: Wān, her mother, and her younger brother. Wān's second reason was her graduate work, which consumed most of her time and became a defining component of her envisioned future.

Although she identifies herself as a steadfast Buddhist and makes merit, eats pork, and does not dress in Malay clothes (e.g., wearing a *tudung*), people living outside the three southernmost provinces identify Wān as a Muslim and a potential militant. Outside the militarized zone, people detect her southern dialect and her darker skin, and falsely conclude that she is a Malay Muslim. In her visits to neighboring universities in Songkhla Province, professors occasionally ask her in a joking manner whether she carries bombs in her bag.

I rendezvoused with Wān in February 2007 at the My Cake Bakery, a café in the capital city of Pattani. She had become deeply troubled after experiencing multiple encounters with racism during her trip to the neighboring province of Songkhla. I detected a whitening cream on her face, which may or may not have been a reaction to her still-vivid memory of that experience. Whitening cream is a popular cosmetic throughout Thailand, but is also a vivid social reminder of the value placed on Whiteness in Thai society. Wān explained that, after spending months working on her research and bearing witness to militant attacks on her campus and around the district, she had decided to take a break from her work.

She took a local bus north to the Songkhla capital district and then caught a motorcycle taxi. When she asked the driver to take her to a guesthouse, he heard her accent and asked her where she was from. When he learned that Wān came from Pattani his demeanor changed dramatically. He wanted to know if she was Muslim and what her purpose was for coming to Songkhla. Numerous other questions followed, such as: "When did you arrive?" "Whom are you visiting?" All of this was followed by the driver's assertion that Wān looked and sounded Muslim. The driver repeatedly told her that Songkhla proper was a developed city, a proper city, and that it did not have the kind of violence found in Pattani. When they arrived at her destination, he charged Wān three times the normal rate. Finally, when Wān paid in coins, the man scoffed at her supposed poverty, saying, "You pay in change, of course you do!"

The taxi driver's comments reflect a common association Thais living outside martial law have of those living within the area. Songkhla Province shares its southern border with Pattani, and also has a large Malay Muslim population; however, aside from a few districts, the province is not under martial law. Hat Yai, located in Songkhla, is the fourth largest city in Thailand and home to Malay Muslims, Thai Chinese, and Thai Buddhists. On September 16, 2006, six blasts exploded in the city, killing a Canadian, a Chinese, and three Thai tourists, and wounding dozens more.[119] This was the first incident in which an American or Eurasian died as a result of militant attacks in Thailand's southernmost provinces. Yet, even after this event and despite the demographics of Pattani,

Songkhla residents saw the people of Pattani as different from themselves. Pattani visitors like Wān were "*khon pattānī*" (Pattani people), as opposed to simply Thais. Two primary causes for this geographic distinction were the Thai State's application of martial law and the continual violence.

Racial designations of space are not specific to times of violence, but rather become more visible during these times of crisis. When the kingdom of Patani was divided into seven principalities, they were referred to as "*khaek jet huamuang*,"[120] displaying the association between religion and space. The majority of the deep south's population is Malay Muslim, but an 80–85% majority is far from homogenous. However, the phenomenon of racial metastasis causes Thais living outside the southernmost provinces to imagine southern Thai identities in association with their violent, chaotic environment, in a sense, blurring environment and collective persona together. Due to polythetic attributes, a populace may identify different races with the same ethno-religious group, such as Thai Buddhists. While Wān is not Malay or Muslim, she lives in the same environment and has dark skin like Malay Muslims. In her particular scenario, racial projects rewrote her perceived religious identification.

Structural and Individual Efficacy

We can gain a greater sense of the social efficacy of religion with its role in reconstituting identity through both the structural efficacy of the State as well as the discrete power of the individual. In either scenario, Buddhist identity becomes a mutable, albeit powerful, signifier of status in the national and global arena.

With respect to structural power, the State's construction of normative identity relies heavily on religion. Within this "regime of truth," rhetoric surrounding religion includes or excludes groups from a society. The late nineteenth century saw the effects of the Eurasian Enlightenment Project in identity-politics. As Peter van der Veer writes, "[r]ace replaced religion as the most important marker of difference, although religion and race were often combined."[121] Orientalist scholars of the day found an audience interested in religious discussions outside of traditional accounts of Christianities. In Eurasia, they restructured Buddhisms to the Eurasian intellectual palate, emphasizing the rationale and scientific, while removing the "localisms" and "supernatural" elements. Cheah writes,

> Having access to Pali and Sanskrit texts, [Brian] Hodgson and [Eugène] Burnouf and their successor, Thomas W. Rhys Davids, attempted to recover 'pure' Buddhism from the layers of cultural accretions that sounded it in the form of cultural practices.[122]

Religion was not only an ideology that was colonized, but also an ideology that was used to rebuke colonial efforts.

King Mongkut and successors saw the role and perception of the Thai *sangha* intimately connected to Siam's global status. Siam sought to refashion Thai Buddhism as a rational and systematic tradition, which would more readily correspond with Eurasian empiricism, science, and modernity (and validate their sovereignty in the colonial world). Eurasian Orientalists' reframing of Buddhisms coupled with Mongkut's reform of Siamese Buddhism would later aid Siam in its efforts to promote itself as a civilized nation-state, preserving its cultures and traditions. A striking comparison to the Siamese State actions is found in its neighbors to the west. King Thibaw Min (r. 1859–1916) used the civilized/barbarian discourse in his attempts to exclude the British from Burmese society. In an effort to dislodge the ever-growing strength of the British, the Burmese king issued proclamations such as "Declaration of War against Burma" and "Royal War Order," which combined the integrity of Buddhism with that of economic and political stability.[123]

Siam's use of Thai Buddhism as a means of aligning herself with a pan-colonial modernity was also akin to the efforts of Japanese Buddhists like D. T. Suzuki and Shaku Sōen, who worked during the same period to present Japanese Zen Buddhism as a tool amenable to Eurasian Enlightenment principles.

In 1893, Chicago hosted the World's Parliament of Religion. It was there that Shaku Sōen, a Zen Buddhist priest, carefully chose a Buddhist topic that would be agreeable to Eurasian scientific progress: causation. Lopez writes,

> Thus, among all the topics that Shaku Sōen, a Zen priest and Mahāyāna master, could have chosen to introduce Buddhism to his American audience, he chose not emptiness or compassion or the Buddha nature, but the comparatively prosaic topic of causation. It is in fact a basic Buddhist doctrine accepted, at least on the conventional level, by all schools of Buddhism across Asia. But it is likely that Shaku Sōen also selected it because it seemed utterly modern, and scientific, explaining both the outer world of matter and the inner world of mind without recourse to God.[124]

After the World's Parliament of Religions, authors like Paul Carus and D. T. Suzuki helped to create a space for Zen Buddhism in Eurasia and the United States. Zen Buddhism's ideological stature in the United States and Eurasia soon became a global phenomenon.

In *Zen in Brazil: The Quest for Cosmopolitan Modernity*, Cristina Rocha traces the Brazilian State's appropriation of Zen Buddhism in an attempt to align Brazilian culture with U.S. and Eurasian notions of modernity.[125] Taking their cue from the French, Brazilians envisioned Zen Buddhism as a cultural commodity that denoted refined and modern tastes in the empirical and rational as opposed to the popular forms of religion that heralded superstitions and magic. While Brazil sought recognition through an appropriation of religion on a global level, within Brazilian society Zen Buddhism became one of the influential dispositions that differentiated social classes. The Brazilian social elite saw Zen Buddhism as a mark of sophistication. As such, the paraphernalia and practices of Zen were identified with elite dispositions and tastes. Like Thai Buddhism, Zen Buddhism became a means that affected the global status of particular nationalisms. By selecting specific characteristics relevant to Eurasian modernity, both Thai and Zen Buddhists refashioned themselves as civilized and respectable global citizens.

Religion was a powerful tool for States, but it was also extraordinarily useful for citizens within the State. Perhaps of all the social characteristics involved in one's racialization, the most mutable is religion. Individual action allows a person to change their status nearly instantaneously so long as the process of transformation is socially accepted. It is in this way that one's religious identity can entrap as well as free a person from her/his prescribed social categories. This evidence is no more apparent than in South Asia, home to the largest Hindu, Muslim, and Sikh populations in the world.

In contrast to the structural forms of racialization, one of the most pronounced and well-known examples of individually invoked transformation occurred in India on October 14, 1956. Dr. Ambedkar led 380,000 Dalits in an outdoor conversion ceremony from their born Hindu identity to his form of Buddhism. Dr. Ambedkar's purpose was to free himself and the thousands of other Dalits from their designated racial identity under the Brahmanic *varna* system. By separating themselves from the Brahmanic system, Dalits sought to reinvent their identity and cast off their pariah status in Indian society. Historian Gyanendra Pandey concludes that the Dalits' conversion to Ambedkar's form of Buddhism was not as effective as Dr. Ambedkar had hoped. The Buddhist tradition originally had been incorporated into Hinduism in India, with the Buddha becoming an avatar of Viṣṇu. Pandey notes that, in contrast to Dalit conversions to Buddhism, their conversions to Islam have been more effective in eschewing the association of Dalits to the Hindu "untouchable" category.[126] The reason for this contrast could be the more drastic change in religious affiliation with Islam because it represents a complete break from the doctrinal system of karma and rebirth. One large Dalit conversion to Islam occurred in 1981, when several hundred Dalit families in the village of Meenakshipuram in Tamil Nadu converted to Islam. Yoginder Sikand explains that after their conversion,

[T]here was a sudden change in the attitude of the local so-called upper castes towards them. Now they could enter village tea-shop, could wear shoes, something that was not possible earlier. This was because the Hindus knew that the Muslims would not let them carry on treating our people who had become Muslims as they had been treating them before. In this way, Islam gave these Dalits a new sense of identity and pride.[127]

Dalits found a way of adopting a new racial identity by changing their religious affiliation. Conversion to Islam is not always a liberating step in society, however. For example, in Israel Jews who convert to Islam face new-found difficulties. Aside from the hurdles and alleged requirements for officially converting, (including a visit to a psychiatrist), they face strident communal reactions from their Jewish neighbors.[128]

The ability to shift religious affiliation becomes more complex when a group's ethnicity is seen as synonymous with their religion. Yet, both the converted Dalits of India and the converted Israeli Muslims demonstrate the power religious conversion has over one's assumed race. For the Dalits, their conversion to Islam or Buddhism affected their racial categories or mores specifically, their status, under the *varna* system. For Israeli Jews who convert to Islam, they similarly find themselves associated with an entirely different racial formation.

In Thailand, a minority's conversion to Thai Buddhism is a powerful means toward assimilation. However, the Malay Muslims find themselves in a quandary. Their religious identification is affixed to their culture and selfhood. Their inability to convert occludes their ability to move toward greater acceptance in Thai society.

Conclusion

The use of Buddhism to construct Otherness in Thai history is not new. King Rama I initiated a discursive campaign against the Burmese. When rewriting the Thai chronicles that had been destroyed during the Burmese invasion in 1767, Rama I's charter insisted on an "iconoclastic violence against the temples and sacred images of Ayutthaya" and "represented the Burmese as impious destroyers of Buddhism as well as enemies of the Thais."[129] Even though most Burmese were followers of Theravāda Buddhism, Rama I demonized them because of their "sacrilegious" actions against Buddhism.[130] The Siamese method of demonizing Burmese became echoed by Buddhist monks with respect to the Malay Muslims in the southernmost provinces. Wan Kadir Che Man argues that Malay Muslims,

> are perceived by many Thais as representing a foreign and undesirable culture. This is because the religious elite symbolizes Malay identity and is well known as a stronghold of culture resistance.[131]

Malay Muslim identity became the embodiment of resistance or anti-nationalism. The image of Islam as an identity of resistance is one of the prompts for notables such as Malcolm X to convert to Islam in the United States. Aminah Beverly McCloud argues, "In this broader usage, 'asabiya designates a key theme in the history of African American Islam—namely, the theme of *nation-building*."

In this fashion, African American Islam can be viewed as "the history of a people attempting to create 'asabiya [kinship relations] in a hostile environment."[132]

In southern Thailand, it is the implicit confluence of Malay ethnicity and Islam that generates an impasse for Malay Muslim acceptance in Thai society. During the inchoation of Thai nation-state building, Thai Buddhism was a means of constructing a nationalist identity, which doubly alienated Malay Muslims. Anthropologist Louis Golomb explains that the word "Malay" connotes "opposition to participation in the Thai polity."[133] These "semi-barbaric" people, according to Chao Phraya Yomarat, were pressured to "assimilate" with heavy-handed tactics from the 1930s onward. Since that time, the Thai State's attempts to assimilate Malay Muslims have been met with violent resistance in the southernmost region.

We can witness the effects of Malay Muslim alienation in Thailand through the actions of Buddhist monks, which we outlined in chapters 2 and 3. It is in the three southernmost provinces where normative identity is most contested that Buddhist monks affirm the dislocation of Malay Muslim identity through their representations and practices. As tensions and violence increase in southern Malay Muslim and Buddhist villages, local perceptions and treatment of Buddhist monks worsen due to a process of identity formation that underwent significant transformations at the close of the nineteenth century.

Conclusion

On a hot October morning in 2008, classes at a public school in Yarang District, Pattani, ended for the day and Muslim and Buddhist students poured out of the classrooms. It was the beginning of their school break. There would have been nothing unusual about this except that police and soldiers kept watch from their posts around the school. While this might have been abnormal in other parts of Thailand, this was a normal scene in the three southernmost provinces. What was not normal, however, was the school's location—inside a *wat*.

In 2008, Wat Amphūanārām was one of only two *wat* in Yarang District that had a school for Muslims. Each of the two schools received financial support from the government as well as from the *wat*. The Rōngrīenchumchonwatamph ūanārām school at Wat Amphūanārām included both elementary and secondary education (*rōngrīenprathom* and *rōngrīenmathayom*, respectively) and had a total of 425 students, 97% of which were Muslim. Ačhān Tat, the abbot of Wat Amphūanārām, was ordained at the age of twenty-five in his home province of Songkhla and has lived in Yarang District for over fifty years. In October of 2008, he was eighty-five years old. He had a hard time walking and suffered from a bad cold. Ačhān Tat also had trouble projecting his voice, so with the assistance of a retired soldier, he explained the situation at the *wat*.

> This school is supported by the *wat*. Because most of the children are Muslim, they come here to study. There are between 400–500 Muslim students, and we can say that there are only 10 Buddhist students to about 390 Muslim students. But, it is fine for them; they get along well with the teachers here. There are teachers who are government officials, and there are temporary teachers as well. Due to this serious situation, most government teachers moved to other schools, so we had to hire Muslim teachers to teach the students.[1]

Ačhān Tat is not engaged in the school's day-to-day activities, nor does he have any official duties at the school, but he does offer scholarships to the school and occasionally meets with the teachers and local imams.

Rōngrīenchumchon is the secondary school. The ratio of Buddhists and Muslims in the student population has fluctuated over the past several years. Khun Mari, a Buddhist who teaches Thai at Wat Amphūanārām, lives down the street from the *wat*. Sitting outside the gated entrance to her convenience store, which also is her home, Khun Mari explained to me that the percentage of Buddhist students has dwindled in recent years. "During the last four years, the Buddhist student population has decreased from 30 to 20 to now 13 students."[2]

Not far away, in the same district of Pattani, is another Buddhist teacher working at a *wat*. Khun Mun, who teaches elementary math at Wat Kowāi, also has noted the decline in the Buddhist student population. In the past, the student body at Khun Mun's school was composed of 50% to 60% Buddhist students. Now, the school is 80% Muslim. Khun Mun explained the situation in this way:

> The Buddhist students learn in the capital district. The Buddhists that do come are fewer than the Muslims and there are quite a lot of Muslims. Because of this, there is an 80/20 differential. 80 percent are Muslim and 20 percent are Buddhist.[3]

Wat Kowāi, also located in Yarang District, also supports a school; however, almost all of the school's students are Muslim. Nearly two hundred Muslim

Figure 6.1 Wat Amphūanārām, by Michael Jerryson on October 17, 2008.

Figure 6. 2 Rōngrīenchumchon, by Michael Jerryson on October 17, 2008.

students attend Wat Kowāi's elementary school, and eight out of its fourteen teachers are Buddhist.[4]

The educational activities at Wat Amphūanārām and Wat Kowāi reflect the not-too-distant past. Before the surge of violence in the three border provinces, predominantly Muslim-populated schools in *wat* were a common occurrence.[5] Southern *wat* served their communities and, because many of these communities were over 50% Muslim, schools in monastic centers catered to both religious groups (figures 6.1 and 6.2).

Wat Kōwai's school is forty years old. Muslims no longer come to visit the *wat* during its ceremonies, but Muslim leaders of the community, district chief (*kamnan*) and village headman (*phūyaibān*), still visit. Wat Amphūanārām's school is much older and celebrated its ninety-sixth anniversary in 2008, at which time both Buddhist monks and Imams were invited to bless the school.[6] While this ethno-religious pluralism was a common occurrence in the past, it has become scarce in recent years due to the rise in ethno-religious tensions and a steady migration of Thai Buddhists out of the region. Wat Amphūanārām continues its tradition of providing public education to the community, but the tensions have not spared schools in and around it. A little over a month before my October 2008 visit, a Buddhist state official was gunned down in front of a neighboring school in Yarang, Pattani.[7]

Buddhist-Muslim relations have not spared the population in Yarang District, Pattani. Much of the district has been identified as part of the red zone where both Khun Mari and Khun Mun live. Khun Mari's experiences serve an example of the violence suffered by those in her area; she has endured multiple attacks on her family and home. In 2006, her husband was shot and killed outside their home while selling gas. A year after the death of her husband, a bomb exploded in front of Khun Mari's house. Yet, even in the aftermath of these attacks, Khun Mari still sees her duty as a teacher to be one who spreads peace through education.

> As teachers we have a duty to teach them to mitigate the violent through peaceful methods. We must teach them to understand each other and not use violence. This is our duty as teachers.[8]

The violence is not a recent phenomenon for Ačhān Tat, who has dealt with attacks on his *wat* for over thirteen years. In 1997, bandits (*čhōn*) set his *wat* on fire. Since that time, there have been repeated attempts to burn it to the ground. This has not deterred Ačhān Tat from supporting his school. In fact, Ačhān Tat explained that if he can live long enough, he would add another floor to the school. He considers education important for all children, regardless of their religion; he also believes that it is equally important for all to respect and adhere to Thai nationalism. Ačhān Tat complains about the way the children sing the Thai national anthem. During our conversation, he added:

> I told the teacher to teach them to sing clearly and loud, because any-where you go, you are a person of Thailand....Between four and five hundred students sing the song so quietly. This is not good. They thought that this land is not their land, so they are not proud to sing it.[9]

Ačhān Tat's request is not an unusual or unique one in a public school such as Rōngrīenchumchon. As discussed in prior chapters, Thai education has been a method of instilling national pride; as a result, public schools are one of the most frequent spaces of conflict in the region.

Both teachers and monks feel threatened when they leave the *wat*, but both groups feel their social demands take precedence over the risks they face. People from each profession expressed confidence that they and their students are safe while within the *wat*. Part of this safety is the result of the local communities' support for Wat Amphūanārām and Wat Kowāi, but the protection provided by the communities is severely limited in scope. Bandits generally come from outside the community. While some local communities like Wat Amphūanārām's and Wat Kowāi's weather the conflict, they still suffer from the greater regional crisis.

It is unclear as to what type of Buddhist support will have the greatest impact in the southernmost provinces. On the one hand, State-monastic representations such as the military monks' covert activities have the potential to destabilize most *wat* in the three southernmost provinces by destroying their communal appearance with armed guards, barbed-wire fences and barracks, and so on, increasing ethno-religious tensions with identity checks based on appearance, military-led Buddhist alms rounds, Buddhist patrols, and so on. Alternately, the preservation and enrichment of monastic-sponsored Muslim educational programs in *wat* could preserve and strengthen Buddhist-Muslim relations in the border provinces. However, one aspect is clear—Thai Buddhism exerts an extensive and significant influence over Thai society and the violence in the southernmost provinces.

The Impact of Violence on Monks

Initially, my decision to examine the activities and perspectives of southern monks was motivated by a desire to find examples of Buddhist monks involved in peace-making activities and interfaith dialogue. When it became clear that there was no substantive activity in these areas, I was left wondering why. Why were monks not talking to the Imams, the *tok gurus* and other Islamic leaders in an attempt to mend cultural and religious divisions? Why were monks becoming silent (or in some cases quite vocal) supporters of the State? In 2004, I found that southern monks perceived the violence as intrinsically political and, therefore, a taboo subject to discuss due to their interpretations of Thai Buddhism. But, the intervening years, which revealed repeated and escalating attacks on monks and *wat* in the border provinces, changed some monks' views and assumptions dramatically. By 2006, monks were becoming more vocal; a few were expressing strong pro-Buddhist nationalism sentiments.

The waning, yet surviving presence of Muslim-populated schools in Buddhist spaces partly diverts Buddhists monks and their *wat* from their current association with the State. While Wat A, Wat B, and Wat Chang Hai appear as merely extensions of a Buddhist State with the encampment of Buddhist soldiers and police in the three southern provinces, the two *wat* in Yarang District contradict such a simplistic association. Wat Kowāi may have fifty soldiers living at the *wat* and only two monks, but it continues to serve as a communal space for both Buddhists and Muslims.

The examination of a finely defined geographical region of the world such as three provinces in Thailand might appear limited; however, the project is useful on a much broader scale. My intention from the very onset was to survey the practices and habits of Buddhist monks who continually live within a violent environment. The purpose was to better understand the role Buddhist monks and the concept "Buddhism" had within the complex social infrastructure of negotiated identities, economies, and politics, and with the resulting violence itself. Ultimately, I found that many southern Buddhist monks retained their Buddhist identifications, but sacrificed their regional affiliations; their communal identities were replaced with identities associated with the State. By adopting the State's Buddhist identity and State and monastic practices (such as militarizing *wat*, or monks collaborating with soldiers), monks served to agitate or, in some circumstances, heighten ethno-religious tensions in the three border provinces. While violence in the region is contingent upon a variety of causes (including ecological, economic, drug trafficking and political factors), *I find that the most pervasive, persistent, and systemic problem is based on identity-formation.* In order to end the upheaval in the southernmost provinces, a space needs to be created for the Malay Muslim identity *within* the conception of *khwāmpenthai* (Thainess). This inclusion will necessitate a reworking of Thailand's concept of racial formations. The current method displaces minority identities by measuring their ethnic and religious identities against a normative of Thai Buddhism.

Monks such as Ačhān Nok, who carries a gun and performs other activities that violate monastic precepts, are a clear and powerful reminder that *idealized religious traditions* are not the same as *lived religious traditions*. In conformance with other religious traditions, Thai Buddhist principles underscore the importance of non-violence. Buddhist religious principles are ideals toward which Thai Buddhists strive; unfortunately, ideals are not always achieved, that is, put into practice. While it is true that the Thai Buddhist *Vinaya* prohibits soldiers from ordination, military monks are a reality in the three border provinces. This disjuncture between ideal and practice are clearly present in Christian and Jewish traditions as well. Although the Judeo-Christian Ten Commandments forbid murder, Christian monks and ministers, rabbis, and Judeo-Christian laity continue to cite justifications for violence in the name of their religious traditions.[10] Thai Buddhist monks who carry firearms, in violation of their religious precepts, reflect a negotiated identity that is often adopted in times of crisis—when the need for safety takes precedence over religious interdictions.

Since the conclusion of my research, I have discussed aspects of it with other Buddhist monks throughout Thailand. To my surprise, I found that the phenomenon of armed Thai Buddhist monks is not limited to the southern provinces. Abbots in provinces such as Nakhon Pathom in the central provinces confide that they, too, own guns. In 2008, a central provincial *wat* was burglarized three times. The abbot of the burglarized *wat* explained he did not intend to harm anyone but (like Ačhān Nok) he needed a gun for protection and to deter potential robbers.[11] In an ideal setting, Thai Buddhist monks would not carry guns, but this ideal is compromised by environments that compromise the safety of monks and their livelihood.

Conditions are constantly changing in southern *wat* as people rotate in and out of Buddhist spaces. Examples are evident at Wat A, Wat B, and Wat Chang Hai. At Wat A, Ačhān Nok's Kathin ceremony in 2008 occurred, but there were 25% fewer participants than the year before and revenues continued to decline. Soldiers who had occupied barracks at Wat A for two years departed, and in their place were fifteen Buddhist policemen. Due to the decline in military protection, over ten volunteer soldiers—both Buddhist and Muslim—from Saiburi, Pattani, helped oversee Wat A's Kathin ceremony. Wat B's Kathin ceremony also occurred in 2008, but with 5–10% fewer participants and lower revenue than in the previous year.

It was interesting to note conditions in the previous *wat* I had visited and reported about. Wat B was without its military monk, Phra Nok. He suffered a neck injury in early 2008 and was sent to Bangkok for medical treatment. Wat Chang Hai continues to serve as a national and international landmark for Lūang Pho Tuat, drawing visitors from the different provinces, as well as Malaysia, Indonesia, and other countries. The number of visitors to Wat Chang Hai still pales in comparison to the number in years prior to martial law, but the fact that visitors continue to attend is testimony to the religious significance of the *wat*. Phra Nirut persists with his work at Wat Chang Hai. Ačhān Tūat's derision of Malay Muslims has sharpened, and Ačhān Tuk left to pursue a doctoral degree in Bangkok. The occupants and participants at these *wat* (and others) will always change, but their *karma* (actions) leave behind cycles of behavior and attitudes that persist well into their absences.

Epistemologies

My initial purpose in this study was to understand the impact violence had on southern Buddhist monks and how they, in turn, affected the violence. However, a second purpose arose during my study, one which became apparent the more I learned about the conflict and the role of Thai Buddhism. I realized during my study that, contrary to popular opinion, Buddhist traditions contribute to the world of violence and conflict just like any other religious tradition. In this respect, I found that my work could not only contribute to the understanding of the conflict, but also counterattack some of the misconceptions about Buddhist traditions in the United States.

Misconceptions about religious traditions are not a new phenomenon, but there is a systemic and enduring misconception about Buddhisms in Eurasia and the United States. Works such as Donald Lopez's *Prisoners of Shangri-La* underscores this misconception. At times, scholars have considered the subject of "Buddhism and violence" inflammatory toward Buddhist traditions and peoples. I concur that Buddhist traditions are replete with examples of non-violent agents, peaceful movements, and pacifist doctrine. This is quite true and there are substantial volumes of primary and secondary texts that attest to this. However, the omission of Buddhist traditions from the study of religion and violence does violence to the discourse and precludes a comprehensive analysis of conflicts such as the one in southern Thailand. In order to maintain the image of Buddhist traditions as non-violent, we would have to create fictitious people and practices—virtual religious models, morally airbrushed to enhance the message. In an effort to avoid this problematic approach, I studied the relationship between Buddhists and the violence in the southernmost Thai provinces. This, in turn, led to the analysis of the active elements interacting in this region of violence, the formation of identities and how they interact with concepts of race, ethnicity, and nationalism.

For over a decade, the version of an idealized and homogenous image of Buddhisms has been presented to me repeatedly. For example, while in Ulaanbaatar, Mongolia, in 1997, a graduate student studying Tibetan Buddhism explained to me in great detail and irritation that "Mongols could not be Buddhists because they ate meat." While there are Buddhist traditions that prohibit the consumption of meat (such as Chinese Buddhist traditions), this is not a universal stance. The graduate student derived his opinion from homogenizing disparate Buddhist traditions into one conceptual model (as well as suffering an acute ignorance of the long-standing Mongolian and Tibetan Buddhist traditions of eating meat). This confusion goes to the heart of distinguishing *lived* and *idealized* religious traditions.

Scholars contribute to peoples' confusion over *lived* and *idealized* Buddhist traditions. At times, they teach or pontificate on ideal and/or conceptual models without clearly identifying them as such, or they interlace these models with practiced forms of the tradition. In a not-too-distant past, when one enrolled in a course on Buddhism(s) in the United States, it inherently meant a course on either Tibetan or Japanese Buddhist philosophy. Students became adept at understanding the meaning of emptiness, or even the concept of the Tibetan Bardo, but struggled to understand the habitual and/or general practices of Buddhists around the world.

The confusion between idealized and lived religion is symptomatic of a greater struggle within U.S. and Eurasian academies to recognize what has been called "Eastern Philosophy." If Asian religious traditions are classified as simply philosophical categories, there is no need to distinguish a course on Hinduism from one on Hindu philosophy; they are one in the same. In order to address the significant absence of study about Indian philosophy, we must first ground the study of Indian religious concepts and traditions within a wider spectrum, one that allows for such diverse explorations.

Scholars such as Charles Hallisey (1995), Gregory Schopen (1997), Bernard Faure (1998), Donald Lopez Jr. (1998, 2008), Tomoko Masuzawa (2005),

Cristina Rocha (2006), Johan Elverskog (2010), and others contest the platonic representation of Buddhisms. In doing so, we learn about different peoples and cultures and gain a better understanding of the interconnected world. On the other hand, many scholars continue to follow what has become an academic tradition of reinforcing the platonic form. This tradition undermines our understanding of issues such as the conflict in southern Thailand.

Social factors such as violence are strong enough to convert monasteries into military compounds, monks into soldiers, and Buddhists' principles into justifications for proto-nationalism. Buddhist traditions change—at times for a specific context—but no change is absolute. A minority of monks, such as those at Wat Amphūanārām, work to retain Thai Buddhism's communal and interfaith characteristics in the southern provinces and suggest an alternate direction for southern Thai Buddhist practices. By reducing their political roles and increasing their community ties, these monks offer hope to the region and, more importantly, a platform of action to develop in the area. While the future of southern Thailand remains uncertain, the role of religion will continue to serve as a powerful component of the conflict. It is my greatest hope that we continue to work toward understanding it.

APPENDIX

1. Name of Wat
2. Age of Wat
3. Contact Information
4. Subject Name
5. Subject Age
6. Number of *phra* (monks), *sāmanēn* (novices), *dekwat* (temple boys)
7. Number of soldiers/police stationed at *wat*
8. How many Buddhists (# and %) do you estimate live around your *wat*?
9. What were the numbers for question 6 last year?
10. Have any *phra* (monk), *sāmanēn* (novice), or *dekwat* (temple boy) left since martial law was declared in January?
11. Have you gained any new members since martial law was declared in January?
12. Have any of your members been threatened, injured, or killed as a result of the violence?
13. Did your *wat* or members have any problems prior to January 2004?
14. When did you realize there was a danger in your area?
15. What do you think is the cause of all the violence?
16. What do you think is a viable solution for the problem at hand?
17. How has the recent events affected your daily lives?
18. How has it affected your alms (daily)?
19. How has it affected the finances for your *wat* (in monthly earnings)?
20. Which Pattani *wat* do you think have been most affected by the violence
21. Why do you think *phra* have been targets for violence?
22. Do you feel that the circumstances are getting better, staying the same, or getting worse?
23. Why?
24. How have the members of your *wat* reacted to martial law and the violence?

25. How have they reacted after April 28th?
26. Has your *wat* been involved in any interfaith events or activities with the mosques in the surrounding area, before or after January 2004?
27. What do you think is the *phra*'s role during all of this?
28. Is there anything about the situation that the public is not aware about?

NOTES

Introduction

* King Vajiravudh, Rama VI, From *The Buddhist Attitude toward National Defense and Administration* (1916)

1. Personal interview over the phone with Ačhān Pim from Pattani, August 14, 2004.
2. Ibid.
3. Srisompob Jitpiromsri, "Sixth Year of the Southern Fire: Dynamics of Insurgency and Formation of the New Imagined Violence," *Deep South Watch* (Prince of Songkhla University: Center for Conflict Studies and Cultural Diversity, 2010), 1.
4. Buddhist monks often discussed the murders of soldiers, police, and other monks. This became a nightly topic under the pavilion. However, monks rarely, if ever, reflected on the increasing number of Muslim deaths around them. Peace Studies scholar Chaiwat Satha-anand observed similar sentiments in 2005: "The divisions are indeed deepening between the Buddhists and the Muslims due to the taboos being violated and the escalating violence." Marwaan Macan-Markar, "Fighting for Peace in Thailand," *Asia Times*, November 3, 2005, accessed at http://www.atimes.com/atimes/Southeast_Asia/GK03Ae01.html on January 28, 2007.
5. "I call such images 'cosmic' because they are larger than life. They evoke great battles of the legendary past, and they relate to metaphysical conflicts between good and evil. Notions of cosmic war are intimately personal but can also be translated to the social plane. Ultimately, though, they transcend human experience." Mark Juergensmeyer, *Terror in the Mind of God: The Global Rise of Religious Violence* (Berkeley: University of California Press, 2001), 146.
6. Kamala Tiyavanich, *Forest Recollections: Wandering Monks in Twentieth-Century Thailand* (Honolulu: University of Hawaii Press, 1997).
7. Political protests and massive demonstrations led to violent clashes between organized protestors and Thai armed personnel—most particularly devastating on April 10, April 22, and May 19 of 2010. "Ajahn, who has been a monk for 22 years, admits that the political situation in the country has broken society into two and that it is hard even for monks to control their thoughts, feelings and rise above the political divide. So, there are red monks who are anti-government and followers of ousted Prime Minister Thaksin Shinawatra and yellow monks who are pro-government and for Prime Minister Abhisit Vejjajiva." Shahanaaz Habib, The Eng Hock, and Brian Moh, "Staying Neutral Is Hard for Monks," *The Star Online*, April 19, 2010.
8. State is capitalized in accordance with Antonio Gramsci's neo-Marxist concepts of domination and hegemony in his State/Civil Society dichotomy. Antonio Gramsci, *Selections from the Prison Notebooks of Antonio Gramsci*, ed. and trans. Quintin Hoare and Geoffrey Nowell Smith (New York: International Publishers, 1971), xiv. While the State cannot be

"found" a priori (Trouillot, 126), and aggregating the State can lead to confusing a system of political and bureaucratic processes with a coherent and unified "thing," the systemic power and influence permeating from these processes requires a reference. See Peter van der Veer, "Writing Violence," in *Contesting the Nation: Religion, Community, and the Politics of Democracy in India*, ed. David Ludden (Philadephia: University of Pennsylvania Press, 1996), 261 and Tony Day, *Fluid Iron: State Formation in Southeast Asia* (Honolulu: University of Hawai'i Press, 2002), 92.

9. "It looks as if, only when Buddhism occupies the sole basis for the definition of Thai cultural identity, could Thai Buddhism exercise religious tolerance toward others." Suwanna Satha-anand, "Buddhist Pluralism and Religious Tolerance in Democratizing Thailand," in *Philosophy, Democracy, and Education*, ed. Philip Cam (Seoul: Korean National Commission for UNESCO, 2003), 212.

10. Ravina Aggarwal, *Beyond Lines of Control: Performance and Politics on the Disputed Borders of Ladakh, India* (Durham: Duke University Press, 2004), 19.

11. Duncan McCargo also notes that most academic discussion and media commentary on the violence has "portrayed the unrest as an example of the 'Islamic militancy'..." "Thai Buddhism, Thai Buddhists and the Southern Conflict," *Journal of Southeast Asian Studies* 40.1 (Feb. 2009), 2.

12. Any historical references will follow Thongchai's practice of using Siam and Siamese for the country and people prior to 1941, and Thailand and Thai for any post-1941 or general context. Thongchai Winichakul, *Siam Mapped: A History of the Geo-Body of a Nation* (Chiang Mai: Silkworm Books, 1998), 18.

13. David Wyatt, *Thailand: A Short History* (Chiang Mai: Trasvin Publications, 1982), 172.

14. See Duncan McCargo, *Tearing Apart the Land: Islam and Legitimacy in Southern Thailand* (Ithaca: Cornell University Press, 2008), 168–74.

15. Andrew Marshall and Don Pathan, "In Death's Shadow" in *Time Magazine Asia*, November 26, 2006, from http://www.time.com/time/magazine/article/0,9171,1563009-2,00.html accessed on November 28, 2006.

16. Marc Askew, "The Killing Fields of the Deep South: A Deadly Mix," *Bangkok Post*, August 9, 2009.

17. Surin Pitsuwan, *Islam and Malay Nationalism: A Case Study of the Malay-Muslims of Southern Thailand* (Bangkok: Thai Khadi Research Institute, Thammasat University, 1985), 216.

18. McCargo, *Tearing*, 2.

19. "Special Operation for the Four Southern Border Provinces," "Ramkamhaeng Operation," and "Special Terrorist Campaign in the Three Border Provinces" were the code names for the Thai operations between 1968 until 1975 that resulted in the deaths of 329 "terrorists." Wan Kadir Che Man, *Muslim Separatism: The Moros of Southern Philippines and the Malays of Southern Thailand*, (New York: Oxford University Press, 1990), 100.

20. "Rebels Die in Bloodbath," *Bangkok Post*, 29 April 2004.

21. There has been confusion over the dates of the Dunsun-nyor revolt, in which local Malay Muslims fought against the Thai military and suffered heavy casualties, and the Khru Se Mosque Affair. The Dunsun-nyor revolt occurred on April 26 and 27 (1948), while the Khru Se Mosque Affair took place on April 28 (2004). The similar month and days have led many Thais to believe that the Khru Se Mosque attacks were connected to the atrocities in Dunsun-nyor.

22. International Crisis Group, "Southern Thailand: The Problem with Paramilitaries," *Asia Report No. 140*, (October 23, 2007): 6.

23. Tak Bai civilians were laid flat on top of each other in the back of military vans. Most suffocated to death.

24. Videos taken at the scene of the Tak Bai massacre were uploaded onto the internet for general viewing. The images displayed the Thai police and soldiers' brutality. One in particular, entitled "Kwāmčhing...tī tāk bai" [The Truth...at Tak Bai], was accessed at http://www.youtube.com on November 15, 2006. There also are English versions, such as "The Tak Bai Massacre: The True Story," edited and submitted by The Patani Support Group, Sweden.

25. Ukrist Pathmanand, "Thaksin's Achilles' Heel: The Failure of Hawkish Approaches in the Thai South," *Critical Asian Studies* 38.1 (2006): 73–93.

26. The four provinces are Songkhla, Pattani, Yala, and Narathiwat. Although Songkhla is not considered part of the violence, a few of its districts bordering Pattani are under martial law. "Update: Extremists Launch Overnight Wave of Violence," *Bangkok Post*, February 19, 2007.

27. Aphisit was elected prime minister. He listed the southern violence as his number one concern in an article, originally published in *Matichon* on July 21, 2006, but reissued due to its political relevance in the 2007 elections. The southern newspaper *Iisrā Samākhom* called it "Phisit hokinwā thī nāyok... chūwāra prachāchon 4 dān" [Aphisit Displays Leader Characteristic as a Prime Minister To Be: Promoting the People's Agenda in Four Areas] on July 22, 2007.

28. *Human Rights Watch*, "Thailand, No One Is Safe: Insurgent Violence against Civilians in Thailand's Southern Border Provinces," (Aug. 2007): 1–102, 6.

29. McCargo, "Thai Buddhism," 1–10, 2.

30. Marc Askew, "Landscapes of Fear, Horizons of Trust: Villagers Dealing with Danger in Thailand's Insurgent South," *Journal of Southeast Asian Studies* 40.1 (February 2009): 59–86, 76.

31. Srisompob Jitpiromsri and Duncan McCargo, "The Southern Thai Conflict Six Years On: Insurgency, Not Just Crime," *Contemporary Southeast Asia* 32.2 (2010): 156–83, 157.

32. Amporn Mardent, "Buddhist Perceptions of Muslims in the Thai South." Paper presented at Asian Area Studies Conference in Boston, 22–25 March 2007. For further details on this association, see chapter 6.

33. International Crisis Group, "Recruiting Militants in Southern Thailand," *Asia Report No. 170* (June 22, 2009): 6.

34. An early, yet passionate, pamphlet on Jihad in Pattani is "Berjihad di Pattani" [Implementing Jihad in Pattani]. It was written by Assulook Ismulyameena (pseudonym), Kelantan, Malaysia, August 2002. Excerpts of this can be found in Greg Fealy and Virgina Hooker, eds., *Voices of Islam in Southeast Asia: A Contemporary Sourcebook* (Singapore: Institute of Southeast Asian Studies, 2006), 396–410. It should be noted here that most of the current leaflets stress nationalist concerns rather than issues of jihad.

35. Thai: 1. *yāy thī nơng rư ŏŏpayop ŏŏknŏk pưn thī sām čhangwatcāyphāktai sīa.* 2. *maihai khwāmrūammư kab nātī thāmrūak tahān.* 3. *hām khlukkhlīa yūrūam kan rư ding kab čhaonātī thāmrūak tahān khaomūbān.* Michael Jerryson, trans. "Anonymous Leaflet," Khokpo District, Pattani Province, Thailand, December 8, 2006. The leaflet was typed in Thai and addressed to "every Thai" (*rīyen khonthai tuk khon*). Malay Muslims primarily communicate in Arabic script and do not refer to themselves as Thai; rather, they refer to themselves as Malay (Bahasa Melayu: *orang melayu, orang nayu*).

36. Che Man, *Muslim Separatism*, 103. See also *Isrā Samākhom*, "Phūnam sūng sut thāng sāsanā islām khong īyip ph.b.ph.l.' surayut nunsandiwithī kāe panhā tai" [One of the Elite Leaders of Egyptian Islam Meets with General Surayud to Show Support for Peaceful Methods of Solving the Southern Problem], June 25, 2007.

37. Starting in 2009, the Abhisit government began to classify the conflict as largely criminal. Instead of references such as "insurgents," authorities and parts of the media use "perpetrators of violence" (*phu ko kwāmrungraeng*). The shift in labels alters the perceived dimension of the conflict from an international to a national affair. Jitpiromsri and McCargo, "Southern Thai Conflict," 156–83, 178.

38. Stanley Jeyaraja Tambiah, *Leveling Crowds: Ethnonationalist Conflicts and Collective Violence in South Asia* (Berkeley: University of California Press, 1996), 257, 266.

39. Asad argues that the term "religion" cannot be applied universally, "not only because its constituent elements and relationships are historically specific, but because that definition is itself the historical product of discursive processes." Talal Asad, *Genealogies of Religion: Discipline and Reasons of Power in Christianity and Islam* (Baltimore: John Hopkins University Press, 1993), 29.

40. Language has its limits and we should be aware of them. That said, the isolation and confinement of language to a specific context restricts constructive comparative studies, as

well as inhibits important dialogue between the author and the reader. Incidentally, there are many other English words (if not all) that fail in their universal applications for similar reasons, such as politics, history, truth, justice, morality, etc.

41. "So far as religion is concerned, the problem becomes one of a particular sort of perspective, a particular manner of interpreting experience, a certain way of going at the world as opposed to other ways, and the implications such a perspective has for conduct." Clifford Geertz, *Islam Observed: Religious Development in Morocco and Indonesia* (Chicago: University of Chicago Press, 1971), 96. Asad critiques Geertz's use of religion, particularly because Geertz invites scholars to "separate it conceptually from the domain of power." Asad, *Genealogies of Religion*, 29–35. However, I do not see Asad's critique as germane to this context; power is embedded in a worldview and a code of conduct.

42. Charles Long, *Signification: Signs, Symbols, and Images in the Interpretation of Religion* (Aurora, CO: Fortress Press, 1995), 7.

43. The Thai *sāsanā* derives from the Pāli *sāsana*, a wide-reaching term that often refers to the Buddha's teachings.

44. Derrida kindly but resolutely reminds us that religion was named in Latin and that it is intrinsically tied to the globalization of Latinity. The genesis of religion may be found in Latin and Eurasian sentiments, but as Dr. Ambedkar persuasively argues, one's birth does not necessitate one's identity. Jacques Derrida, "Faith and Knowledge: The Two Sources of 'Religion' at the Limits of Reason Alone," in *Religion*, ed. Jacques Derrida and Gianni Vattimo (Stanford: Stanford University Press, 1996), 29.

45. Gayatri Spivak, "Can the Subaltern Speak?" in *Marxism and the Interpretation of Culture*, ed. Cary Nelson and Lawrence Grossberg (Urbana: University of Illinois Press, 1988), 280.

46. Walter Benjamin, "Critique of Violence," in *Reflections: Essays, Aphorisms, Autobiographical Writings*, ed. Peter Demetz (New York: Schocken Books, 1978), 278. Benjamin finds within these legal parameters mythical and divine acts of violence, for "If mythical violence is lawmaking, divine violence is law-breaking." While divine violence is lawbreaking, Benjamin considers it a form of sovereign violence. Ibid., 297, 300.

47. Juergensmeyer, *Terror in the Mind of God*, 10.

48. James Aho, *This Thing of Darkness* (Seattle: University of Washington Press, 1994), 25.

49. Jacob Dalton, Taming of the Demons: A History of Violence in Tibetan Buddhism (forthcoming, 2011).

50. See Paul Demiéville, "Buddhism and War," in *Buddhist Warfare*, ed. Michael Jerryson and Mark Juergensmeyer (New York: Oxford University Press, 2010).

51. Saskia Sassen, "The World's Third Spaces: Novel Assemblages of Territory, Authority, and Rights," at the Religion and Globalization in Asia Conference: Prospects, Patterns and Problems for the 21st Century, University of San Francisco, March 13–14, 2009.

52. National Statistical Office, "Population and Households Census 1970, 1980, 1990, 2000: Southern Provinces" (Bangkok: Prime Minister Office, 2003). Since the recent escalation in violence in 2004, we can only speculate that Buddhist population levels have decreased further.

53. From 2006 through 2010, Thailand has witnessed a revolving door of prime Ministers, with the current prime minister Abhisit Vejjajiva the fifth in five years. The continued instability of the central government in Bangkok has diverted attention and resources to addressing the problems in the southernmost province.

54. Trevor Ling uses the term "Buddhisms" to underline the importance history, politics and society have on a transnational religion such as Buddhism. For more information on this, see "Introduction," in Trevor Ling ed., *Buddhist Trends in Southeast Asia* (Sinagpore: Institute of Southeast Asian Studies, 1993) 1.

55. The Malay Muslim nomenclature is quite long and, although it stresses the complexity of their identity, which is stratified along religious, ethnic, and national lines, it does not reflect their self-identification or their contested space in Thailand (for an in-depth discussion of this, see chapter 5:. "Identity"). Thus, for the purposes of this book, I will use the label Malay Muslim even though this identity does not differentiate the Malay Muslims of Thailand from the Malay Muslims of the Philippines, Malaysia, Indonesia, etc.

56. See McCargo, "Thai Buddhism," Duncan McCargo, "The Politics of Buddhist Identity in Thailand in Thailand's Deep South: The Demise of Civil Religion?" (11-32), Michael Jerryson, "Appropriating a Space for Violence: State Buddhism in Southern Thailand" (33-57), and Askew, "Landscapes of Fear," (59-86)which are in the special edition of the *Journal of Southeast Asian Studies* 40.1 (Feb. 2009). ." Another account that seeks to fill this void comes from Lorraine M. Gesick, *In the Land of Lady White Blood: Southern Thailand and the Meaning of History* (Ithaca, NY: Southeast Asia Program, Cornell University, 1995).

57. In accordance with the arguments articulated by Judith Butler and Diana Taylor, who argue that cultural identities are performed, I understand the performative to be an aural and physical way of describing one dimension of cultural identity: religious identity. See Judith Butler, *Gender Trouble: Feminism and the Subversion of Identity* (New York: Routledge, 1990) and Diana Taylor, *The Archive and the Repertoire: Performing Cultural Memory in the Americas* (Durham, NC: Duke University Press, 2003).

58. Ordinarily, Thai monks instruct laity or other monks about Buddhisms .The Thai laity does not instruct monks on Buddhisms. According to the Pinit Ratanakul, director of the College of Religious Studies at Mahidol University, this is an unusual circumstance resulting from special permission granted to the College to enhance the monks' awareness of different religious traditions. Personal communication, Mahidol University, August 2003.

59. The reason for having a local Buddhist translator was twofold. First and foremost, in 2004 I was not proficient enough in Thai to deal with the very distinctly southern variant. Second, I wanted to mitigate my outsider-non-Buddhist persona.

60. I have maintained the Thai Buddhist graduate student's anonymity upon her request. She felt it was too dangerous to disclose her name in reference to this subject matter.

61. Personal communication with Phra Man on August 13, 2004 in the southernmost provinces.

62. Askew, "Landscapes of Fear," 59–86, 64.

63. The distinction between red, yellow, and green zones is subject to debate. Local Buddhists and Muslims told me that the colors indicate how dangerous a place is. In this way, one monk told me a few areas in Narathiwat and Yala were "black zones" (*boriwen sī dam*) because he considered them the most dangerous places in the three southernmost provinces. The International Crisis Group cites the Thai security forces' grouping of three levels of danger in the southernmost provinces: the red zones are Malay Muslim militant strongholds, the yellow zones are places where the militants have sought shelter, and green zones "less violence prone" areas. International Crisis Group, "Thailand's Emergency Decree: No Solution," *Asia Report No. 105* (November 18, 2005): 7.

64. Personal communication with an abbot from Yaring district of Pattani province, August 14, 2004.

65. Personal communication with Ačhān Subin from Wat Mutjalin in Nongčhik district, Pattani province, August 14, 2004.

66. Juergensmeyer, *Terror in the Mind of God*, 5.

67. Monks gave different accounts about Wat Chang Hai. Some felt it was in the yellow zone, others in the green zone. I eventually chose it due to its very high Buddhist population and its fortifications. Because of Wat Chang Hai's prestige and the academic attention it drew, I was unable to maintain its anonymity. Even a brief description of the *wat* and its history would identify it. However, unlike at Wat A and B, I did not promise the high-ranking monks from Wat Chang Hai complete anonymity. Other monks I interviewed from Wat Chang Hai have subsequently left for other regions or professions.

68. On March 14, 2007, a similar minivan was driving in Yala when it was ambushed. The minivans are very reliable transportation from Hat Yai, Songkhla, to the capital districts of Pattani, Yala, and Narathiwat, which leave as soon as they fill their quota of passengers. Unfortunately, their daily routines made them very viable targets for attack. One of these attacks made international deadlines due to its extremely gruesome details. Suspected Muslim militants ambushed a van going from Hat Yai to Yala Province. Most passengers were beheaded and only one person survived the encounter, albeit with a coma that lasted

several months. See Rungrawee C. Pinyorat, "Eight Killed in Attack on Van in Thailand," *Associated Press*, March 14, 2007 and Muhammad Ayub Pathan, "Eight Massacred in Van Ambush," *Bangkok Post*, March 15, 2007.

69. Hazard pay was common starting in 2004. In August 2004, I learned that teachers in the conflict region received an additional 1,000 baht a month, and police receive an additional 2,500 baht a month. These increases are quite substantial; however, they are for good reason. Teachers and police are common targets of violence by militants.

70. For example, the very reliable commercialized vans that travel from Hat Yai, Songkhla, to the capital districts of Pattani, Yala, and Narathiwat left as soon as they filled their quota of passengers. Unfortunately, their daily routines made them very viable targets for attack. One of these attacks made international deadlines due to its extremely gruesome details. Suspected Muslim militants ambushed a van going from Hat Yai to Yala Province. Most passengers were beheaded and only one person survived the encounter, albeit with a coma that lasted several months. Rungrawee C. Pinyorat, "Eight Killed in Attack on Van in Thailand," *Associated Press*, March 14, 2007.

71. See chapter 4: "Militarization" for more details on soldier and police duties and activities in the *wat*.

Chapter 1

1. Personal communication with Ačhān Dolmanach Baka in his office at the College of Islamic Studies, Prince of Songkhla University, Pattani, October 15, 2008.

2. Prior to 2004, teachers at private Islamic schools were free from the State or any central Islamic body to design their own curriculum. International Crisis Group, "Recruiting Militants in Southern Thailand," *Asia Report No. 170* (June 22, 2009), 4.

3. Thai students study the Sukhothai dynasty, followed by the Ayutthaya, Thonburi, and Chakri dynasties. In each case, they learn about the peripheral regions surrounding each dynasty, but only in relation to the dynasty's growth and power. The focal point throughout this historiography is the central reign, which today continues with Bangkok.

4. Surin Pitsuwan, *Islam and Malay Nationalism: A Case Study of the Malay Muslims of Southern Thailand* (Bangkok: Thai Khadi Research Institute, Thammasat University, 1985), 200.

5. The Associated Press reports that over 80 Buddhist teachers had been killed by January 24, 2008. "Buddhist Teacher Shot in Thailand," *Associated Press*, January 24, 2008. The International Crisis Group lists 290 public schools and 111 public school teachers and education officials killed as of June, 2009. International Crisis Group, "Recruiting," 5.

6. Johan Elverskog, *Buddhism and Islam on the Silk Road* (Philadelphia: University of Pennsylvania Press, 2010), 2.

7. Richard J. Evans, *In Defense of History* (New York: W. W. Norton, 2000), 128.

8. Janet Abu-Lughod, "On the Remaking of History: How to Reinvent the Past," in *Remaking History*, ed. Barbara Kruger and Phil Mariani (New York: New Press, 1998), 118.

9. Patani refers to the kingdom that included the southernmost provinces from the fifteenth century until the twentieth century. Pattani refers to the Thai southern province of the twentieth and twenty-first centuries. Most Malays from the southernmost province of Pattani still use the term "Patani" to refer to their province. The term Malay, like the term Chinese, is a blanket designation for various groups that live in a region mapped out by colonial powers. Although they infer a uniformity that does not implicitly exist, I will not note their complexities unless data is available and it is productive to do so.

10. Chris Baker and Sunait Chutintaranond, eds., *Recalling Local Pasts: Autonomous History in Southeast Asia* (Chiang Mai: Silkworm Books, 2002), vii.

11. One of the oldest Thai historical accounts is a product of royal design: a Buddhist cosmology entitled *Three Worlds According to King Ruang (trai phum phra ruang)*. Frank Reynolds considers it the first "truly literary" work in Thai, and the author Sukhothai King Phaya Lithai (r. 1347–1368) was heir-apparent during its composition .in 1345. Frank E. Reynolds, "Introduction," in *Three Worlds According to King Ruang: A Thai Buddhist*

Cosmology, translated by Frank E. Reynolds and Mani B. Reynolds (Berkeley: University of California Press, 1982), 5.

12. He isolates three discrete chronological categories for Thai history-making: *tamnan, phongsawadan,* and *prawatsat. Tamnan* histories existed largely in the fifteenth to seventeenth centuries and connect Thai history to the origins of Buddhism. *Phongsawadan* histories developed in the seventeenth to nineteenth centuries and orient on the development of kings and dynasties. The most recent *prawatsat* histories engage in the development of the nation-state (and are heavily influenced by technological advents such as printing presses and library services). Charnvit Kasetsiri largely views these categories as discrete, acting in succession to one another, although he cites the pervading presence of *phongsawadan* in contemporary historiographies. However, contemporary Thai historiography contains all three in varying degrees: Buddhist, monarchical, and nation-building, and thus suggests a more coterminous relationship among the three styles. Charnvit Kasetsiri, "Thai Historiography from Ancient Times to the Modern Period," in *Perceptions of the Past in Southeast Asia*, ed. Anthony Reid and David Marr (Singapore: Heinemann Educational Books (Asia) Ltd., 1979), 156.

13. See Fred Riggs, *Thailand: The Modernization of a Bureaucratic Polity* (Honolulu: East-West Center Press, 1966) and Duncan McCargo, "Network Monarchy and Legitimacy Crises in Thailand," *Pacific Review* 18.4 (December 2005): 499–519.

14. Benedict Anderson, *Imagined Communities: Reflections on the Origins and Spread of Nationalism* (London: Verso, 1991), 204.

15. Craig J. Reynolds, "Religious Historical Writing and the Legitimation of the First Bangkok Reign," in *Perceptions of the Past in Southeast Asia*, ed. Anthony Reid and David Marr (Singapore: Heinemann Educational Books (Asia) Ltd., 1979), 90.

16. Kenneth Landon, *Siam in Transition: A Brief Survey of Cultural Trends in the Five Years since the Revolution of 1932* (Chicago: University of Chicago Press, 1939), 84.

17. Chavivun Prachuabmoh, "The Role of Women in Maintaining Ethnic Identity and Boundaries: A Case of Thai-Muslims (The Malay Speaking Group) in Southern Thailand," (PhD diss., Department of Anthropology, University of Hawai'i, 1980), 91.

18. Francis R. Bradley, "The Social Dynamics of Islamic Revivalism in Southeast Asia: The Rise of the Patani School, 1785–1909," (PhD diss., Department of History, University of Wisconsin–Madison, 2010), 7.

19. Thongchai Winichakul, *Siam Mapped: A History of the Geo-Body of a Nation* (Chiang Mai: Silkworm Books, 1998), 4. For more information on the role of Thainess, see chapter 5.

20. Peter Jackson argues that the modern idealization of Sukhothai originates with King Mongkut and his reforms of the Thai *sangha* in the nineteenth century. Peter A. Jackson, "Thai-Buddhist Identity: Debates on the *Traiphum Phra Ruang*," in *National Identity and Its Defenders: Thailand Today*, ed. Craig J. Reynolds (Chiang Mai: Silkworm Books, 2002), 172.

21. Personal communication with Mr. Adam, secondary education history teacher at Thamavitya Mulniti School in the capital district of Yala, October 17, 2008.

22. Chavivun Prachuabmoh, "The Role of Women in Maintaining Ethnic Identity and Boundaries: A Case of Thai-Muslims (The Malay Speaking Group) in Southern Thailand," (PhD diss., Department of Anthropology, University of Hawai'i, 1980), 92.

23. Thai: *phūmi phāk ēsīataweanōkchīengtai mī kānpokkhrong lāi rūp bāeb nai raya rāek dairab itthiphon čhak indīa thang nāeo khwāmkhit rūang sammattēp lae khatthām čhāk phraphutthasāsanā kānpokkhrong bāebnī chai kan nai lāi ānāčhak chen thai phamā kamphūchā lāo indonīsīa malāyū tomā mūangindonīsīa lae malāyū dai plīenpai naptū sāsanāislām kānpokkhrong čhung plīenpai dōi mī sultān pen pramuk khong prathēt. Prawatisāt m. 5: chan mathayom sūksā pī thī 5* [History, Year 5: Fifth Year Education for Secondary Education] (Bangkok: Aksončharōenthat, 2007), 66.

24. *Prawatisāt m. 1: chan mathayom sūksā pī thī 1* [History, Year 1: First Year Education for Secondary Education] (Bangkok: Aksončharōenthat, 2007), *Prawatisāt m. 2: chan mathayom sūksā pī thī 2* [History, Year 2: Second Year Education for Secondary Education] (Bangkok: Aksončharōenthat, 2007), *Prawatisāt m. 3: chan mathayom sūksā pī thī 3* [History, Year 3:

Third Year Education for Secondary Education] (Bangkok: Aksončharõenthat, 2007), *Prawatisāt m. 4: chan mathayom sūksā pī thī 4* [History, Year 4: Fourth Year Education for Secondary Education] (Bangkok: Aksončharõenthat, 2007), *Prawatisāt m. 5: chan mathayom sūksā pī thī 5* [History, Year 5: Fifth Year Education for Secondary Education] (Bangkok: Aksončharõenthat, 2007), *Prawatisāt m. 6: chan mathayom sūksā pī thī 6* [History, Year 6: Six Year Education for Secondary Education] (Bangkok: Aksončharõenthat, 2007).

25. Personal communication with Mr. Ali at a private Islamic school in the capital district of Yala, October 17, 2008.

26. Ibid.

27. Pattani has two Educational Administrations, Yala has two Educational Administrations, and Narathiwat has three Educational Administrations. Each administration oversees the educational system for its area.

28. Personal conversation with Mr. Wali, principle of Bengama School in the capital district of Pattani Province, October 17, 2008.

29. Personal communication with Ačhān Dolmanach Baka in his office at the College of Islamic Studies, Prince of Songkhla University, Pattani, October 15, 2008.

30. *Prawatisāt m. 2: chan mathayom sūksā pī thī 2* [History, Year 2: Second Year Education for Secondary Education] (Bangkok: aksončharõenthat, 2007), 156, 157.

31. Srīsakon Walliphōdom collected and synthesized oral narratives from the southernmost provinces in *Lao kān tamnāna tai* [The Numerous Utterances and Myths of the South] (Bangkok: Mahidol University, 2007).

32. Derek Elley, "Queen of Langkasuka," *Variety Magazine*, June 30, 2008, accessed at http://www.variety.com/index.asp?layout=festivals&jump=review&reviewid=VE1117937586&cs=1 on November 11, 2008.

33. A. Teeuw and D. K. Wyatt, eds. and trans., *Hikayat Patani: The Story of Patani* (The Hague: Koninklijk Instituut, 1970), 2.

34. Wayne Bougas, *The Kingdom of Patani: Between Thai and Malay Mandala* (Bangi, Selangor: University of Kebangsaan Malaysia: Institute of the Malay World and Civilization, 1994), 7.

35. Nik Hassan Shuaimi Nik Abdul Rahman, "Srivijaya" in *The Encyclopedia of Malaysia*, vol. 4, ed. Nik Hassan Shuhaimi Nik Abdul Rahman (Singapore: Didier Millet, 1998): 118–21, 119.

36. Hermann Kulke, *Kings and Cults: State Formation and Legitimation in India and Southeast Asia* (New Delhi: Manohar, 1993), 304.

37. George Coedès, *The Indianized States of Southeast Asia*, ed. Walter F. Vella and trans. Susan Brown Cowing (Honolulu: East-West Center Press, 1968), 81.

38. Akin to Antonio Gramsci's observations on northern and southern Italy, we find in the context of Thailand that the State bias is not only religious, but regional as well.

39. Prachuabmoh, "Role of Women," 190.

40. Personal communication with Ačhān Kaimōk, professor of history at the Prince of Songkhla University, Pattani, John F. Kennedy Library, October 14, 2008.

41. Francis R. Bradley, "The Social Dynamics of Islamic Revivalism in Southeast Asia: The Rise of the Patani School, 1785–1909," (PhD diss., Department of History, University of Wisconsin–Madison, 2010), 5.

42. In 2007, 91,982 students studied at Islamic schools whereas only 15,071 students studied at the 249 *pondoks*. Ibrahem Narongraksakhet, "Kānsuksā nai dindaenmalāyū," [Education in the Malay Region] in *Rāyngān krongkānprachum tāng wichākān rūang malāyū kab ratthai nai mitbrawatisāt lāe āryatham kab kānsāngkwāmpentham* [Report on an Academic Conference on Melayu and the Thai State in Aspects of History, Civilization and Justice] (Pattani, 2008 [B.E. 2551]), 195, 201.

43. Bradley criticizes that al-Fatani's chronology for Patani's seventeenth-century political history is more plausible than the chronology found Teeuw and Wyatt's version of the *Hikayat Patani*. See Francis R. Bradley, "Moral Order in a Time of Damnation: The *Hikayat Patani* in Historical Context," *Journal of Southeast Asian Studies* 40.2 (2009): 267–93, 274–76.

44. In the *Malay Annals* , the word Patani comes from the actions of a Siamese prince who had converted to Islam. Having conquered the kingdom of Cota Meliyei, the prince ordered a search for a location to establish his capital. His followers came upon land suitable for a capital that was well positioned near the sea. As the narrative explains, the only inhabitants of the land were a fisherman and his son, Tani. It is from the name Pa-tani, Tani's father, that we get the name of the newly formed city, Patani. John Leyden trans., *Malay Annals: with an Introduction by Sir Thomas Stamford Raffles* [Microfilm] (London: Longman, Hurst, Reese, ORMF, and Brown, Paternoster-row, 1821), 319, 320. The *Hikayat Patani* has a slightly different version with the king's subjects spotting a mystical white moose-deer on the shore next to the fisherman's hut. Wyatt and Teeuw review other Malay accounts of Patani's origins in their commentary. Teeuw and Wyatt, *Hikayat Patani*, 146–47, 217–21.

45. Ibrahim Syukri, *History of the Malay Kingdom of Patani*, trans. Conner Bailey and John N. Miksic (Athens: Ohio University, Center for International Studies, 1985). Francis Bradley considers the publication in or around 1950, with the English translation 35 years later. Bradley, "Social Dynamics," 26.

46. Syukri argues that Patani lost its autonomy for the first time in 1785. "This defeat was the first in the history of the Malay Kingdom of Patani, and signified the loss of independence of the Malay Kingdom of Patani and the abolition of the sovereignty of the Malay Rajas which had been defended for hundreds of years." He then notes the second defeat that came in 1791. This had greater impact, however, because it resulted in the division of Patani into "several provinces." Ibrahim Syukri, *History of the Malay Kingdom* , 44, 53.

47. International Crisis Group, "Recruiting," 6.

48. Personal communication with Ačhăn Kaimŏk, professor of history at the Prince of Songkhla University, John F. Kennedy Library, October 14, 2008.

49. For historian William Green, the periodization of world history is inherently political: "Ideally, all periodizations should be rooted in disciplined concepts of continuity and change," but in trying to map the theory of historical change he concedes, "We cannot hope to be value-free in our formulation of theory. Our theories reflect our priorities." William A. Green, "Periodizing World History," *History and Theory* 34.2 (May 1995): 99–111, 101.

50. One extreme example comes from the *Bangkok Post*, one of Thailand's English newspapers, which keeps a count of beheadings in the southernmost provinces.

51. One of many accounts comes from *The Nation*, another Thai English-language newspaper. The newspaper has devoted a separate web page to chronicle the violence in the southernmost provinces. "Fire on South: Violence and Peace Building," the title of the page, begins its query with January 4, 2004. http://www.nationmultimedia.com/specials/south2-years/index.php, accessed last on September 17, 2007. Exceptions to this form of periodization come from such notable scholars such as Chaiwat Satha-anand, who has submitted editorials for the *Bangkok Post*, or Nidhi Aeusrivongse's column in *Matichon*.

52. Translated from Thai in "Faitai ĭk dăn lang măn khwan" [The Southern Fire: Another Perspective behind the Smoke Screen], *Pāčhārisăn* (April–June 2007): 34–43, 35.

53. Thai: *tāe čhŏn samkhan khŭ khrai pen phŭčhĕračhă čhĕračhă kab khrai*. Phk. Phongtĕp Suthĭrwut, "Panhă wikrit cäidăenphăktai" [The Problem of the Southern Border Crisis], *Matichon* 30.10719, July 16, 2007.

54. Newspapers generally assign responsibility to the newest separatist movement, the Runda Kumbulan Kecil.

55. See Andrew Marshall, "Thailand's Endless Woe," *Time Magazine Asia*, July 19, 2007, and "In Death's Shadow," *Time Magazine Asia*, November 28, 2006.

56. Nidhi Aeursriwongse, "Understanding the Situation in the South as a 'Millenarian Revolt,'" *Kyoto Review of Southeast Asia* (March 2005), accessed at http://kyotoreview.cseas.kyoto-u.ac.jp/issue/issue5/article_380.html on February 15, 2007.

57. See David Forgacs, ed., *The Antonio Gramsci Reader: Selected Writings 1916–1935* (New York: New York University Press, 2000). Subaltern Studies develops the notion of uninterpretability further and connects Gramsci's theory to India. For a comprehensive example

of this, see Ranajit Guha's *Elementary Aspects of Peasant Insurgency in Colonial India* (Delhi: Oxford University Press, 1992).

58. Davisakd Puaksom interprets the phrase "since time immemorial" to mean the Sukhothai kingdom. Puaksom references Prince Damrong Rajanubhab, "Historical Background to the Dispatches of Luang Udomsombat," in *Rama III and the Siamese Expedition to Kedah in 1839: The Dispatches of Luang Udomsombat*, ed. Justin Corfield, trans. Cyril Skinner (Center of Southeast Asian Studies, Melbourne: Monash University, 1993), 1. "Of a Lesser Brilliance: Patani Historiography in Contention," in *Thai South and Malay North: Ethnic Interactions on a Plural Peninsula*, ed. Michael J. Montesano and Patrick Jory (Singapore: NUS Press, 2008).

59. Thanet Aphornsuvan, "Origins of Malay Muslim 'Separatism' in Southern Thailand" *Thai South and Malay North: Ethnic Interactions on a Plural Peninsula*, ed. Michael J. Montesano and Patrick Jory (Singapore: NUS Press, 2008), 91.

60. For detailed examples of this colonial pressure, see David Streckfuss, "The Mixed Colonial Legacy in Siam: Origins of Thai Racialist Thought, 1890–1910," in *Autonomous Histories, Particular Truths: Essays in Honor of John Smail*, ed. Laurie Sears (Madison, WI: Center for Southeast Asian Studies) and Tamara Loos, *Subject Siam: Family, Law, and Colonial Modernity in Thailand* (Ithaca: Cornell University Press, 2006).

61. Maurizio Peleggi, *Thailand: The Worldly Kingdom* (Singapore: Talisman Publishing, 2007), 156.

62. Mongkut used *wat* as cultural perimeter posts to demarcate the borders of Siamese territory and "culture" from that of the Malay Muslim regions of Kedah, Kelantan, Terengganu, and other southern Malay principalities occupied by the British. Personal conversation with Irving Johnson at National University of Singapore, February 20, 2006.

63. Thongchai, *Siam Mapped*, 141, 142

64. Loos, *Subject Siam*, 3.

65. For more information on the conflict at the Khru Se Mosque affair, please see the Introduction.

66. Wan Kadir Che Man, *Muslim Separatism: The Moros of Southern Philippines and the Malays of Southern Thailand* (New York: Oxford University Press, 1990), 66.

67. The seven demands are listed in Surin, *Islam and Malay Nationalism*, 152.

68. Hajji Sulong was an accomplished scholar who ran an Islamic school in Saudi Arabia before returning to his home in Pattani. After being arrested in 1948, he was tried for slandering the government and was imprisoned until 1952. In 1954, he was summoned to police headquarters by the police chief in the neighboring province of Songkhla and immediately thereafter disappeared. His death remains a mystery. Che Man, *Muslim Separatism*, 66–68.

69. Surin, *Islam and Malay Nationalism*, 161.

70. Thanet, "Origins."

71. Thanet goes into great detail about this historical collapsing of events in "Origins."

72. Chaiwat Satha-anand, "The Silence of the Bullet Monument: Violence and 'Truth' Management, Dusun-Ynor 1948, and Kru-Ze 2004," *Critical Asian Studies* 38.1 (2006): 11–37, 22–26. One noteworthy example is a police officer's explanation that the top of the Bullet monument contained the actual bones of policemen, commemorating those who fell in battle during this two-day conflict.

73. For instance, historians such as Chaiwat Satha-anand and Davisakd Puaksom state that the Dusun-Ynor revolt occurred on April 28, 1948. Chaiwat, "Silence of the Bullet Monument," 11–37, 22–26 Puaksom, "Of a Lesser Brilliance," 86.

74. Thanet, "Origins," 96.

75. Alessandro Portelli, "The Death of Luigi Trastulli: Memory and the Event," in *The Death of Luigi Trastulli and Other Stories: Form and Meaning in Oral History*, ed. Michael Frisch (New York: State University of New York Press, 1991), 1–26, 26.

76. G. W. Skinner states that prior to 1893, Chinese women almost never immigrated to Siam. Cantonese women were the first to immigrate to Siam in large numbers in the early 1900s.

They were followed by the Teo Chiu women in the early 1920s. Prior to 1905, only some of the wealthy Chinese merchants were able to bring their wives to Siam, and "most of the other China-born females were prostitutes." G. W. Skinner, *Chinese Society in Thailand: An Analytical History*, (Ithaca: Cornell University Press,1957), 126, 196, 197. Kenneth Landon notes that the majority of Chinese prostitutes at this time were either Cantonese or Hainanese. *The Chinese in Thailand* (London: Oxford University Press, 1941), 97.

77. These *lūkčhin*, who are typically identified as Thai Chinese, have a distinctly different relationship with Thais and Malays than their Chinese ancestors. As a result of constant and heavy immigration, the vast majority of Thais claim some Chinese ancestry. When asked about their genealogy, Thais will usually give their Thai and Chinese percentage. Richard J. Coughlin, *Double Identity: The Chinese in Modern Thailand* (Hong Kong: Cathay Press, 1960), 89.

78. Landon, *Siam in Transition*, 87.

79. See Jovan Maud's "The Nine Emperor Gods at the Border: Transnational Culture, Alternate Modes of Practice, and the Expansion of the Vegetarian Festival in Hat Yai" in *Dynamic Diversity in Southern Thailand*, ed. Wattana Sugunnasil (Chiang Mai: Silkworm Books, 2005): 153–78.

80. Kenneth Landon notes that many of the Chinese dentists immigrated from British Malay or China (his specific account is of a Cantonese dentist proprietor); see *Chinese in Thailand*, 86. W. W. Skeat also notes the small-scale businesses and specialties owned and/or managed by the Chinese in the southernmost provinces. On May 13, 1899, he tried to inspect some Malay pottery and found to his surprise that "business was entirely in the hands of Chinese, and conducted on purely Chinese lines." Skeat, "Reminiscences of the Expedition, by the late W. W. Skeat, M.A., leader of the Expedition," *Journal of the Malaysian Branch Royal Asiatic Society* 26.4 (Dec. 1953): 9–147, 31.

81. Coughlin, *Double Identity*, 119. Skinner found that two-thirds of miners in the southernmost province of Yala were Cantonese. Skinner, *Chinese Society in Thailand*, 351.

82. The second largest entry of Chinese settlement was British Malaya with 1.7 million. Landon, *Chinese in Thailand*, 26. Figures from Landon's citation come from Li Chang-fu's *History of Chinese Colonization* (1937), and official figures from the National Overseas Commission of 1935.

83. In the late 1970s, Chavivun Prachuabmoh examined the main commercial areas of Pattani and found 266 Chinese stores, 25 Malay Muslim stores, and 46 Thai Buddhist stores. "Ethnic Relations among Thai, Thai Muslim and Chinese in South Thailand," in *Ethnicity and Interpersonal Interactions: A Cross Cultural Study*, ed. David Y. H. Wu (Hong Kong: Maruzen Asia, 1982): 62–83, 67.

84. Louis Golomb, *An Anthropology of Curing in Multiethnic Thailand* (Urbana: University of Illinois Press, 1985), 27.

85. Alexander Horstmann, "Hybrid Processes of Modernization and Globalization: The Making of Consumers in South Thailand," International Conference on Globalization, Development and the Making of Consumers: What Are Collective Identities for? The Hague, Netherlands, (March 13–16, 1997): 1–27, 8.

86. Local Thai Malay and Tais see Thai Chinese comprising the bourgeoisie class that has gained power in Thailand since the 1990s. Many Sino-Thais are known to be prejudiced against Thai Malays, considering them lazy or incompetent, a view unfortunately shared just a hundred kilometers south by the Thai Malays' kin in Malaysia. According to Horstmann, from the Chinese perspective "[t]he Malays are said to 'be illiterate,' 'dirty,' 'fanatic,'" while Malays feel the Chinese "exploit the Malay peasantry without mercy," and "would sell their grandmother." "Hybrid Processes," 8, 9.

87. Chaiwat gives a detailed account of the Khru Se Mosque's symbolism in *The Life of This World: Negotiated Muslim Lives in Thai Society* (Singapore: Marshall Cavendish 2005), 60–77.

88. Jovan Maud, "The Sacred Borderland: A Buddhist Saint, the State, and Transnational Religion in Southern Thailand," (PhD diss., Department of Anthropology, Macquarie University, 2007), xxi.

89. See Maud, "Nine Emperor Gods," 153–78.
90. Peter van der Veer, *Imperial Encounters: Religion and Modernity in India and Britain* (Princeton: Princeton University Press, 2001), 6, 85–104.
91. Since 2004, over 225 public schools have been destroyed in the three southernmost provinces. For a detailed and personal account about the role of public education in Afghanistan and Pakistan, see Greg Mortenson and David Relin, *Three Cups of Tea: One Man's Mission to Promote Peace . . . One School at a Time* (New York: Penguin, 2007).
92. Hans-Dieter Bechstedt, "Identity and Authority in Thailand," in *National Identity and Its Defenders: Thailand Today*, ed. Craig J. Reynolds (Chiang Mai: Silkworm Books, 2002), 246.
93. For an in-depth analysis of the absence of women in modern Iranian historiography, see Staci Scheiwiller, "Mirrors of Memory: Nineteenth-Century Imagery in Contemporary Iranian Photography," (PhD diss., Art History Department, University of California–Santa Barbara, 2009).
94. Leonard Thompson, *A History of South Africa* (New Haven: Yale University Press, 2000), 198.
95. Michael Jerryson, *Mongolian Buddhism: The Rise and Fall of the Sangha* (Chiang Mai: Silkworm Books, 2007), 69–96.
96. See Gyanendra Pandey, *The Construction of Communalism in Colonial North India* (Delhi: Oxford University Press, 1990).
97. The Israeli Education Ministry announced plans to include in the third-grade primer acknowledgements of Palestinian suffering in the first years of the Israeli state, which would be the first time such information was included in the official Israeli curriculum. This decision instantly prompted Israeli rightists to defend the Israeli school system's traditional one-sided teaching of history. Richard Boudreaux, "Israeli Textbook Tells of Arab Plight: The New Edition for Minority Third-graders Recognizes the Hardships to Palestinians Caused by the Nation's Creation," *Los Angeles Times*, July 23, 2007.
98. According to Michael Sells, the ideology of genocide is a "set of symbols, rituals, stereotypes, and partially concealed assumptions that dehumanize a people as a whole, [to] justify the use of military power to destroy them, and are in turn reinforced by the economic, political, and military beneficiaries of that destruction." *The Bridge Betrayed: Religion and Genocide in Bosnia* (Berkeley: University of California, 1996), 28.
99. For a look into the politics of myth and history, see Bruce Lincoln, *Discourse and the Construction of Society: Comparative Studies of Myth, Ritual and Classification* (New York: Oxford University Press, 1989), 21–26.
100. Walpola Rāhula's *The Heritage of the Bhikkhu* serves as an excellent example of the use of religious historical narratives. H. L. Seneviratne rightly points out that Rāhula's narrative of Buddhist monks is more an activist document than a scholarly treatise, making claims based off the mytho-historical *Mahāvaṃsa*. *The Work of Kings: The New Buddhism in Sri Lanka*, (Chicago: University of Chicago Press, 1999), 168.

Chapter 2

1. Thailand is a country that has no constitutional provisions for Thai Buddhism and is often heralded as secular (*rathabān thāng lok*). One defining characteristic for secular governments is the legal sequestering of religiosity to the private sphere. While Thailand officially maintains its platform as a secular country, its allowance of *shar'ia* in Muslim-dominated provinces and the intermingling of Buddhist ecclesiastical departments with its central governmental departments provide ample justification to critique this platform.
2. Personal communication and observations on July 29 and 30, 2004, in the capital district of Pattani Province.
3. In a 2009 report, Amnesty International noted an increase in reported tortures and ill-treatment of Malay Muslims and Malay Muslim families in the south between mid-2007 and mid-2008. Although there were reports and evidence of torture, Amnesty International could not locate any evidence to "indicate that the use of torture or ill-treatment is

pursuant to a written or verbal policy of the security forces, and torture has been consistently condemned at various levels of the Thai military and government both publicly and in private discussions with Amnesty International." Amnesty International, "Thailand: Torture in the Southern Counter-Insurgency," (London: Amnesty International Publications, 2009), 5. Amnesty International, Human Rights Watch, and the International Crisis Group all argue that the precedence for structural violence and disregard for human rights began before martial law with the Thai State's "war on drugs" in the southernmost provinces.

4. Wassana Nanuam and Yuwadee Tunyasiri, "Curfew May Be Imposed; 12 Arrested," *Bangkok Post*, January 28, 2004.

5. Stanley Jeyaraja Tambiah, *Leveling Crowds: Ethnonationalist Conflicts and Collective Violence in South Asia* (Berkeley: University of California Press, 1996), 22, 337.

6. Pierre Bourdieu's term "symbolic capital" is applicable for describing how one can become (and thereby embody the capital of) the job one performs. Pierre Bourdieu defines symbolic capital as "nothing more than economic or cultural capital which is acknowledged and recognized, when it is acknowledged in accordance with the categories of perception that it imposes, the symbolic power relations tend to reproduce and to reinforce the power relations which constitute the structure of the social space." Pierre Bourdieu, *In Other Words: Essays Towards a Reflexive Sociology*, trans. Matthew Adamson (Stanford: Stanford University Press, 1990), 135.

7. Local Buddhists didactically apply the Jātakas in their sermons in order to emphasize Thai Buddhist morality. Patrick Jory discusses King Bhumibol Adulyadej's application of the Mahājānaka Jātaka in a 1996 publication that led to alternative means of distribution, such as the re-creation of the story as a cartoon in 1999. For Jory, the use of the Jātaka was more for the king's benefit than that of the monks because the newly adapted story was a "thinly disguised allegory of the king's own career." "Thai and Western Buddhist Scholarship in the Age of Colonialism: King Chulalongkorn Redefines the Jātakas," *Journal of Asian Studies* 61.3 (August 2002): 891–918, at 891, n. 3.

8. For more information on femininity and Thai Buddhism, see Chatsumarn Kabilsingh (Dhammananda Bhikkhuni), *Thai Women in Buddhism* (Berkeley, CA: Parallax Press, 1991) and Penny Van Esterik, "Laywoman in Theravada Buddhism," in *Women of Southeast Asia*, ed. Penny Van Esterik (DeKalb: Northern Illinois University, 1982).

9. Tambiah also notes that the amulets are "really 'political' prizes providing access to and control of good things of this world." Stanley Jeyaraja Tambiah, *The Buddhist Saints of the Forest and the Cult of Amulets: A Study of Charisma, Hagiography, Sectarianism, and Millennial Buddhism* (Cambridge: Cambridge University Press, 1984), 344.

10. Donald Swearer, "Hypostatizing the Buddha: Buddhist Image Consecration in Northern Thailand," *History of Religions* 34 (1995): 263–80.

11. In this context, the simulacra would be the representation of the Buddhist monk, which Thai society (and the greater society of the world) perceives and relies upon more heavily than the actual thing in itself. Jean Baudrillard, *Simulacra and Simulation*, trans. Sheila Faria Glaser (Ann Arbor: University of Michigan, 1994).

12. Thomas Kirsch, "Complexities in the Thai Religious System: An Interpretation," *Journal of Asian Studies* 37.2 (February 1977): 241–66, 248.

13. The *wai* is not a formal way of greeting used by Malay Muslims in southern Thailand. According to the International Crisis Group, "even *wai*, a Thai way of greeting or showing respect by putting one's palms together at chest level, is considered by some Malay Muslims to be alien to their culture." "Recruiting Militants in Southern Thailand," *Asia Report No. 170* (June 22, 2009): 1–28, 5.

14. Thai newspapers are replete with scandals involving monks, but it is their social sacrality that makes their transgressions scandalous.

15. I use the term awaken instead of enlightenment, following Richard Cohen's argument (and that of many others, including his teacher Luis Gómez) that the correct translation of the Sanskrit verbal root *budh-* from which we get *buddha-* is "to wake up," and that the term enlightenment comes from a specific European intellectual context from the

seventeenth and eighteenth centuries. Richard Cohen, *Beyond Enlightenment: Buddhism, Religion, Modernity* (London: Routledge, 2009), 1, 9.

16. Craig J. Reynolds, "Power," in *Critical Terms for the Study of Buddhism*, ed. Donald S. Lopez Jr. (Chicago: University of Chicago Press, 2005), 224.

17. While Buddhist laity see monks as fields-of-merit, the term is not often applied (Pāli: *puñ-ñakkhetta*, Thai: *nā bun*). Stanley Jeyaraja Tambiah notes, "The layman, by giving material gifts, expects to accumulate merit in the form of ethical energy; the monk in turn in accepting these gifts confers merit on the donor." *Buddhism and the Spirit Cults in Northeast Thailand* (Cambridge: Cambridge University Press, 1970), 213.

18. Tambiah, *Leveling Crowds*, 334, 335.

19. Krishan Kumar and Ekaterina Makarova, "An Interview with José Casanova" *The Hedgehog Review* 4.2 (Summer 2002): 91–108, reprinted in *Global Studies 1*, ed. Giles Gunn (Dubuque, IO: Kendall/Hunt Publishing Company, 2003), 36.

20. Personal communication with a monk in the southernmost provinces, August 7, 2004.

21. "Another paradox is that it is generally thought that a monk should stay out of politics and should not use his spiritual powers for political purposes because a political monk does damage to the sangha; yet, the political monk has emerged from time to time in Buddhist countries. For example, he antedates the colonial period in Burma, and he was not unknown in Sri Lanka." Stanley Jeyaraja Tambiah, *World Conqueror, World Renouncer: A Study of Buddhism and Polity in Thailand against a Historical Background* (Cambridge: Cambridge University Press, 1976), 519.

22. There are other religions that have founders with royal lineages, such as Mahāvīra of Jainism and Kṛṣṇa of Vaiṣṇavism, often subsumed under the term Hinduism.

23. Uma Chakravarti, *The Social Dimensions of Early Buddhism* (Delhi: Munshiram Manoharlal Publishers, 1999), 7. While the same can be said of the Roman Catholic Church, this institutional structure was a later development in Christianity, occurring over three hundred years after Jesus's crucifixion. From the onset, Siddhattha Gotama established a social infrastructure that mirrored the political framework of polities indigenous to his time and region.

24. Balkrishna Govind Gokhale, "Dhamma as a Political Concept," *Journal of Indian History* 44 (August 1968): 249–61, 251.

25. I. B. Horner, trans., *The Book of the Discipline*, vol. 1, *Suttavibhanga* (Oxford: Pali Text Society, 1992), 74. For a further glimpse into a Buddhist king's role in torture, see Stephen Jenkins, "Making Merit through Warfare According to the *Ārya-Bodhisattva-gocara-upāyaviṣaya-vikurvaṇa-nirdeśa Sūtra*," in *Buddhist Warfare*, ed. Michael Jerryson and Mark Juergensmeyer (New York: Oxford University Press, 2010).

26. Chakravarti, *Social Dimensions*, 150.

27. Tambiah, *World Conqueror*, 515.

28. Justin McDaniel, *Gathering Leaves and Lifting Words: Histories of Buddhist Monastic Education in Laos and Thailand* (Seattle: University of Washington Press, 2008), 121.

29. Peter Jackson writes,

"[E]ach new political regime in the past century has attempted to restructure the organization of the order of Buddhist monks in its political image in order to maintain a legitimatory [sic] parallelism between the symbolic religious domain and the secular power structure.

Buddhism, Legitimation and Conflict: The Political Functions of Urban Thai Buddhism (Singapore: Institute of Southeast Asian Studies, 1989), 2.

30. For Kamala Tiyavanich, modern State Buddhism was a product of the Chulalongkorn administration (1873–1910). Advocates of State Buddhism treated Prince Wachirayan's printed religious texts, which determined degrees, examinations, and ranks in the *sangha* hierarchy, as authoritative. A distinct difference between State and Popular Buddhism was that State Buddhist orators emphasized a Bangkok interpretation of sermons and used Bangkok Thai stories about the Buddha's last life rather than using local dialects and stories about the Buddha's previous births. Kamala Tiyavanich, *Forest Recollections: Wandering Monks in Twentieth-Century Thailand* (Honolulu: University of Hawaii Press, 1997), 8, 9, 34.

31. Perhaps the most extreme example of this is the Emerald Buddha (*phra kāeo morakot*), a jasper sculpted buddha seated in a lotus posture. As a Thai palladium, the Emerald Buddha protects the country with its power and its physical form (Pāli: *rūpaka*) signifies the wholeness of the country. Most notably, it denotes the sovereignty of the current Chakri Dynasty, which has been the official custodian of the palladium since Rama I (1782–1809). For a comparative look at the Emerald Buddha and other Southeast Asian palladia, see Frank E. Reynolds, "The Holy Emerald Jewel: Some Aspects of Buddhist Symbolism and Political Legitimation in Thailand and Laos," in *Religion and Legitimation of Power in Thailand, Laos, and Burma*, ed. Bardwell L. Smith (Chambersburg, PA: ANIMA Books, 1978).

32. Reynolds, "Power," 211.

33. Christine Gray, "Thailand: The Soteriological State in the 1970s," (PhD diss., Department of Anthropology, University of Chicago, 1986), 42.

34. Craig Reynolds, "The Buddhist Monkhood in Nineteenth Century Thailand," (PhD diss., Cornell University, 1972), 270.

35. This is eloquently explained in Benedict Anderson's seminal book on nationalism: *Imagined Communities: Reflections on the Origin and Spread of Nationalism* (London: Verso, 1991), 1–8.

36. The Mahānikai became a school due to the emergence of a contrasting one, the Thammayut.

37. Wachirayan Warorot, *Autobiography*, trans. Craig Reynolds (Athens: Ohio University Press, 1979), 249, 250.

38. David Wyatt, *The Politics of Reform in Thailand: Education in the Reign of King Chulalongkorn* (New Haven: Yale University Press, 1969), 102–44

39. Yoneo Ishii, *Samgha, State, and Society: Thai Buddhism in History*, trans. Peter Hawkes (Honolulu: University of Hawaii Press, 1986), 68.

40. According to Tambiah, this connection between the Thai *sangha* and the State was most clearly evident in education. The Ministry of Education oversaw the promotion and improvement of ecclesiastical education, published religious textbooks and periodicals, established libraries, and revised syllabi. Tambiah, *World Conqueror*, 313.

41. Charles Keyes, "Buddhism and National Integration in Thailand," *Journal of Asian Studies* 30.3 (May 1971): 551–67, 555.

42. Tambiah, *World Conqueror*, 434–56.

43. Brawit Dandlanugul, *The History of wat Srisoda: Where the Regional Dhamma Jarika Project Is Situated in Chiang Mai, Thailand* (Chiang Mai: Saeng Silpa Printing Press, 2002), 36–38.

44. Paul Handley, *The King Never Smiles: A Biography of Thailand's Bhumibol Adulyadej* (New Haven: Yale University Press, 2006), 214–30.

45. Thai socialists also criticized Buddhism. Jit Phomisak, one of the most prominent Thai socialist writers in the 1950s and 1960s, disparaged Thai Buddhism (under the pseudonym City Slave) in "The Spirits of the Yellow Leaves," trans. Craig Reynolds (unpublished essay, University of Sydney, 1993).

46. Somboon Suksamran, *Political Buddhism in Southeast Asia: The Role of the Sangha in the Modernization of Thailand* (London: C. Hurst & Company, 1977), 23.

47. Handley, *King Never Smiles*, 230.

48. Handley, *King Never Smiles*, 235.

49. Somboon Suksamran, *Buddhism and Politics in Thailand* (Singapore: Institute of Southeast Asian Studies, 1982), 54.

50. Tambiah uses the term "political monk" as well, but in reference to Theravāda monks throughout South and Southeast Asia. As in the case of Thailand, he views political monks embodying a paradoxical role: "Another paradox is that, while the general norm is that a monk should keep away from politics and should not use his spiritual power for political purposes—because a political monk does damage to the *sangha*, yet the political monk has emerged from time to time in Buddhist countries." *World Conqueror*, 519.

51. Suwanna Satha-anand, "Buddhist Pluralism and Religious Tolerance in Democratizing Thailand," in *Philosophy, Democracy, and Education*, ed. Philip Cam (Seoul: Korean National Commission for UNESCO, 2003), 206.

52. Personal communication with Dr. Amnat at the Office of National Buddhism in Buddhamonthon, Nakhon Pathom, February 10, 2004.

53. Julian Kusa writes, "in 1992 under the auspices of the *Sangha* Council, the police monks were the *Sangha*'s answer and response to the spate of clerical misdemeanors exposed by the media and the burgeoning public perception that the *Sangha* was inert, morally decadent and lagging behind changes in society." "'Bad Boys, Bad Boys, Watcha Gonna Do? Watcha Gonna Do When They Come for You?'—Police monks (*Tamruat Phra*): The Thai *Sangha*'s Covert Disciplinary Enforcement Agency" The Ninth International Conference on Thai Studies, Northern Illinois University, April 4, 2005.

54. According to the *Vinaya* (monastic guidelines), monks are not allowed to handle money directly. This is circumvented through various means, such as placing money in an envelope and then passing the envelope on to a monk. Dr. Amnat explained that the Office of National Buddhism deposits money into monks' bank accounts on a monthly basis, leaving it up to the monk's discretion as to when and how they use it. Personal communication with Dr. Amnat at the Office of National Buddhism in Buddhamonthon, Nakhon Pathom, February 10, 2004.

55. Duncan McCargo, "Buddhism, Democracy and Identity in Thailand," *Democratization* 11.4 (August 2004): 155–70, 158.

56. In his analysis of Thai bureaucracies and organizations, anthropologist Richard Basham finds that highly vaulted individuals are often protected by a moral division of labor.

   As long as such individuals are seen as generous, honest, and devoted to the populace at large, people accept their legitimacy and will tolerate great deviation from the ideal from those in the lower and middle level.

   Richard Basham, "'False Consciousness' and the Problem of Merit and Power in Thailand," *Mankind* 19.2 (August 1989): 126–37, 134.

57. Nidhi Aeursriwongse argues that Thai Buddhism's vitality can be revitalized only by severing its intimacy between the *sangha* and the state. "'Onākhot khōng 'ongkonson" [The Future of the Sangha Organization], in *Mōng 'Onākhot: Botwikhrō phūa Praplīan Thisthāng Sangkhom Thai* [Looking to the Future: Analytical Essays to Change the Direction of Thai Society], ed. Nidhi Aeursriwongse et al. (Bangkok: Munithi Phumipnaya, 1993): 114–51.

58. *Bangkok Post*, "Bulls in China Shop Tend to Cause Havoc," January 28, 2004.

59. Kunsiri Olarikkachat, "Queen Again Calls for Peace in South: Inhumane Cruelties Must Be Condemned," *Bangkok Post*, August 12, 2005.

60. "Thai Official Says Queen's Projects Not Aimed at Dividing Buddhists, Muslims," translated from *Daily News*, July 8, 2005, BBC Monitoring International Reports, cited in Duncan McCargo, "The Politics of Buddhist Identity in Thailand's Deep South: The Demise of Civil Religion?" *Journal of Southeast Asia Studies* 40.1 (February 2009): 11–32, 22.

61. W. K. Che Man estimated that over 100,000 Thai Buddhists relocated to the southernmost provinces in order to receive land grants from the Self-Help Colony program. *Muslim Separatism: The Moros of Southern Philippines and the Malays of Southern Thailand* (New York: Oxford University Press, 1990), 38.

62. Personal communication with a volunteer monk at Wat A, 2007.

63. *The Nation*, "Monks Head to South to Spread Message of Peace," July 26, 2007.

64. Personal communication with Nopparat Benjawatthananant, director of the Office of National Buddhism, in Nakhon Pathom on December 25, 2006.

65. Abdulloh Benyakaj, "Scarecrows Carry Mean Message for Thaksin," *Bangkok Post*, November 4, 2005.

66. Personal communication with a volunteer monk at Wat A in 2007.

67. *The Nation*, "148 Buddhist Monks Deployed to Temples in Deep South," July 3, 2009.

68. Bruce Lincoln, *Discourse and the Construction of Society: Comparative Studies of Myth, Ritual, and Classification* (New York: Oxford University Press, 1989), 117.

69. *Bangkok Post*, "Monk, Temple Boys Killed in Pattani," October 16, 2005.

70. *The Nation*, "Buddhist Temple Attacked," October 16, 2005.

71. Personal communication with Pattani Thai Chinese, Thai Buddhist, and Malay locals in September 2006.

72. Michael Taussig, *Defacement: Public Secrecy and the Labor of the Negative* (Stanford: Stanford University Press, 1999), 1.

73. Anand Panyarachun et al., "Report of the National Reconciliation Commission: Overcoming Violence through the Power of Reconciliation," 53. Unofficial translation accessed at http://thailand.ahrchk.net/docs/nrc_report_en.pdf on August 15, 2006.

74. McCargo, "Politics of Buddhist Identity," 11–32, 15.

75. Personal communication with the abbot of Wat Phromprasit, Panāre, Pattani, on December 26, 2006.

76. When I asked the abbot about these other factors, he compared the southern violence to the U.S. war on "Islamic terrorism" and explained that President George W. Bush and Prime Minister Thaksin Shinawatra were fighting the same fight against extreme Muslims.

77. Tambiah, *Leveling Crowds*, 81.

78. Personal communication with Phra Kwāmsūk at Wat A, 2006.

79. There are a few national reports on Buddhist monk using drugs. For an example, Sanitsuda Ekachai's "The Booze is Part of General Decline," *Bangkok Post*, March 29, 2001.

80. Mark Juergensmeyer, *Terror in the Mind of God: The Global Rise of Religious Violence* (Berkeley: University California Press, 2000).

81. *Human Rights Watch*, "No One Is Safe, Insurgent Violence against Civilians in Thailand's Southern Border Provinces," vol. 19, no. 13C (August 2007): 1–102, 66–67.

82. A monk living in Panāre told Human Rights Watch "They should be tough in dealing with Muslim militants, otherwise soon there will be no Buddhists left here in Pattani and other southern provinces. There used to be 20 Buddhist monks in my temple. After Pra Kaeo was killed most of them have packed up and gone." *Human Rights Watch*, "No One Is Safe," 1–102, 68.

83. Rungrawee C. Pinyorat, "Thai Buddhist Vigilante Squads Suspected," *Associated Press*, August 7, 2007. It is difficult to assess the level of Buddhist vigilantism because of the militants' anonymity. For instance, on June 8, 2010, a drive-by bombing injured twenty-three people outside of a mosque in Yala. Police blame the attack on Muslim insurgents. However, a Muslim insurgent attack in this scenario "does not make sense" to Don Pathan. Buddhist vigilantism may also be the cause. "23 Hurt by Bomb near Mosque in Southern Thailand," *Associated Press*, June 9, 2010.

84. International Crisis Group, "Southern Thailand: The Problem with Paramilitaries," *Asia Report No. 140* (October 23, 2007): 19.

85. Marc Askew, "Landscapes of Fear, Horizons of Trust: Villagers Dealing with Danger in Thailand's Insurgent South," *Journal of Southeast Asian Studies* 40.1 (February 2009): 59–86, 84

86. Tambiah, *Leveling Crowds*, 236.

87. Thailand never had an order of nuns. Thai women can take the eight precepts, shave their heads, and don white robes, thereby becoming associated with the Buddhist clergy. Thais recognize these women as nominally sacred, and call them *māechī*, but they are not officially ordained. In 2004, Dhammanada Bhikkhuni became the first fully ordained Thai Buddhist nun.

88. Seth Mydans, "Under Desert Sun, Mourners Pray for 9 Killed at Temple," *New York Times*, August 12, 1991, accessed at http://query.nytimes.com/gst/fullpage.html?res=9D0CE2D F163AF931A2575BC0A967958260&sec=&spon=&pagewanted=print on October 12, 2007.

89. *The Nation*, August 18, 1991.

90. Charles Keyes, "Thai Buddhism: From State Religion to Religion beyond the State," a paper presented for the panel "Buddhism in the Contemporary World: Universalism and Particularism Association" at the Asian Studies Conference, Boston, March 1994.

91. *The Nation*, August 18, 19 and 28, 1991.

92. Keyes, "Thai Buddhism."

93. Angela Cara Pancrazio, "Time to Remember 1991 Massacre at Thai Buddhist Temple," *The Arizona Republic*, August 9, 2006, accessed at http://buddhistchannel.tv/index. php?id=64,3025,0,0,1,0 on October 12, 2007.

94. The Arizona massacre section was greatly enhanced by suggestions from Charles Keyes and Juliane Schober at the "Workshop on Buddhism and the Crises of Nation-States in Asia" at the Asia Research Institute of National University of Singapore, June 19, 2008.

95. See Susan Darlington, "Ritual and Risk: Environmental Buddhism in Practice," accessed at http://72.14.253.104/search?q=cache:Zb6QcGnsRLoJ:www.hds.harvard.edu/cswr/resources/print/dongguk/darlington.pdf+Susan+Darlington+%22Ritual+and+Risk%22&hl=en&ct=clnk&cd=1&gl=us on October 13, 2007.

96. Ong-ard Decha, "Phra Supoj's Mysterious Death: a Buddhist Monk Falls Victim to Capitalist Greed," *Prachatai*, October, 7 2007, accessed at http://www.prachatai.com/english/news.php?id=289 on October 13, 2007.

97. It is probable that the equation for religiously motivated violence extends beyond the boundaries of Buddhist traditions. The Sikh conflict with the Indian government and Indira Gandhi's assassination led to a massive demonstration of violence, catalyzed by Gandhi's death.

98. Mark Juergensmeyer, *Global Rebellion: Religious Challenges to the Secular State from Christian Militias to Al Qaeda* (Berkeley: University of California Press, 2008), 2.

99. James D. Fearon and David D. Laitin, "Ethnicity, Insurgency, and Civil War," *American Political Science Review* 97.1 (February 2003): 75–90.

100. A *tudung* is a Malaysian Muslim headdress for women.

101. Amartya Sen, *Identity and Violence: The Illusion of Destiny* (New York: W. W. Norton, 2006), xiii.

102. Duncan McCargo, "Thai Buddhism, Thai Buddhists and the Southern Conflict," *Journal of Southeast Asian Studies* 40.1 (February 2009): 1–10, 4.

103. Lincoln, *Discourse*, 118.

104. Ibid, 120.

105. Buddhist monks helped galvanize nearly 100,000 laity in a public display of defiance to the military overlords. For many of the Burmese, it was what the monks symbolized that made their participation significant. When the junta applied violence against the Buddhist monks, it was as if the junta had struck at the very heart of the resistance. According to the *Associated Press*, "The corralling of monks was a serious blow. They carry high moral authority in this predominantly Buddhist nation of 54 million people and the protests had mushroomed when the clergymen joined in. 'The monks are the ones who give us courage. I don't think that we have any more hope to win,' said a young woman who had taken part in a huge demonstration Thursday that broke up when troops shot protesters." *Associated Press*, "Troops Take Back Control of Myanmar," September 29, 2007.

106. One legend underscores the importance of the Buddhist monk's body and how the violence attributed it sacred properties: "Following his death, Thich Quang Duc was cremated and legend has it that his heart would not burn. As a result, his heart is considered Holy and is in the custody of the Reserve Bank of Vietnam." "Self Immolation," accessed at http://www.buddhistinformation.com/self_immolation.htm on September 30, 2007.

Chapter 3

1. Personal communication with Ǎchǎn Nok at Wat A, August 2004.

2. One of the most infamous occasions occurred under the direction of Phra Fang, who organized an army composed of laymen and monks and who overtook the governorship of Phitsanulok in northern Siam. King Thaksin (1767–1782). Eventually Phra Fang's growing insurrection was quelled in 1768, but this was not the end of Siamese monastic warfare. Chatthip Nartsupha writes about the "Holy Men Revolts" in the northeastern provinces that occurred from 1699–1959. Buddhist monks were either a part of the revolts or led them. Chatthip Nartsupha, "The Ideology of 'Holy Men' Revolts in North East Thailand," in *History and Peasant Consciousness in Southeast Asia*, ed. Andrew Turton and Shigeru Tanabe (Osaka: National Museum of Ethnology, 1984): 111–34.

3. Monks' devotion to combating the vices and sufferings of the world might infer a lack of fear, or at least a strong, sound psychological engagement with it. Monks are people who

can come from ordinary backgrounds, yet don the saffron robes and offer their pledges. They are not instantly immune to problems because of the robes or the pledges and, although they devote themselves to otherworldly aspirations, this does not depose them from falling prey to social vices and afflictions.

4. This is analogous to Robert Sharf's claim that those proponents of the performative model are more concerned with "how participants come to do what they do," rather than "what does the performance mean?" An analysis of performativity encourages an observer to examine the mechanics of an action. Robert Sharf, "Ritual," in *Critical Terms for the Study of Buddhism*, ed. Donald Lopez Jr. (Chicago: University of Chicago Press, 2005), 250.

5. Stanley Jeyaraja Tambiah, *Leveling Crowds: Ethnonationalist Conflicts and Collective Violence in South Asia* (Berkeley: University of California Press, 1996), 222.

6. In this chapter, I use Erving Goffman's definition of performance:

A "performance" may be defined as all the activity of a given participant on a given occasion which serves to influence in any way any of the other participants. Taking a particular participant and his performance as a basic point of reference, we may refer to those who contribute to the other performances as the audience, observers, or co-participants.

Erving Goffman, *The Presentation of Self in Everyday Life* (Garden City, NY: Doubleday, 1959), 15, 16.

7. Thailand's population is more than 92% Buddhist. For the most part, Buddhist monks are not concerned with converting people to Buddhism, but rather supporting ethical and religious practices for Buddhists by disseminating the *dhamma*. The Theravāda traditions are not removed from missionary work. Burmese Buddhists performed work in Nepal among the Newaris. Sarah LeVine considers the impact of Burmese and Tibetan Buddhist missions among the Newari in "The Theravada Domestic Mission in Twentieth-Century Nepal," in *Buddhist Missionaries in the Era of Globalization*, ed. Linda Learman (Honolulu: University of Hawaii Press, 2005).

8. Thomas Kirsch, "Complexities in the Thai Religious System: An Interpretation," *Journal of Asian Studies* 37.2 (February 1977): 241–66, 248.

9. Since January 2004, the Fourth Army has been charged with maintaining martial law in the three southernmost provinces.

10. *Bangkok Post*, "Alms-gathering Not Halted," October 26, 2004.

11. Edmund Leach, "On Certain Unconsidered Aspects of Double Descent Systems," *Man* 62 (1962): 130–34, 133.

12. Paul Schmelzer writes, "Many of the products are devised by 'Thailand's Q' (a reference to James Bond's gadget guy), Major Songphon Eiamboonyarith, a defense contractor who has also invented bulletproof tuk-tuks (motorcycle taxis), umbrellas that shoot rubber bullets, bullet-proof baseball caps and a hand-held device to fire a man-sized net 30 feet (10 m) to stop a villain in his tracks." Paul Schmelzer, "Monkmobiles and Bulletproof Robes," *Eyeteeth*, October 15, 2005, accessed at http://eyeteeth.blogspot.com/2005/10/monkmobiles-and-bulletproof-robes.html on February 18, 2006.

13. Catherine Bell, *Ritual: Perspectives and Dimensions* (New York: Oxford University Press, 1997), 73.

14. Samuels develops this theory within a progression of scholarship that questions the monolithic status of the Pāli Canon. He argues, "...in addition to performing texts in ritual contexts, certain ritualized activities such as eating, walking, and sweeping formed an integral component to the training of newcomers to the Sangha and provided them with a growing understanding of monastic life." "Toward an Action-Based Pedagogy: Buddhist Texts and Monastic Education in Contemporary Sri Lanka," *Journal of the American Academy of Religion* 72.4 (2004): 955–71, 968.

15. Mark Juergensmeyer, *Terror in the Mind of God: The Global Rise of Religious Violence* (Berkeley: University of California Press, 2001), 121–47.

16. Tambiah is the first to point out the applicability of Geertz's theater-state in Thailand. Stanley Jeyaraja Tambiah, *Culture, Thought and Social Action: An Anthropological Perspective* (Cambridge, MA: Harvard University Press, 1985), 317. For further information, see

Clifford Geertz, *Negara: The Theater-State in Nineteenth-Century Bali* (Princeton, NJ: Princeton University Press, 1980), and Tambiah, *Leveling Crowds*, 221–43.

17. Seth Mydans, "Muslim Insurgency Stokes Fear in Southern Thailand," *International Herald Tribune*, February 25, 2007, accessed at http://www.iht.com/articles/2007/02/25/news/ thailand.php on September 28, 2008.

18. According to the National Reconciliation Commission, 15.7% of the southernmost province (257 out of 1,638 villages) are red zones and nearly half of these red zones have experienced conflicts over natural resources. Anand Panyarachun et al., "Report of the National Reconciliation Commission: Overcoming Violence through the Power of Reconciliation," 6. Unofficial translation accessed at http://thailand.ahrchk.net/docs/nrc_report_en.pdf, on August 15, 2006. Wat A's classification and statistics come from an anonymous survey compiled for the abbot and the military of Wat A's district, called *khomūn phūntī*ʾ.XXX čh.XXX. The survey covered maps, contact information, and records of over thirteen subdistricts and fifty-eight villages in Wat A's district. It also recorded the number of attacks, government workers, religious and gender population statistics in each sub-district. The district and province names were removed in order to maintain Wat A's anonymity.

19. Stanley Jeyaraja Tambiah, *Buddhism and the Spirit Cults in North-east Thailand* (Cambridge: Cambridge University Press, 1970), 147.

20. Kirsch, "Complexities," 241–66, 249.

21. Linda Green, "Living in a State of Fear," in *Fieldwork under Fire: Contemporary Studies of Violence and Survival*, ed. Carolyn Nordstrom and Antonius M. Robben (Berkeley: University of California Press, 1995): 105–27, 108.

22. *The Nation*, "Southern Violence," January 28, 2004.

23. *Human Rights Watch*, "Thailand: No One Is Safe: Insurgent Violence against Civilians in Thailand's Southern Border Provinces," (August 2007): 1–102, 50.

24. Since it is considered the most auspicious time to do so, it is custom for Thai and Thai Chinese Buddhists to ordain during the Rain Retreat (*khaophansā*).

25. Personal communication with Ačhān Nok by phone, August 2004.

26. Personal communication with ONB worker, December 2006.

27. Personal communication with Ačhān Luk, August 2004.

28. Duncan McCargo, "The Politics of Buddhist Identity in Thailand's Deep South: The Demise of Civil Religion?" *Journal of Southeast Asia Studies* 40.1 (February 2009): 11–32, 18.

29. Marc Askew, "Landscapes of Fear, Horizons of Trust: Villagers Dealing with Danger in Thailand's Insurgent South," *Journal of Southeast Asian Studies* 40.1 (February 2009): 59–86, 83, 84.

30. *Bangkok Post*, "Government Official Beheaded in South," September 10, 2008.

31. Zachary Abuza, "The Role of Foreign Trainers in Southern Thailand's Insurgency," *Terrorism Monitor* 5.11 (June 7, 2007), accessed at http://www.jamestown.org/terrorism/news/ article.php?articleid=2373451 on September 28, 2008.

32. Thai: *dai mī ustās thī son sāsanā nai phūn thī čh. yalā lae kōei pai rīyen sāsanā thī pratēt indōnīsīya lae ʾdīt khommāndō thī ko hētrāi ʾyū nai phūn thī khong čh. yalā dai klāo yomrab rawāng kānsak thāmwā dairab kānfuk chai āwut dōichapo withī kānchai mīt tat kho čhāk klum phūkokānrāi čhāk āčhe. Isrā Samākhom*, "Khommāndō čhāk khabūankān bāengyāek dindāen dairab kānfukkān chai mī tat kho čhāk klum tidāwut hūarunrāeng čhāk āčhe" [Commando from Separatist Movement Received Training for Beheadings from an Arms Group from Aceh], January 23, 2008, accessed at http://www.isranews.org/cms/index. php?option=com_content&task=view&id=3109&Itemid=47 on October 7, 2008.

33. The *Bangkok Post* started a tally of militant beheadings in southern Thailand, the first occurring on May 29, 2004, that includes two others before Iraq's public surge in January 2005. *Bangkok Post*, "Militants Behead 25th Southern Victim," March 7, 2007.

34. When a State's monopoly of control is broken and there is no clear indication of who *is* in control, people's worldviews begin to unravel. German sociologist Max Weber described the State in a 1918 speech as an agency that has the monopoly on all legitimate acts of violence. Max Weber, "Politics as a Vocation" in *From Max Weber: Essays in Sociology*, trans. H. H. Gerth and C. Wright Miller (New York: Oxford University Press, 1958): 77–128, 78.

35. Freud argues that civilization, among other things, provides an order and repetitive-compulsion that society needs. This order and structure are requisites in a society's life, as to be bereft of this would incur severe psychological ramifications. Sigmund Freud, *Civilization and Its Discontents*, trans. Joan Riviere (London: Hogarth Press, 1949), 55–57.

36. "This may well be the case. Nevertheless, I shall argue that food in South Asia can serve two diametrically opposed semiotic functions. It can serve to indicate and construct social relations characterized by equality, intimacy, or solidarity; or, it can serve to sustain relations characterized by rank, distance, or segmentation." Arjun Appadurai, "Gastro-Politics in Hindu South Asia," *American Ethnologist* 8.3 (August 1981): 494–511, 496.

37. Buddhists and Muslims in Ladakh, India, have had repeated conflicts that stem from the Muslim food restrictions. For examples, see Ravina Aggarwal, *Beyond Lines of Control: Performance and Politics on the Disputed Borders of Ladakh, India* (Durham: Duke University Press, 2004), 50, 80–82.

38. Personal communication with Saroja Dorairajoo at National University of Singapore, November 2006.

39. Eating habits have divided the eating spaces of the southernmost provinces. Muslims will attend the *halal*-endorsed restaurants. Buddhists will attend the *haram* restaurants. Most Chinese restaurants are *haram*, serving mainly pork. This works well with Thai Buddhists, since they prefer pork or chicken to beef. In Theravāda Buddhism, it is generally considered better to eat the meat of an animal that is less intelligent and/or smaller than the opposite.

40. I followed up on the story of this attack with an interview with the abbot who was allegedly attacked. The abbot in question confirmed the details of the occurrence. According to him, in April of 2004 at 2:00 A.M., men came and cut off the power at his *wat*. Dogs began barking and the volunteer Buddhists staying at the *wat* woke up. The Buddhist volunteers shot their guns into the air and chased the men away. Later, there were rumors that one of them was injured and possibly died from the warning shots. Personal communication with an abbot, August 2004.

41. Personal interview over the phone with Ačhān Pim from Pattani, August 14, 2004.

42. This assertion is not entirely true. Ačhān Pim's comments pertain to the period on or before the Khru Se Mosque attacks. After the Khru Se Mosque and the Tak Bai attacks in 2004, the Thai State offered compensation to Muslim families that suffered losses. In both incidences, the Thai officials were implicated of wrongdoing and the financial compensation was offered in an attempt to make amends. The Thai media publicized these actions, provoking many monks' complaints that lasted into 2007.

43. Like the abbot, some monks living in the red zone believe that the Buddhist-Muslim problems date further back than 2004. They cite occurrences, like a bomb attempt on Wat Chang Hai in 2002, as evidence that the religious feud is an old issue that is fomenting; however, in many ways their vision of the past is painted by the fear and violence of the present.

44. One story recounts how a wealthy Brahmana, when asked for food, became enraged and said, "You shaven head! You would do better to work rather than beg. Look at me! I plow and sow; when I have plowed and sowed, I can eat. If you did the same, you would have something to eat." Mohan Wijayaratna, *Buddhist Monastic Life: According to the Texts of the Theravada Tradition*, trans. Claude Grangier and Steven Collins (Cambridge: Cambridge University Press, 1990): 59.

45. There has been a communal effort to defend the *wat*. In early 2006, the military initiated a project called "The Wat Community Watch," (*bānrakwat*), in which local volunteers keep watch and work to make the *wat* safer (for example, by building fences around the Buddhist monks' living quarters, the kuti). "Rongnāyok...suwačhsong chāydāentai tēngob 96 lān čhadbānrakwat phūchīan" [Deputy Prime Minister Sawajan Goes to the Southern Borders and Budgets 96 Million Baht for the Wat Community Watch Project], *Isrā Samākhom*, February 4, 2006.

46. Cited in *Human Rights Watch*, "Thailand: No One Is Safe,"1–102, 66.

47. Personal communication at Wat A, 2006.

48. In the same interview with the anonymous representative of the Office of National Buddhism, I was told that 5,000 baht (roughly $120 USD in 2006) was given to *wat* no longer performing morning alms.

49. Personal conversation with an abbot in the southernmost provinces, September 2006.

50. In one of his early works, Tambiah assesses the power of ritual words and finds that ritual words are at least as important as other kinds of ritual acts: "the power is in the 'words' even though the words only become effective if uttered in a very special context of other action." Stanley Jeyaraja Tambiah, "The Magic Power of Words," *Man* 3.2 (June 1968): 175–208, 176.

51. These monks canvass for national elections and, in some ways, avoid the public criticism. Daniel Arghiros, *Democracy, Development and Decentralization in Provincial Thailand* (Richmond, Surrey: Curzon Press, 2001), 151.

52. These interviews took place in Pattani Province between May and August 2004, shortly after the Khru Se Mosque attacks, a conflict that resulted in the deaths of over 100 Malay Muslims.

53. He attended an interfaith dialogue conference at the C.S. Pattani Hotel in the capital district of Pattani on August 11, 2004. Since then, he occasionally has spoken with key Muslim figures in his village, but only in passing.

54. The survey covered 80% of the districts in Pattani Province and primarily focused on abbots. Questions took place either over the phone or at the *wat* during the summer of 2004. While it is beyond the parameters of this chapter to explore, it is important to note that Burmese and Sinhala Theravāda monks have different parameters and degrees of allowances engaging in political affairs.

55. Local government officials requested that The Mahidol University Research Center for Peace Building hold interfaith workshops in their areas between 2007 and 2008. One of the mediators Parichart Suwanbubbha notes that twenty monks participated in these workshops in 2008. Once southern locals saw that the organization was not affiliated with the government, people felt more comfortable participating. For monks, this distinction is important because a non-government sponsored event could be seen as less "political." Personal communication with Parichart Suwanbubbha, Mahidol University, October 8, 2008.

56. Environmental monks are Buddhist monks who utilize their cultural and symbolic capital in order to protect and promote ecological interests. There is a burgeoning field of study centered on environmental Buddhist monks in Northern Thailand. For examples, see Susan Darlington's "The Ordination of a Tree: the Buddhist Ecology Movement in Thailand," *Ethnology* 37.1 (Winter 1998): 1–15; Australian National University's National Thai Studies Centre and Murdoch University's Asia Research Centre, eds., *Seeing Forests for Trees: Environment and Environmentalism in Thailand* (Chiang Mai: Silkworm Books, 1999).

57. Somboon Suksamran coins the phrase "Political Monk" for the rise of conservatively inclined Thai Buddhist monks in the 1970s and early '80s. *Buddhism and Politics in Thailand* (Singapore: Institute of Southeast Asian Studies, 1982). The term "Development Monk" (Thai: *phrasongphathanā*) first appeared in Phinit Laphathanan's 1986 master's thesis, "Bothbāt phrasing nai kānphathanā chonabot," [The Role of Buddhist Monks in Rural Development] (Chulalongkon University Social Science Lab, 1986).

58. Over 1,000 Santi Asoke Buddhist monks protested the Thaksin administration on February 26, 2006. Their protests sparked a much larger protest involving more than 40,000 people. *The Nation*, "From Royal Palace to Sanam Luang," February 26, 2006.

59. *Bangkok Post*, "The Bhikkhu Who Does Battle," June 22, 2006.

60. The Thai *sangha* had Photirak disrobed in 1975. Aside from public and political denouncements of Photirak, the Santi Asoke center was bombed on February 23, 2006. This may have been a reaction to his Dhamma Army's political actions. See Kosol Nakachol, "Santi Asoke Centre Bombed," *Bangkok Post*, February 23, 2006.

61. Non-governmental organizations suffer from a social stigma within Thai popular culture and are often considered "foreign" forces. *Bangkok Post*, "Bhikkhu Who Does Battle."

62. Somboon Suksamran speculates that this view is due to a historically based conscious fear from the Thai government of the Sangha's potential influence over Thai sovereignty. He refers to the example of the monk Phra Fang who led a revolt against King Thaksin and seized for some time the northern capital of Pitsanulok in the late 1700s. *Buddhism and Politics in Thailand*, 25.

63. Anand Panyarachun justified the NRC's attention to Muslims due to the fact "that the violence was mostly caused by conflict between local Muslims and the government, while Buddhists have no problem with the authorities." *The Nation*, "National Reconciliation Commission: Anand, Monks Exchange Words," November 12, 2005, accessed at http://www.nationmultimedia.com/specials/south2years/nov1205.php on January 28, 2007. Media coverage of the southern Buddhists has changed slightly. In January 2007, Thai Channel 9 began airing programs concerning the Buddhists in southern Thailand. One particular show called "The Visitors" (*phūmāyūan*) talked about the refugees and the monks at Wat Nirotsangkaratham.

64. Personal communication with Ačhān Nok at Wat A, November 2006.

65. Southern monks began to channel their feelings about the violence into their speeches and sermons. As with other global religions, sermons are the oldest performative acts in Buddhism. It began with Siddhattha Gotama, who offered a sermon to five wandering ascetics (Pāli: *samaṇas*) at a park in Sārnāth and won over the first Buddhist converts. Buddhists worldwide have memorialized this event, naming the area Deer Park (Pāli: *isipatana*) after the deer that collected during the Buddha's sermon. The event is further symbolized in Buddhist iconography as two deer on either side of a *cakra* (a wheel, which represents the Buddhist teachings).

66. While it is impractical to assume one cause would lead to such a widespread social phenomena, it is also important not to underestimate the power of nation-building.

67. This argument is in line with Christine's Gray's discussion on Thai Buddhist rituals and kingship during the colonial period. "I also argue that Buddhist ritual and Buddhist kingship acquired new functions during and after the colonial period, to mediate antinomies in order to maintain the political autonomy of the Thai State and status as a soteriological state." Christine Gray, "Thailand: The Soteriological State in the 1970s," (PhD diss., Department of Anthropology, University of Chicago, 1986), 68.

68. First cited in Kamala Tiyavanich, *Forest Recollections: Wandering Monks in Twentieth-Century Thailand* (Honolulu: University of Hawaii Press, 1997), 34, 35.

69. Kamala, *Forest Recollections*, 36.

70. Kamala, *Forest Recollections*, 34–36. According to the official educational administrators, southern monks relied mostly on the stories of the Buddha and the *Questions of King Milinda* to propagate the Buddhist doctrine. The *Questions of King Milinda* or the *Milindapañha* is a Theravāda scripture that follows a Socratic form of dialogue between a monk called Nagasena and the Greek king Menander. The conversation covers both metaphysical and epistemological questions about Buddhism.

71. Personal communication with Ačhān Tam, April 19, 2007.

72. Personal communication with Ačhān Nok at Wat A, September 2006.

73. Ibid.

74. It is important to note that Ačhān Nok's influence is limited. Right before the end of the Rain Retreat in 2006, one of his own monks left and returned to Central Thailand, sick with fear. However, this monk was a volunteer monk and, thus, was less invested in southern issues. He also held less respect for Ačhān Nok than the locals who lived in the community.

75. One volunteer monk from Isan eventually arrived in mid-2007, prior to the beginning of the Rain Retreat.

76. Personal conversation with the Ačhān Tuk from Wat B, August 2004.

77. These are soldiers who stay and guard the king in his residence a few days every month.

78. Personal communication with Lieutenant Colonel Surathep Nukagow at Ingkayut Camp, December 28, 2006.

79. The number nine is deeply venerated in Buddhism for its mathematical properties and its divisibility into the auspicious number 108. In addition, nine is a homonym in Thai for "moving forward" (nine: *gao*, and to progress: *gāo*).

80. Ačhān Tuk, "Sermon to Ingkayut Camp," at Ingkayut Camp, December 26, 2006.
81. Ibid.
82. In fact, when I first spoke with him about these issues, Ačhān Tuk was so guarded about these issues that he would not allow a recording of his answers.
83. Daniel Kent, "Onward Buddhist Soldiers: Preaching to the Sri Lankan Army," in *Buddhist Warfare*, ed. Michael Jerryson and Mark Juergensmeyer (New York: Oxford University Press, 2010), 171.
84. This view and context is not restricted to Theravāda Buddhist traditions. In a more recent example, the Fourteenth Dalai Lama may have intended a similar message when he issued his statement in support of England's Armed Forces Day on June 18, 2010,

    Although the public may think that physical strength is what is most important, I believe that what makes a good soldier, sailor or airman, just as what makes a good monk, is inner strength. And inner strength depends on having a firm positive motivation. The difference lies in whether ultimately you want to ensure others' well being or whether you want only wish to do them harm.

    Tenzin Gyatso (the Fourteenth Dalai Lama), "Message for Who's Supporting Armed Forces Day," Department of Defence, United Kingdom, accessed at http://www.armed-forcesday.org.uk/celebrity-supporters.aspx#Dalai-Lama on June 18, 2010. The Fourteenth Dalai Lama's statement was later removed from the official website; however, a commentary on the initial message is still available at Mark Vernon, "The Dalai Lama on Violence," *The Guardian*, June 21, 2010, accessed at http://www.guardian.co.uk/commentisfree/andrewbrown/2010/jun/21/dalai-lama-armed-forces-day-message on June 21, 2010.
85. Prince Wachirayan, *The Buddhist Attitude towards National Defence and Administration: A Special Allocution by His Holiness Prince Vajiranana (1916)*, trans. Vajiravudh (Ithaca: Cornell University Library, 2010), 19.
86. Wassana Nanuam, "Troops Make Merit after Mosque Fight," *Bangkok Post*, May 2, 2004.
87. Gray, "Thailand," 52.
88. Katherine A. Bowie, *Rituals of National Loyalty: An Anthropology of the State and the Village Scout Movement in Thailand* (New York: Columbia University Press, 1997), 8.
89. This is in reference to the great Buddhist Mauryan emperor of India Aśoka in the 5th century B.C.E., who used his political capital to spread and convert people to Buddhism.
90. Charles Keyes, "Buddhism and National Integration in Thailand," *Journal of Asian Studies* 30.3 (May 1971): 551–67, 562.
91. For more information on the process of using religion to nationalize and assimilate, see chapter 6.
92. "Thaelaengkan khanasong jangwat pattani ruang khwam mai sangop nai 3 jangwat chaid-aen phak tai, karani Wat Phromprasit, Tambon Bannok, Amphoe Panare, Jangwat Pattani" [Declaration of the Sangha Council of Pattani Province on the Subject of the Unrest in the Three Southern Border Provinces, case of Wat Phromprasit, Tambon Ban Nok, Panare District, Pattani Province] (2 page faxed document), October 20, 2005, point 18, cited by Duncan McCargo in "Politics of Buddhist Identity," 11–32, 11.
93. *The Nation*, "National Reconciliation Commission."
94. McCargo, "Politics of Buddhist Identity," 11–32, 30.
95. Thai: *sūnsongsöenkičhakānphraphutthasāsanā 3 čhangwatchāidāenphāktai.*
96. In May 2006, an anonymous Buddhist monk distributed an unpublished short essay explaining the newly formed foundation to Buddhist monks in the south. In his essay, he outlined six core conditions, problems, and principles concerning the violence:

    1.1 The unrest in the southern three border provinces has impacted the life and property of Buddhists who are a minority in the area. Some Buddhists have moved to other areas out of fear.

    1.2 Temples, which are important places for Buddhists, have been destroyed and burned down by the terrorists. Some Buddhist monks and novices have been murdered or left injured and disabled.

    1.3 Usual religious and ritual ceremonies of Buddhists have changed, which causes the suffering of many Buddhists.

1.4 Buddhism was very prosperous in the border provinces during the period of Srivijaya and Langkasuka, which lasted more than 1,000 years. There are many ancient places, art, objects and evidences that relate to the prosperity Buddhism brings. However, as Buddhism has been neglected, new generations cannot succeed in these productive and prosperous ways.

1.5 The government does not make a sincere effort to develop Buddhist affairs in government, being aware only of Muslims who are the majority in the area. So, the emphasis of development is put on Islamic affairs.

1.6 If Buddhists move out of the area, temples and Buddhism will also fade away from this area. Her Majesty the Queen Sirikit is very concerned about Buddhists in these three border provinces that number around 300,000. Her Majesty the Queen is seeking the way to help Buddhists live with peace and happiness, as their countrymen.

"Anonymous Letter," trans. Michael Jerryson, unpublished article, Thailand, May 2006.

97. This stance was confirmed by Phra Nirut at Wat Chang Hai through personal communication on February 22, 2007.

98. In 1906, the anthropologist Charles Blagden wrote that "it is worth mention that Langkasuka still lies in the memory of the local Malays. It has developed into a myth, being evidently the 'spirit-land' referred to as Lakan Suka. . . ." Roland Braddell, *A Study of Ancient Times in the Malay Peninsula and the Straits of Malacca and Notes on Ancient Times in Malaya* (Kuala Lumpur: Art Printing Works Sdn. Bhd., 1980), 357.

99. In a speech entitled "What Are the Wild Tigers?" on May 26, 1911, King Vajiravudh claimed that "the Buddha believed that the military was essential for protecting the nation, and that the strength and vitality of the religion was dependent on national security. Vajiravudh went further by suggesting that if instability developed, Buddhism would be doomed, thereby precipitating the total collapse of the Thai nation, which would then become the 'slave' of other more unified powers." A.J. Brown, "An Annotated Translation with Introduction," bachelor's honors thesis (Canberra: Australian National University, 1983), 47, 48. Cited by Scot Barmé in *Luang Wichit Wathakan and the Creation of a Thai Identity* (Singapore: Institute of Southeast Asian Studies, 1993), 33.

100. Charles Keyes, "Political Crisis and Militant Buddhism," in *Religion and Legitimation of Power in Thailand, Laos, and Burma*, ed. Bardwell L. Smith (Chambersburg, PA: ANIMA Books, 1978): 147–63, 153.

101. Leftist groups, especially students, protested Kittiwuttho's behavior. However, despite the editorial attacks on him and his political posturing, the Mahātherasammakhon refused to conduct a full investigation. Keyes cites Heinz Bechert, who suggested that "[t]he Buddhist public [accepts] political activity of the Sangha as legitimate only in periods of crisis when the survival of Buddhism itself [is] considered to be at stake." Keyes, "Political Crisis," 159, citing Bechert, "Sangha, State, Society, 'Nation': Persistence of Tradition in 'Post-Traditional' Buddhist Studies," *Daedalus* 102 (1973): 1:90. I would differ only slightly here in that it is not merely a period of crisis, but a stance in support of the State that tends to favor political activism for monks.

102. Charles Hallisey, "Devotion in the Buddhist Literature of Medieval Sri Lanka," (PhD diss., University of Chicago, 1988). Cited in Samuels, "Toward an Action-Based Pedagogy," 955–71, 966.

103. Hundreds of monks protested for the inclusion of Buddhism and the official Thai religion in front of the Thai Parliament on April 16, 2007. Newspapers around the country speculated at their turnout and how much of an impact they would have on the writing of the constitution. Ultimately, parliament rejected their proposal. *Bangkok Post*, "Monks to Lead Mass Political Rally," April 15, 2007; Penchan Charoensuthipan, "Constitution Contains No State Religion," *Bangkok Post*, April 17, 2007.

104. Phra Sripariyattimoli (Somchai Kulaacitto) "Why Should Buddhism Become the National Religion," unpublished article, June 20, 2005.

105. Phra Sripariyattimoli is not the first monk to publicly advocate this stance. Tamara Loos notes that there have been occasions wherein people demanded that the State adopt Buddhism as its national religion. *Subject Siam: Family, Law, and Colonial Modernity in Thailand* (Ithaca: Cornell University Press, 2006), 186.

106. Personal communication with Ačhān Nok at Wat A, 2006.

107. In September and October of 2008, I met abbots in central and northern Thailand who also secretly kept guns. There are not many abbots who do this, and they are scattered across different provinces. The abbots did not reveal that they owned guns until I told them about the southern monks' habits. In each scenario the abbot would explain that the *wat* was threatened or had been attacked and that the gun was there simply to scare off robbers. This correlation only strengthens the supposition that monks will own a gun if they are living in a dangerous or volatile environment.

108. Rungrawee C. Pinyorat, "Distrust, Brutality and Glut of Guns Puts Thai South at Risk of Communal Combat," *Associated Press*, April 27, 2007.

109. Personal communication with Ačhan Tam in the southern provinces, 2006.

110. Akira Hirakawa, *A History of Indian Buddhism: From Śākyamuni to Early Mahāyāna*, vol. 1, trans. Paul Groner (Honolulu: University of Hawaii Press, 1990), 31.

111. This is perhaps why in later Buddhist scriptures, Buddhists are advised to practice meditation in lands devoid of strife between kings. I would like to thank Vesna Wallace for pointing out this connection.

Chapter 4

1. Thai: *khao thahān ton āyu yīsibet pī pho fuk čhob thahān āyu yīsibsong pī po yīsibsām ko mā būat ton yīsibsong pai sob nāi sib dai lāeo tamngān 'yū pramān hok dūan lāeo yot ko čhamā ēng.* Personal communication with a military monk at Wat B, 2006.

2. Academic books that offer a cursory study of Buddhism do not address militarism and the word military is absent in their indices. For example, Peter Harvey, *An Introduction to Buddhism: Teachings, History and Practices* (Cambridge: Cambridge University Press, 1990), Peter Harvey, *An Introduction to Buddhist Ethics* (Cambridge: Cambridge University Press, 2000), Donald Mitchell, *Buddhism: Introducing the Buddhist Experience* (New York: Oxford University Press, 2002), Richard Robinson and Willard Johnson, *The Buddhist Religion: A Historical Introduction* (Belmont, CA: Wadsworth Publishing Company, 1997), John Snelling, *The Buddhist Handbook: A Complete Guide to Buddhist Schools, Teaching, Practice, and History* (Rochester, VT: Inner Traditions, 1998), Kevin Trainor, *Buddhism: The Illustrated Guide* (Oxford: Oxford University Press, 2004), and Paul Williams, *Buddhist Thought: A Complete Introduction to the Indian Tradition* (London: Routledge, 2000).

3. Kurt Lang, "Military" in *International Encyclopedia of the Social Sciences*, vol. 10, ed. David L. Sills (New York: Macmillan and Free Press, 1968), 305. Some political scientists such as Kjell Skjelsbaek consider the terms military and militarism words that escape attempts to universally define it. Kjell Skjelsbaek, "Militarism, Its Dimensions and Corollaries: An Attempt at Conceptual Clarification," *Journal of Peace Research* 16.3 (1979): 213–29, 213.

4. Michael Mann, *The Sources of Social Power*, vol. 2, *The Rise of Classes and Nation-States, 1760–1914* (Cambridge: Cambridge University Press, 1993), 8–9.

5. I draw this definition from Peace Educator Betty Reardon's work on peace education in *Militarization, Security, and Peace Education: A Guide for Concerned Citizens* (Valley Forge: United Ministries in Education, 1982), 3.

6. Paul Demiéville's essay was first published in 1957 and offers a cornucopia of historical examples linking the military and Buddhist monasticism in countries such as India, Korea, Japan, and China. This work was just recently translated in the edited volume, *Buddhist Warfare*. Paul Demiéville, "Buddhism and War," trans. Michelle Kendall, in *Buddhist Warfare*, ed. Michael Jerryson and Mark Juergensmeyer (New York: Oxford University Press, 2009).

7. For notable examples, see Stanley Jeyaraja Tambiah, *Sri Lanka: Ethnic Fraticide and the Dismantling of Democracy* (Chicago: University of Chicago Press, 1986) and H. L.

Seneviratne, *The Work of Kings: The New Buddhism in Sri Lanka* (Chicago: University of Chicago Press, 1999).

8. Military monks continued to receive monthly salaries for their connection to the military (typical salaries range from 9,000–10,000 baht a month, roughly $250 USD). While there are military monks who come from the Thai army, navy, air force, and marines, the majority of military monks work for the army (and comprise the data for this chapter).

9. Hayashi Yukio, *Practical Buddhism among the Thai-Lao: Religion in the Making of Religion* (Kyoto: Kyoto University Press, 2003), 1.

10. See Michael Jerryson and Mark Juergensmeyer, eds., *Buddhist Warfare* (New York: Oxford University Press, 2010).

11. Charles F. Keyes, *Thailand: Buddhist Kingdom as Modern Nation-State* (Boulder: Westview Press, 1987), 138, 139.

12. Mohan Wijayaratna, *Buddhist Monastic Life: According to the Texts of the Theravāda tradition*, trans. Claude Grangier and Steven Collins (Cambridge: Cambridge University Press, 1990), 15.

13. Monks are clearly warned against interacting with or becoming involved with the military in the *Vinaya*. In the Buddhist monastic code, under the "Etiquette of a Contemplative," it is a *pacittiya* offense for monks to go to a battlefield, see a review of the battle units, or even watch a field army—or similar large military force—on active duty, unless there is a suitable reason. T. W. Rhys Davids and Hermann Oldenberg, trans., *Vinaya Texts*, part 1, *The Pātimokkha, The Mahāvagga, I–IV* (Delhi: Motilal Banarsidass, 1968), 43, 48, 49.

14. Richard Gombrich, *Theravāda Buddhism: A Social History from Ancient Benares to Modern Colombo* (London: Routledge & Kegan Paul, 1988), 116..

15. Temporary ordinations occur in other Southeast Asian Buddhist traditions, such as the Burmese. I would like to thank one of Oxford University Press's anonymous reviewers for this reminder.

16. Duncan McCargo, "The Politics of Buddhist Identity in Thailand's Deep South: The Demise of Civil Religion?" *Journal of Southeast Asia Studies* 40.1 (February 2009): 11–32, 24. Duncan McCargo notes that the seventy-five soldiers were ordained in honor of the Thai queen's birthday. Personal communication, National University of Singapore, February 22, 2007.

17. Personal communication with Nopparat Benjawatthananant, director of the Office of National Buddhism, in Nakhon Pathom, December 25, 2006.

18. Craig Reynolds, *Seditious Histories: Contesting Thai and Southeast Asian Pasts* (Seattle: University of Washington Press, 2006), 237.

19. I have also heard unsubstantiated reports of military monks in the northern province of Chiang Rai, which suggest that their deployment might be systemic rather than regionally motivated.

20. There are no official reports on military monks, the only substantiations of their existence coming from interviews, personal observations, and local rumors in southern Thailand. Part of the process of unraveling the mystery of the military monk is explicating the secrecy behind these rumors.

21. Michael Taussig, *Defacement: Public Secrecy and the Labor of the Negative* (Stanford: Stanford University Press, 1999), 2.

22. Personal communication with Ačhān Hom in the southernmost provinces, 2004.

23. It is important to distinguish my use of the public secret from that of Michael Taussig's. In this specific scenario, I apply Taussig's idea of the public secret as a less encompassing and overarching social phenomenon. Public in this context is the military monk's specific community. The identity of the military monk is a public secret for his immediate community; it is not a public secret for an entire district, province, or region. Most people in a district, province, or region are unaware of military monks.

24. Personal communication in English with Ačhān Nirut at Wat Chang Hai, 2007.

25. McCargo, "Politics of Buddhist Identity," 11–32, 24.

26. Another State-sponsored program similar to this was the Thammathud, launched in 1964. For more information on this project, see Stanley Jeyaraja Tambiah, *World Conqueror,*

World Renouncer: A Study of Buddhism and Polity in Thailand against a Historical Background (Cambridge: Cambridge University Press, 1976), 434–56.

27. Personal communication with Ačhān Tim at Wat Chang Hai, 2007.

28. Military monks have offered estimates as to the number of active military monks currently dispersed throughout the three southernmost provinces. The numbers are said to be around two hundred, although this number is in flux and changes according to the level of violence and the need for them.

29. Thai: *tong prapom mā kab phrasing hai kwām romyen kab khao to pai phra nai sām čhangwat phāk tai ko mot rao tong mā hai kam langčhai khao phūachāt sāsanā lae kong tap phūa pen an nung an dīeo kan mai tāekyāek kan phūa mai hai khrai mā rang kāe.* Personal communication with Phra Eks at Wat B, 2006.

30. Monthly salaries differ for soldiers. Every month, an electronic transfer of 9,000 baht is deposited into Phra Eks account (nearly $250 USD).

31. In chapter 4 of the *Vinaya* (Buddhist monastic code), the third *pārājika* for a monk is depriving another human being of life. The offense is so specific in this rule that to merely insinuate or persuade a person to end their life constitutes such an offense and results in permanent excommunication from the *sangha*.

32. Some Buddhist scriptures condone monks committing violence so long as the intentions are pure. For instance, Asáṅga in the *Yogācārabhūmi* makes it the Bodhisattva's duty to commit the sin of killing so as to prevent another from doing so. Paul Demiéville, "Buddhism and War," trans. Michelle Kendall, in *Buddhist Warfare*, ed. Michael Jerryson and Mark Juergensmeyer (New York: Oxford University Press, 2009).

33. Thai: *thā chāt pratētchāt mai mī phraphutthasāsanā ko pen mūang čhon phro mai mī phraphutthasāsanā thā mī phutthasāsanā khōi chūai khadklao kilēt hai khonrao rū čhak la lōph krōt lang hai 'yū bāeb klāng klāng thā maim ī trongčhut nī maim ī phraphutthasāsanā khao mā chūamsangsōn dūlāe khongčha pen mūang thī wunwāi khon čhahen kāe tūa...mūakhrai mā tamrāi phraphiksu nai wat chēn mā phao lāeo rao hen mā tī mā fan phra mā ying phra tōng ao būi ōk mā ying 'yāng dīeo.* Personal communication with Phra Eks at Wat B, 2006. Phra Eks referenced a specific arson attack on Wat B in his response, but it was omitted in the translation.

34. *Caturat* 2.51 (June 29, 1976 [B.E. 2519]): 28–32, 31 and 32, cited in Charles Keyes, "Political Crisis and Militant Buddhism," in *Religion and Legitimation of Power in Thailand, Laos, and Burma*, ed. Bardwell L. Smith (Chambersburg, PA: ANIMA Books, 1978), 153.

35. Kittiwuttho reaffirms this stance later in a speech to monks at Cittabhāvana College by first asking, "Did the Lord Buddha teach us to kill or not? He taught [us to do]. He taught us to kill. Venerable sirs, you are likely to be suspicious about this teaching. I will tell you the sutta and you can investigate it: [It is] the *Kesi-sutta* in the *Kesiya-vagga*, the *suttanipiṭaka, aṅguttara-nikāya, catukaka-nipāta.* If you open [this text] venerable sirs, you will find in the sutta that the Lord Buddha ordered killing." Kittiwuttho Bhikkhu, *Khā Khōmmūnit Mai Bāp* [Killing Communists Is Not Demeritorious] (Bangkok: Abhidhamma Foundation of Wat Mahādhātu, 1976), 49, cited in Keyes, "Political Crisis," 154.

36. In the *Kesi Sutta* of the *Aṅguttara Nikāya*, the Buddha parallels the training of a horse with the moral training of a human to a horse trainer named Kesi. At one point Kesi asks the Buddha what happens to a human who does not submit to the moral training of the mind and body, and the Buddha responds, "If a tamable person does not submit either to a mild training or to a harsh training or to a mild and harsh training, then I kill him, Kesi." The Buddha proceeds to explain that such a person is not worth being spoken to or admonished, a person of comparable status to the Mahāyāna term *icchantika* (one who is beyond the capabilities of being liberated through the power of the Buddha). Thanissaro Bhikkhu, trans., "Kesi Sutta: To Kesi the Horsetrainer," in *Aṅguttara Nikāya* 4.111, accessed at http://www.accesstoinsight.org/tipitaka/an/an04/an04.111.than.html on July 1, 2010. For an analysis of *icchantika* in the *Mahāparinirvaṇa Sūtra*, see Ming-Wood Liu, "The Problem of the *Icchantika* in the Mahāyāna *Mahāparinirvaṇa Sūtra*," *Journal of the International Association of Buddhist Studies* 7.1 (1984): 57–81.

37. Monks explained to the Sinhalese king that "[o]nly one and a half human beings have been slain here by thee, O lord of men. The one had come unto the (three) refuges, the other had taken on himself the five precepts Unbelievers and men of evil life were the rest, not more to be esteemed than beasts." Wilhelm Geiger, trans. *Mahāvaṃsa: The Great Chronicle of Lanka from 6th century B.C. to 4th Century A.D.* (New Delhi: Asian Educational Services, 1993), 178.

38. For a comprehensive background to this, see Stanley Jeyaraja Tambiah, *Buddhism Betrayed? Religion, Politics and Violence in Sri Lanka* (Chicago: University of Chicago Press, 1992).

39. Ananda Abeysekara, "The Saffron Army, Violence, Terror(ism): Buddhism, Identity, and Difference in Sri Lanka" *Numen* 48.1 (2001): 1–46, 31, 32.

40. This latent tendency in Theravāda traditions is socio-historically founded on the strong interrelationship between *sangha* and State in Southeast Asia. The construction of a national religion permits the militancy of that religion if the nation is threatened. By isolating this tendency in Theravāda tradition, I do not mean to infer that other Buddhist traditions are absent of militant traits, nor that Theravāda traditions are more violent than other Buddhist traditions. I would like to thank Betty Nguyen of University Wisconsin–Madison for reminding me to make these distinctions.

41. Although Chinese Buddhist scriptures prohibited the retaining of arms within *wat*, Christoph Kleine notes that spears, bows and arrows, and shields were discovered in Chinese *wat* as early as 446 C.E. "Evil Monks with Good Intentions? Remarks on Buddhist Monastic Violence and Its Doctrinal Background," in *Buddhism and Violence*, ed. Michael Zimmermann (Kathmandu: Lumbini International Research Institute, 2006), 76.

42. J. J. M. De Groot, "Militant Spirit of the Buddhist Clergy in China," *T'oung Pao* 2 (1891): 127–39, 139.

43. For detailed accounts of these and other examples, see Demiéville, "Buddhism and War."

44. Melvyn C. Goldstein, "A Study of the *Ldab Ldob*," *Central Asiatic Journal* 1.2 (1964): 123–41, 132.

45. Melvyn C. Goldstein, *A History of Modern Tibet, 1913–1951: Demise of the Lamaist State* (Berkeley: University of California Press, 1989), 488–518.

46. Mikael S. Adolphson, *The Gates of Power: Monks, Courtiers, and Warriors in Premodern Japan* (Honolulu: University of Hawai'i Press, 2000), 75.

47. Kleine, "Evil Monks," 74.

48. Brian Victoria, *Zen at War* (New York: Weatherhill, 1997), 137.

49. One of the more prominent of these is found in Buddhaghoṣa's commentary on the *Aṅguttara Nikāya*, which talks of five periods during the great age of decline. The third of these periods is marked by the disappearance of sacred texts, the rise of evil kings, and the popular failure to support the community of monks. John Strong, *Relics of the Buddha* (Princeton: Princeton University Press, 2004), 222.

50. Chatthip Nartsupha, "The Ideology of 'Holy Men' Revolts in North East Thailand," in *History and Peasant Consciousness in Southeast Asia*, ed. Andrew Turton and Shigeru Tanabe (Osaka: National Museum of Ethnology, 1984): 111–34.

51. The Burmese accounts follow other Theravāda accounts. After the disappearance of analytical insight, path, and fruition states, practice, and texts comes the disappearance in the *sangha* itself. Chit Tin, William Pruitt, *The Coming Buddha Ariya Metteyya*, The Wheel Publication No. 381/383 (Kandy: Buddhist Publication Society, 1992), 27–28, cited in Alicia Marie Turner, "Buddhism, Colonialism and the Boundaries of Religion: Theravada Buddhism in Burma, 1885–1920," vol. 1, (PhD diss., University of Chicago, the Divinity School, 2009), 64.

52. Turner, "Buddhism, Colonialism," 83.

53. One could postulate that the reason for the lack of violence in the Burmese scenario is due to the presence of a superior physical force, namely, the British. Maurice Bloch suggests a similar line of reasoning in his analysis of rebounding violence with the Orokaiva of Papua New Guinea.

   When the actors of the ideology of rebounding conquest are weak and in retreat they will, like the Buid, develop the potential of the structure so that it is only concerned with reproduction. Then the image of the consumption of vitality and aggression will stop at the animals. But in different historical circumstances, when expansionist aggression is a real possibility, as it sometimes was for the Ilongot, the symbolism of the reconsumption of vitality is expanded and becomes a legitimation of outwardly directed aggression.

Maurice Bloch, *Prey into Hunter: The Politics of Religious Experience* (Cambridge: Cambridge University Press, 1992), 45.

54. Personal communication with Ačhān Tim at Wat Chang Hai, 2007.

55. Thai: *khwāmpenthai ko khū kwāmmīmanutsampan thī dī ōbōmārī chūai lūa kan tāe dīeo nī pen 'yāng nan tāe khonthai phutth ko yang mūan dōem ōbōmārī kan mūan dōem tāe khonthai muslim mī tāe khwāmrunrāeng.* Personal communication with Phra Eks at Wat B, 2007.

56. Although southern monks conceded in interviews that it was appropriate for military monks to exist and to live within the *wat*, they did not, however, condone the military monk remaining armed in the monks' quarters. Personal communications in the southernmost provinces, 2004.

57. Richard H Jones, "Theravāda Buddhism and Morality," *Journal of the American Academy of Religion* 47.3 (September 1979): 371–87, 383, 384.

58. Military monks believe that most parties and individuals involved in their daily lives are aware of their true identity and help to conceal the secret, but those outside of their shared habits and lifestyles are oblivious to their existence. Phra Eks granted me permission to talk about our conversations, but forbid me from disclosing any personal information that would identify him.

59. Tambiah, *Buddhism Betrayed*, 99.

60. The public secret is now shared by more than just the monks and some Buddhist laity. Phra Eks told me in 2007 that the terrorists (*phūkokānrai*) now know he is a military monk. According to his friend, who has contacts with militant groups, the terrorists are now watching him very closely. Because of this, he must be constantly vigilant. So far, there are no reports of military monks having been killed in southern Thailand; with regard to Phra Eks, there is no confirmation that his identity has been compromised.

61. *Bangkok Post*, "Yala Buddhists Flee to Temple Safety," November 9, 2006.

62. According to the *Bangkok Post*, by December 24, 2006, 161 refugees were at the *wat*. *Bangkok Post*, "Buddhist 'Refugees' Demand New Home," December 24, 2006. However, on December 8, 2006, from personal communications with refugees and the abbot at the *wat*, I received different statistics. I was told that refugees numbered 228 at the beginning of December. This number decreased by sixty during the first week of December. Some moved away, others rented different places to stay, and about fourteen moved back to their villages. On December 8, there were exactly 157 people still present.

63. Statistical information translated from Thai into English from the National Statistical Office, "Sūn padibatkān čhangwat pattānī" [Centralized Practices in Pattani Province], (Bangkok: Prime Minister Office, 2003) accessed at http://poc.pattani.go.th/report. php?report_id=26 on October 10, 2007.

64. In this chapter, the term "secular" is used to denote that which is not overtly or publicly recognized as religious.

65. This is comparable to the function served by mosques, churches, and Jewish temples throughout the world.

66. Donald Swearer, *Becoming the Buddha: The Ritual of Image Consecration in Thailand* (Princeton: Princeton University Press, 2004), 40.

67. Personal communication with Nopparat Benjawatthananant, director of the ONB in Nakhon Pathom, December 25, 2006.

68. In comparison to Yala's 127,442 Buddhists, Pattani has 113,205 Buddhists and Narathiwat has 112,250. There was an overall population of 1,7488,682 people in the southernmost provinces. Less than 2% of this population is classified in a category other than "Buddhist" or "Muslim," most hailing from the small Christianity population present. Narathiwat's population was 680,303 with an 83.5% Muslim majority (the Buddhist growth rate was –2.65 as opposed to the Muslim growth rate of 1.59). Yala's population contained the largest percentage of Buddhists. It had 439,456 people with a 71% Muslim majority (the

Buddhist growth rate was –0.29 as opposed to the Muslim growth rate of 2.70). Pattani's population was 628,922 with an 82% Muslim majority (the Buddhist growth also dropped at –1.39 as opposed to the Muslim growth rate 2.24). Information translated from Thai into English from the National Statistical Office, "Population and Households Census 1970, 1980, 1990, 2000: Southern Provinces," (Bangkok: Prime Minister Office, 2003).

69. Personal communication with Wat Kūaanai abbot in Khokpo district, Pattani Province, August 13, 2004.
70. Tamara Loos writes that the Siamese government used *wat* as government training centers during the reign of King Chulalongkorn, a practice that "unsurprisingly failed to attract the local Muslim population." *Subject Siam: Family, Law, and Colonial Modernity in Thailand* (Ithaca, NY: Cornell University Press, 2006), 22.
71. Chavivun Prachuabmoh, "Ethnic Relations among Thai, Thai Muslim and Chinese in South Thailand," in *Ethnicity and Interpersonal Interactions: A Cross Cultural Study*, ed. David Y. H. Wu (Hong Kong: Maruzen Asia, 1982): 62–83, 77.
72. Nearly every southern monk who has lived in the border provinces for more than a decade has mentioned the previous Muslim patronage to their *wat*. This comment was especially prominent in a phone interview conducted on August 15, 2004, with the abbot at Wat Tanapimo. The abbot remarked about the difference in patronage since the recent surge in violence and how Muslims no longer come to his *wat*. "Before this [recent surge in the conflict] began, Muslims used to come over and borrow things from the *wat*. But, last year they stopped coming and stopped communicating with me." Political Scientist Duncan McCargo also offers an example of Muslim patronage. He notes that Muslims still come to *wat*, such as one in Panāre District of Pattani, for problems of a religious nature, in this particular case, de-hexing. Chavivun Prachuabmoh also mentions Malays going to visit Buddhist monks for healing purposes. Chavivun Prachuabmoh, "The Role of Women in Maintaining Ethnic Identity and Boundaries: A Case of Thai-Muslims (The Malay Speaking Group) in Southern Thailand," (PhD diss., Department of Anthropology, University of Hawai'i, 1980), 171. For Buddhist and Islamic medicinal practices in southern Thailand, see Louis Golomb, *An Anthropology of Curing in Multiethnic Thailand* (Urbana: University of Illinois Press, 1985).
73. Kenneth Landon, *Siam in Transition: A Brief Survey of Cultural Trends in the Five Years since the Revolution of 1932* (Chicago: University of Chicago Press, 1939), 84.
74. Personal communication with Irving Johnson at the National University of Singapore, February 10, 2007.
75. Ryoko Nishii, "A Way of Negotiating with the Other within the Self: Muslims' Acknowledgement of Buddhist Ancestors in Southern Thailand" a working paper from *The Southern Thailand Homepage*, accessed at http://72.14.253.104/search?q=cache:pWFcvngTFuAJ:www.uni-muenster.de/Ethnologie/South_Thai/working_paper/Nishii_Negotiation.pdf+Nishii+%22A+Way+of+Negotiating+with+the+Other%22&hl=en&ct=clnk&cd=3&gl=us on September 20, 2006. Nishii also notes that Malays have a ritual to break their ties with Buddhism and rejoin the faith of Islam once they have defrocked. Ryoko Nishii, "Coexistence of Religions: Muslim and Buddhist Relationship on the West Coast of Southern Thailand," *Tai Culture: International Review on Tai Cultural Studies* 4.1 (June 1999): 77–92, 88.
76. Personal communication in English with southern officer of National Buddhism, December 6, 2006.
77. Personal communication with a refugee at Wat Nirotsangkatham, December 8, 2006.
78. The article references sixty wounded and eight dead. Casualties included: "28 bombs and three murders targeted foreign tourist sites, Thai-Chinese celebrating the Lunar New Year, hotels, karaoke bars, power grids, telephone lines and commercial sites in the country's southernmost provinces. Two public schools were torched." *Bangkok Post*, "Update: Extremists Launch Overnight Wave of Violence," February 19, 2007.
79. Patrick Jory, "*Luang Pho Thuat* as a Southern Thai Cultural Hero: Popular Religion in the Integration of Patani," in *Thai South and Malay North: Ethnic Interactions on the Plural Peninsula*, ed. Michael J. Montesano and Patrick Jory (Singapore: NUS Press, 2008), 295.

80. Personal communication with a Thai Buddhist restaurant owner adjacent to Wat Chang Hai, February 19, 2007.

81. According to the National Statistical Office in 2007 (B.E. 2550) Khokpo district had 30,934 Buddhists residents, making it the largest Buddhist populated district in Pattani. http://poc.pattani.go.th/report.php?report_id=10 accessed on September 16, 2007.

82. Personal communication with the Ačhān Tuk in Pattani Province, August 8, 2004.

83. Personal communication with a policeman at Wat B, 2006.

84. Pierre Bourdieu, *Outline of a Theory of Practice* (Cambridge: Cambridge University Press, 1977), 214.

85. Thai *wat* were used as military bases during and after World War II in southern Thailand. Personal communication with Irving Johnson at National University of Singapore, February 27, 2007. Kamala Tiyavanich also noted the historical presence of the Thai military in *wat* during King Vajiravudh's reign; personal communication at Cornell University, April 22, 2006.

86. Reports on military occupation during the 1970s comes from personal communications with monks in Pattani Province, September 2006. For information on the Village Scouts, see Marjorie A. Muecke, "The Village Scouts of Thailand," *Asian Survey* 20.4 (April 1980): 407–27 and Katherine Bowie, *Rituals of National Loyalty: An Anthropology of the State and the Village Scout Movement in Thailand* (New York: Columbia University Press, 1997).

87. This information comes from personal communication with commanding officers at the *wat* I visited and from Lieutenant Colonel Surathep Nukaeow of Ingkayut Camp, Pattani on December 28, 2006. In 2008, Surathep received a promotion and became the Deputy Chief in Hat Yai, Songkhla. The Thai armed forces have had difficulty acquiring local Malay Muslim recruits. The International Crisis Group records that, although the Thai military set out to make the Rangers out of local Malay Muslims, they ended up with less than 30%. International Crisis Group, "Southern Thailand: The Problem with Paramilitaries," *Asia Report No. 140* (October 23, 2007), 1.

88. Muslim soldiers are stationed around Islamic schools (*pondoks*) and near Islamic centers. Authorities have explained to me that this is done in order to honor religious sensitivities. Though there has never been any explanation offered for why only Buddhist soldiers are present in *wat*, the same rationale (honoring religious sensitivities) could apply. However, because the national police and soldiers use the *wat* as a State facility and because there is no Buddhist interdiction concerning non-Buddhists living in a *wat*, the presence of only Buddhist soldiers results in an air of State preferentiality.

89. *Human Rights Watch*, "Thailand: Government Covers Up Role in 'Disappearance'. Two Years on, Authorities Must Ensure Justice in Somchai Case," March 11, 2006.

90. Personal communication in English with Lieutenant Colonel Surathep Nukaeow of Ingkayut Camp, Pattani, December 28, 2006.

91. Monks have told me that it is more expensive to have soldiers stay in a *wat*, and if funding is cut for a specific area, police are usually brought in. Personal communication in the southernmost provinces, 2006.

92. Personal communication with Ačhān Dī at Wat Chang Hai, 2007.

93. Personal communication with an Ačhān Nok at Wat A, 2006.

94. In my own experience, I have found soldiers either refrain from drinking alcohol in the *wat*, or drink in the privacy of their buildings (thus in a more private and discreet manner).

95. Personal communication with police at Wat B, 2006.

96. Personal communication by telephone with Ačhān Mahāwichī, August 15, 2004.

97. I want to thank Irving Johnson for calling this to my attention.

98. Personal communication with a monk at Wat A, 2006.

99. These examples come from Ačhān Nok's military files at Wat A. I have omitted personal information from the photos.

100. Amnesty International, "Thailand: Torture in the Southern Counter-Insurgency," (London: Amnesty International Publications, 2009), 17.

101. Amnesty International does not have any evidence linking Buddhist monks to the tortures taking place in their *wat*. Personal communication with Amnesty International Southeast Asian Researcher Benjamin Zawacki, April 30, 2009.

102. International Crisis Group, "Southern Thailand: The Problem with Paramilitaries," *Asia Report No. 140* (October 23, 2007), 19, 20.

103. International Crisis Group, "Southern Thailand: The Problem," 18, 19. The subject of Buddhist militia in the southernmost provinces introduces a wider and more pervasive element of Buddhist militarism. For more analysis on this phenomenon, see McCargo, "Politics of Buddhist Identity," 11–32, 24–28 and Marc Askew, "Landscapes of Fear, Horizons of Trust: Villagers Dealing with Dangers in Thailand's Insurgent South," *Journal of Southeast Asian Studies* 40.1 (February 2009): 59–86, 67–69.

104. The population of the southernmost provinces is predominantly Muslim. Hence, the number of Muslim deaths may be higher, but the percentage of casualties from the Buddhist population is still greater. Srisompob Jitpiromsri and Panyaksak Sobhonvasu, "Unpacking Thailand's Southern Conflict: The Poverty of Structural Explanations," *Critical Asian Studies* 38.1 (2006): 95–117, 95. By January 2010, the disparity still remained: 58.95% of the deaths were Muslim, 38.09% Buddhist. Srisompob Jitpiromsri, "Sixth Year of the Southern Fire: Dynamics of Insurgency and Formation of the New Imagined Violence," *Deep South Watch* (Prince of Songkhla University: Center for Conflict Studies and Cultural Diversity, 2010): 1–24, 1.

105. Malay Muslims still come to the *wat*, although their purposes, numbers, and frequency have decreased dramatically since martial law was declared.

106. Personal communication by phone with Phra Arhom in the southernmost provinces, 2004.

107. Buddhist monks suffer the second lowest fatality rates at 21.8%, and military personnel suffer the lowest at 17.7%. The most telling statistic is the disparity between the fatality rates of Buddhist monks and Islamic religious leaders. Islamic religious leaders suffer the greatest fatalities at 83.9%. Jitpiromsri, "Sixth Year," 1–24, 17.

108. Though one could argue that the targeting and killing of monks on their morning alms rounds already signifies how southern militants see monks.

109. Surin Pitsuwan, *Islam and Malay Nationalism: A Case Study of the Malay Muslims of Southern Thailand* (Bangkok: Thai Khadi Research Institute, Thammasat University, 1985), 183.

Chapter 5

1. Personal communication with a teaching assistant from Bangkok, February 10, 2007.

2. As Peter Jackson succinctly explains, the primacy of Buddhism in the definition of "Thainess" is accepted by every Thai Buddhist. Peter A. Jackson, "Thai-Buddhist Identity: Debates on the *Traiphum Phra Ruang*," in *National Identity and Its Defenders: Thailand Today*, ed. Craig J. Reynolds (Chiang Mai: Silkworm Books, 2002), 156.

3. Liah Greenfeld, *Nationalism: Five Roads to Modernity* (Cambridge, MA: Harvard University Press, 1992), 11.

4. In the Preamble of Patronage of Islam Act of 1945, the Thai State officially referred to Malay Muslims as "the Thai people who profess Islam" (*prachāchon čhao thai thī nabthua islam*).

5. Michel Gilquin, *The Muslims of Thailand*, trans. Michael Smithies (Chiang Mai: Silkworm Books, 2002), 51.

6. Michael Omi and Howard Winant, *Racial Formation in the United States: From the 1960s to the 1980s* (London: Routledge, 1991), 55.

7. Omi and Winant, *Racial Formation*, 60 and 68. It is interesting to note that in most English-Thai dictionaries there is no listing for "racism;" in its place there is only the word "racialist." See SE-ED's *English-Thai Thai-English Dictionary (Contemporary Edition)* (Bangkok: SE-Education, 2002), 414.

8. Stanley Jeyaraja Tambiah, *Leveling Crowds: Ethnonationalist Conflicts and Collective Violence in South Asia* (Berkeley: University of California Press, 1996), 20.

9. See Michael Moerman, "Ethnic Identity in a Complex Civilization: Who Are the Lue?" *American Anthropologist* 76 (1974): 1215–30.

10. Thomas Hylland Eriksen, *Ethnicity and Nationalism: Anthropological Perspectives* (London: Pluto Press, 2002), 12.

11. Jan Weisman argues persuasively that *khaek* is a racialized term that is based at least partially in phenotype and not solely contingent upon culture or citizenship. Jan Weisman, "Tropes and Traces: Hybridity, Race, Sex, and Responses to Modernity in Thailand," (PhD diss., University of Washington, 2000), 128.

12. Weisman, "Tropes and Traces," 128.

13. Cultural Studies scholar Paul Gilroy labels the phenomenon of modernity as a catalyst for distinctive regimes of truth as "raciology." He discloses early links between anthropology and colonial modernity's corresponding inventions of race. In cases such as Immanuel Kant's discussion of enslaved Africans (through David Hume's accounts) or Hegel's anthropological view of the Ashanti, conceptions of race travel with modernity to create "workings of the great imperial systems it battles to control." Paul Gilroy, *Against Race: Imagining Political Culture beyond the Color Line* (Cambridge, MA: Belknap Press of Harvard University Press, 2000), 57, 58.

14. In his discussion of the neo-colonial education and its affect on Hindu Studies, Shrinivas Tilak notes the propensity of scholars to use Western paradigms to assume "Western ideas about the most fundamental things are the only ideas possible to hold, certainly the only rational ideas, and the only ideas that can make sense of the world, of reality, of social life, and of human beings." Shrinivas Tilak, "Hinduism for Hindu Studies: Taking Back Hindu Studies," in *The Life of Hinduism*, ed. John Stratton Hawley and Vasudha Narayanan (Berkeley: University of California Press, 2006), 274.

15. Kenneth Perry Landon, "The Problem of the Chinese in Thailand," *Pacific Affairs* 13.2 (June 1940): 149–61, 154. Landon concludes that the Siamese State discriminated against the Chinese through economic and social policies. "Problem of the Chinese," 149–61, 161.

16. See Richard J. Coughlin, "The Status of the Chinese Minority in Thailand," *Pacific Affairs* 25.4 (December 1952): 378–89; Eliezer B. Ayal, "Private Enterprise and Economic Progress in Thailand," *Journal of Asian Studies* 26.1 (November 1966): 5–14; Frederic C. Deyo, "Ethnicity and Work Culture in Thailand: A Comparison of Thai and Thai-Chinese White-Collar Workers," *Journal of Asian Studies* 34.4 (August 1975): 995–1015.

17. G. William Skinner, "Chinese Assimilation and Thai Politics," *Journal of Asian Studies* 16.2 (February 1957): 237–50, 249.

18. Keyes' view of ethnicity is in accordance with those placed under the ethnicity-theory paradigm, in which ethnicity is the result of a group formation process based on culture and descent. William Peterson, "Concepts of Ethnicity," in *Concepts of Ethnicity: Selections from the Harvard Encyclopedia of American Ethnic Groups*, ed. W. Peterson, M. Novak, and P. Gleason (Cambridge, MA: Harvard University Press, 1982), 2, quoted in Omi and Winant, *Racial Formation*, 15. In his comparative paper on Thailand and Vietnam, Keyes considers the Thai State dominated by inclusivist policies, which "accommodate considerable diversity within a national community" in contrast to other countries that have constricted policies, which exclude peoples from the national community. Charles Keyes "Ethnicity and the Nation-States of Thailand and Vietnam," in *Challenging the Limits: Indigenous Peoples of the Mekong Region*, ed. Prasit Leepreecha, Don McCaskill, and Kwanchewan Buadaeng, 13–53 (Chiang Mai: Mekong Press, 2008), 13–15.

19. Charles Keyes, "Toward a New Formulation of the Concept of Ethnic Group," *Ethnicity* 3 (1976): 202–13, 208.

20. Chan Kwok Bun and Tong Chee Kiong, "Rethinking Assimilation and Ethnicity: The Chinese in Thailand," *International Migration Review* 27.1 (Spring 1993): 140–68.

21. Surin Pitsuwan, *Islam and Malay Nationalism: A Case Study of the Malay-Muslims of Southern Thailand* (Bangkok: Thai Khadi Research Institute, Thammasat University, 1985), 24. Malay identification with Islam began in the 1600s and did not fully become an implicit association until the twentieth century.

22. Anthony Reid writes that the "farther away from the heartland of Sumatra and the Peninsula one travelled, the more likely it was that the trading community of Muslims would be known collectively as Melayu, whatever their ethnic or geographic origin." Anthony Reid, "Understanding *Melayu* (Malay) as a Source of Diverse Modern Identities," in *Contesting Malayness: Malay Identity across Boundaries*, ed. Timothy P. Barnard, 1–24 (Singapore: Singapore University Press, 2006), 7. Malay Buddhists populated the border provinces long before the introduction of Islam, but this ethno-religious identity has not been noted, nor considered since the early 1900s. Writing on the popular religion of Patani Malay in the early twentieth century, Nelson Annandale notes, "Neither Malays nor Siamese (*i.e.*, neither Mahommedans nor Buddhists)..." Nelson Annandale, "Notes on the Popular Religion of the Patani Malays," *Man* 3 (1903): 27–28, 28.

23. Surin, *Islam and Malay Nationalism*, 224.

24. Timothy P. Barnard and Hendrik M. J. Maier, "Melayu, Malay, Maleis: Journeys through the Identity of a Collection," in *Contesting Malayness: Malay Identity across Boundaries*, ed. Timothy P. Barnard, ix–xiii (Singapore: Singapore University Press, 2006), ix.

25. Trinh Minh-ha, *Woman, Native, Other* (Bloomington: Indiana University Press, 1989), 6. I would like to thank Staci Scheiwiller for reminding me of this parallel.

26. See Frantz Fanon, *The Wretched of the Earth*, Richard Philcox trans. (New York: Grove Press, 2004).

27. In his comparison between the Moros of the Philippines and the Malays of southern Thailand, Wan Kadir Che Man considers the conflict between the Malay Muslims and the Thai government an ethnic reaction to internal colonialism. Che Man, *Muslim Separatism: The Moros of Southern Philippines and the Malays of Southern Thailand* (Singapore Oxford University Press, 1990), 7. Surin holds a similar position, arguing that the Thai State forces Malay Muslims to assimilate into an alien cultural identity. Surin, *Islam and Malay Nationalism*, 216. The Thai State's internal colonialism of the Malay Muslims follows theories offered by Thongchai Winichakul, Chaiyan Rajchagool, Michael Herzfeld, and Tamara Loos, all of whom delivered papers during a roundtable discussion, "Discussion Thailand: Anything but 'Never Colonized'" at the Ninth International Conference on Thai Studies at Northern Illinois University, April 3–6, 2005.

28. For a close look at the identity conflicts of the Khache, see Rohit Singh "History, Narrative, and Identity among Tibetan Muslims in Kashmir: A Rethinking of Tibetan-ness," unpublished master's thesis (University of California–Santa Barbara, Department of Religious Studies, 2010).

29. Juliane Schober, "Buddhism, Violence, and the State in Burma (Myanmar) and Sri Lanka," in *Religion and Conflict in South and Southeast Asia: Disrupting Violence*, ed. Linell E. Cady and Sheldon W. Simon (New York: Routledge, 2007), 55.

30. Anand Panyarachun et al., "Report of the National Reconciliation Commission: Overcoming Violence through the Power of Reconciliation," 30. Unofficial translation accessed at http://thailand.ahrchk.net/docs/nrc_report_en.pdf on August 15, 2006.

31. Scott L. Malcomson, One Drop of Blood: The American Misadventure of Race (New York: Farrar Straus Giroux, 2000), 356.

32. Antonio Sérgio Alfredo Guimarães, "Racism and Anti-Racism in Brazil," in *Racism and Anti-Racism in World Perspective*, ed. Benjamin P. Bowser (Thousand Oaks: Sage Publications, 1995), 214.

33. Thais generally consider people from Eurasia as *khon farang*, from South Asia as *khon khaek*, and from the continent of Africa as *khon kham nigon*. However, there is an assumed appearance corresponding with these geographies. Thais will not call a Pakistani American visiting Thailand a *khon farang*, nor will they identify a White South African as *khon kham nigon*. The common reference for Native Americans is *indiyen dæng* (red Indian).

34. Gary Hamilton and Tony Waters state that, no longer members of a "harassed, inward-looking minority group, the Chinese in Thailand have embraced the outside world and reaffirmed their Chinese identity, as well as maintaining their Thai identity." "Ethnicity and Capitalist Development: The Changing Role of the Chinese in Thailand," in *Essential Outsiders: Chinese and Jew in the Modern Transformation of Southeast Asia and Central*

Europe, ed. Daniel Chirot and Anthony Reid (Seattle: University of Washington Press, 1997): 258–84, 262.

35. For information on the Godfather era see William A. Callahan and Duncan McCargo, "Vote-Buying in Thailand's Northeast: The July 1995 General Election," *Asian Survey* 36.4 (April 1996): 376–92, and Nishizaki Yorinoshi, "The Moral Origin of Thailand's Provincial Strongman: The Case of Banharn Silpa-acha," *South East Asia Research* 13.2 (2005): 184–234.

36. Chris Baker and Pasuk Phoongpaichit comment on the changing trends, and how it is now chic to claim Chinese roots in *Thailand's Boom and Bust* (Chiang Mai: Silkworm Books, 1998), 174. Anthropologist Ara Wilson presents Thai prime minister Thaksin Shinawatra as the embodiment of change for Chinese identity in Thailand: he embodies the transformation from Chinese merchant to ethnic Chinese *tao kae* businessman, and last to "Thai" tycoon, representing the Thai nation in the region and on the global stage. Ara Wilson, *Intimate Economies of Bangkok: Tomboys, Tycoons, and Avon Ladies in the Global City* (Berkeley: University of California Press, 2004), 141.

37. There are a myriad of amalgamations of Thai and Chinese Buddhism, each one providing impetus and support for Chinese immigrants to adopt Thai Buddhist customs and practices. One of these was the deification of the famous Chinese Muslim explorer, Zheng He (as San-pao), in a Thai Buddhist *wat*. The most famous San-pao *wat* in Thailand was founded by Rama I. G. W. Skinner, *Chinese Society in Thailand: An Analytical History* (Ithaca, NY: Cornell University Press, 1957), 129, 130. The differences were still evident within the southernmost provinces in 2007. While Chinese still frequently visit and donate money to Thai *wat*, funeral rituals for Chinese are often practiced at Chinese temples. *Wat* generally have affiliations with local Chinese communities and monks commute to perform the rituals in specific Chinese locations (rather than at their own *wat*).

38. Thongchai Winichakul, *Siam Mapped: A History of the Geo-Body of a Nation* (Chiang Mai: Silkworm Books, 1998), 5.

39. We can find similar constructions of religious identity and alterity in the neighboring country of Myanmar. In the Thai and Burmese scenario, religious identity acts as a social solvent, absorbing other identity markers into its identity construction. Reflecting on the identity construction of Burmese, Joseph Cheah writes,

> *Bamahsan gyin* (Burmeseness) is best expressed in a Burmese who exhibits the quality of *ah nah day*, and who has a deep respect for others, especially one's elders. Because *bamahsan gyin* is part and parcel of Burmese Buddhism, any discussion of adaptations of the practice of Burmese Buddhism must take *bamahsan gyin* into account.

> Joseph Cheah, "Race and Religion in American Buddhism: A Case Study of a Burmese Buddhist Congregation of the Dhammananda Monastery," (PhD diss., Graduate Theological Union, 2004), 23–24.

40. Patrick Jory, "From 'Melayu Pattani' to 'Thai Muslim': The Spectre of Ethnic Identity in Southern Thailand," *Asia Research Institute's Working Paper Series No. 84*, February 2007, accessed at http://www.ari.nus.edu.sg/showfile.asp?pubid=643&type=2 on March 1, 2007.

41. Charles Keyes, "Muslim 'Others' in Buddhist Thailand," paper presented at a conference on Buddhism and Islam: Encounters, Histories, Dialogues and Representation (Numata Conference Center, McGill University, May 29–30, 2009).

42. There are lighter skinned people who are identified as *khaek*, but these identifications are relative to different environments and altered nomenclatures. For instance, Arabs and Persians are referred to as *khaek khāo* (white *khaek*) as opposed to African and African Americans, who are called *khaek dam* (black *khaek*). Personal communication with Thai linguist Titima Suthiwan, National University of Singapore, March 9, 2007.

43. The term "*khaek*" may derive from the Teo Chiu, Hokkien, and Hainanese term *k'e*, which also means guests. G. W. Skinner notes that the Hokkien and Teo Chiu, the most prominent Chinese immigrants in Thailand, pronounced the word as "*Kheh*" and generally used it to refer to the Hakka Chinese, who, coincidentally, are also a significant Chinese immigrant group in Thailand. Skinner, *Chinese Society in Thailand*, 39. *Khaek* and the term nation have

interesting etymological parallels. "Nation" comes from the Latin term *natio*, which in the early Roman context meant foreigner, with negative connotations. Gradually through the centuries, the term developed a positive context that continues today. *Khaek* also means foreigner, but initially had a positive connotations. During the formative years of nation-state building, Thainess became a focal point, making distinctions from Thainess, like *khaek*, pejorative.

44. One of the more popular of these books is P. A. Payutto, *A Constitution for Living: Buddhist Principles for a Fruitful and Harmonious Life*, trans. Bruce Evans (Bangkok: Office of National Buddhism Press, 1997).

45. Chart Korbjitti, *The Judgment*, trans. Phongdeit Jiangphatthana-kit and Marcel Barang (Nakhon Rachasima, Thailand: Howling Books, 2003), 14.

46. Sameskybooks Chatroom, "'Khon thai tang pēn khon phut?' [Do Thais have to be Buddhist?]," accessed at http://www.sameskybooks.org/board/lofiversion/index.php?t3413.html, on March 8, 2008. McCargo also cites examples of anti-Muslim sentiments found on Thai-language internet bulletin boards such as panthip.com. Duncan McCargo, "The Politics of Buddhist Identity in Thailand's Deep South: The Demise of Civil Religion?" *Journal of Southeast Asian Studies* 40.1 (February 2009): 11–32, 14.

47. Personal communication by telephone with Āčhān Subin, August 14, 2004.

48. I would like to thank Charles Keyes for raising this issue. General Sonthi Boonyaratglin was the first Muslim to lead a largely Buddhist army in Thailand, and was the leader of the coup that displaced Thaksin Shinawatra in 2006. A multimillionaire, Sonthi possesses both military and economic power in Thailand. His ancestor, Sheikh Ahmad Qomi was an Iranian expatriate trader who lived in Thailand for twenty-six years. Phangčhūdī Phosamūa, "Chīwit lae pholngān pholēk sonthi boonyaratglon phūbaychākārthahārbok [Life and Accomplishments of General Sonthi Boonyaratglin, Commander in Chief]," *Khui khui khāo* [Teenee News], February 27, 2007.

49. For example, political scientists James Fearon and David Laitin hypothesize that it is not ethnicity or religion, but rather a government's finances, organization, and politics that dramatically affect the probability of a civil war. "Ethnicity, Insurgency, and Civil War," *American Political Science Review* 97.1 (February 2003): 75–90, 75.

50. Although a majority of Malay Muslims live in the three southern provinces and endure widespread poverty, all three provinces are rich in natural resources, such as timber and rubber.

51. Chaiwat Satha-anand, *The Life of This World: Negotiated Muslim Lives in Thai Society* (Singapore: Marshall Cavendish International, 2005), 6.

52. Supara Janchitfah, *Violence in the Mist: Reporting on the Province of Pain in Southern Thailand* (Bangkok: Kobfai Publishing Company, 2005), 152.

53. Walter Mignolo, "Citizenship, Knowledge, and the Limits of Humanity," *American Literary History* 18.2 (2006): 312–31, 320.

54. Similar to the terms East Asia and South Asia, I use Eurasia for the western part of Asia, otherwise known as Europe.

55. Ann Laura Stoler and Frederick Cooper, "Between Metropole and Colony: Rethinking a Research Agenda," in *Tensions of Empire: Colonial Cultures in a Bourgeois World*, ed. Frederick Cooper and Ann Laura Stoler (Berkeley: University of California Press, 1997), 7.

56. Gilroy, *Against Race*, 64.

57. David Streckfuss, "The Mixed Colonial Legacy in Siam: Origins of Thai Racialist Thought, 1890–1910," in *Autonomous Histories, Particular Truths: Essays in Honor of John Smail*, ed. Laurie Jo Sears and John Smails (Madison, WI: Center for Southeast Asian Studies, 1993): 123–53, 141.

58. The verbal root *jan* (to become, change into, or to be born) is the base for *jāti*, as well as the noun *jana*, which denotes a person, race (as in the *panca janās*, the five races), political subjects or, when used collectively, a "divine race." Monier Monier-William, *A Sanskrit-English Dictionary*, digital facsimile edition (Los Angeles: Bhaktivedanta Book Trust, 2002), 410.

59. Herman Tull, *The Vedic Origins of Karma: Cosmos as Man in Ancient Indian Myth and Ritual* (Albany: State University of New York Press, 1989), 17.

60. Donald S. Lopez Jr., *Buddhism and Science: A Guide for the Perplexed* (Chicago: University of Chicago Press, 2008), 78.

61. Prajāpati, who appears earlier in the Yajur Veda, was a reworking of an earlier cosmogony of Puruṣa in the Ṛg Veda. Both deities, in their self-destruction (Sanskrit: *tapas*), have been used to explain the construction of the *varṇa* system. Eurasian scholars have been criticized for overemphasizing the presence of caste in India today and rightly so. With the information revolution in full force, there are different practices in play that directly oppose the traditional rules of the caste system. Jeffrey Samuels makes similar points about the presence of *jāti* in the Theravādin Sri Lankan society. "Saving the Buddhist Religion: Caste Discrimination and the Establishment of New Temples in Twentieth- and Twenty-First Century Sri Lanka," Annual American Academy of Religion Conference, Philadelphia 2005.

62. International Studies scholar Vijay Prashad writes,
    ...if we borrow from recent theories of nationalism, *jati* itself might be seen as an "imagined community" founded in opposition to other "imagined communities" and linked by relations of power and production.
    Vijay Prashad, *The Karma of Brown Folk* (Minneapolis: University of Minnesota Press, 2000), 96.

63. A. J. Brown, "Awakening the Wild Tigers (An Annotated Translation with Introduction)," B.A. honors thesis (Canberra: Australian National University, 1983), 47–48. As Scot Barmé has already noted, T. W. S Wannapho was the first to introduce this notion in 1893. *Luang Wichit Wathakan and the Creation of a Thai Identity* (Singapore: Institute of Southeast Asian Studies, 1993), 17.

64. It is also worthy to note that Vajiravudh's uncle and supreme patriarch of the Thai *sangha*, Prince Wachirayanawarorot, claimed that King Vajiravudh had formed the Wild Tiger Corps "to teach civilians the art of war." Prince Wachirayan, *The Buddhist Attitude towards National Defence and Administration: A Special Allocution by His Holiness Prince Vajiranana (1916)*, trans. Vajiravudh (Ithaca, NY: Cornell University Library, 2010), 21.

65. In light of this and other information pointing to the relevance of religion in Siam's early nation-building, historian Maurizio Peleggi amended Streckfuss's work with the acknowledgement that there was a Buddhist dimension to *chāt*. However, Peleggi does not unravel the full implications of this Buddhist dimension for the Malay Muslims, nor does he address the overarching dimension of race. Maurizio Peleggi, *Thailand: The Worldly Kingdom* (Singapore: Talisman Publishing, 2007), 118.

66. Barmé, *Luang Wichit Wathakan*, 30.

67. Tamara Loos, *Subject Siam: Family, Law, and Colonial Modernity in Thailand* (Ithaca: Cornell University Press, 2006), 3 and 76.

68. The notion of "civilized" existed in Siam prior to the colonial period, but still rested upon Buddhist affiliations. Ronald Renard writes that during the Ayutthaya period, the prisoners of war might have entered the kingdom as members of a captive or lower class of people, but "many among them were not considered foreigners because they practiced some kind of Buddhism and followed 'civilized' lifestyles similar to many *tai*." Ronald D. Renard, "Creating the Other Requires Defining Thainess against Which the Other Can Exist: Early-Twentieth Century Definitions," *Southeast Asian Studies* 44.8 (December 2006): 295–320, 301.

69. James C. Scott, *The Art of Not Being Governed: An Anarchist History of Upland Southeast Asia* (New Haven: Yale University Press, 2009), 123.

70. Thongchai Winichakul, "The Quest for 'Siwilai': A Geographical Discourse of Civilizational Thinking in the Late Nineteenth and Early Twentieth-Century Siam," *Journal of Asian Studies* 59.3 (August 2000): 528–49, 529.

71. For example, see Craig Reynolds, "The Buddhist Monkhood in Nineteenth Century Thailand," (PhD diss., Cornell University, 1972), 125 and 135.

72. The concept of heralding reason over faith did not originate in Eurasia; this intellectual phenomenon has roots in India, the Middle East, and elsewhere, but Eurasia provided the context for the Siamese at the time.

73. "For the past half-century, however, the gradient of available identities has, as it were, been radically tilted in favor of various degrees of state control. The classical narrative of 'raw' barbarian peoples being brought to civilization has been replicated by a narrative of development and nation-building." Scott, *Art of Not Being Governed*, 281.

74. Alicia Marie Turner, "Buddhism, Colonialism and the Boundaries of Religion: Theravada Buddhism in Burma, 1885–1920," vol. 1 (PhD diss., University of Chicago, the Divinity School, 2009), 112–14.

75. Peleggi, *Thailand*, 50.

76. Chulalongkorn encouraged the Islamic moral code of *sharia* in the southern provinces. Pitsuwan, *Islam and Malay Nationalism*, 12.

77. This spatial distinction is important when considering the more successful "assimilation" of Haw Chinese, Cham, Pathan, Tamil, Persian, Arab, and Sam Sam Muslims in Central Siam during the Ayutthaya period. This point was raised during personal communication with Chris Joll on March 9, 2007.

78. Loos, *Subject Siam*, 80–81.

79. (Vajiravudh), *The Jews of the Orient* (Bangkok: Siam Observer, 1914).

80. Somchot Ongsakun, "Kānpatirūp kānpokkhrong monthon pattānī (p.s. 2449–2474)" [The Administrative Reform of Monthon Pattani (1906–1931)] (Master's thesis Sri Nakharinwirot University, Bangkok, 1978), 134.

81. In this chapter, "assimilate" is used to denote the hegemonic efforts of State ideology to co-opt power from, and legitimate the co-opting through, a discourse of "naturalizing" citizens on an inferred normative identity, in this case the Tai Buddhist (Tai as an ethnic group as opposed to Thai, the national identity created in 1939).

82. Wa Thiong'o locates language as an internal aspect of colonialism in the African subject: "In my view language was the most important vehicle through which that power [of imperialism] fascinated and held the soul prisoner. The bullet was the means of the physical subjugation. Language was the means of the spiritual subjugation." Ngũgĩ Wa Thiong'o, *Decolonizing the Mind: The Politics of Language in African Literature* (Oxford: James Currey, 2006), 9.

83. On June 24, 1940, Thai Chinese were notified of a "Thai-ification" policy that promoted the use of the Thai language. This policy was designed to put pressure specifically on the Chinese community. Barmé, *Luang Wichit Wathakan*, 155.

84. "During the early Bangkok period, *chat*, meaning 'race,' was widely used and appears to have been virtually interchangeable with the term *phasa* (meaning 'language')." S. Phlai Noi, "Wat Pho," in *Phumisat Wat Pho* [The Geography of Wat Pho], ed. Sa'nga Kanchanakhaphan (Bangkok: Sansawan, 1966), 109–10.

85. Chavivun Prachuabmoh, "The Role of Women in Maintaining Ethnic Identity and Boundaries: A Case of Thai-Muslims (The Malay Speaking Group) in Southern Thailand," (PhD diss., Department of Anthropology, University of Hawai'i, 1980), 98.

86. Ann Laura Stoler, "Sexual Affront and Racial Frontiers: European Identities and the Cultural Politics of Exclusion in Colonial Southeast Asia," in *Tensions of Empire: Colonial Cultures in a Bourgeois World*, ed. Frederick Cooper and Ann Laura Stoler (Berkeley: University of California Press, 1997), 217–18.

87. Malays call the Thais who convert to Islam Sam Sam, though this reference is mostly used by Malays from northern Malaysia. During my fieldwork between 2004 and 2007, I found that there were still marriages that resulted in spousal conversions to Islam.

88. Chavivun Prachuabmoh, "Ethnic Relations among Thai, Thai Muslim and Chinese in South Thailand," in *Ethnicity and Interpersonal Interactions: A Cross Cultural Study*, ed. David Y. H. Wu (Hong Kong: Maruzen Asia, 1982): 62–83, 71.

89. Louis Golomb, *An Anthropology of Curing in Multiethnic Thailand* (Urbana: University of Illinois Press, 1985), 27.

90. In one district where I have been working more closely, the abbot told me there had not been any converts to Buddhism in the last ten years. I want to thank Irving Johnson for calling my attention to Thai Buddhist conversions.

91. Surin, *Islam and Malay Nationalism*, 88.

92. Thanet Aphornsuvan contextualizes Prime Minister Phibun's application of Malay Muslim assimilation as a product of the wider influences of Japanese imperialism. "At the same time, the rise of militarism in Japan and the threat of war in Europe brought Phibun into close and cordial contact with the Japanese government. To Phibun and his advisors, Thailand could become a strong nation as well as a modern—'civilized'—country by following the example of Japan, whose successes had made it 'the light of Asia.'" Thanet, "Origins of Malay Muslim 'Separatism,'" in *Thai South and Malay North: Ethnic Interactions on the Plural Peninsula*, ed. Michael J. Montesano and Patrick Jory (Singapore: NUS Press, 2008), 105.

93. Craig Reynolds, *Seditious Histories: Contesting Thai and Southeast Asian Pasts* (Seattle: University of Washington Press, 2006) 260.

94. Raymond Scupin, "Muslim Accommodation in Thai Society," *Journal of Islamic Studies* 9.2 (1998): 229–58, 231.

95. Chavivun Prachuabmoh, "Ethnic Relations among Thai, Thai Muslim and Chinese in South Thailand: Ethnicity and Interpersonal Interaction," in *Ethnicity and Interpersonal Integration*, ed. D. Y. H. Wu (Singapore: Maruzen Asia, 1982), 74, 75.

96. Chavivun, "Role of Women," 89 and 169.

97. Scupin, "Muslim Accommodation," 229–58, 236.

98. Thai: *dai song phra ōk pai čhārik obrom sangson chāokhao lae chon thin kendān phưa hai khao dai dranekthưng khwām pen chāt dīeo kan nabthư sāsanā dīeo kan lǽ rakphakdī to phra mahākasat ong dīeo kan lae hai khao dai yưd thư sthāban lak tang sām nī wai pen thī phưng todpai.* Brawit Dandlanugul, *The History of Wat Srisoda: Where the Regional Dhamma Jarika Project Is Situated in Chiang Mai, Thailand* (Chiang Mai: Chiang Mai Publishing House, 2002), 35.

99. The director-general of the Department of the Public Welfare outlined the Thammačarik policy in a speech that included among its objectives "To induce the hill tribes to accept the important role of helping to maintain the security of national frontiers, by instilling in them a sense of belonging and national loyalty to the nation." Charles Keyes, "Buddhism and National Integration in Thailand," *Journal of Asian Studies* 30.3 (May 1971): 551–67, 564.

100. Another state-sponsored activity that engendered assimilation through conversion was the organization of Village Scouts of the 1970s and early 1980s. This mandatory five-day training course for millions of Village Scouts usually took place in *wat* or in public schools owned by *wat*. Marjorie Muecke notes that the Village Scout program focused on infusing a sense of Thai identity that included a profound respect for the king, for Buddhism, and "the sense of an ethnic Thai 'specialness.'" She adds that "[r]einforcement of these aspects of Thai identity is unquestionably gratifying to most Thai, and is apparently a very effective Village Scout strategy for gaining members as well as for encouraging nationalism." Marjorie A. Muecke, "The Village Scouts of Thailand," *Asian Survey* 20.4 (April 1980): 407–27, 413.

101. Thomas Fraser, *Rusembilan: A Malay Fishing Village in Southern Thailand* (Ithaca, NY: Cornell University Press, 1960), 69.

102. McCargo writes that the "politics in the deep south from the 1980s onward were characterized by two main forms of transformation: the domestication of dissent and a parallel dissent from domestication." Duncan McCargo, *Tearing Apart the Land: Islam and Legitimacy in Southern Thailand* (Ithaca & London: Cornell University Press, 2008), 55.

103. In light of Subaltern Studies and Ranajit Guha's work, we can read militant actions, which are largely considered by the media and Thai State to be disparate actions, collective and organized. Guha explains that this ambiguity of being either criminality or insurgency can be distinguished through four separate criteria: the violence being public, collective, destructive, and total. Failure to explicate these criteria, Guha notes, leads the historian to be "resigned to the point of view which sees in insurgency nothing but chaos, confusion, and disorder," rather than a contemplative, conscious, and orderly attack. Ranajit Guha, *Elementary Aspects of Peasant Insurgency in Colonial India* (Delhi: Oxford University Press, 1992), 109, 136.

104. Personal conversation with Ačhān Tūat at Wat Chang Hai, February 18, 2007.

105. At midnight on February 19, 2007, local Thai television such as ITV reported that the previous night's attacks by terrorists (*phūkokānrāi*) in southern Thailand were the worst in the last 3 years...According to military reports, there were eleven separate small-scale attacks, an arson attack on Wat Nabradu in Khokpo District, Pattani, and numerous other attacks on civilian areas. Over fifty people were injured and more than six died during these attacks throughout Yala and Pattani provinces. Personal communication with Don Pathan and participant observations in Pattani Province, February 18, 2007.

106. "The police went to pick up the nails in front of the wat...and could not catch the attackers because the police were collecting the nails that the terrorists put out. The bombs were two kilometers away, so they could not get there in time." Personal communication with a monk at Wat B, 2007.

107. Ukrist Pathmanand, "Thaksin's Achilles' Heel: The Failure of Hawkish Approaches in the Thai South," *Critical Asian Studies* 38.1 (2006): 73–93.

108. As events were unfolding, one female student from Prince of Songkhla University (PSU) informed me that she and others witnessed two people dressed in black and white Islamic garb (covering their heads) cheering right behind PSU after the generators were bombed. The police kept chasing suspects well into the night. One chase in particular started just outside of Pattani's Yaring District, with police and helicopters in pursuit of seven teenagers on motorbikes. The chase led them out from Pattani into Narathiwat.

109. *The Nation*, "Surayud Apologises for Govt's abuses in South," November 3, 2006.

110. Muhamad Ayub Pathan and Wassana Nanuam, "Blacklisting of Teachers to Stop," *Bangkok Post*, November 9, 2006.

111. One may be tempted to conclude that the conflict is only about ethnicity between Chinese and Malays, but this is not the case. Just as there is resentment in the United States between Blacks and other racial groups considered closer to White normativity, Malays see Chinese in the same fashion. This resentment includes ethnic and class, as well as religious, distinctions. The Chinese (who are mostly Buddhists) enjoy considerable economic status in southern Thailand, and are associated with consumerism that is linked to the State.With respect to the targeting of Buddhist and Chinese locations, an English newspaper reported: "At least 28 bombs and three murders targeted foreign tourist sites, Thai Chinese celebrating the Lunar New Year, hotels, karaoke bars, power grids, telephone lines and commercial sites in the country's southernmost provinces. Two public schools were torched." *Bangkok Post*, "Update: Extremists Launch Overnight Wave of Violence," February 19, 2007. Additional newspaper articles urged Thais to be alert during special Buddhist times, e.g. "Buddhist Holiday Alert Urged for South," *Bangkok Post*, February 19, 2007.

112. Personal communication in English with Ačhān Nirut at Wat Chang Hai, February 22, 2007.

113. Cornel West, *Race Matters* (Boston: Beacon Press Books, 1993), 26, 85.

114. bell hooks stresses this connection of sexism and racism under the colonial discourse, particularly white supremacy in the United States, and how the two prejudices complement one another in the subjugation of Blacks in *Killing Rage: Ending Racism* (New York: Henry Holt and Company, 1995).

115. Amporn Mardent, "From Adek to Mo'ji: Identities and Social Realities of Southern Thai People" *Kyoto Review of Southeast Asia* Vol. 8, March 2007, accessed at http://kyotoreview-sea.org/Amporn.htm on September 30, 2006.

116. Informal communication with Ačhān Tuk at Wat Chang Hai, Pattani Province, February 20, 2007.

117. Marc Askew, "Landscapes of Fear, Horizons of Trust: Villagers Dealing with Danger in Thailand's Insurgent South," *Journal of Southeast Asian Studies* 40.1 (February 2009): 59–86, 70.

118. "Also and paradoxically, this term is used of foreigners coming from the same geographic areas as Thai Muslims, even if they are not themselves Muslim." Gilquin, *Muslims of Thailand*, 23.

119. *CBC News*, "Canadian Dies in Thai Bomb Attack," September 16, 2006, accessed at http://www.cbc.ca/world/story/2006/09/16/thai.html on March 16, 2008 and *The Nation*, "Six Blasts Rock Hat Yai," September 17, 2006.

120. Kobkua Suwannathat-Pian, *Thai-Malay Relations: Traditional Intra-Regional Relations from the Seventeenth to the Early Twentieth Centuries* (Singapore: Oxford University Press, 1988), 161.

121. Peter van der Veer, *Imperial Encounters: Religion and Modernity in India and Britain* (Princeton: Princeton University Press, 2001), 22.

122. Cheah, "Race and Religion," 48.

123. However, unlike the Siamese, the Burmese nation was under attack by the British. The barbarians became the English, and the desire became the preservation of Buddhism. Alicia Marie Turner, "Buddhism, Colonialism and the Boundaries of Religion: Theravada Buddhism in Burma, 1885–1920, Volume One," (PhD diss., University of Chicago, the Divinity School, 2009), 112–14.

124. Lopez, *Buddhism and Science*, 21.

125. Cristina Rocha, *Zen in Brazil: The Quest for Cosmopolitan Modernity* (Honolulu: University of Hawaii Press, 2006), 15.

126. Gyanendra Pandey, "The Question of Conversion in the Dalit Struggle," Department of Religious Studies, University of California–Santa Barbara, March 7, 2008.

127. Rashid Salim Adil and Yoginder Sikand, "Politics of Conversion," *CounterCurrent.org*, accessed at http://www.countercurrents.org/dalit-sikander030404.htm on March 21, 2008.

128. "2006: More Jews Converting to Islam," *Ynet News.com*, accessed at http://www.ynetnews.com/articles/0,7340,L-3274735,00.html on March 21, 2008

129. Peleggi, *Thailand*, 194.

130. This is no different than Japanese Buddhists who demonized Chinese Buddhists during Sino-Japanese wars. Brian Victoria, *Zen at War* (New York: Weatherhill, 1997), 20.

131. Che Man, *Muslim Separatism*, 134.

132. Aminah Beverly McCloud, *African American Islam* (New York: Routledge, 1995), 4.

133. Golomb, *Anthropology of Curing*, 35.

Conclusion

1. Personal communication with Ačhān Tat, abbot of Wat Amphūanārām, Yarang District, Pattani, October 16, 2008.

2. Personal communication with Khun Mari, a secondary-school Thai teacher, outside her home, Yarang District, Pattani, October 16, 2008.

3. Personal conversation with Khun Mun, an elementary-school math teacher at Wat Kōwai, Yarang District, Pattani, October 16, 2008.

4. Ibid.

5. In the 1970s, Chavivun Prachuabmoh realized that Buddhist teachers felt uneasy teaching Muslims; furthermore, they could not speak Malay. These systemic challenges were still prevalent in 2008. "The Role of Women in Maintaining Ethnic Identity and Boundaries: A Case of Thai-Muslims (The Malay Speaking Group) in Southern Thailand," (PhD diss., Department of Anthropology, University of Hawai'i, 1980), 86.

6. The Islamic and Buddhist rituals occurred at different locations and at different times. Personal communication with Khun Mari, a secondary-school teacher, outside her home, Yarang District, Pattani, October 16, 2008.

7. Police found twenty-nine spent M-16 bullets around the pickup truck of the victim, identified as twenty-six-year-old Attapong Gonlom, after at least two gunmen opened fire on him at a school in Pattani, one of four southern provinces hit by the violence. "After the attack, the gunmen dragged his body out of the truck and chopped his head off, to the horror of students and teachers," a police incident report said. *Reuters*, "State Official Beheaded in Thai Muslim South," September 9, 2008, accessed at http://uk.reuters.com/article/worldNews/idUKBKK16575420080909?rpc=401&feedType=RSS&feedName=wo

rldNews&rpc=401 on October 23, 2008. For more information on beheadings in the southernmost provinces, see chapter 3.

8. Personal communication with Khun Mari, a secondary-school teacher, outside her home, Yarang District, Pattani, October 16, 2008.

9. Personal communication with Ačhān Tat, abbot of Wat Amphūanārām, Yarang District, Pattani, October 16, 2008.

10. See Mark Jurgensmeyer, *Terror in the Mind of God* (Berkeley: University of California Press, 2001), 19–60.

11. Personal communication in English with a Buddhist monk in Nakhon Pathom Province, October 2008.

BIBLIOGRAPHY

[in Thai]

Aksončharōenthat. *Prawatisāt m. 1: chan mathayom sūksā pī thī 1* [History, Year 1: First Year Education for Secondary Education]. Bangkok: Aksončharōenthat, 2007.

———. *Prawatisāt m. 2: chan mathayom sūksā pī thī 2* [History, Year 2: Second Year Education for Secondary Education]. Bangkok: Aksončharōenthat, 2007.

———. *Prawatisāt m. 3: chan mathayom sūksā pī thī 3* [History, Year 3: Third Year Education for Secondary Education]. Bangkok: Aksončharōenthat, 2007.

———. *Prawatisāt m. 4: chan mathayom sūksā pī thī 4* [History, Year 4: Fourth Year Education for Secondary Education]. Bangkok: Aksončharōenthat, 2007.

———. *Prawatisāt m. 5: chan mathayom sūksā pī thī 5* [History, Year 5: Fifth Year Education for Secondary Education]. Bangkok: Aksončharōenthat, 2007.

———. *Prawatisāt m. 6: chan mathayom sūksā pī thī 6* [History, Year 6: Sixth Year Education for Secondary Education]. Bangkok: Aksončharōenthat, 2007.

Anonymous. "Anonymous Leaflet." Khokpo District, Pattani Province, Thailand, December 8, 2006.

Anonymous. "Anonymous Letter." Thailand, May 2006.

Caturat 2.51 (June 29, 1976 [B.E. 2519]): 28–32.

Isrā Samākhom. "'Phisit chokinwā thī nāyok...chūwāra prachāchon 4 dān" [Aphisit Displays Leader Characteristic as a Prime Minister to be: Promoting the People's Agenda in Four Areas]. July 22, 2007.

———. "Phūnam sūng sut thāng sāsanā islām khong īyip ph.b.ph.l.' surayut nunsandiwithī kāe panhā tai" [One of the Elite Leaders of Egyptian Islam Meets with General Surayud to Show Support for Peaceful Methods of Solving the Southern Problem]. June 25, 2007.

———. "Khommāndō čhāk khabūankān bāengyāek dindāen dairab kānfukkān chai mī tat kho čhāk klum tidāwut hūarunrāeng čhāk āčhe" [Commando from Separatist Movement Received Training for Beheadings from an Arms Group from Aceh]. January 23, 2008. Accessed at http://www.isranews.org/cms/index.php?option=com_content&task=view&id =3109&Itemid=47 on October 7, 2008.

Kittiwuttho, Bhikkhu. *Khā khōmmūnit mai bāp* [Killing Communists Is Not Demeritorious]. Bangkok: Abhidhamma Foundation of Wat Mahādhātu, 1976.

"Kwāmčhing...tī tāk bai." [The Truth...at Tak Bai]. Accessed at http://www.youtube.com on November 15, 2006.

Narongraksakhet, Ibrahem. "Kānsuksā nai dindāenmalāyū," [Education in the Malay Region], in *Rāyngān krongkānprachum tāng wichākān rūang malāyū kab ratthai nai mitbrawatisāt lāe āryatham kab kānsāngkwāmpentham*, [Report on An Academic Conference on Melayu and the Thai State in Aspects of History, Civilization and Justice]. Pattani, 2008 [B.E. 2551].

National Statistical Office. "Rāydai-rāyčhāy čhangwat [Provincial Income and Expenditures]." Bangkok: Prime Minister Office, 2003.

————. "Population and Households Census 1970, 1980, 1990, 2000: Southern Provinces." Bangkok: Prime Minister Office, 2003.

————. "Sūn padibatkān čhangwat pattānī" [Centralized Practices in Pattani Province]. Bangkok: Prime Minister Office, 2003. Accessed at http://poc.pattani.go.th/report.php?report_id=26 on October 10, 2007.

Nidhi Aeursriwongse. "'Onākhot khōng 'ongkonson" [The Future of the Sangha Organization]. In *Mōng 'onākhot: botwikhrō phūa praplīan thisthāng sangkhom thai* [Looking to the Future: Analytical Essays to Change the Direction of Thai Society], edited by Nidhi Aeursriwongse et al. Bangkok: Munithi Phumipnaya, 1993.

Pāčhārisān. "Faitai īk dān lang mān khwan" [The Southern Fire: Another Side behind the Smoke Screen]. (April–June 2007): 34–43.

Phangčhūdī Phosamūa, "Chīwit lae pholngān pholēk sonthi boonyaratglon phūbaychākārtha hārbok [Life and Accomplishments of General Sonthi Boonyaratglin, Commander in Chief]." *Khui khui khāo* [Teenee News], February 27, 2007.

Phinit Laphathanan. "Bothbāt phrasing nai kānphathanā chonabot" [The Role of Buddhist Monks in Rural Development]. Unpublished master's thesis. Chulalongkon University Social Science Lab, 1986.

Gen. Phongtēp Suthīrwut. "Panhā wikrit cāidāenphāktai" [The Problem of the Southern Border Crisis]. *Matichon* 30.10719. July 16, 2007.

"Rongnāyok...suwačhsong chāydāentai tēngob 96 lān čhadbānrakwat phūchīan" [Deputy Prime Minister Sawajan Goes to the Southern Borders and Budgets 96 Million Baht for the Wat Community Watch Project]. *Isrā Samākhom*, February 4, 2006.

S. Phlai Noi. "Wat Pho." In *Phumisat Wat Pho* [The Geography of Wat Pho], ed. Sa'nga Kancha nakhaphan. Bangkok: Sansawan, 1966.

Sameskybooks Chatroom. "'Khon thai tang pēn khon phut?' [Do Thais have to be Buddhist?]." Accessed at http://www.sameskybooks.org/board/lofiversion/index.php?t3413.html, on March 8, 2008.

Somchot Ongsakun. "Kānpatirūp kānpokkhrong monthon pattānī (p.s. 2449–2474)" [The Administrative Reform of Monthon Pattani (1906–1931)]. Master's thesis, Sri Nakharinwirot University, Bangkok, 1978.

Srīsakon Walliphōdom. *Lao kān tamnāna tai* [The Numerous Utterances and Myths of the South]. Bangkok: Mahidol University, 2007. "Sūn padibatkān čhangwat pattānī" [Centralized Practices in Pattani Province]. National Statistical Office. Bangkok: Prime Minister Office, 2003. Accessed at http://poc.pattani.go.th/report.php?report_id=26 on October 10, 2007.

[in English]

Abdulloh Benyakaj, "Scarecrows Carry Mean Message for Thaksin." *Bangkok Post*, November 4, 2005.

Abeysekara, Ananda. "The Saffron Army, Violence, Terror(ism): Buddhism, Identity, and Difference in Sri Lanka." *Numen* 48.1 (2001): 1–46.

Abu-Lughod, Janet. "On the Remaking of History: How to Reinvent the Past." In *Remaking History*, edited by Barbara Kruger and Phil Mariani, 111–30. New York: New Press, 1998.

Abuza, Zachary. "The Role of Foreign Trainers in Southern Thailand's Insurgency." *Terrorism Monitor* 5.11 (June 7, 2007). Accessed at http://www.jamestown.org/terrorism/news/article.php?articleid= 2373451 on September 28, 2008.

Adil, Rashid Salim, and Yoginder Sikand. "Politics of Conversion." *CounterCurrent.org*. Accessed at http://www.countercurrents.org/dalit-sikander030404.htm on March 21, 2008.

Adolphson, Mikael S. *The Gates of Power: Monks, Courtiers, and Warriors in Premodern Japan.* Honolulu: University of Hawai'i Press, 2000.

Aggarwal, Ravina. *Beyond Lines of Control: Performance and Politics on the Disputed Borders of Ladakh, India.* Durham: Duke University Press, 2004.

Aho, James. *This Thing of Darkness: A Sociology of the Enemy.* Seattle: University of Washington Press, 1994.

Amnesty International. "Thailand: Torture in the Southern Counter-Insurgency." London: Amnesty International Publications, 2009.

Amporn Mardent. "From Adek to Mo'ji: Identities and Social Realities of Southern Thai People." *Kyoto Review of Southeast Asia* Vol. 8, March 2007. Accessed at http://kyotoreviewsea.org/Amporn.htm on September 30, 2006.

Anand Panyarachun, et al. "Report of the National Reconciliation Commission: Overcoming Violence through the Power of Reconciliation." Unofficial translation. Accessed at http://thailand.ahrchk.net/docs/nrc_report_en.pdf on August 15, 2006.

Anderson, Benedict. *Imagined Communities: Reflections on the Origin and Spread of Nationalism.* London: Verso, 1991.

Annandale, Nelson. "Notes on the Popular Religion of the Patani Malays." *Man* 3 (1903): 27–28.

Appadurai, Arjun. "Gastro-Politics in Hindu South Asia." *American Ethnologist* 8.3 (August 1981): 494–511.

Arghiros, Daniel. *Democracy, Development and Decentralization in Provincial Thailand.* Richmond, Surrey: Curzon Press, 2001.

Asad, Talal. *Genealogies of Religion: Discipline and Reasons of Power in Christianity and Islam.* Baltimore: John Hopkins University Press, 1993.

———. *Formations of the Secular: Christianity, Islam, Modernity.* Stanford: Stanford University Press, 2003.

Askew, Marc. "Landscapes of Fear, Horizons of Trust: Villagers Dealing with Danger in Thailand's Insurgent South." *Journal of Southeast Asian Studies* 40.1 (February 2009): 59–86.

———. "The Killing Fields of the Deep South: A Deadly Mix." *Bangkok Post*, August 9, 2009.

Associated Press. "Troops Take Back Control of Myanmar." September 29, 2007.

———. "Buddhist Teacher Shot in Thailand." January 24, 2008.

———. "23 Hurt by Bomb near Mosque in Southern Thailand." June 9, 2010.

Australian National University's National Thai Studies Centre and Murdoch University's Asia Research Centre, eds. *Seeing Forests for Trees: Environment and Environmentalism in Thailand.* Chiang Mai: Silkworm Books, 1999.

Ayal, Eliezer B. "Private Enterprise and Economic Progress in Thailand." *Journal of Asian Studies* 26.1 (November 1966): 5–14.

Baker, Chris, and Pasuk Phoongpaichit. *Thailand's Boom and Bust.* Chiang Mai: Silkworm Books, 1998.

Baker, Chris, and Sunait Chutintaranond, eds. *Recalling Local Pasts: Autonomous History in Southeast Asia.* Chiang Mai: Silkworm Books, 2002.

Bangkok Post. "Bulls in China Shop Tend to Cause Havoc." January 28, 2004.

———. "Monk, Temple Boys Killed in Pattani." October 16, 2005.

———. "Alms-gathering Not Halted." October 26, 2004.

———. "The Bhikkhu Who Does Battle." June 22, 2006.

———. "Yala Buddhists Flee to Temple Safety." November 9, 2006.

———. "Buddhist 'Refugees' Demand New Home." December 24, 2006.

———. "Buddhist Holiday Alert Urged for South." February 19, 2007.

———. "Update: Extremists Launch Overnight Wave of Violence." February 19, 2007.

———. "Militants Behead 25th Southern Victim." March 7, 2007.

———. "Monks to Lead Mass Political Rally." April 15, 2007.

———. "Government Official Beheaded in South." September 10, 2008.

Barmé, Scot. *Luang Wichit Wathakan and the Creation of a Thai Identity.* Singapore: Institute of Southeast Asian Studies, 1993.

Barnard, Timothy P., and Hendrik M. J. Maier. "Melayu, Malay, Maleis: Journeys through the Identity of a Collection." In *Contesting Malayness: Malay Identity across Boundaries*, edited by Timothy P. Barnard, ix–xiii. Singapore: Singapore University Press, 2006.

Basham, Richard. "'False Consciousness' and the Problem of Merit and Power in Thailand." *Mankind* 19.2 (August 1989): 126–37.

Baudrillard, Jean. *Simulacra and Simulation.* Translated by Sheila Faria Glaser. Ann Arbor: University of Michigan Press, 1994.

Bechert, Heinz. "Sangha, State, Society, 'Nation': Persistence of Tradition in 'Post-Traditional' Buddhist Studies." *Daedalus* 102 (1973): 1–90.

Bechstedt, Hans-Dieter. "Identity and Authority in Thailand." In *National Identity and Its Defenders: Thailand Today*, edited by Craig J. Reynolds, 238–54. Chiang Mai: Silkworm Books, 2002.

Bell, Catherine. *Ritual: Perspectives and Dimensions*. New York: Oxford University Press, 1997.

bell hooks. *Killing Rage: Ending Racism*. New York: Henry Holt and Company, 1995.

Benjamin, Walter. "Critique of Violence." In *Reflections: Essays, Aphorisms, Autobiographical Writings*, edited by Peter Demetz, 277–300. New York: Schocken Books, 1978.

Berger, J. M. "New Terror Tactic: 'Sidewalk Beheadings' Hit Iraq." *Intelwire*. Accessed at http://intelwire.egoplex.com/2005_01_21_exclusives.html on September 28, 2008.

Bloch, Maurice. *Prey into Hunter: The Politics of Religious Experience*. Cambridge: Cambridge University Press, 1992.

Bougas, Wayne. *The Kingdom of Patani: Between Thai and Malay Mandala*. Bangi, Selangor: University of Kebangsaan Malaysia: Institute of the Malay World and Civilization, 1994.

Bourdieu, Pierre. *Outline of a Theory of Practice*. Cambridge: Cambridge University Press, 1977.

————. *In Other Words: Essays Towards a Reflexive Sociology*. Translated by Matthew Adamson. Stanford: Stanford University Press, 1990.

Boudreaux, Richard. "Israeli Textbook Tells of Arab Plight: The New Edition for Minority Third-Graders Recognizes the Hardships to Palestinians Caused by the Nation's Creation." *Los Angeles Times*. July 23, 2007.

Bowie, Katherine A. *Rituals of National Loyalty: An Anthropology of the State and the Village Scout Movement in Thailand*. New York: Columbia University Press, 1997.

Braddell, Roland. *A Study of Ancient Times in the Malay Peninsula and the Straits of Malacca and Notes on Ancient Times in Malaya*. Kuala Lumpur: Art Printing Works Sdn. Bhd., 1980.

Bradley, Francis R. "Moral Order in a Time of Damnation: The *Hikayat Patani* in Historical Context." *Journal of Southeast Asian Studies* 40.2 (2009): 267–93.

————. "The Social Dynamics of Islamic Revivalism in Southeast Asia: The Rise of the Patani School, 1785–1909." PhD diss., Department of History, University of WisconsinMadison, 2010.

Brawit Dandlanugul. *The History of Wat Srisoda: Where the Regional Dhamma Jarika Project Is Situated in Chiang Mai, Thailand*. Chiang Mai: Saeng Silpa Printing Press, 2002.

Brown, A. J. "Awakening the Wild Tigers (An Annotated Translation with Introduction)." Unpublished bachelor's honors thesis. Canberra: Australian National University, 1983.

Bun, Chan Kwok, and Tong Chee Kiong. "Rethinking Assimilation and Ethnicity: The Chinese in Thailand." *International Migration Review* 27.1 (Spring 1993): 140–68.

Butler, Judith. *Gender Trouble: Feminism and the Subversion of Identity*. New York: Routledge, 1990.

Callahan, William A., and Duncan McCargo. "Vote-Buying in Thailand's Northeast: The July 1995 General Election." *Asian Survey* 36.4 (April 1996): 376–92.

CBC News. "Canadian Dies in Thai Bomb Attack." September 16, 2006. Accessed at http://www.cbc.ca/world/story/2006/09/16/thai.html on March 16, 2008.

Chaiwat Satha-anand. *The Life of This World: Negotiated Muslim Lives in Thai Society*. Singapore: Marshall Cavendish, 2005.

————. "The Silence of the Bullet Monument: Violence and 'Truth' Management, Dusun-Ynor 1948, and Kru-Ze 2004." *Critical Asian Studies* 38.1 (2006): 11–37.

Chakravarti, Uma. *The Social Dimensions of Early Buddhism*. Delhi: Munshiram Manoharlal Publishers, 1999.

Charnvit Kasetsiri. "Thai Historiography from Ancient Times to the Modern Period." In *Perceptions of the Past in Southeast Asia*, edited by Anthony Reid and David Marr, 156–70. Singapore: Heinemann Educational Books (Asia), 1979.

Chart Korbjitti. *The Judgment*. Translated by Phongdeit Jiangphatthana-kit and Marcel Barang.

Chatsumarn Kabilsingh (Dhammanada Bhikhuni). *Thai Women in Buddhism*. Berkeley: Parallax Press, 1991.

Chatthip Nartsupha. "The Ideology of 'Holy Men' Revolts in North East Thailand." In *History and Peasant Consciousness in Southeast Asia*, edited by Andrew Turton and Shigeru Tanabe, 111–34. Osaka: National Museum of Ethnology, 1984.

Chavivun Prachuabmoh. "The Role of Women in Maintaining Ethnic Identity and Boundaries: A Case of Thai-Muslims (The Malay Speaking Group) in Southern Thailand." PhD diss., Department of Anthropology, University of Hawai'i, 1980.

———. "Ethnic Relations among Thai, Thai Muslim and Chinese in South Thailand." In *Ethnicity and Interpersonal Interactions: A Cross Cultural Study*, edited by David Y. H. Wu, 62–83. Hong Kong: Maruzen Asia, 1982.

Che Man, Wan Kadir. *Muslim Separatism: The Moros of Southern Philippines and the Malays of Southern Thailand*. Singapore: Oxford University Press, 1990.

Cheah, Joseph. "Race and Religion in American Buddhism: A Case Study of a Burmese Buddhist Congregation of the Dhammananda Monastery." PhD diss., Graduate Theological Union, 2004.

Coedès, George. *The Indianized States of Southeast Asia*. Edited by Walter F. Vella and translated by Susan Brown Cowing. Honolulu: East-West Center Press, 1968.

Cohen, Richard. *Beyond Enlightenment: Buddhism, Religion, Modernity*. London: Routledge, 2009.

Coughlin, Richard. "The Status of the Chinese Minority in Thailand." *Pacific Affairs* 25.4 (December 1952): 378–89.

———. *Double Identity: The Chinese in Modern Thailand*. Hong Kong: Cathay Press, 1960.

Dalton, Jacob. *Taming of the Demons: A History of Violence in Tibetan Buddhism*. Forthcoming, 2011.

Damrong Rajanubhab, Prince. "Historical Background to the Dispatches of Luang Udomsombat." In *Rama III and the Siamese Expedition to Kedah in 1839: The Dispatches of Luang Udomsombat*, edited by Justin Corfield and translated by Cyril Skinner. Center of Southeast Asian Studies, Melbourne: Monash University, 1993.

Darlington, Susan. "The Ordination of a Tree: the Buddhist Ecology Movement in Thailand." *Ethnology* 37.1 (Winter 1998): 1–15.

———. "Ritual and Risk: Environmental Buddhism in Practice." Accessed at http://72.14.253.104/search?q=cache:Zb6QcGnsRLoJ:www.hds.harvard.edu/cswr/resources/print/dongguk/darlington.pdf+Susan+Darlington+%22Ritual+and+Risk%22&hl=en&ct=clnk&cd=1&gl=us on October 13, 2007.

Davisakd Puaksom. "Of a Lesser Brilliance: Patani Historiography in Contention." In *Thai South and Malay North: Ethnic Interactions on a Plural Peninsula*, edited by Michael J. Montesano and Patrick Jory, 71–90. Singapore: NUS Press, 2008.

Day, Tony. *Fluid Iron: State Formation in Southeast Asia*. Honolulu: University of Hawai'i Press, 2002.

Demiéville, Paul. "Buddhism and War." Translated by Michelle Kendall. In *Buddhist Warfare*, edited by Michael Jerryson and Mark Juergensmeyer, 17–58. New York: Oxford University Press, 2010.

Derrida, Jacques. "Faith and Knowledge: The Two Sources of 'Religion' at the Limits of Reason Alone." In *Religion*, edited by Jacques Derrida and Gianni Vattimo, 1–78. Stanford: Stanford University Press, 1996.

Deyo, Frederic C. "Ethnicity and Work Culture in Thailand: A Comparison of Thai and Thai-Chinese White-Collar Workers." *Journal of Asian Studies* 34.4 (August 1975): 995–1015.

Elverskog, Johan. *Buddhism and Islam on the Silk Road*. Philadelphia: University of Pennsylvania Press, 2010.

Eriksen, Thomas Hylland. *Ethnicity and Nationalism: Anthropological Perspectives*. London: Pluto Press, 2002.

Evans, Richard J. *In Defense of History*. New York: W. W. Norton, 2000.

Fanon, Frantz. *The Wretched of the Earth*. Translated by Richard Philcox. New York: Grove Press, 2004.

Faure, Bernard. *The Red Thread: Buddhist Approaches to Sexuality*. New Jersey: Princeton University Press, 1998.

Fealy, Greg, and Virgina Hooker, eds. *Voices of Islam in Southeast Asia: A Contemporary Sourcebook.* Singapore: Institute of Southeast Asian Studies, 2006.

Fearon, James D., and David D. Laitin. "Ethnicity, Insurgency, and Civil War." *American Political Science Review* 97.1 (February 2003): 75–90.

Forgacs, David, ed. *The Antonio Gramsci Reader: Selected Writings 1916–1935.* New York: New York University Press, 2000.

Fraser, Thomas. *Rusembilan: A Malay Fishing Village in Southern Thailand.* Ithaca, NY: Cornell University Press, 1960.

Freud, Sigmund. *Civilization and Its Discontents.* Translated by Joan Riviere. London: Hogarth Press, 1949.

Geertz, Clifford. *Negara: The Theater-State in Nineteenth-Century Bali.* Princeton, NJ: Princeton University Press, 1980.

———, *Islam Observed: Religious Development in Morocco and Indonesia.* Chicago: University of Chicago Press, 1971.

Geiger, Wilhelm, trans. *Mahāvaṃsa: The Great Chronicle of Lanka from 6th Century B.C. to 4th Century A.D.* New Delhi: Asian Educational Services, 1993.

Gesick, Lorraine M. *In the Land of Lady White Blood: Southern Thailand and the Meaning of History.* Ithaca, NY: Southeast Asia Program, Cornell University, 1995.

Gilquin, Michel. *The Muslims of Thailand.* Translated by Michael Smithies. Chiang Mai: Silkworm Books, 2002.

Gilroy, Paul. *Against Race: Imagining Political Culture beyond the Color Line.* Cambridge, MA: Belknap Press of Harvard University Press, 2000.

Goffman, Erving. *The Presentation of Self in Everyday Life.* Garden City, NY: Doubleday, 1959.

Gokhale, Balkrishna Govind. "Dhamma as a Political Concept." *Journal of Indian History* 44 (August 1968): 249–61.

Goldstein, Melvyn C. "A Study of the *Ldab Ldob.*" *Central Asiatic Journal* 1.2 (1964): 123–41.

———. *A History of Modern Tibet, 1913–1951: Demise of the Lamaist State.* Berkeley: University of California Press, 1989.

Golomb, Louis. *An Anthropology of Curing in Multiethnic Thailand.* Urbana: University of Illinois Press, 1985.

Gombrich, Richard. *Theravāda Buddhism: A Social History from Ancient Benares to Modern Colombo.* London: Routledge & Kegan Paul, 1988.

Gramsci, Antonio. *Selections from the Prison Notebooks of Antonio Gramsci.* Edited and translated by Quintin Hoare and Geoffrey Nowell Smith. New York: International Publishers, 1971.

Gray, Christine. "Thailand: The Soteriological State in the 1970s." PhD diss., Department of Anthropology, University of Chicago, 1986.

Green, Linda. "Living in a State of Fear." In *Fieldwork under Fire: Contemporary Studies of Violence and Survival,* edited by Carolyn Nordstrom and Antonius M. Robben, 105–27. Berkeley: University of California Press, 1995.

Green, William A. "Periodizing World History." *History and Theory* 34.2 (May 1995): 99–111.

Greenfeld, Liah. *Nationalism: Five Roads to Modernity.* Cambridge, MA: Harvard University Press, 1992.

Groot, J. J. M. de. "Militant Spirit of the Buddhist Clergy in China." *T'oung Pao* 2 (1891): 127–39.

Guha, Ranajit. *Elementary Aspects of Peasant Insurgency in Colonial India.* Delhi: Oxford University Press, 1992.

Guimarães, Antonio Sérgio Alfredo. "Racism and Anti-Racism in Brazil." In *Racism and Anti-Racism in World Perspective,* edited by Benjamin P. Bowser, 208–26. Thousand Oaks: Sage Publications, 1995.

Gyatso, Tenzin (the Fourteenth Dalai Lama). "Message for Who's Supporting Armed Forces Day." Department of Defence, United Kingdom. Accessed at http://www.armedforcesday.org.uk/celebrity-supporters.aspx#Dalai-Lama on June 18, 2010.

Habib, Shahanaaz, The Eng Hock, Brian Moh. "Staying Neutral Is Hard for Monks." *The Star.* Accessed at http://thestar.com.my/news/nation/default.asp?pdate=/2010/4/19 on April 19, 2010.

Hallisey, Charles. "Devotion in the Buddhist Literature of Medieval Sri Lanka." PhD diss., University of Chicago, the Divinity School, 1988.

———. "Roads Taken and Not Taken in the Study of Theravāda Buddhism." In *Curators of the Buddha: The Study of Buddhism under Colonialism*, edited by Donald Lopez Jr., 31–62. Chicago: University of Chicago Press, 1995.

Hamilton, Gary, and Tony Waters. "Ethnicity and Capitalist Development: The Changing Role of the Chinese in Thailand." In *Essential Outsiders: Chinese and Jew in the Modern Transformation of Southeast Asia and Central Europe*, edited by Daniel Chirot and Anthony Reid, 258–84. Seattle: University of Washington Press, 1997.

Handley, Paul. *The King Never Smiles: A Biography of Thailand's Bhumibol Adulyadej*. New Haven, CT: Yale University Press, 2006.

Harvey, Peter. *An Introduction to Buddhism: Teachings, History and Practices*. Cambridge: Cambridge University Press, 1990.

———. *An Introduction to Buddhist Ethics: Foundations, Values and Issues*. Cambridge: Cambridge University Press, 2000.

Hirakawa, Akira. *A History of Indian Buddhism: From Śākyamuni to Early Mahāyāna*. Volume 1. Translated by Paul Groner. Honolulu: University of Hawai'i Press, 1990.

Horner, I. B., trans. *The Book of the Discipline*. Vol. 1, *Suttavibhanga*. Oxford: Pali Text Society, 1992.

Horstmann, Alexander. "Hybrid Processes of Modernization and Globalization: the Making of Consumers in South Thailand." A paper presented at the "International Conference on Globalization, Development and the Making of Consumers: What are Collective Identities For?" The Hague, Netherlands, March 13–16, 1997.

Human Rights Watch. "Thailand: No One Is Safe: Insurgent Violence against Civilians in Thailand's Southern Border Provinces." *Human Rights Watch Report* 19.13C (August 2007): 1–102.

———. "Thailand: Government Covers Up Role in 'Disappearance'. Two Years on, Authorities Must Ensure Justice in Somchai Case." March 11, 2006.

———. "Thailand, No One Is Safe: Insurgent Violence against Civilians in Thailand's Southern Border Provinces." (August 2007): 1–102.

International Crisis Group. "Southern Thailand: Insurgency, Not Jihad." *Asia Report No. 98*. May 18, 2005.

———. "Thailand's Emergency Decree: No Solution." *Asia Report No. 105*. November 18, 2005.

———. "Southern Thailand: The Problem with Paramilitaries." *Asia Report No. 140*. October 23, 2007.

———. "Recruiting Militants in Southern Thailand." *Asia Report No. 170*. June 22, 2009.

Ishii, Yoneo. *Sangha, State, and Society: Thai Buddhism in History*. Translated by Peter Hawkes. Honolulu: University of Hawai'i Press, 1986.

Jackson, Peter. *Buddhism, Legitimation and Conflict: The Political Functions of Urban Thai Buddhism*. Singapore: Institute of Southeast Asian Studies, 1989.

———. "Thai-Buddhist Identity: Debates on the *Traiphum Phra Ruang*." In *National Identity and Its Defenders: Thailand Today*, edited by Craig J. Reynolds, 155–88. Chiang Mai: Silkworm Books, 2002.

Jenkins, Stephen. "Making Merit through Warfare According to the *Ārya-Bodhisattva-gocara-upāyaviṣaya-vikurvaṇa-nirdeśa Sūtra*." In *Buddhist Warfare*, edited by Michael Jerryson and Mark Juergensmeyer, 59–76. New York: Oxford University Press, 2010.

Jerryson, Michael. *Mongolian Buddhism: The Rise and Fall of the Sangha*. Chiang Mai: Silkworm Books, 2007.

———. "Appropriating a Space for Violence: State Buddhism in Southern Thailand." *Journal of Southeast Asian Studies* 40.1 (February 2009): 33–57.

———, and Mark Juergensmeyer, eds. *Buddhist Warfare*. New York: Oxford University Press, 2010.

Jit Phomisak (City Slave). "The Spirits of the Yellow Leaves." Translated by Craig J. Reynolds. Unpublished essay. University of Sydney, 1993.

Jones, Richard H. "Theravāda Buddhism and Morality." *Journal of the American Academy of Religion* 47.3 (September 1979): 371–87.

Jory, Patrick. "Thai and Western Buddhist Scholarship in the Age of Colonialism: King Chulalongkorn Redefines the Jātakas." *Journal of Asian Studies* 61.3 (August 2002): 891–918.

———. "From 'Melayu Pattani' to 'Thai Muslim': The Spectre of Ethnic Identity in Southern Thailand." *Asia Research Institute's Working Paper Series No. 84.* February 2007. Accessed at http://www.ari.nus.edu.sg/showfile.asp?pubid=643&type=2 on March 1, 2007.

———. "*Luang Pho Thuat* as a Southern Thai Cultural Hero: Popular Religion in the Integration of Patani." In *Thai South and Malay North: Ethnic Interactions on the Plural Peninsula,* edited by Michael J. Montesano and Patrick Jory, 292–303. Singapore: NUS Press, 2008.

Juergensmeyer, Mark. *The New Cold War? Religious Nationalism Confronts the Secular State.* Berkeley: University of California Press, 1993.

———. *Terror in the Mind of God: The Global Rise of Religious Violence.* Berkeley: University of California Press, 2001.

———. *Global Rebellion: Religious Challenges to the Secular State, from Christian Militias to Al Qaeda.* Berkeley: University of California, 2008.

Kamala Tiyavanich. *Forest Recollections: Wandering Monks in Twentieth-Century Thailand.* Honolulu: University of Hawai'i Press, 1997.

Kent, Daniel. "Onward Buddhist Soldiers: Preaching to the Sri Lankan Buddhist Army." In *Buddhist Warfare,* edited by Michael Jerryson and Mark Juergensmeyer, 157–78. New York: Oxford University Press, 2009.

Keyes, Charles. "Buddhism and National Integration in Thailand." *Journal of Asian Studies* 30.3 (May 1971): 551–67.

———. "Toward a New Formulation of the Concept of Ethnic Group." *Ethnicity* 3 (1976): 202–13.

———. "Political Crisis and Militant Buddhism." In *Religion and Legitimation of Power in Thailand, Laos, and Burma,* edited by Bardwell L. Smith, 147–64. Chambersburg, PA: ANIMA Books, 1978.

———. *Thailand: Buddhist Kingdom as Modern Nation-State.* Boulder: Westview Press, 1987.

———. "Thai Buddhism: From State Religion to Religion beyond the State." A paper presented for the panel "Buddhism in the Contemporary World: Universalism and Particularism Association" at the Asian Studies Conference, Boston, March 1994.

———. "Ethnicity and the Nation-States of Thailand and Vietnam." In *Challenging the Limits: Indigenous Peoples of the Mekong Region,* edited by Prasit Leepreecha, Don McCaskill, and Kwanchewan Buadaeng, 13–53. Chiang Mai: Mekong Press, 2008.

———. "Muslim 'Others' in Buddhist Thailand." Paper presented at a conference on Buddhism and Islam: Encounters, Histories, Dialogues and Representation. Numata Conference Center, McGill University, May 29–30, 2009.

Kirsch, Thomas. "Complexities in the Thai Religious System: An Interpretation." *Journal of Asian Studies* 37.2 (February 1977): 241–66.

Kleine, Christoph. "Evil Monks with Good Intentions? Remarks on Buddhist Monastic Violence and Its Doctrinal Background." In *Buddhism and Violence,* edited by Michael Zimmermann, 65–98. Kathmandu: Lumbini International Research Institute, 2006.

Kobkua Suwannathat-Pian. *Thai-Malay Relations: Traditional Intra-Regional Relations from the Seventeenth to the Early Twentieth Centuries.* Singapore: Oxford University Press, 1988.

Kosol Nakachol. "Santi Asoke Centre Bombed." *Bangkok Post,* February 23, 2006.

Kulke, Hermann. *Kings and Cults: State Formation and Legitimation in India and Southeast Asia.* New Delhi: Manohar, 1993.

Kumar, Krishan, and Ekaterina Makarova. "An Interview with José Casanova." *The Hedgehog Review* 4.2 (Summer 2002): 91–108.

Kunsiri Olarikkachat. "Queen again Calls for Peace in South: Inhumane Cruelties Must Be Condemned." *Bangkok Post,* August 12, 2005.

Kusa, Julian. "'Bad Boys, Bad Boys, Watcha Gonna Do? Watcha Gonna Do When They Come for You?'—Police Monks (*Tamruat Phra*): The Thai *Sangha's* Covert Disciplinary Enforcement

Agency." Paper presented at the Ninth International Conference on Thai Studies. Northern Illinois University, April 4, 2005.

Landon, Kenneth. *Siam in Transition: A Brief Survey of Cultural Trends in the Five Years since the Revolution of 1932*. Chicago: University of Chicago Press, 1939.

———. "The Problem of the Chinese in Thailand." *Pacific Affairs* 13.2 (June 1940): 149–61.

Lang, Kurt "Military." In *International Encyclopedia of the Social Sciences*. Vol. 10, edited by David L. Sills, 305–11. New York: Macmillan Company and Free Press, 1968.

Leach, Edmund." On Certain Unconsidered Aspects of Double Descent Systems." *Man* 62 (1962): 130–34.

LeVine, Sarah. "The Theravada Domestic Mission in Twentieth-Century Nepal." In *Buddhist Missionaries in the Era of Globalization*, edited by Linda Learman, 51–76. Honolulu: University of Hawai'i Press, 2005.

Leyden, John, trans. *Malay Annals: With an Introduction by Sir Thomas Stamford Raffles* [Microfilm]. London: Longman, Hurst, Reese, ORMF, and Brown, Paternoster-row, 1821.

Liu, Ming-Wood. "The Problem of the *Icchantika* in the Mahāyāna *Mahāparinirvaṇa Sūtra*." *Journal of the International Association of Buddhist Studies* 7.1 (1984): 57–81.

Lincoln, Bruce. *Discourse and the Construction of Society: Comparative Studies of Myth, Ritual, and Classification*. New York: Oxford University Press, 1989.

Ling, Trevor. "Introduction." In *Buddhist Trends in Southeast Asia*, edited by Trevor Ling, 1–5. Singapore: Institute of Southeast Asian Studies, 1993.

Long, Charles. *Signification: Signs, Symbols, and Images in the Interpretation of Religion*. Aurora, CO: Fortress Press, 1995.

Loos, Tamara. *Subject Siam: Family, Law, and Colonial Modernity in Thailand*. Ithaca, NY: Cornell University Press, 2006.

Lopez Jr., Donald. S. *Prisoners of Shangri-La: Tibetan Buddhism and the West*. Chicago: University of Chicago Press, 1998.

———. *Buddhism and Science: A Guide for the Perplexed*. Chicago: University of Chicago Press, 2008.

McCargo, Duncan. "Buddhism, Democracy and Identity in Thailand." *Democratization* 11.4 (August 2004): 155–70.

———. "Network Monarchy and Legitimacy Crises in Thailand." *Pacific Review* 18.4 (December 2005): 499–519.

———. *Tearing Apart the Land: Islam and Legitimacy in Southern Thailand*. Ithaca, NY: Cornell University Press, 2008.

———. "Thai Buddhism, Thai Buddhists and the Southern Conflict." *Journal of Southeast Asian Studies* 40.1 (February 2009): 1–10.

———. "The Politics of Buddhist Identity in Thailand's Deep South: The Demise of Civil Religion?" *Journal of Southeast Asia Studies* 40.1 (February 2009): 11–32.

McCloud, Aminah Beverly. *African American Islam*. New York: Routledge, 1995.

McDaniel, Justin. *Gathering Leaves and Lifting Words: Histories of Buddhist Monastic Education in Laos and Thailand*. Seattle: University of Washington Press, 2008.

Macan-Markar, Marwaan. "Fighting for Peace in Thailand." *Asia Times*, November 3, 2005. Accessed at http://www.atimes.com/atimes/Southeast_Asia/GK03Ae01.html on January 28, 2007.

Malcomson, Scott L. *One Drop of Blood: The American Misadventure of Race*. New York: Farrar Straus Giroux, 2000.

Mann, Michael. *The Sources of Social Power*. Vol. 2, *The Rise of Classes and Nation-States, 1760–1914*. Cambridge: Cambridge University Press, 1993.

———. "Buddhist Perceptions of Muslims in the Thai South." Paper presented at Asian Area Studies Conference in Boston, March 22–25, 2007.

Marshall, Andrew. "Thailand's Endless Woe." *Time Magazine Asia*, July 19, 2007.

———, and Don Pathan. "In Death's Shadow." *Time Magazine Asia*, November 26, 2006. Accessed at http://www.time.com/time/magazine/article/0,9171,1563009-2,00.html on November 28, 2006.

Masuzawa, Tomoko. *The Invention of World Religions: Or, How European Universalism Was Preserved in the Language of Pluralism*. Chicago: University of Chicago Press, 2005.

Maud, Jovan. "The Nine Emperor Gods at the Border: Transnational Culture, Alternate Modes of Practice, and the Expansion of the Vegetarian Festival in Hat Yai." In *Dynamic Diversity in Southern Thailand*, edited by Wattana Sugunnasil, 153–78. Chiang Mai: Silkworm Books, 2005.

———. "The Sacred Borderland: A Buddhist Saint, the State, and Transnational Religion in Southern Thailand." PhD diss., Department of Anthropology, Macquarie University, 2007.

Mignolo, Walter. "Citizenship, Knowledge, and the Limits of Humanity." *American Literary History* 18.2 (2006): 312–31.

Minh-ha, Trinh. *Woman, Native, Other*. Bloomington: Indiana University Press, 1989.

Mitchell, Donald. *Buddhism: Introducing the Buddhist Experience*. New York: Oxford University Press, 2002.

Moerman, Michael. "Ethnic Identity in a Complex Civilization: Who Are the Lue?" *American Anthropologist* 76 (1974): 1215–30.

Monier-Williams, Sir Monier. *A Sanskrit-English Dictionary*. Digital facsimile edition. Los Angeles: Bhaktivedanta Book Trust, 2002.

Mortenson, Greg, and David Relin. *Three Cups of Tea: One Man's Mission to Promote Peace . . . One School at a Time*. New York: Penguin, 2007.

Muecke, Marjorie A. "The Village Scouts of Thailand." *Asian Survey* 20.4 (April 1980): 407–27.

Muhammad Ayub Pathan. "Eight Massacred in Van Ambush." *Bangkok Post*, March 15, 2007.

Mydans, Seth. "Under Desert Sun, Mourners Pray for 9 Killed at Temple." *New York Times*, August 12, 1991. Accessed at http://query.nytimes.com/gst/fullpage.html?res=9D0CE2DF163AF9 31A2575BC0A967958260&sec=&spon=&pagewanted=print on October 12, 2007.

———. "Muslim Insurgency Stokes Fear in Southern Thailand." *International Herald Tribune*, February 25, 2007. Accessed at http://www.iht.com/articles/2007/02/25/news/thailand. php on September 28, 2008.

Pathan, Muhamad Ayub and Wassana Nanuam. "Blacklisting of Teachers to Stop." *Bangkok Post*, November 9, 2006.

The Nation. "Southern Violence." January 28, 2004.

———. "Buddhist Temple Attacked." October 16, 2005.

———. "National Reconciliation Commission: Anand, Monks Exchange Words." November 12, 2005. Accessed at http://www.nationmultimedia.com/specials/south2years/nov1205.php on January 28, 2007.

———. "From Royal Palace to Sanam Luang." February 26, 2006.

———. "Six Blasts Rock Hat Yai." September 17, 2006.

———. "Surayud Apologises for Govt's abuses in South." November 3, 2006.

———. "Monks Head to South to Spread Message of Peace." July 26, 2007.

———. "Family of Burma's Super Boss Are in Laos." September 29, 2007.

———. "148 Buddhist Monks Deployed to Temples in Deep South." July 3, 2009.

Nidhi Aeursriwongse. "Understanding the Situation in the South as a 'Millenarian Revolt." *Kyoto Review of Southeast Asia*. March 2005. Accessed at http://kyotoreview.cseas.kyoto-u.ac.jp/issue/issue5/article_380.html on February 15, 2007.

Nishii, Ryoko. "Coexistence of Religions: Muslim and Buddhist Relationship on the West Coast of Southern Thailand." *Tai Culture: International Review on Tai Cultural Studies* 4.1 (June 1999): 77–92.

———. "A Way of Negotiating with the Other within the Self: Muslims' Acknowledgement of Buddhist Ancestors in Southern Thailand." A working paper from *The Southern Thailand Homepage*. Accessed at http://72.14.253.104/search?q=cache:pWFcvngTFuAJ:www.unim-uenster.de/Ethnologie/South_Thai/working_paper/Nishii_Negotiation.pdf+Nishii+%22A+Way+of+Negotiating+with+the+Other%22&hl=en&ct=clnk&cd=3&gl=us on September 20, 2006.

Nordstrom, Carolyn, and Antonius C.G. M Robben. "Introduction." In *Fieldwork under Fire: Contemporary Studies of Violence and Culture*, edited by Carolyn Nordstrom and Antonius C.G. M. Robben, 1–24. Berkeley: University of California Press, 1995.

Omi, Michael, and Howard Winant. *Racial Formation in the United States: From the 1960s to the 1980s*. London: Routledge, 1991.

Ong-ard Decha. "Phra Supoj's Mysterious Death: A Buddhist Monk Falls Victim to Capitalist Greed." *Prachatai*, October 7, 2007. Accessed at http://www.prachatai.com/english/news.php?id=289 on October 13, 2007.

Pancrazio, Angela Cara. "Time to Remember 1991 Massacre at Thai Buddhist Temple." *Arizona Republic*, August 9, 2006. Accessed at http:// buddhistchannel.tv/index.php?id= 64,3025,0,0,1,0 on October 12, 2007.

Pandey, Gyanendra. *The Construction of Communalism in Colonial North India*. Delhi: Oxford University Press, 1990.

———. "The Question of Conversion in the Dalit Struggle." Department of Religious Studies, University of California–Santa Barbara, March 7, 2008.

The Patani Support Group. "The Tak Bai Masscre: The True Story." Accessed at http://www.youtube.com/watch?v=fk_ZEuE-70M on November 15, 2006.

Payutto, P. A. *A Constitution for Living: Buddhist Principles for a Fruitful and Harmonious Life*. Translated by Bruce Evans. Bangkok: Office of National Buddhism Press, 1997.

Peleggi, Maurizio. *Thailand: The Worldly Kingdom*. Singapore: Talisman Publishing, 2007.

Penchan Charoensuthipan. "Constitution Contains No State Religion." *Bangkok Post*, April 17, 2007.

Peterson, William "Concepts of Ethnicity." In *Concepts of Ethnicity: Selections from the Harvard Encyclopedia of American Ethnic Groups*, edited by W. Peterson, M. Novak, and P. Gleason. Cambridge, MA: Harvard University Press, 1982.

Pinyorat, Rungrawee C. "Distrust, Brutality and Glut of Guns Puts Thai South at Risk of Communal Combat." *Associated Press*, April 27, 2007.

———. "Eight Killed in Attack on Van in Thailand." *Associated Press*, March 14, 2007.

———. "Thai Buddhist Vigilante Squads Suspected." *Associated Press*, August 7, 2007.

Portelli, Alessandro. "The Death of Luigi Trastulli: Memory and the Event." In *The Death of Luigi Trastulli and Other Stories: Form and Meaning in Oral History*, edited by Michael Frisch, 1–26. New York: State University of New York Press, 1991.

Prashad, Vijay. *The Karma of Brown Folk*. Minneapolis: University of Minnesota Press, 2000.

Rahman, Nik Hassan Shuaimi Nik Abdul. "Srivijaya." In *The Encyclopedia of Malaysia*. Vol. 4, edited by Nik Hassan Shuhaimi Nik Abdul Rahman, 118–21. Singsapore: Didier Millet, 1998.

Rāhula, Walpola. *The Heritage of the Bhikkhu: A Short History of the Bhikkhu in Educational, Cultural, Social and Political Life*. New York: Grove Press, 1974.

Reardon, Betty. *Militarization, Security, and Peace Education: A Guide for Concerned Citizens*. Valley Forge: United Ministries in Education, 1982.

Reid, Anthony. "Understanding *Melayu* (Malay) as a Source of Diverse Modern Identities." In *Contesting Malayness: Malay Identity across Boundaries*, edited by Timothy P. Barnard, 1–24. Singapore: Singapore University Press, 2006.

Renard, Ronald D. "Creating the Other Requires Defining Thainess against Which the Other Can Exist: Early-Twentieth Century Definitions." *Southeast Asian Studies* 44.8 (December 2006): 295–320.

Reuters. "State Official Beheaded in Thai Muslim South." September 9, 2008. Accessed at http:// uk.reuters.com/article/worldNews/idUKBKK16575420080909?rpc=401&feedType=RSS& feedName=worldNews&rpc=401 on October 23, 2008.

Reynolds, Craig J. "The Buddhist Monkhood in Nineteenth Century Thailand." PhD diss., Ithaca, NY: Cornell University, 1972.

———. "Religious Historical Writing and the Legitimation of the First Bangkok Reign." In *Perceptions of the Past in Southeast Asia*, edited by Anthony Reid and David Marr, 90–107. Singapore: Heinemann Educational Books (Asia), 1979.

———, ed. *National Identity and Its Defenders: Thailand Today*. Chiang Mai: Silkworm Books, 2002.

———. "Power." In *Critical Terms for the Study of Buddhism*, edited by Donald S. Lopez Jr., 211–28. Chicago: University of Chicago Press, 2005.

————. *Seditious Histories: Contesting Thai and Southeast Asian Pasts*. Seattle: University of Washington Press, 2006.

Reynolds, Frank E. "The Holy Emerald Jewel: Some Aspects of Buddhist Symbolism and Political Legitimation in Thailand and Laos." In *Religion and Legitimation of Power in Thailand, Laos, and Burma*, edited by Bardwell L. Smith, 175–93. Chambersburg, PA: ANIMA Books, 1978.

————, and Mani B. Reynolds trans. *Three Worlds according to King Ruang: A Thai Buddhist Cosmology*. Berkeley: University of California Press, 1982.

Rhys Davids, T. W., and Hermann Oldenberg, trans. *Vinaya Texts*. Part 1, *The Pātimokkha, The Mahāvagga, I–IV*. Delhi: Motilal Banarsidass, 1968.

Riggs, Fred. *Thailand: The Modernization of a Bureaucratic Polity*. Honolulu: East-West Center Press, 1966.

Robinson, Richard, and Willard Johnson. *The Buddhist Religion: A Historical Introduction*, 4th ed. Belmont, CA: Wadsworth Publishing Company, 1997.

Rocha, Cristina. *Zen in Brazil: The Quest for Cosmopolitan Modernity*. Honolulu: University of Hawai'i Press, 2006.

Samuels, Jeffrey. "Toward an Action-Based Pedagogy: Buddhist Texts and Monastic Education in Contemporary Sri Lanka." *Journal of the American Academy of Religion* 72.4 (2004): 955–71.

————. "Saving the Buddhist Religion: Caste Discrimination and the Establishment of New Temples in Twentieth- and Twenty-First Century Sri Lanka." Paper presented at Annual American Academy of Religion Conference, Philadelphia, 2005.

Sanitsuda Ekachai. "The Booze is Part of General Decline." *Bangkok Post*, March 29, 2001.

Elley, Derek. "Queen of Langkasuka." *Variety Magazine*, June 30, 2008. Accessed at http://www.variety.com/index.asp?layout=festivals&jump=review&reviewid=VE1117937586&cs=1 on November 11, 2008.

Sassen, Saskia. "The World's Third Spaces: Novel Assemblages of Territory, Authority, and Rights." A paper presented at the Religion and Globalization in Asia Conference: Prospects, Patterns and Problems for the 21st Century. University of San Francisco, March 13–14, 2009.

Scheiwiller, Staci. "Mirrors of Memory: Nineteenth-Century Imagery in Contemporary Iranian Photography." PhD diss., Art History Department, University of California–Santa Barbara, 2009.

Schmelzer, Paul. "Monkmobiles and Bulletproof Robes." *Eyeteeth*, October 15, 2005. Accessed at http://eyeteeth.blogspot.com/2005/10/monkmobiles-and-bulletproof-robes.html on February 18, 2006.

Schober, Juliane. "Buddhism, Violence, and the State in Burma (Myanmar) and Sri Lanka." In *Religion and Conflict in South and Southeast Asia: Disrupting Violence*, edited by Linell E. Cady and Sheldon W. Simon, 51–69. New York: Routledge, 2007.

Schopen, Gregory. *Bones, Stones, and Buddhist Monks: Collected Papers on the Archaeology, Epigraphy, and Texts of Monastic Buddhism in India*. Honolulu: University of Hawai'i Press, 1997.

Scott, James C. *The Art of Not Being Governed: An Anarchist History of Upland Southeast Asia*. New Haven, CT: Yale University Press, 2009.

Scupin, Raymond. "Muslim Accommodation in Thai Society." *Journal of Islamic Studies* 9.2 (1998): 229–58.

"Self Immolation." Accessed at http://www.buddhistinformation./self_immolation.htm on September 30, 2007.

Sells, Michael. *The Bridge Betrayed: Religion and Genocide in Bosnia*. Berkeley: University of California, 1996.

Sen, Amartya. *Identity and Violence: The Illusion of Destiny*. New York: W. W. Norton, 2006.

Seneviratne, H. L. *The Work of Kings: The New Buddhism in Sri Lanka*. Chicago: University of Chicago Press, 1999.

Sharf, Robert. "Ritual." In *Critical Terms for the Study of Buddhism*, edited by Donald Lopez Jr., 245–70. Chicago: University of Chicago Press, 2005.

Singh, Rohit. "History, Narrative, and Identity among Tibetan Muslims in Kashmir: A Rethinking of Tibetan-ness." Unpublished master's thesis. Department of Religious Studies, University of California–Santa Barbara, 2010.

Skeat, W. W. "Reminiscences of the Expedition, by the late W. W. Skeat, *M.A.*, leader of the Expedition." *Journal of the Malaysian Branch Royal Asiatic Society* 26.4 (December 1953): 9–147.

Skinner, G. W. *Chinese Society in Thailand: An Analytical History.* Ithaca, NY: Cornell University Press, 1957.

———. *The Chinese in Thailand.* London: Oxford University Press, 1941.

Skjelsbaek, Kjell. "Militarism, Its Dimensions and Corollaries: An Attempt at Conceptual Clarification." *Journal of Peace Research* 16.3 (1979): 213–29.

Smith, Bardwell L., ed. *Religion and Legitimation of Power in Thailand, Laos, and Burma.* Chambersburg, PA: ANIMA Books, 1978.

Snelling, John. *The Buddhist Handbook: A Complete Guide to Buddhist Schools, Teaching, Practice, and History.* Rochester, VT: Inner Traditions, 1998.

Somboon Suksamran. *Political Buddhism in Southeast Asia: the Role of the Sangha in the Modernization of Thailand.* New York: St. Martin's Press, 1977.

———. *Buddhism and Politics in Thailand.* Singapore: Institute of Southeast Asian Studies, 1982.

Spivak, Gayatri. "Can the Subaltern Speak?" In *Marxism and the Interpretation of Culture*, edited by Cary Nelson and Lawrence Grossberg, 271–313. Urbana: University of Illinois Press, 1988.

Sripariyattimoli, Phra (Somchai Kulaacitto). "Why Should Buddhism Become the National Religion." Unpublished article. June 20, 2005.

Srisompob Jitpiromsri. "Sixth Year of the Southern Fire: Dynamics of Insurgency and Formation of the New Imagined Violence." *Deep South Watch.* Prince of Songkhla University: Center for Conflict Studies and Cultural Diversity (2010): 1–24.

———, and Duncan McCargo. "The Southern Thai Conflict Six Years On: Insurgency, Not Just Crime." *Contemporary Southeast Asia* 32.2 (2010): 156–83.

——— and Panyaksak Sobhonvasu. "Unpacking Thailand's Southern Conflict: The Poverty of Structural Explanations." *Critical Asian Studies* 38.1 (2006): 95–117.Stoler, Ann Laura. "Sexual Affront and Racial Frontiers: European Identities and the Cultural Politics of Exclusion in Colonial Southeast Asia." In *Tensions of Empire: Colonial Cultures in a Bourgeois World*, edited by Frederick Cooper and Ann Laura Stoler, 198–237. Berkeley: University of California Press, 1997.

Stoler, Ann Laura, and Frederick Cooper. "Between Metropole and Colony: Rethinking a Research Agenda." In *Tensions of Empire: Colonial Cultures in a Bourgeois World*, edited by Frederick Cooper and Ann Laura Stoler, 1–58. Berkeley: University of California Press, 1997.

Streckfuss, David. "The Mixed Colonial Legacy in Siam: Origins of Thai Racialist Thought, 1890–1910." In *Autonomous Histories, Particular Truths: Essays in Honor of John Smail*, edited by Laurie Jo Sears and John Smail, 123–53. Madison, WI: Center for Southeast Asian Studies, 1993.

Strong, John. *Relics of the Buddha.* Princeton, NJ: Princeton University Press, 2004.

Surin Pitsuwan. *Islam and Malay Nationalism: A Case Study of the Malay Muslims of Southern Thailand.* Bangkok: Thai Khadi Research Institute, Thammasat University, 1985.

Supara Janchitfah. *Violence in the Mist: Reporting on the Province of Pain in Southern Thailand.* Bangkok: Kobfai Publishing Company, 2005.

Suwanna Satha-anand. "Buddhist Pluralism and Religious Tolerance in Democratizing Thailand." In *Philosophy, Democracy, and Education*, edited by Philip Cam, 193–213. Seoul: Korean National Commission for UNESCO, 2003.

Swearer, Donald. "Hypostatizing the Buddha: Buddha Image Consecration in Northern Thailand." *History of Religions* 34 (1995): 263–80.

———. *Becoming the Buddha: The Ritual of Image Consecration in Thailand.* Princeton, NJ: Princeton University Press, 2004.

Syukri, Ibrahim. *History of the Malay Kingdom of Patani.* Translated by Conner Bailey and John N. Miksic. Athens: Ohio University, Center for International Studies, 1985.

Tambiah, Stanley Jeyaraja. "The Magic Power of Words." *Man* 3.2 (June 1968): 175–208.

———. *Buddhism and the Spirit Cults in North-east Thailand.* Cambridge: Cambridge University Press, 1970.

————. *World Conqueror and World Renouncer: A Study of Buddhism and Polity in Thailand against a Historical Background.* Cambridge: Cambridge University Press, 1976.

————. *The Buddhist Saints of the Forest and the Cult of Amulets: A Study of Charisma, Hagiography, Sectarianism, and Millennial Buddhism.* Cambridge: Cambridge University Press, 1984.

————. *Culture, Thought and Social Action: An Anthropological Perspective.* Cambridge, MA: Harvard University Press, 1985.

————. *Sri Lanka: Ethnic Fraticide and the Dismantling of Democracy.* Chicago: University of Chicago Press, 1986.

————. *Buddhism Betrayed? Religion, Politics and Violence in Sri Lanka.* Chicago: University of Chicago Press, 1992.

————. *Leveling Crowds: Ethnonationalist Conflicts and Collective Violence in South Asia.* Berkeley: University of California Press, 1996.

Taylor, Diana. *The Archive and the Repertoire: Performing Cultural Memory in the Americas.* Durham, NC: Duke University Press, 2003.

Taussig, Michael. *Defacement: Public Secrecy and the Labor of the Negative.* Stanford: Stanford University Press, 1999.

Teeuw, A., and D. K. Wyatt, ed. and trans. *Hikayat Patani: The Story of Patani.* The Hague: Koninklijk Instituut, 1970.

Thanet Aphornsuvan. "Origins of Malay Muslim 'Separatism' in Southern Thailand." In *Thai South and Malay North: Ethnic Interactions on the Plural Peninsula,* edited by Michael J. Montesano and Patrick Jory, 91–123. Singapore: NUS Press, 2008.

Thanissaro Bhikkhu trans. "Kesi Sutta: To Kesi the Horsetrainer." In *Anguttara Nikāya* 4.111. Accessed at http://www.accesstoinsight.org/tipitaka/an/an04/an04.111.than.html on July 1, 2010.

Thiong'o, Ngũgĩ Wa. *Decolonizing the Mind: The Politics of Language in African Literature.* Oxford: James Currey, 2006.

Thompson, Leonard. *A History of South Africa.* New Haven, CT: Yale University Press, 2000.

Thongchai Winichakul. *Siam Mapped: A History of the Geo-Body of a Nation.* Chiang Mai: Silkworm Books, 1998.

————. "The Quest for 'Siwilai': A Geographical Discourse of Civilizational Thinking in the Late Nineteenth and Early Twentieth-Century Siam." *Journal of Asian Studies* 59.3 (August 2000): 528–49.

Tilak, Shrinivas. "Hinduism for Hindu Studies: Taking Back Hindu Studies." In *The Life of Hinduism,* edited by John Stratton Hawley and Vasudha Narayanan, 271–87. Berkeley: University of California Press, 2006.

Trainor, Kevin. *Buddhism: The Illustrated Guide.* Oxford: Oxford University Press, 2004.

Trouillot, Michel-Rolph. "The Anthropology of the State in the Age of Globalization: Close Encounters of the Deceptive Kind." *Current Anthropology* 42.1 (2001): 125–38.

Tull, Herman. *The Vedic Origins of Karma: Cosmos as Man in Ancient Indian Myth and Ritual.* Albany: State University of New York Press, 1989.

Turner, Alicia Marie. "Buddhism, Colonialism and the Boundaries of Religion: Theravada Buddhism in Burma, 1885–1920." Volume 1. PhD diss., University of Chicago, the Divinity School, 2009.

Ukrist Pathmanand. "Thaksin's Achilles' Heel: The Failure of Hawkish Approaches in the Thai South," *Critical Asian Studies* 38.1 (2006): 73–93.

(Vajiravudh). *The Jews of the Orient.* Bangkok: Siam Observer, 1914.

van der Veer, Peter. "Writing Violence." In *Contesting the Nation: Religion, Community and the Politics of Democracy in India,* edited by David Ludden, 250–69. Philadelphia: University of Pennsylvania Press, 1996.

————. *Imperial Encounters: Religion and Modernity in India and Britain.* Princeton, NJ: Princeton University Press, 2001.

Van Esterik, Penny. "Laywoman in Theravada Buddhism." In *Women of Southeast Asia,* edited by Penny Van Esterik, 55–78. DeKalb: Northern Illinois University, 1982.

Vernon, Mark. "The Dalai Lama on Violence." *The Guardian*, June 21, 2010. Accessed at http://www.guardian.co.uk/commentisfree/andrewbrown/2010/jun/21/dalai-lama-armed-forces-day-message on June 21, 2010.

Victoria, Brian. *Zen at War*. New York: Weatherhill, 1997.

Wachirayan, (Prince). *The Buddhist Attitude towards National Defence and Administration: A Special Allocution by His Holiness Prince Vajiranana (1916)*. Translated and with a foreword by Vajiravudh. Ithaca, NY: Cornell University Library, 2010.

Wachirayan Warorot. *Autobiography*. Translated by Craig Reynolds. Athens: Ohio University Press, 1979.Weber, Max. "Politics as a Vocation." In *From Max Weber: Essays in Sociology*. Translated by H. H. Gerth and C. Wright Miller. New York: Oxford University Press, 1958.

Wassana Nanuam, and Yuwadee Tunyasiri. "Curfew May Be Imposed; 12 Arrested." *Bangkok Post*, January 28, 2004.

———. "Troops Make Merit after Mosque Fight." *Bangkok Post*, May 2, 2004.

Weisman, Jan. "Tropes and Traces: Hybridity, Race, Sex, and Responses to Modernity in Thailand." PhD diss., University of Washington, 2000.

West, Cornel. *Race Matters*. Boston: Beacon Press Books, 1993.

Wijayaratna, Mohan. *Buddhist Monastic Life: According to the Texts of the Theravāda Tradition*. Translated by Claude Grangier and Steven Collins. Cambridge: Cambridge University Press, 1990.

Williams, Paul. *Buddhist Thought: A Complete Introduction to the Indian Tradition*. London: Routledge, 2000.

Wilson, Ara. *Intimate Economies of Bangkok: Tomboys, Tycoons, and Avon Ladies in the Global City*. Berkeley: University of California Press, 2004.

Wyatt, David. *The Politics of Reform in Thailand: Education in the Reign of King Chulalongkorn*. New Haven, CT: Yale University Press, 1969.

———. *Thailand: A Short History*. Chiang Mai: Trasvin Publications, 1982.

Ynet News.com. "2006: More Jews Converting to Islam." Accessed at http://www.ynetnews.com/articles/0,7340,L-3274735,00.html on March 21, 2008.

Yorinoshi, Nishizaki. "The Moral Origin of Thailand's Provincial Strongman: The Case of Banharn Silpa-acha." *South East Asia Research* 13.2 (2005): 184–234.

Yu, Xue. *Buddhism, War, and Nationalism: Chinese Monks in the Struggle against Japanese Aggression, 1931–1945*. New York: Routledge, 2005.

Yukio, Hayashi. *Practical Buddhism among the Thai-Laos: Religion in the Making of a Region*. Kyoto: Kyoto University Press, 2003.

INDEX